MDX Solutions
With Microsoft® SQL Server Analysis Services

George Spofford

Wiley Computer Publishing

John Wiley & Sons, Inc.

NEW YORK • CHICHESTER • WEINHEIM • BRISBANE • SINGAPORE • TORONTO

For Giancarlo, who shows how much work and reward a second edition can be.

Publisher: Robert Ipsen
Editor: Robert M. Elliott
Assistant Editor: Emilie Herman
Managing Editor: John Atkins
Associate New Media Editor: Brian Snapp
Text Design & Composition: MacAllister Publishing Services, LLC

Designations used by companies to distinguish their products are often claimed as trademarks. In all instances where John Wiley & Sons, Inc., is aware of a claim, the product names appear in initial capital or ALL CAPITAL LETTERS. Readers, however, should contact the appropriate companies for more complete information regarding trademarks and registration.

Published by John Wiley & Sons, Inc.

Published simultaneously in Canada.

This publication is designed to provide accurate and authoritative information in regard to the subject matter covered. It is sold with the understanding that the publisher is not engaged in professional services. If professional advice or other expert assistance is required, the services of a competent professional person should be sought.

Library of Congress Cataloging-in-Publication Data:

ISBN: 0-471-40046-7

Printed in the United States of America.

10 9 8 7 6 5 4 3

CONTENTS

For a number of reasons, applications that provide users with multidimensional analysis of data are becoming widespread, and in a few years may even be considered pervasive. Whether the user is aware of the analysis or not, it is there or will be there soon. Basic analytical operations can be handled by SQL and relational databases, but SQL is very cumbersome and lacks important semantics for dimensional analysis. OLAP databases, however, have been designed for analytical use. *Multidimensional Expressions* (MDX) is a language that helps unlock the capabilities of OLAP databases.

The decision to create this book grew out of our experience with how people have been using the databases that support MDX. The people who create the analytical databases need to know about the database design and implementation, whereas the people who create applications for these databases may not. Everyone involved needs to know MDX, however.

If you are familiar with SQL, be prepared for something new. There is very little that is the same between SQL and MDX. In some respects, SQL's strengths are MDX's weaknesses, and vice versa.

Since its release in commercial products in 1998, MDX has quickly grown in acceptance and use by the analytical application community. As of this writing, servers that support MDX are provided by Applix, Microsoft, Microstrategy, SAS, SAP, and Whitelight. Many client tools generate MDX to provide sophisticated capabilities to users, although the users need only point and click to use them.

MDX is the language component of the OLE DB for OLAP specification, which was created and is maintained by Microsoft. OLE DB for OLAP specifies a set of COM interfaces through which a program can gain access to the services of an OLAP data provider. The overall OLE DB for OLAP specification includes data structures and protocols for issuing queries to and exchanging data with a data provider. Being COM-based, it and MDX have been primarily considered for use on Windows-based computers. However, as with SQL, there is nothing inherently COM-oriented or Windows-oriented about MDX, and it could be used in systems that are completely divorced from these technologies.

Although the official MDX specification is contained in a larger specification that pertains to client-side access to databases, MDX can also be used in many places at the database server itself. For example, in Microsoft's Analysis Services 2000, all calculations defined at the server are defined in MDX. With the exception of some important keywords, it is exactly the same MDX that a client application might itself use. For this reason, understanding MDX is crucial for anyone designing or implementing a database in Microsoft's products.

In order to effectively develop an OLAP-based analytical system, there are two things to master. One is the dimensional design, which forms the framework for all queries and calculations. The other thing is the language and use of the language in which queries and calculations are formed. The queries and calculations are limited by the dimensional design as to what they can request and compute. MDX is a capable enough language that even with an inefficient or less-expressive underlying database structure, a wide variety of useful queries can be answered. However, the better the underlying dimensional design, the easier the MDX will be to create (and perhaps the more efficiently it will be executed). Awesome MDX can make up for an awkward database, and an awesome database can truly unleash MDX. In our experience, designing and implementing OLAP systems based on Microsoft's OLAP Services 7 and Analysis Services 2000 and mentoring others in them, we have ascertained that understanding MDX is an important skill for the database designer, as well as for the developer of applications based on the databases.

However, whereas we want you to become an MDX expert, sometimes the simplest solution to your needs is actually a relatively minor tweak to your database.

How This Book Is Organized

This book is organized roughly from introduction to the language into applications and details. Chapters 1, 2, 3, and 4 introduce the language and provide examples of common usage. Chapters 5 and 6 delve into the details of executing an MDX query. Chapter 7 looks at augmenting MDX native capabilities with external, user-defined functions. We take a more detailed look at building MDX queries in Chapter 8. Chapter 9 covers more advanced and specialized MDX for supporting drill-through and actions, whereas Chapter 10 covers use of MDX in a client session to alter the overall dimension and cube environment. Chapter 11 discusses more advanced MDX that you should consider when building Analysis Services dimensions and cubes. We discuss the basics of client programming for using MDX results in Chapter 12. Chapter 13 covers the capabilities of and MDX syntax for building disconnected "local cubes" that users can access without attaching to a Microsoft Analysis Services server. Basic optimization of Analysis Services queries and expressions is covered in Chapter 14. Along the way, we try to cover a broad range of features and uses for MDX in general and Microsoft Analysis Services 2000 in particular. Appendix A is a detailed reference for MDX operators and functions. You should refer to it while you go through this book; not every function could be covered in the main body. The remaining appendixes are references for operators and settings that are important for use of MDX.

Who Should Read This Book

This book is targeted to professionals and students who need to understand and apply the MDX language. Application designers, OLAP database administrators, advanced analysts, and front-end developers will all need to understand how to formulate and interpret MDX when building and using systems.

What's Not in This Book

OLAP-based analysis requires some database structure. Creating this structure usually requires a lot of conceptual work and implementation work in some database. We'd like to cover all of that as well, to help tie MDX more closely to your databases. However, we're going to focus this book on MDX, which we think will make it a more potent guide and make less overlap with the other books on your shelf. Conceptual fundamentals for OLAP are covered in Erik Thomsen's *OLAP Solutions* (John Wiley & Sons, 1997). *Microsoft OLAP Solutions* (Thomsen, Spofford, and Chase; John Wiley & Sons, 1999) covered conceptual and implementation details for Microsoft's OLAP Services 7.0 product. That product has been superseded by Microsoft's Analysis Services 2000, which would require a book at least twice as large as this to do justice to. Rather than create a book over 1,000 pages in length, this book focuses on MDX.

We've tried to cover the entirety of standard MDX. The only vendor's extensions to MDX that we've explored belong to Microsoft, owing to our familiarity with the product and the extent of their user community. If you'd like to see us cover other vendors' variations on MDX in a future edition, please send us a note.

What's on the CD-ROM

This book is supplemented with a CD-ROM and a Web site. The CD-ROM contains a set of sample queries based on the contents of the book and additional tools for working with MDX. We will also be posting corrections and updates at http://www.dsslab.com/MDXSolutions.html.

A Note on Our MDX Style

Within MDX, some functions and operators are optional in certain circumstances. Our examples in this book will frequently include some of these optional functions and operators for the sake of creating a consistent style. However, we may leave optional operators out if an expression is short and sweet, and including the operators would generate a relatively high amount of syntactic noise. We will also frequently break up queries and statements onto multiple lines so the components of each will be a little clearer. This style will also allow us to easily reuse snippets of text from one query to the next.

MDX function syntax is fairly irregular. Some functions use the standard function format-Function (Arguments); other functions use an object method format-Object.Function (Arguments). There is no intuitive way to determine which functions are expressed in which format, and functions that are conceptually quite related will nonetheless use different formats. Furthermore, those object-style functions that take no arguments use no parentheses (in the style of Pascal and current versions of Visual Basic, unlike C++, Java, and SQL functions, which do use parentheses even when a function takes no arguments). Even after you have used MDX for some time, it is easy to trip up on which functions use which format. In this text, we will therefore use the following convention for referring to MDX functions by name: If a function ThisFunction is written in standard function format, we will refer to it as "ThisFunction()." An example of this usage might be the sentence, "The Order() function sorts information based on data values." If a function ThatFunction is written in object method format and it takes arguments, we will refer to it as ".ThatFunction()", as in "The .Lag() function lets you reference data elements some number of members away." If a function OtherFunction is written in object method format but it takes no arguments, we will refer to it as ".OtherFunction", as in "The .Children function returns all child members of a parent member." In using this style, we hope the text will not only describe functions and their semantics but also help reinforce their actual syntax.

From Here

We hope that you find MDX engaging, even fun. It's very flexible for what it does, and many different challenges can get solved with no more than a little cleverness and a good understanding of the functions and operators available. Towards that end, we've put great care into the MDX reference in Appendix A. Like any dictionary, it holds terms that you may not need yet and haven't come across before, but the more familiar you are with it, the better equipped you'll be.

ACKNOWLEDGMENTS

This book has only been possible through the efforts of many. Joanna Loveluck explored many of the newly available language features. Erik Thomsen helped keep everything in perspective. Nick Dowd and Deanna Young helped keep the wheels running inside, and Lisa Santoro helped keep them running outside. There are too many correspondents that have stimulated ideas and solutions to name all of them; Chris Webb and Harsha Munasinghe seem to have shared a similar interest in fully exploiting MDX. Amir Netz, Mosha Pasumansky, Marin Bezic, Matt Carroll, and Cristian Petculescu of Microsoft (among others) have all contributed knowledge over the past two years, while Bill Baker and Mike O'Connell have assisted greatly in support of our work with Microsoft's analytical products. Emilie Herman, Bob Elliott, and John Atkins at John Wiley & Sons helped steer this project through a demanding personal and professional schedule.

CHAPTER 1

A First Introduction to MDX

This chapter introduces the syntax and semantics of the MDX (MultiDimensional eXpressions) language, primarily as a general overview but with a look at the dialect implemented by Microsoft OLAP/Analysis Services. This chapter will introduce queries and some of the modular nature of MDX expressions. When implementing an OLAP/Analysis Services solution, you will create calculations before users execute any queries, so the order of usage might be "design calculations, then design queries." However, we will look at queries first because MDX calculations and expressions will be easier to understand within the context of queries.

The specification for Object Linking and Embedding Data Base for Online Analytical Processing (or OLE DB for OLAP) describes the full relationship between MDX queries and the data structures that convey the queried information back to the client program. In this chapter, we mention a few of the relevant aspects of this relationship, but we primarily focus on the more logic-related side of what queries are asking for, rather than the programming-oriented aspect of how queries come out.

The Very Basics

We will start off by looking at MDX queries that don't involve what appear to be calculations. Even if an application only uses aggregations of base measures, the end user will still only access the data through MDX queries. Throughout this chapter, we will mix descriptions of the abstract properties of a query in with concrete examples to build up a more comprehensive picture of MDX.

To prepare you for the concrete examples used in this chapter, imagine the following very simple sample database. It uses a time dimension that has three base members: June-2001, July-2001, and August-2001. It also contains a store dimension that has two base members: Downtown and Uptown. The cube is called TrivialCube, and it has two base measures: Sales and Costs. We can have 12 cells (three months for two stores for two measures), and some initial values for this example are shown in Figure 1.1 in a tabular format. We will expand the example as we go, but these initial values will give us some explanatory mileage.

Let's say we want to look at a grid of numbers that has our downtown store's sales and costs for two months, June and July. MDX queries result in grids of cells. The grid can have two dimensions, like a spreadsheet or table, but it can also have one, three, or more. (It can also have zero; we'll talk about that in the section "Data Model: Queries"). The grid we want to see is shown in Figure 1.2.

The MDX query in the following example would specify the cells we want to see:

```
SELECT
   { [Measures].[Sales], [Measures].[Costs] } on columns,
   { [Time].[June-2001], [Time].[July-2001] } on rows
FROM TrivialCube
WHERE ( [Stores].[Downtown] )
```

Stores	Time	Sales	Costs
Downtown	June-2001	1200	1000
Downtown	July-2001	1300	1050
Downtown	August-2001	1300	1050
Uptown	June-2001	1000	800
Uptown	July-2001	1000	900
Uptown	August-2001	1300	1050

Figure 1.1 A trivial data set in TrivialCube.

Store: Downtown

Measures

	Sales	Costs
June-2001	1200	1000
July-2001	1300	1050

Time (labels June-2001 and July-2001)

Figure 1.2 A trivial data set in TrivialCube.

Like SQL, an MDX query includes SELECT, FROM, and WHERE. (Although MDX and SQL share these keywords in form, don't look for too many similarities in their meaning.) Whereas SQL only lets you put columns of tables into columns of a query, the result of an MDX query is itself another cube, and you can put any dimension (or combinations of dimensions) on any *axis* of that result. In MDX terminology, the term *axis* applies to an edge or dimension of the query result. Referring to "axis" rather than "dimension" makes it simpler to distinguish the dimensions of the cube being queried from the dimensions of the results. (Furthermore, each axis can hold a combination of multiple cube dimensions.)

You may be able to make a number of generalizations immediately from this example. Let's break this simple query down into pieces:

1. MDX uses curly braces, { and }, to enclose a set of elements from a particular dimension or set of dimensions. Our simple query has only one dimension on each of the two axes of the query (the measures dimension and the time dimension).

2. In an MDX query, you specify how dimensions from your database map onto axes of your result cube. Each query may have a different number of result axes. The first three axes have the names "columns," "rows," and "pages" so as to conceptually match a typical printed report. (You can refer to them in other ways, as we will see in "Axis Numbering and Ordering.") Though our simple query does not show more than one dimension on a result axis, when more than one dimension maps to a result axis, each cell slot on the axis is related to a combination of one member from each of the mapped dimensions.

3. "Columns" always comes before "rows" (and "rows" always comes before "pages"). We'll see why in the section "Axis Numbering and Ordering" in Chapter 2 "MDX in More Detail."

4. The FROM clause in an MDX query names the cube from which the data is being queried. This is similar to the FROM clause of Structured Query

Language (SQL) that specifies the tables from which data is being queried. Microsoft's OLAP products only support a single cube in the FROM clause.

5. Any other dimensions that don't appear in the columns or rows (or other axes) will nevertheless still have some member involved in the query. The WHERE clause provides a place to specify any such member(s). If you don't specify any such members, then the database will assume some reasonable defaults. The use of parentheses in our simple query will be explained in the section "Data Model: Tuples and Sets."

Once the database has determined the cells of the query result, it fills them with data from the cube being queried. So, every query has at least a SELECT ... FROM ... WHERE framework.

To reinforce this, let's look at another example. To generate the result grid shown in Figure 1.3, with costs shown over all three months across the columns and for both stores down the rows, we can use the following query:

```
SELECT
   { [Time].[June-2001], [Time].[July-2001], [Time].[August-2001] }
on columns,
   { [Stores].[Downtown], [Stores].[Uptown] } on rows
FROM TrivialCube
WHERE ([Measures].[Costs] )
```

MDX has a number of other relevant aspects that we will devote the remainder of this chapter to describing:

- The MDX data model
- How meta data entities are named in MDX
- Simple MDX construction
- Dimensional calculations as calculated members
- Named sets
- Detailed parts of MDX queries

Measure: Costs			Time	
		June-2001	July-2001	August-2001
Store	Downtown	1000	1050	1050
	Uptown	800	900	1050

Figure 1.3 A second result grid.

You can skip ahead to the section "Simple MDX Construction," later in this chapter, if you want to jump right into learning more MDX vocabulary. In the discussion of the first two topics—the MDX data model and how meta data entities are named—we will present a lot of detail that may seem boring or picayune at first. However, the details are important for almost every query, and really understanding any MDX that is more sophisticated than what we have explored already requires some degree of understanding of these topics. By breaking them out, we hope that you will be able to refer to them later on when you need to refresh yourself on some detail or other.

The MDX Data Model

MDX uses a data model that is based on dimensions and cubes, but it is even richer (and somewhat more complex, though not terribly so). Understanding it is the key to unlocking powerful analyses and even to understanding why some basic operations and syntax work the way they do. In this section, we will explore what this data model is.

Data Model: Tuples and Sets

The terminology of MDX includes tuples and sets in addition to all the other OLAP terms we have used so far. Tuples and sets are very similar to members and dimensions, but a little more generalized. Because they are the basic elements of many MDX operations, we need to explain them before exploring how they are used.

Tuples are combinations of members from some number of dimensions, with only one member from each dimension. Tuples are essentially multidimensional members. A single member is a simple tuple (for example, [Time].[June-2001]). A tuple combining a store member and a time member would be ([Store].[Downtown], [Time].[June-2001]). However, ([Store].[Downtown], [Time].[June-2001], [Time].[July-2001]) is not a valid tuple since it has two time members in it. The "dimensionality" of a tuple refers to the set of dimensions whose members compose it. The order in which dimensions appear in a tuple is an important part of a tuple's dimensionality. Any and all dimensions can be part of a tuple, including members of the measures dimension.

Syntactically, a tuple can be specified in the following ways. If it is comprised of a member from only one dimension, that dimension can be listed by itself (as with [Product].[Leather Jackets]). If it is comprised of members from more than one dimension, the members must be surrounded by parentheses (as with ([Time].[2001], [Product].[Leather Jackets])). You can always put a single member within parentheses, but it's not required if the tuple is defined by just that member.

In OLAP Services 7.0, until SP2, there was an exception to this rule. In the WHERE clause of a query, even a single member was required to have parentheses around it. In OLAP Services SP2 and Analysis Services 2000, this is changed, and a WHERE clause of a single member doesn't need parentheses any more.

In calculations and queries, MDX identifies cells based on tuples. Each cell value can conceptually be identified by a tuple comprised of one member from each dimension in the cube. (This is sort of like a spreadsheet, in which Sheet1, Column B, Row 22 identifies a cell.) In a query, some of these members' dimensions may be placed on rows, others on columns, others on pages, and yet others on the query slicer. However, the intersection of two or more tuples is yet another tuple, so combining them all together yields a cell in the end. The tuple ([Product].[Leather Jackets], [Time].[June-2001], [Store].[Fifth Avenue NYC], [Measures].[Sales]) may completely define a cell with a value of $13,000.

Note, however, that a tuple refers to a slice of the cube (with an individual cell being the ultimate slice). Depending on the context or the function that it is used in, a tuple either refers to that combination of members or to the value(s) in the cell(s) that the tuple specifies. This is a little point that makes a big difference when trying to understand what some of the MDX functions do.

Sets are simply ordered collections of tuples. A set may have more than one tuple, only one tuple, or it may be empty. Unlike a set in mathematical terms, an MDX set may contain the same tuple more than once. Also, ordering is significant in an MDX set. Although sets might be better called "collections," we are stuck with the term set for now. Depending on the context in which a set is used, it either refers to that set of member combinations or to the value(s) in the cell(s) that its tuples specify.

Syntactically, a set may be specified in a number of ways. Generally, a set can be specified by enclosing its members in curly braces. One such example is the expression {[Time].[June-2001], [Time].[July-2001]} from our earlier trivial query. An example of a query that uses a set involving multiple dimensions would be the following:

```
SELECT
{ ([Time].[June-2001], [Store].[Downtown]),
  ([Time].[July-2001], [Store].[Uptown])
} on columns
FROM TrivialCube
WHERE ([Measures].[Costs])
```

This query yields the result grid shown in Figure 1.4. (This result has columns and no rows, which is just fine in MDX.)

Whenever one or more tuples are explicitly listed, you will need to enclose them within braces. Some MDX operators and functions also return sets. The expressions that use them do not need to be enclosed in braces if the set is not being combined with more tuples, but we will tend to enclose set expressions with braces for the sake of style.

Although a single member is by default a tuple of one dimension, a set that has only one tuple is not equivalent to a tuple. As far as MDX is concerned, the following two are quite different:

```
    ([Time].[2001 Week 1], [Product].[HyperGizmos])
 { ([Time].[2001 Week 1], [Product].[HyperGizmos]) }
```

The first of these is a tuple, and the second is a set containing that tuple. You might think it reasonable that wherever a set is called for, you can use a single tuple and it would be interpreted as a set of one. However, that is not the case. Instead, you will need to wrap the tuple in curly braces as in the second sample just given. Hence, the following is not a valid query (it needs braces around the tuple to become valid):

```
SELECT
([Time].[June-2001], [Store].[Downtown]) on columns
FROM TrivialCube
WHERE ([Measures].[Costs])
```

The following is valid:

```
SELECT
{ ([Time].[June-2001], [Store].[Downtown]) } on columns
FROM TrivialCube
WHERE ([Measures].[Costs])
```

Measure: Costs

Time

Store

June-2001	July-2001
Downtown	Uptown
1000	900

Figure 1.4 Result from multidimensional set query.

Similarly, a set that happens to contain only one tuple is still considered to be a set. To use it in a context that calls for a tuple (for example, in a WHERE clause), even if you have guaranteed that it only contains one tuple, you must still employ an MDX function (such as .Item( )) that takes a tuple from a set.

Every tuple in a set must have the same dimensionality (that is, the dimensions represented and their order within each tuple). This means that we can also refer to the dimensionality of a set, which by implication also refers to the dimensionality of each tuple within it. You can construct a query that uses the following two tuples:

```
([Time].[2001], [Store].[Downtown])
([Store].[Uptown], [Time].[2001])
```

However, combining them into the same set will result in an error.

Data Model: Queries

An MDX query result is just another cube that is a transformation of the cube that is being queried. This is analogous to a standard SQL query result, which is essentially another table. The result cube can have one, two, three, four, or more axes (up to 64 in Microsoft OLAP/Analysis Services). It is also possible for a query to be considered to have zero axes, but it will still return a single-cell value. Each tuple in a result axis is essentially a member of the result cube.

As described earlier, each axis of the query result is composed of a set of tuples, each of which can have one or more dimensions. When multidimensional tuples end up on the axis of a query, the order in which the dimensions appear in the tuples affects the nesting order in the axis. The first dimension listed becomes the outermost dimension, the second becomes the next outermost, and so on. The last dimension is the innermost. For example, suppose the following set were placed on the "rows" axis in a query:

```
SELECT
...
  { ([Time].[2001], [Product].[Leather Jackets]),
    ([Time].[2001], [Product].[Silk Scarves]),
    ([Time].[1997], [Product].[Leather Jackets]),
    ([Time].[1997], [Product].[Silk Scarves] } ON ROWS
...
```

In this case, the expected presentation for data brought back to a client through OLE DB for OLAP or ADO would be as shown in Figure 1.5. Note that the layout shown in Figure 1.5 is simply conventional; your applications may do something different with the results.

---	---	---
2001	Leather Jackets	*cell values*
2001	Silk Scarves	*cell values*
2000	Leather Jackets	*cell values*
2000	Silk Scarves	*cell values*
---	---	---

Figure 1.5   Typical expected client data layout.

Two examples of zero-axis queries would be

```
SELECT FROM SalesCube
```

and

```
SELECT FROM SalesCube
WHERE ([Time].[1994], [Geography].[Quebec],
       [Product].[Snorkels], [Channel].[Superstores])
```

Since no members were assigned to any (non-slicer) axis in the query, the result is considered to have zero axes and by convention would be a single unlabeled cell. In OLE DB for OLAP, all slicer information is returned as part of the query result. Whether you consider the results here to be zero-dimensional depends on whether or not you choose to ignore the dimensional information conveyed in the slicer information returned with the cell. A one-dimensional query, which selects only columns, will show tuples on one axis and on only one column of numbers and will lack a descriptive header apart from the slicer information.

Note that all MDX queries return cells. Many useful OLAP and decision-support system (DSS) queries are of the form "What members belong in this set?," where the result that is of real interest is not cell data, but members that are associated with cell data or member property values. A query of this form, such as "Show me the top customers that make up the top 10 percent of our revenue," will at least implicitly prepare a set of cell values as well. (It may not actually retrieve their values due to internal optimizations, though.) This is in contrast to SQL, which will return only the columns that you request. There are uses for queries that have no interest in cells; we will look at an example of this in Chapter 8 "Buildng Queries in MDX."

Simple MDX Construction

Now that we have explored the basics of tuples and sets, let's look at some additional ways to create them. A few MDX operators and functions are used very commonly to create sets. We will introduce them here and describe how they are frequently used. Learning how they work will let us introduce and explore more sophisticated and complex areas of MDX later in the chapter. (More complete and detailed descriptions can be found in Appendix A, which is a detailed reference on MDX functions and operators.) The most common MDX operators and functions, apart from parentheses and curly braces, are as follows:

- Comma (,) and colon (:)
- .Members
- CrossJoin( )
- Filter( )
- Order( )

In this discussion (and in many to follow) we will show the operators in use both within whole queries and as fragments of MDX. MDX is much more modular than SQL, and an expression can usually be plugged into a larger expression as well as a query. Therefore, we encourage you to begin trying to understand what MDX provides in terms of building blocks as well as finished products; each fragment itself could be re-used in a variety of ways. The MDXBuilder tool included on the accompanying CD-ROM graphically leverages this modular nature.

Comma (,) and colon (:)

We have already seen the comma operator used to construct sets; let's talk about them more here. The tuples that form a set can be enumerated by separating them with commas, as with

```
{[Time].[January 2001], [Time].[February 2001], [Time].[March 2001]}
```

This expression results in a set that holds the first three months of 2001.

In every level in every dimension in OLE DB for OLAP, the members of that level are arranged in a particular order (by member key or by name). When it makes sense, we can specify a set as a range of members in that order by listing two members from the same level as endpoints and putting a colon between them to mean "These members and every member between them." (This is similar to a syntax used to specify ranges of cells in spreadsheets like Excel.) For example, the expression

```
{ [Time].[January 2001] : [Time].[April 2001] }
```

is the set of months January through April 2001, inclusive. Most frequently, expressions using the colon to define sets will be used when the database ordering corresponds to a useful real-world ordering, as with time. The colon takes two members on the same level as its endpoints; you cannot use it with more tuples that have more than one dimension. It is not an error to put the same member on both sides of the colon; you will just get a range of one member.

The comma operator can be used anywhere within a set specification to add tuples or subsets to an overall set. For example

```
{ { [Time].[January-2001] : [Time].[March-2001] } ,
  { [Time].[October-2001] : [Time].[December-2001] } }
```

creates a set of the first three and last three months of 2001, while

```
{ [Time].[2001], { [Time].[January-2001] : [Time].[March-2001] } }
```

creates a set of 2001 and its first three months. When tuples or subsets are concatenated by commas, the order in which the commas join them is the order in which they are returned.

New Functionality in Analysis Services 2000

In Analysis Services 2000, regardless of whether the member on the left of the colon is before or after the member on the right in terms of database ordering, the set that results will have all members between the two in the correct database ordering. That is, {[Time].[April-2001] : [Time].[January-2001]} will return exactly the same set as {[Time].[January-2001] : [Time].[April-2001]}.

In OLAP Services 7, the colon only produced members in one direction. Because of the internal mechanics of OLAP Services, { [Time].[April-2001] : [Time].[January-2001] } created the range { [Time].[April-2001] : last member on level }.

.Members

Getting the set of members for a dimension, hierarchy, or level is a very common starting point for further operations. The .Members operator takes a dimension, hierarchy, or level on its left-hand side, and it results in a set of all members associated with that meta data scope. For example, [Customer].Members results in the set of all customers, whereas [Product].[Product Category] .Members returns all members of the Product Category level in the Product dimension. For example, the query

```
SELECT
{ [Scenario].Members } on columns,
{ [Store].Members } on rows
FROM Budgeting
```

lays out all members of the scenario dimension across the columns and all members of the store dimension down the rows.

The following two points will hopefully illuminate the use of the .Members operator more than obscure:

- **First, in Microsoft's OLAP servers, hierarchies are implemented as dimensions, and multiple dimensions have different sets of members.** As a result, in a Microsoft OLAP/Analysis Services dimension that contains multiple hierarchies, you cannot simply express [Dimension].Members. If you do, it will complain of an unknown dimension. For example, given a logical [Time] dimension that contains two hierarchies, [Time].[Fiscal] and [Time].[Calendar], a client taking meta data from OLE DB for OLAP will see one time dimension. However, the expression [Time].Members will result in an error rather than result in all members on all time hierarchies. To obtain a set of members, the client must request either [Time].[Fiscal].Members or [Time].[Calendar].Members. If the dimension has only one hierarchy and that hierarchy does not have an explicit name, then Dimension.Members will work. For example, if time has only one hierarchy, then [Time].Members will work.

- **Second, when a client uses .Members (or other meta data functions that return the set of members associated with some meta data element), OLAP/Analysis Services will not automatically include any calculated members in the returned set.** This means that the preceding request for [Scenario].Members, as written, will not return any calculated members in the scenario dimension. We can always ask for them by name, however, and OLAP Services provides the AddCalculatedMembers( ) (Analysis Services provides the .AllMembers functions as well) to add them into a set. We'll show an example of AddCalculatedMembers( ) in Chapter 2 in the section "Named Sets."

CrossJoin( )

In many cases we will want to take the cross-product of members (or tuples) in two different sets (that is, specify all of their possible combinations). The CrossJoin( ) function is the most direct way of combining the two sets in this way. For example, we may want to lay out on the columns of a query for all months in 1999 and all product categories. We would generate this set with the following expression:

```
CrossJoin (
   { [Time].[Jan 1999] : [Time].[Dec 1999] },
   { [Product].[Product Category].members }
)
```

We would use it like this:

```
SELECT
CrossJoin (
   { [Time].[January 1999] : [Time].[December 1999] },
   { [Product].[Product Category].Members }
) on columns,
{ [Store].[East Region], [Store].[West Region] } on rows
FROM Budgeting
```

This would create a result grid that looks like the one shown in Figure 1.6. CrossJoin( ) only takes two sets as inputs. If you want to take the CrossJoin( ) of three or more sets, such as times, scenarios, and products, you can do it in one of two ways:

```
CrossJoin (
  [Time].Members,
  CrossJoin (
    [Scenario].Members,
    [Product].Members
  )
)

CrossJoin (
  CrossJoin(
    [Time].Members,
    [Scenario].Members
```

	Jan 1999	Jan 1999	Jan 1999	Feb 1999	Feb 1999	Feb 1999	...	Dec 1999	Dec 1999	Dec 1999
	Toys	Games	Clothing	Toys	Games	Clothing	...	Toys	Games	Clothing
East Region	45	60	120	45	60	120	...	350	500	800
West Region	60	30	90	60	30	90	...	400	400	750

Figure 1.6 CrossJoined dimensions on columns.

```
   ),
   [Product].Members
 )
```

Notice that each of these results in a set whose dimensionality is, in order, time, scenario, product.

CrossJoin( ) is standard MDX. Microsoft OLAP/Analysis Services also has a non-standard technique for doing the same thing by using * (asterisk):

```
{ [Time].Members } * { [Scenario].Members } * { [Product].Members }
```

This performs the same operation as CrossJoin( ).

One of the common uses for CrossJoin( ) is to combine a single member on one dimension with a set of members on another dimension, such as creating a set in which a particular measure is referred to over a set of tuples from other dimensions. When the formula of one calculated measure involves the count of non-empty cells for another measure, this construct is required. Although it might seem preferable, you cannot construct tuples on multiple dimensions by using range operators. For example, to express the range "toothpaste in stores 1 through 10," you might want to write something like the following:

```
([Product].[Toothpaste],
 {[Geography].[Store 1] : [Geography].[Store 10] })
```

Instead, you will need to use CrossJoin( ) (or the * variant). The phrasing for this would be something like this:

```
CrossJoin (
  { [Product].[Toothpaste] },
  [Geography].[Store 1] : [Geography].[Store 10]
)
```

In the phrasing in the CrossJoin( ) example, we did not use curly braces around the set; they were not needed there. However, since the function requires a set, we did use them around the single member [Toothpaste] so we could convert the tuple to a set.

Filter( )

Operators like CrossJoin( ) and : help us construct sets. In contrast, Filter( ) lets us reduce a set by including in the resulting set only those elements that meet some criteria. Filter( ) takes one set and one Boolean expression as its arguments and returns that subset where the Boolean expression is true. For example, the expression

```
Filter (
  { [Product].[Product Category].Members },
```

```
      [Measures].[Sales] >= 500
   )
```

will return a set of all product category members in which the associated sales measure value was at least 500. This is the first time we have used comparisons. Any Boolean expression may be used to filter the set. For example, the expression

```
   Filter (
      { [Product].[Product Category].Members },
      ([Measures].[Sales] >= 1.2 * [Measures].[Costs])
        AND [Measures].[Sales] >= 150
   )
```

will return a set of all product category members in which the associated sales measure value was at least 1.2 times the associated cost measure value and the sales value was greater than 150.

Filter( ) works on general sets, not just on sets of one dimension's members, so the following expression returns the set of all (product category, city) tuples in which the associated sales value was at least 500:

```
   Filter (
      CrossJoin (
        [Product].[Product Category].Members,
        [Store].[City].Members
      ),
      [Measures].[Sales] >= 500
   )
```

In determining the value of sales associated with each product category, or each (product category, city) tuple, you must take into account the other dimensions that are associated with sales values. For example, the first two Filter( ) expressions and the last one did not account for the time or times with which the sales values were associated. We can specify any additional dimensions' members that we need to in either the Boolean condition or in the set. For example, if we wanted to specify that we wished to filter 2000's sales in Baton Rouge, we simply say

```
   Filter (
      [Product].[Product Category].Members,
      ([Measures].[Sales], [Time].[2000], [Store].[Baton Rouge, LA]) >= 500
   )
```

Within the filtering operation, the cell value will be taken from the 2000 Baton Rouge sales at each product category. The result is a set of product category members.

On the more advanced side, we can also specify more members in the set. For example, the preceding operation could be specified as follows:

```
Filter (
  CrossJoin (
    {([Time].[2000], [Store].[Baton Rouge, LA]) },
    [Product].[Product Category].Members
  ),
  [Measures].[Sales] >= 500
)
```

This expression filters a set of tuples that all include 2000 and Baton Rouge, thus fixing on the correct time and store. However, the set returned would consist of tuples with dimensionality:

```
([Time], [Store], [Product]).
```

These Filter( ) expressions have introduced the concept of query context (the relevant members for dimensions not listed in the set being filtered or the filter condition). Every MDX expression ultimately operates in a context that is set up outside of it. Nested MDX operations are resolved within the context of the operation that invokes the nested operation. We'll defer discussion of contexts here; Chapter 5, "MDX Context and Execution," explains query evaluation and context in detail.

Order( )

To put the tuples in a set into some ordering based on associated data values, we need to use the Order( ) function. Order( ) takes a set, a criterion for ordering the set, and, optionally, a flag that indicates what sorting principle to use (ascending or descending, including or ignoring hierarchical relationships between the tuples). Order( ) returns a set that consists of the original set's tuples in the new order. The precise operations of the orderings that include hierarchical relationships are fairly complex. Appendix A includes a complete description. Here we will use the examples that don't show this complexity in order to demonstrate Order( ) in simpler terms.

For example, given the set of product categories in our database, we may want to sort them in descending order by profit realized in 2000 over all customers. This would be expressed by the following:

```
Order (
  [Product].[Product Category].Members,
  ([Measures].[Profit], [Time].[2000], [Customer].[All Customers]),
  BDESC
)
```

Since Order( ) works on tuples, we can also sort our interesting (product and store) combinations by their profit. For example, the following expression orders each (product and store) tuple according to its profit and returns tuples; Figure 1.7 shows the resulting order.

```
Order (
  Filter(
    CrossJoin(
      [Product].[Product Category].Members
      ,[Store].[City].Members)
    )
    , [Measures].[Sales] >= 500
  )
  , ([Measures].[Profit], [Time].[2000], [Customer].[All Customers])
  , BDESC
)
```

Note that the BDESC variant breaks (that is, ignores) the hierarchy. We'd get back a more complex and possibly more interesting ordered set if we instead chose DESC, which respects the hierarchy and the dimensional components of tuples. See the section "Ordering Sets" in Appendix A for a full description of ordering sets.

Comments in MDX

With the advent of Analysis Services 2000 and the OLE DB for OLAP 2.0 specification, comments are now supported in MDX. One of the uses for MDX is for humans to communicate about the semantics of queries and calculations, and being able to embed comments regarding these is important. Three variations of comment syntax are provided, which will suit a variety of styles.

Product	Store	Associated Sales	Associated Profit
(Leather Jackets	Las Vegas, NV)	6,000	3,500
(Silk Blouses	Honolulu, HI)	5,000	1,700
(Attache Cases	Nyack, NJ)	2,500	1,300
(Golf Umbrellas,	Nyack, NJ)	1,900	1,200
(Golf Umbrellas,	Augusta, GA)	8,000	1,150

Figure 1.7 Result of ordering tuples.

The first style uses the symbols /* and */ to delimit a comment. All characters between the /* and the */ are ignored by the MDX parsing machinery. This enables comments to be placed within a line, and for the comment to span lines. The following is an example of this style of comment:

```
SELECT /* Put products
on columns */ [Product].Members
on columns FROM Cube
```

The second style uses the // symbol to begin a comment, and the comment will extend to the end of the line. The following is a re-phrasing of the previous query that uses this style of comment:

```
SELECT // Put products on columns
[Product].Members
on columns FROM Cube
```

The third style is identical to the second style but uses a pair of dashes (--) to begin a comment. The following is a re-phrasing of the previous query that uses this style of comment:

```
SELECT -- Put products on columns
[Product].Members
on columns FROM Cube
```

Comments can be placed anywhere white space could be used. For example, [Product]./* whole dimension */ Members will work just fine. They can be used in queries or expressions. Don't use them inside a name, though!

If you use comments to selectively include and exclude portions of a query or expression (for example, while debugging it), keep in mind that the /* */ comments do not nest. That is,

```
/* /* comment */ */
```

is not a valid comment, while

```
/* /* comment */
```

is a valid comment. In the first of these two examples, the first */ ends the overall comment, so the second */ is a token that the MDX parser will try to parse (and fail on).

Summary

We have covered only the basics of MDX queries. We have gone over the basic structure of a query, what the MDX data model is, and some of the functions that are commonly used in queries. We have also tried to emphasize the modular nature of MDX and explain expressions as an independent concept from queries. In the next chapter, we will build on this understanding to get a detailed understanding of queries and a beginning understanding of calculations.

CHAPTER 2

MDX in More Detail

I n this chapter, we introduce more details on using MDX. This includes a greater degree of detail on Microsoft's own implementations of MDX and OLE DB for OLAP. In the last chapter, we simply introduced the form of a query. In this chapter, we will get more nitty-gritty and cover the following:

- How to reference OLAP meta data
- Dimensional calculations
- Named sets
- More detail on query structure

We took meta data more or less for granted in the last chapter, but it's important enough (even if a little boring) to cover straightaway. One of the most important aspects of using MDX is calculation and set expressions, but we wanted to make sure that queries were understood first. Now that we've explained queries, we're ready to handle dimensional calculations and named sets. Finally, we've omitted a number of salient details for many queries, and we will revisit the structure of a query to fill those details in.

How to Reference OLAP Meta Data in MDX

We need to look at how meta data entities are named in MDX because we will need to refer to OLAP meta data wherever we use MDX. Dimensions, cubes, levels, members, and member properties all have names that need to be expressed in MDX queries. Two key aspects of MDX identifiers, as they are used in Microsoft OLAP/Analysis Services, are the delimiting of names within surrounding text and the multi-part nature of many names.

Delimited and Multi-part Names

When you write a name in MDX, it can be *delimited* or *undelimited*. Undelimited names, as in SQL and many other languages, start with a letter, and one or more letters, numbers, or underscores may follow them. For example, Production is a legal name. Names in OLAP/Analysis Services can also be delimited by square brackets, [and], in which case spaces, periods, commas, and other characters can be used. For example, [Production of Widgets] and [2000] are also both legal names. OLAP/Analysis Services does not have any published limitations on valid member names except with regard to measures.

Member names with embedded single quotes (such as [Stores].[Armando's Deli]) create special challenges when used as part of a calculation. We will cover this in Chapter 8, "Building Queries in MDX."

When the name of a member at any level is enclosed within brackets, any characters may be used in that name. In OLAP/Analysis Services's way of handling names, the leading bracket starts the name, and every character until the closing bracket is acceptable. Names can even contain the open and closing bracket characters. Leading and trailing spaces are part of the name. Moreover, the member can have an empty name too, which you would reference with [].

If a closing bracket symbol is part of a member name, then in Microsoft's MDX you have to use double closing brackets ("]]") to represent it. For example, the literal name "Table [with chairs]" would be written as [Table [with chairs]]].

MDX makes use of identifiers that have more than one name part, and in these identifiers the names are separated by a period. Cubes and dimensions form the primary part of these names. For example, [Time].[2001] and Time.[2001] both identify the [2001] member of the time dimension, and [SalesCube].[Measures].[Profit] identifies the Profit member of the Measures dimension of the SalesCube cube. Notice that [2001] is listed in brackets. If it weren't, it would be interpreted as a number. Also, notice that the periods are placed between the bracketed sections: [Time].[2001.Quarter1] is a different member name than [Time].[2001].[Quarter1].

Names Versus Unique Names

When you reference meta data entities like levels and members in a query, you need to understand the importance of the distinction between a name and a unique name. Microsoft OLAP/Analysis Services can handle names that don't clearly spell out what the entity is, but it will usually be to your advantage to use unique names where possible. For example, if only one member in your cube has the name "Profit" or "[2001]," then referring simply to Profit or [2001] in a query or expression will be adequate. However, for any member, its name in that level may not be unique. (For example, "Springfield" is a city name shared by 31 U.S. states.) If you were simply to refer to [Springfield] in MDX, OLAP/Analysis Services will pick one of the Springfields and use it, but you won't have much control over which one. The solution to this problem is to use the unique name of the appropriate member.

Software tools that help you construct MDX queries will relieve you of most of the burden of constructing unique names. These tools may not always be available for the MDX you write, however, so you should understand how unique names are constructed. We devote the remainder of this section to a description of the unique names for the various OLAP/Analysis Services structures.

Dimensions

The unique name for a dimension is simply the name of that dimension (such as [Time] or [Measures]).

Analysis Services 2000 Enhancement to Unique Member Names

Microsoft Analysis Services 2000 adds more options for how unique member names can be formed. Whereas OLAP Services 7 enabled only one way to construct a unique member name, Analysis Services 2000 offers several different ways, and any of them can be used anywhere in queries and definitions.

Hierarchies

The unique name for a hierarchy is the name of the dimension, followed by a period, followed by the name of the hierarchy (such as [Time].[Fiscal] or [Product].[ByManufacturer]). If the dimension has only one implicit hierarchy, then the name of the dimension is the name of the hierarchy, so no *.Hierarchy* needs to be added to the dimension's name. That is, you would write [Time] instead of [Time].[Time]. Note that in OLAP Services 7.0, you sometimes needed to write a hierarchy name as [Dimension.Hierarchy].

Levels

The unique name for a level is the unique name for its hierarchy, followed by a period, followed by the name of the level. For example, the sole level of the measures dimension of a cube is named [Measures].[Measures Level]. Levels of other dimensions might be named [Geography].[State] or, in the case of a multiple time hierarchies, [Time].[Fiscal].[Quarter].

Members

In OLAP Services 7, the following algorithm was used to generate or parse the unique name for a member (and it is still valid in Analysis Services):

1. Start with the name of the dimension.
2. Starting at the top level (the All level if there is one), append a dot (.) followed by the (non-unique) name of the desired member's ancestor at that level (or the name of the member if you've reached its level).
3. Moving down levels, repeat the last step until you've reached the level of the member.

For example, depending on your choice of names for the All member caption, the root member in a time dimension that has an All level would be named [Time].[All Time]. If this dimension has levels of Years, Quarters, and Months, then the unique names for the year 2000, the first quarter of the year 2000, and January 2000 would be [Time].[All Time].[2000], [Time].[All Time].[2000].[Quarter 1], and [Time].[All Time].[2000].[Quarter 1].[January].

In Analysis Services 2000, the following additional techniques will also work for generating unique names:

■ When the dimension itself has its Member Names Unique property set to true, then simply placing the name of the member after the name of the dimension will function as a perfectly fine unique name. The unique name [Time].[Oct 19, 2001] is an example.

- When a level of the dimension has a setting of Member Names Unique, then joining the level's unique name with the name of the member will create a unique name. (This will also work if the dimension has Member Names Unique set.) The unique name [Time].[Month].[Oct 2001] is an example.

Analysis Services 2000 also introduces a way of identifying members based on their member keys, not just their names. Although powerful, this belongs to a more advanced discussion than we want to undertake here; we discuss it in detail in Chapter 8.

TIP   Although it won't occur in every database, it is possible (in Analysis Services) for two members in a dimension to have exactly the same unique name, following the algorithm shown. If you query for a member using "unique" name that is not unique, all the members that share that unique name will be returned. The key-based naming discussed in Chapter 8 can be used to avoid this happening.

Member Properties

The unique name for a database-defined member property is the unique name for its level, followed by a dot, followed by the name of the property. For example, a store square-footage property in a geography dimension might have [Geography].[Store].[SquareFootage] as its unique name.

Other Considerations

If you are constructing a unique name outside the context of a cube, then you need to put the cube's name and a dot at the very beginning, followed by the name of the dimension and all the other parts, as we detailed earlier. This situation arises when you create or drop named sets or calculated members from a client (or when you are constructing server-side commands, although you can use a CURRENTCUBE tag then too; see Chapter 13, "Working with Local Cubes"). For example, the unique name of the January 2001 member in a cube named Production History might be [Production History].[Time].[All Time].[2001].[Quarter 1].[January 2001].

Throughout our discussions of MDX, we will tend toward using simpler names for the sake of brevity. For example, we will place an unambiguous member name immediately after the dimension's name, as in [Time].[January 2001]. If we actually have an unambiguous member named [January 2001] in the time dimension, then this is a perfectly adequate way to reference it in Microsoft OLAP/Analysis Services. We will, however, generally enclose names in the square-bracket delimiters even when special characters like spaces aren't part of the name. You can see an example of this in the trivial query with which we started the last chapter.

TIP

Delimiting all names (in square brackets for Microsoft's OLAP) and qualifying member names with at least the name of the dimension should be done for another reason: If the name is not delimited, it may be interpreted as the name of an external function or an MDX operator (perhaps an operator that is only added to the language in a subsequent version of the language). When you are constructing calculated members, named sets, saved MDX queries, or external functions, you cannot really anticipate all the other names that may come into play when they are used in new ways later on.

Dimensional Calculations as Calculated Members

The phrases "multidimensional calculations" and "hypercube calculations" may be a bit daunting to some. However, one goal of this chapter is to show that these calculations are actually fairly easy to perform using MDX. If you have some experience with SQL, you will find that the numerical calculations that are straightforward in SQL are also straightforward in MDX. However, a great many calculations that are very difficult in SQL are also straightforward in MDX. If you have experience with spreadsheet formulas (with their absolute and relative cell references in two or three dimensions), then you are already familiar with some of the basic concepts of dimensional calculations. MDX provides a much clearer language in which to create calculations, however, and you don't have to put a formula into each cell to calculate the cell. Rather, you can specify a formula and control the range of cells that all share that formula.

It is useful to consider SQL and spreadsheet cell formulas as starting points for understanding how to use MDX. Like SQL, MDX lets you form queries that request a particular set of data to be returned to a client. (Also, like SQL, MDX has its SELECT . . . FROM . . . WHERE framework for queries.) In a query, you need to explicitly state from which cube data is to be selected and which ranges of cells should be included on each dimension. However, similar to a spreadsheet, OLAP/Analysis Services uses equations (MDX expressions) as formulas for defining cell values for calculated members. When defining calculated members, you do not specify a SELECT . . . FROM . . . WHERE framework, nor do you need to define, on any dimension, the sets of members to select from. (There are reasons why you might define sets of members from some dimensions, and we will introduce these in the section "Named Sets.")

Let us use SQL as a baseline for understanding how MDX works. We won't go too far with SQL, just enough to make MDX more comprehensible. First, in SQL, if you submit a query like SELECT store, time, sales-cost AS profit FROM table, the calculation of sales-cost AS profit is carried out once per row. More complex calculations are possible in SQL, but the process of forming them always boils down to trying to line up all of the fields of all of the tables involved onto a single row so a result for the row being returned may be calculated.

Second, in SQL you can also build this profit calculation into the database schema by defining it in a view. For example, the query

```
CREATE VIEW profits (store, time, profit) AS
SELECT store, time, sales - cost AS profit FROM table
```

creates a new table-like entity with a calculated profit column. In SQL, you have no real way to define calculations in the database without phrasing them as queries. Third, in a spreadsheet, you don't really build calculations into queries as you do in SQL. Instead, you put calculations into cells, and when you want to see their results you simply bring those cells into view.

Fourth, in MDX queries you put calculations in the axes of a query as new members of dimensions, and the cells get filled in with the results. You never select an expression like sales-cost. Instead, you define a new member whose formula is sales-cost and select that. In this way, the model of an MDX query is a little more like a spreadsheet than SQL. We discuss the basic syntax for this in the next section.

TIP   Whenever you are trying to perform a calculation in MDX, you need to define a calculated member (or perhaps some other calculated entity in Analysis Services) to contain it and then reference this entity in a query.

Under the hood of the OLAP Services OLAP Manager and the Analysis Services Analysis Manager, the user interface generates exactly the same MDX statements that create the calculated members we will be discussing in the remainder of this chapter. So, although the calculated members are meta data entities, they are also MDX language constructs. Two of the purposes of this chapter are to give you an understanding of MDX queries and of how to create calculated members for cubes in databases.

Calculations in Analysis Server 2000

Calculated members are only one of six different ways to compute the value of a cell in Microsoft Analysis Server 2000, and five of those ways involve MDX. This section focuses on calculated members because they are a workhorse, and one of only two ways that an OLAP client can define without special permissions. The concepts you gain in understanding how calculated members work go a long way towards helping you understand how to use the other techniques.

Calculated Members and WITH Sections in Queries

The core syntax for defining a calculated member on a dimension is as follows:

```
MEMBER MemberName AS 'member-formula'
```

There are other aspects of a calculated member that can be specified, but we are focusing on the formula part here. The member must be associated with a dimension of a cube, so MemberName must contain a dimension name as a component. Earlier in this chapter we talked about the formation of the unique names that an MDX query uses when it references meta data. The rules for constructing the member name are the same as the rules for referencing members in a query.

MDX provides two variations on this core syntax to define calculated members. One variation defines a calculated member purely within a query. This is like the sales-costs AS profit expression within an SQL query that creates a new column named Profit that only exists for the life of the query. The other variation defines a calculated member that will be available to more than one query. We will focus on the first variation here. A calculated member that is defined only for a query is defined in a section of the query that we will call the "WITH section."

The WITH section of a query comes before the SELECT keyword and forms a section where the definitions private to the query are made. Calculated members and named sets (described in the section titled "Named Sets") are two of the four things that may be specified in the WITH section.[1] More than one cal-

---

[1]In Analysis Server, declaring a cell calculation and a cache of data to be loaded would be the other two things. We will cover cell calculations in Chapter 6, "The Many Ways To Calculate in Microsoft Analysis Services." Caches are purely a physical optimization that we will discuss in Chapter 14, "Optimizing MDX."

Why Define a Calculated Member Only within a Query?

Some kinds of calculations can only be performed by calculated members in a WITH clause. In particular, any calculation on members that are picked by a user in the course of a session cannot be stored in the database. We'll talk about this in Chapter 8.

culated member and named set may be defined in a WITH section. For example, the following query will augment our trivial query at the beginning of this chapter with a profit calculation. We show its result in Figure 2.1 with the profit calculation shaded in.

```
WITH
MEMBER [Measures].[Profit] AS
'[Measures].[Sales] - [Measures].[Costs]'
SELECT
  { [Measures].[Sales], [Measures].[Costs], [Measures].[Profit]} on
columns,
  { [Time].[June-2001], [Time].[July-2001] } on rows
FROM TrivialCube
WHERE ( [Stores].[Downtown] )
```

As a member of the measures dimension, the calculated Profit member intersects all members of the other dimensions (of which Time is the only important one in this example). Calculated members can be on any dimension, so we can also query for the growth in sales and costs between June and July with the following query (its results are shown in Figure 2.2 with the growth calculation shaded in):

```
WITH
MEMBER [Time].[June to July] AS
'[Time].[July-2001] - [Time].[June-2001]'
SELECT
```

		Measures		
		Sales	Costs	Profits
Time	June-2001	1200	1000	200
	July-2001	1300	1050	250

Figure 2.1 Query result with calculated profit measure.

Measures

	Sales	Costs
June-2001	1200	1000
July-2001	1300	1050
June to July	100	50

(left side label: **Time**)

Figure 2.2 Query result with calculated time growth member.

```
 { [Measures].[Sales], [Measures].[Costs] } on columns,
 { [Time].[June-2001], [Time].[July-2001], [Time].[June to July]} on
rows
FROM TrivialCube
WHERE ( [Stores].[Downtown] )
```

Suppose we were trying to perform this same calculation in SQL, and each time period's values were on different rows of the data table. We would have a difficult time accomplishing this with a single query. In MDX, it is quite simple, however. Notice that our syntax for calculating measures and for calculating members on other dimensions is the same.

Formula Precedence (*Solve Order*)

So far, we have only considered formulas for members of one dimension. We will very likely have formulas on members of more than one dimension, which raises the issue of what we should do when these formulas intersect. For example, consider the set of base and calculated cells shown in Figure 2.3. They are combined from the queries for Figures 2.1 and 2.2, where each calculated slice is shaded.

In the example in Figure 2.3, we have formulas in two different dimensions; the cell in which they overlap is shaded in. This cell has two possible formulas: (July Profit − June Profit) or (June-to-July difference in Sales − June-to-July Difference in Costs). In either case, the answer will be the same, so picking one or the other doesn't make a difference. However, consider Figure 2.4, in which profit is replaced by Margin Pct calculated as (Sales − Costs)/Costs.

The example in Figure 2.4 also has formulas on two different dimensions. The cell in which the formulas overlap, which is shaded in, has two numbers in it. One is the result of (July Margin − June Margin), and the other is the result of

Measures

	Sales	Costs	Profit
June-2001	1200	1000	200
July-2001	1300	1050	250
June to July Difference	100	50	50

Figure 2.3 3x3 cells with formulas: A difference and a sum.

Measures

	Sales	Costs	Margin Pct.
June-2001	1200	1000	0.20
July-2001	1300	1050	0.24
June to July Difference	100	50	0.04 / 1.00

Figure 2.4 3x3 cells with formulas: Ratio and a sum.

((Difference in Sales − Difference in Costs)/Difference in costs). We are going to be interested in one result or the other, depending on the question we want to answer. The issue that has arisen here is sometimes called dimensional precedence, or formula overlap. How do we control the ordering of calculations among dimensions?

The particular mechanism in MDX for dealing with dimensional formula precedence is termed the member's *solve order* and is specified when the member is created. Every calculated member has an associated solve order property, which is a non-negative integer that says what the calculation priority of the member is. A higher number indicates that the member is calculated using the values that result from calculations that have a lower number. If you don't specify a number when you specify the formula for the member, it defaults to 0. The number is fixed when you create the calculation, and cannot be changed without dropping and re-creating it. The numbers are simply relative precedence numbers, so there is no requirement that the smallest number you use be 0. Nor is there any requirement that you use 2 or 1 if the highest number in use is 3 and the lowest is 0. (Microsoft Analysis Services supports solve order numbers down to -8191. See Chapter 6 for a detailed discussion on solve orders.)

For the example in Figure 2.4, let us say that we are interested in seeing the difference in Margin Pct rather than the Percentage Growth of sales to costs. We would simply give the [Time].[June to July] member a higher solve order number. For example, the following query controls the solve order to give us the growth calculation that is shown in Figure 2.5:

```
WITH
MEMBER [Measures].[Margin Percent] AS
'([Measures].[Sales] - [Measures].[Costs]) / [Measures].[Costs]',
SOLVE_ORDER = 1
MEMBER [Time].[June to July] AS
'[Time].[July-2001] - [Time].[June-2001]', SOLVE_ORDER = 2
SELECT
  { [Measures].[Sales], [Measures].[Costs],
    [Measures].[Margin Percent] }
on columns,
  { [Time].[June-2001], [Time].[July-2001], [Time].[June to July] }
on rows
FROM TrivialCube
WHERE ( [Stores].[Downtown] )
```

A few paragraphs ago we referred to other parts of a calculated member that we can specify in the member definition. The solve order property shown in the preceding query is one of them.

Note the following syntactic point about defining multiple calculated members in the WITH section of the query. Each member definition is simply followed by the next one. A comma is used to separate the formula definition from the solve order definition, but no punctuation, such as a comma, semicolon, or other device, is used to separate the end of one from the beginning of the next. Instead, they are separated by the MEMBER keyword.

		Measures		
		Sales	**Costs**	**Margin Pct.**
	June-2001	1200	1000	0.20
Time	**July-2001**	1300	1050	0.24
	June to July Difference	100	50	0.04

Figure 2.5 Controlled solve order in a query.

You should keep two other points in mind regarding solve orders. First, if members on two different dimensions have the same priority, you should consider the order in which Microsoft's PivotTable Services will evaluate them as being random. (It won't be at random, but we'd rather not rely on the details of the behavior.) You should only let formulas on different dimensions have the same solve order number when the formulas are commutative (either when they all involve only addition and subtraction or when they all involve only multiplication and division). Second, the solve order only affects the priority of calculation between dimensions. The database still uses actual formula dependencies to determine what to calculate first. For example, consider the following four formulas. Figure 2.6 shows these four formulas and their inputs laid out on a grid, together with the formula that is actually in use for any given cell.

```
[Measures].[Profit]
  AS '[Measures].[Sale Amount] - [Measures].[Total Cost]',
  SOLVE_ORDER = 0
[Scenario].[Amount of Variance]
  AS '[Scenario].[Actual] - [Scenario].[Planned]',
  SOLVE_ORDER = 1
[Measures].[Percentage Margin]
  AS '[Measures].[Profit] / [Measures].[Sale Amount]',
  SOLVE_ORDER = 2
[Scenario].[Percentage Variance]
  AS '[Scenario].[Amount of Variance] / [Scenario].[Planned]',
  SOLVE_ORDER = 3
```

Calculated members for a cube's dimension may be defined at the server or at the client. Calculated members defined at the server will be visible to all client sessions that can query the cube and can be used in any number of queries. A client can also define such calculated members as well. Clients and servers do this by using the second variation of the syntax for creating calculated members: the CREATE MEMBER command. Calculated members defined with the CREATE MEMBER command must be named with the cube as well as the dimension that they are to be a part of. The CREATE MEMBER command is not part of a query that uses SELECT but is its own statement. Other than that, the

	Sale Amount	Total Cost	Profit	Percentage Margin
Actual				
Planned				
Amount of Variance				
Percentage of Variance				

Figure 2.6   Map of calculated member definitions and overlap on a grid.

core syntax for naming the member and defining its formula and other properties is basically the same as a WITH-defined member. For example, the following MDX statement will create [Scenario].[Amount of Variance] on the Scenario dimension used by the [Sales Cube] cube:

```
CREATE MEMBER [Sales Cube].[Scenario].[Amount of Variance] AS
 '[Scenario].[Actual] - [Scenario].[Planned]', SOLVE_ORDER = 1
```

This calculated member will only be visible to queries on the [Sales Cube] cube. Queries to other cubes, even if they also use the scenario dimension, will not be able to see this calculated member, just like they cannot see any other information about another cube. The CREATE MEMBER statement defines a calculated member for a dimension that can be used by any query (until the member is dropped or the client exits), and additionally will exist in the dimension's meta data visible through OLE DB for OLAP. (In Microsoft's OLAP, this meta data will only be visible on that client; that meta data will not be visible at the server or at any other client attached to that server.)

When a query uses calculated members, all solve order numbers from all the calculated members in the query are thrown together regardless of their source. A formula defined in the WITH section of a query as having solve order = 2 will be evaluated before a formula defined in a CREATE MEMBER statement as having solve order = 3. At the time a query is constructed, you can know the solve orders for all calculated members included in the cube definition on the server. However, when a database is constructed, you obviously cannot know the formulas used in queries and their solve orders. Furthermore, since solve orders are integer numbers, you cannot slip a calculated member into a query between two members whose solve orders are 1 and 2 by giving the new member a solve order of 1.5.

For these reasons, you may want to leave gaps in the solve order numbers that are used for calculated members created as part of a cube's definition (with OLAP/Analysis Manager or through DSO if you are creating them through your own code). For example, the lowest-precedence number at the server might be 10, the next one 20, and so on. If you ever programmed in classic BASIC, this procedure should be familiar (remember line numbers running 10, 20, 30, and so on?). OLAP/Analysis Services' solve order numbers can run up to 2,147,483,647, so you have plenty of headroom here. OLAP Services ignores larger numbers and makes them equivalent to zero, while Analysis Services complains if you use a larger number. (The Analysis Manager suggests a range of up to 65,536.) When we look at constructing queries in Chapter 8, we will see reasons for leaving gaps in the numbers.

The solve order of calculated members is one facet of the concept of formula application ranges. Basically, every formula that you will create will apply to some set of locations in your database. As far as MDX semantics are concerned, the formula that you define for a calculated member will be calculated over every cell in the database that intersects that member. This may or may not be what you want, depending on your circumstances. You may, at times, want some formulas to calculate differently, depending on what level they are at in a dimension. Profitability may be calculated differently in different countries, for example. A formula to compute GNP will not apply to a sub-national level of data. We will explore techniques for controlling application ranges in depth in Chapter 4 "Advanced MDX Application Topics."

Defining Named Sets

In addition to providing you with the ability to define calculations, MDX also enables you to define named sets that represent sets of interest. Named sets are a fairly powerful feature that can be used for several purposes. They can be used as placeholders to hold interesting products, ingredients, measures, and so on between one query and the next. They can also be used to greatly simplify the logic of a query by breaking up complex set operations into discrete units. They can also be used to simplify the substance of a total query by abstracting the logic used to generate the sets from a query template that uses the sets, and they may be used to increase the efficiency of a query's execution.

Named sets behave like any other sets in a query. The syntax for creating a named set is similar to the syntax for creating a calculated member, both in the WITH section of a query and in the CREATE SET command. The basic syntax is

```
SET setname AS 'set-expression'
```

For example, the following two queries return identical results:

```
SELECT
{ [Time].[1996] : [Time].[2001] } on columns,
{ [Measures].Members } on rows
FROM InventoryCube


WITH
SET [3 Years] AS '{ [Time].[1996] : [Time].[2001] }'
SELECT
{ [3 Years] } on columns,
{ [Measures].Members } on rows
FROM InventoryCube
```

We can also create the named set [3 Years] for use in multiple queries on the [InventoryCube] cube through the following CREATE SET statement:

```
CREATE SET [InventoryCube].[3 Years] AS
'{ [Time].[1996] : [Time].[2001] }'
```

Note that we needed to include the name of the cube in the name of the set when we created a named set that would be accessible by multiple queries. However, we did not need to include the name of any dimension. We also didn't include the name of a dimension in the WITH SET definition. Any set may have tuples of more than one dimension, but whether it is a set of one-dimensional tuples (members) or multidimensional tuples, it is not part of any dimension.

As with calculated members, a named set is defined within the scope of a single cube and cannot be referenced from another cube. Even if a dimension is used identically by two different cubes, a set in one cube that contains only members of that dimension cannot be used in a query on the other cube.

Like calculated members, named sets can be stored with a cube's definition on the server so that they can be easily accessed by client queries. With the advent of the OLE DB for OLAP 2.0 specification and Analysis Services 2000, named sets can be accessed as meta data through OLE DB for OLAP. Also, named sets can be defined for cubes in Microsoft's Analysis Manager console.

The logic required to create a named set is executed once within the scope that it is defined in, and the resulting set is reused after that. This means that in addition to helping to clarify the logic involved in a query, named sets have the potential to greatly increase the efficiency of query execution. For example, in the following query, the set [Top Custs] is evaluated once at the beginning of the query execution, and then the set of members that it results in is used for the sum, the count, and the formation of rows in the overall query:

```
WITH
   SET [Top Custs] AS
   'TopCount (
     [Customer].[Cust City].Members,
     25,
     ([Measures].[Profit], [Time].[2001])
   )'
   MEMBER [Measures].[Avg Sale] AS
   'Sum ([Top Custs], [Measures].[Sales]) /
   Count ( CrossJoin ( [Topcusts],  { [Measures].[Sales] }))'
SELECT
  { AddCalculatedMembers ([Measures].Members) } on columns,
  { [Top Custs] } on rows
FROM SalesCube
WHERE ([Product].[All Products])
```

When Sets Are Resolved into Members

Named sets are actually evaluated (resolved into members and tuples) the first time they are used within a particular scope. For a WITH SET declaration within a query, of course, occurs at the commencement of the query (they are computed in the order in which they are referenced while evaluating the query). For a CREATE SET that a client issues in its session or connection, the set is calculated at the instant that the statement is executed. For a CREATE SET that is stored with the cube definition on the server, the set expression is actually evaluated the first time that the named set is invoked in a query.

For the sets that are defined at the session level (with CREATE SET statements retrieved from the cube definition on the server or created by the client application), the tuples that the set describes are cached until either the session is terminated or until a DROP SET statement is issued by the client. For example, say that you create a session-level set of the top 10 products that sell within your sales area. If the underlying cubes are updated with new data that would change which products are in the top 10, the set will remain unchanged. As with calculated members, it is possible within a client session to drop a set defined on the server.

MDX Queries: More Detail

Now that we've covered the components of MDX in some depth, let's return to MDX queries. We've taken a look at most of the parts of a query, but some we haven't seen at all yet, including the following:

- Axis numbering and ordering
- Removing entirely empty slices from a query
- Querying for member properties
- Querying for specific cell properties

The following two parts of MDX queries deserve some further explanation in this chapter:

- WITH Sections
- MDX Cube Slicers

Axis Numbering and Ordering

To use an abstract syntax notation, the core of a query is as follows:

```
[WITH set-or-member-declarations]
SELECT
  [axis-expression1 on axis1 [, axis-expression on axis2 . . .]]
FROM cube
[WHERE slicer]
```

Each axis expression can be a simple set expression or a complex set expression. You can specify from 0 to 64 axis expressions. If you specify zero axis expressions, you probably will specify a slicer expression in the WHERE clause. You do not need to, but if you leave out the slicer, you will get the default measure at the intersection of the default members of all other dimensions (usually the global aggregate), which is rarely of interest.

Each axis is numbered, starting at 0. The numbering of axes in the query corresponds with the positioning of the axis in the data structures that are related to the query results returned by the OLE DB for OLAP driver. You can refer to any axis by its number, as in axis(0) or axis(2). You can also refer to each of the first five axes by their aliases: COLUMNS, ROWS, PAGES, CHAPTERS, and SECTIONS, respectively. If a query uses only two axes, then the axis numbers that are used must be 0 and 1. If it uses only three axes, then the axis numbers that are used must be 0, 1, and 2. In general, if a query returns N axes, then axis numbers 0 through N − 1 must be used. In Analysis Services, they may appear in any order: you may list axis(0) first and axis(1) second, or axis(1) first and axis(0) second, for example. Skipping numbers, however, will generate an MDX parser error. For example, the following is fine: SELECT . . . on Columns, . . . on Rows, . . . on Pages FROM Cube. So is this, which changes the order and mixes the aliases: SELECT . . . on axis(1), . . . Columns, . . . on Pages FROM Cube. However, this is not acceptable, as it skips an axis [axis(0) or Columns]: SELECT on Rows, . . . on Pages FROM Cube.

A Microsoft extension to the MDX specification enables you to skip the Axis( ) and row/column/page/etc. verbiage and simply provide the axis number. For example,

```
SELECT
{ [Product].Members } on Axis (0),
{ [Time].Members } on Axis (1),
{ [Region].Members } on Axis (2)
FROM Cube
```

can be written as the following:

```
SELECT
{ [Product].Members } on 0,
{ [Time].Members } on 1,
{ [Region].Members } on 2
FROM Cube
```

Removing Empty Slices from a Query Axis

It is quite possible that a query will result in some of the tuples along an axis generating entirely empty slices along the result. For example, consider the following query:

```
SELECT
{ Filter (
  [Geography].[State].Members,
  ([Measures].[Unit Sales], [Time].[2000],
   [Product].[All Products]) > 3000)
} on columns,
{[Product].[Snow Shovels], [Product].[Sidewalk Salt],
 [Product].[Suntan Lotion]} on rows
FROM Sales
WHERE ([Measures].[Revenue], [Time].[July-2000])
```

This query will include all states in which more than 3,000 units of all products together were sold and three products of interest (snow shovels, sidewalk salt, and suntan lotion) for the time slice of July 2000. Clearly, if the states returned for the Geography dimension are within 450 miles of the equator, there are going to be a lot of empty product-by-geography tuples across the result set. Less whimsically, in any given month, most of your customers may not make any purchases, so asking for individual customer-by-month-level sales will result in an unpredictable pattern of missing intersections across products.

You can have the query suppress entirely empty result slices from a query by using the NON EMPTY keywords. When NON EMPTY is specified on an axis, any tuples on that axis that correspond to entirely empty slices of data within the result set are removed from the result set before they are delivered to the client. For example, the query

```
SELECT
NON EMPTY { [Geography].[Nashville, TN].Children } on columns,
{ CROSSJOIN (
  { [Product].[Category].Members},
  { [Outlets].[Direct], [Outlets].[Small Retail] }
  ) } on rows
FROM Sales
WHERE ([Measures].[Units Sold], [Time].[July 3, 1999])
```

will return only those children of Nashville for which at least one Product category had a non-empty Units Sold measure on July 3, 1999. Notice that the

Geography members are included or excluded here as determined by slices formed from the other axes of the query. NON EMPTY operates on a querywide basis, so in this way it is different than Filter( ). You could construct Filter( ) expressions to remove empty tuples from sets that represented the axis queries, but these filters would have to employ cross-joins of all sets from all other axes, including the query slicer. Using NON EMPTY is much more convenient.

Querying for Member Properties

Within an MDX query, you can also query for member properties defined for members in a cube. A member property is defined for a single level of a dimension, while the axes of a query are sets that may contain multiple dimensions. However, OLE DB for OLAP and MDX enable the properties to be included on the axis anyway. On whatever axis a dimension is mapped to, you can query one or more member properties for each of the dimensions and levels as well as the identities of the members. If a member is repeated in a result axis, its related member property value will be repeated too.

You specify the member properties that you want to have returned on an axis by using the PROPERTIES keyword in the axis specification. For example, the following will query for the zip code and hair color of customers returned in the query:

```
SELECT
  { [Customer].[Akron, OH].Children }
PROPERTIES [Customer].[Zip Code],
          [Customer].[Individual].[Hair Color] on columns,
  { [Product].[Category].Members} on rows
FROM Sales
WHERE ([Measures].[Units Sold], [Time].[July 3, 1999])
```

Properties can be identified either by using the name of the dimension and the name of the property, as with the zip code property just given, or by using the unique name of the dimension's level and the name of the property, as with the hair color property.

NOTE

While the values of properties requested with the PROPERTIES statement in an MDX query are returned, along with all other result information, in the Dataset object returned by OLE DB for OLAP, it is up to the client application to retrieve and utilize this information from the Dataset. For example, after running an MDX query using the MDX Sample application distributed with OLAP/Analysis Services, double-clicking on a member name in the results pane will bring up a dialog that will include the values of any properties requested in the MDX query.

Two general types of properties can be queried. One type is the member properties that you defined for the dimension. The other type is the intrinsic member properties that exist for all members. The intrinsic member properties are named KEY, NAME, and ID, and every level of every dimension has them. For example, the KEY property of a Product dimension's SKU level is named [Product].[SKU].[KEY]. The member key property contains the values of the member keys as represented in the dimension table. The member name property contains the values of the member names as represented in the dimension table. The ID property contains the internal member number of that member in the dimension-wide database ordering. (Since these properties are maintained internally, your application should not use them to avoid problems with ambiguous names.)

When property names between levels of a dimension are ambiguous, you can get ambiguous results if you query for member properties on the axis of a query. For example, every layer of an organizational dimension may have a Manager property for each member above the leaf. Consider the following query fragment:

```
SELECT { Descendants ([Organization].[All Organization],
[Organization].[Junior Staff], SELF_AND_ABOVE }
PROPERTIES [Organization].[Manager] on columns
   ...
```

When the query is executed, it will return the specific Manager property for only one level. It is not a good idea to rely on whatever level that would happen to be. (In our experience, it would be the lowest level in the query, or the Junior Staff level in this case.) Members belonging to that level will have a valid [Manager] value; members belonging to other levels won't. Suppose that, instead, you queried for each level's properties independently, as with the following:

```
SELECT { Descendants ([Organization].[All Organization],
         [Organization].[Junior Staff], SELF_AND_ABOVE }
PROPERTIES
[Organization].[Executive Suites].[Manager],
[Organization].[Middle Managers].[Manager],
[Organization].[Junior Staff].[Manager] on columns
   ...
```

In this case, the property for each level at each level's member will arrive appropriately filled in (and be empty at members of the other levels). However, when you access properties in member calculations, there won't be any ambiguity. Suppose, for example, that some calculated member referred to [Organization].CurrentMember.Properties ("Manager"). (Appendix A provides a detailed reference to this function, and we also use it in the "Using Member Properties in MDX Expressions" section of Chapter 3 "MDX in Use.") The lookup of this value is done on a cell-by-cell basis, and at each cell the particular manager is unambiguous (though the level of manager to which it refers may change). For this case, you can easily and simply reference member properties on multiple levels that share the same name.

WITH Section

Earlier in the chapter we took a brief look at the WITH section of an MDX query. We'll finish our description of it here. The WITH section of a query is the location where all definitions of calculated members and named sets that are specific to the query are made. Both calculated members and named sets may be defined within a single WITH section. For example, the following is fine MDX:

```
WITH
SET [3 Years] AS '{ [Time].[1996] : [Time].[2001] }'
MEMBER [Measures].[Avg Value Returned] AS
'[Measures].[Units Returned]/ [Measures].[Value Returned]', SOLVE_ORDER
= 10
SELECT
{ [3 Years] } on columns,
{ [Measures].[Units Returned], [Measures].[Avg Value Returned] } on rows
FROM InventoryCube
```

The order of members and sets does not matter as long as no set or member is referred to before it is defined. As you can see, it is the presence of each SET or MEMBER keyword that ends any definition and begins the next, and the appearance of the SELECT keyword ends the WITH section and begins the axis/cell specifications.

Querying Cell Properties

Querying for specific cell properties is fairly tightly bound to the programming layer that retrieves results from a query. In keeping with the non-programming thrust of this book, we won't cover all of the programming details here. However, we will explain the basic model that querying for specific cell properties supports and how an application might use it.

Every query is a specification of one or more result cells and, most frequently, one or more members of one or more dimensions. Much as each member is able to have one or more related properties, each result cell also has more than one possible related result property. If a query specifies no cell properties, then three properties are returned by default: an ordinal number that represents the index of the cell in the result set, the raw value for the cell, and the formatted textual value for the cell. If the query specifies particular cell properties, then only the cell properties actually specified are returned to the client. We discuss formatting the raw value into text in the section "Precedence of Display Formatting with Calculated Members" in Chapter 6. The ordinal cell index value is germane to client tools that are querying the data that has been generated through OLE DB for OLAP. Other cell properties can be queried for, which can be specified for any measure or calculated member in the cube. The full list of cell properties and how they are used in OLE DB for OLAP and ADO MD is found in Appendix C.

The way to specify cell properties in a query is to follow the slicer (if any) with the CELL PROPERTIES keywords and the names of the cell properties. For example, the following query

```
SELECT
{ [Measures].[Units Returned], [Measures].[Value Returned] } on columns,
{ [Time].[2000], [Time].[2001] } on rows
FROM InventoryCube
CELL PROPERTIES FORMATTED_VALUE
```

returns to the client only the formatted text strings that correspond to the query results. Generally speaking, clients that render their results as text strings (such as spreadsheet-style report grids) will be most interested in the formatted values. Clients that render their results graphically (such as in bar charts where each height of each bar represents the value of the measure at that intersection) will be most interested in the raw values. Other OLE DB for OLAP-standard properties available in Microsoft OLAP/Analysis Services enable string formatting, font, and color information to be stored and retrieved for measures and calculated members. This gives you server-side control over useful client rendering operations. Analysis Services adds more cell properties covering cell calculation specifics.

Our discussion of CREATE MEMBER in Chapter 6 describes how to specify the various cell properties that should be associated with calculated members. In Chapter 5 "MDX Context and Execution," we describe how calculated members influence cell properties in queries.

MDX Cube Slicers

Astute readers may by now have noticed a remarkable logical similarity between the slicer clause of a cube query and an axis, albeit one whose interpretation is limited to a single tuple. In fact, this similarity is real. The primary reason for using the slicer is as a convenience and convention for the software portions of a client that interpret the data structures returned as a result of executing the query. If you think of the query result as a sub-cube of the original cube being queried, the chief advantage of a slicer is that it essentially parks unnecessary dimensions on the side. They aren't lost for most client queries. In the OLE DB for OLAP API, they are placed on a special edge in the IMDDataset structure resulting from an MDX query, and a front end will hopefully relay the slicer tuple information to the user. However, the number of (non-slicer) result edges implies to the client the number of dimensions in which it should lay out its reporting framework. (When an MDX query results in a regular OLE DB rowset or ADOMD recordset, dimensional information placed in the slicer is indeed lost.)

For example, the following two queries are identical in substance as well as being virtually identical in what they return to the client:

```
SELECT
{ [Measures].Members } on columns,
{ Time.Members } on rows
FROM cube
WHERE ([Product].[Ceiling Tiles], [Store].[Lincoln, NE])

SELECT
{ [Measures].Members } on columns,
{ Time.Members } on rows,
{ ([Product].[Ceiling Tiles], [Store].[Lincoln, NE]) } on pages
FROM cube
```

Ordinarily, clients would expect to lay out the first version of the query as a 2-D grid that has a product and store as context. Clients would expect to lay out the second version as a 3-D grid that has only one tuple on one of its axes.

Complex Slicers

Slicers need not be composed of simple base members from the cube. For example, it is perfectly fine to have the slicer include a calculated member from more than one dimension, including the measures dimension:

```
WITH
MEMBER [Measures].[Avg Sales per Employee Hour] as '. . .'
MEMBER [Time].[Sum to Date] AS '. . .'
SELECT ...
FROM ...
WHERE ([Measures].[Avg Sales per Employee Hour], [Time].[Sum to Date])
```

More advanced still would be a query that took the first member of a sorted set with the .Item( ) operator and used that as its slicer, as in:

```
CREATE SET SalesCube.OrderedProducts AS 'ORDER(
  [Product].[Product Family].Members,
  ([Measures].[Profit], [Time].[2000], [Customer].[All Customers],
```

```
BDESC)
)'

WITH ...
SELECT ...
FROM SalesCube
WHERE (OrderedProducts.Item (0))
```

[.Item( ) takes a set on its left side and an index, based at zero, as its argument, and it returns the tuple at that position in the set. CREATE SET creates a named set that can be referenced in a query like any other set.]

Sets in the Slicer

According to the MDX specification, it is also acceptable for the slicer expression to contain a set of tuples rather than a single tuple. (However, no version of Microsoft's OLAP supports this.) Although the expression may contain a set, the database would only return a single tuple of data as the slicer by aggregating the result cells found for that tuple along the set. The aggregation performed would be as if the MDX Aggregate( ) function were used: Each base measure will be aggregated across the set by its associated aggregation function. (See Appendix A for information on the Aggregate( ) function.)

For example, the following two queries are basically equivalent:

```
SELECT
{ [Measures].[Sales], [Measures].Units } on columns,
{ Stores.[Las Vegas, NV], Stores.[San Ysidro, CA] } on rows
FROM Cube
WHERE { ([Time].[2000], [Product].[Rain Coats]),
        ([Time].[2000], [Product].[Umbrellas]) }

WITH
Member [Product].[CrossDimAggregate] AS
'Aggregate( { [Product].[Rain Coats], [Product].[Umbrellas] } )'
SELECT
{ [Measures].[Sales], [Measures].Units } on columns,
{ Stores.[Las Vegas, NV], Stores.[San Ysidro, CA] } on rows
FROM Cube
WHERE ( [Time].[2000], [Product].[CrossDimAggregate] )
```

These two queries will generate the same cell results at the client. However, the second variation returns the name of the calculated member to the client in the resulting slicer information, while the first returns the tuples that composed the aggregate.

Summary

We have now covered all of the basics of MDX queries and expressions. In this chapter and the last, we have gone over all of the components of a query, how we can refer to meta data in queries, what the MDX data model is, and some of the functions that are commonly used in queries. We have also seen how calculated members in a database relate to expressions in queries. With all these points fresh in our minds, we are ready to explore MDX in greater depth. In the next chapter, we take a look at using MDX to solve common calculation and query requirements.

CHAPTER 3

MDX in Use

This chapter covers a variety of topics around the construction and use of MDX, as well as some pointers on building databases that leverage the MDX constructs. This chapter aims to be a broader reference than any chapter titled "MDX for Insurance Claim Analysis" or "MDX for Manufacturing Quality and Process Optimization" would be. Of course, detailed examples in insurance and manufacturing would be worthwhile, but this book and chapter are a bit more general in scope. Along the way, we show some ways that the various operators and functions of MDX can be used together.

The topics presented in this chapter are among the most common calculation and analysis techniques that a variety of applications will use. Different application domains may use different terminology for the same technique. For example, analyses of insurance claims, production quality control, and customer shopping preferences may all require the calculation of an item's percentage contribution to an aggregated item. In an insurance claim analysis, this calculation may be required to see which claimants, treatments, or plans consume the largest proportion of resources. In a production quality control analysis, this calculation may be used to see which products or production steps produce the greatest proportion of defects. In a customer shopping preference analysis, this calculation may be used to see which products contribute the highest proportion of profits for a customer or set of customers, or which customers are the proportionately highest volume shoppers for a store. However, they all use the same basic dimensional calculation.

This chapter is divided into three main sections. The first is devoted to commonly required straightforward expressions which describe bread-and-butter calculations required by many applications. The second section is devoted to more advanced expressions and analytical queries that will be used by more sophisticated applications and reports. In the last section of the chapter, we will work through the construction of a detailed series of analytical queries. Working through all of the examples and techniques we provide in this chapter should give you a good grasp of the principles underlying their construction and the tools available for constructing whatever MDX you need to solve a particular problem.

If you are familiar with data warehousing already, then you may be looking to solve certain tasks that are well defined in data warehousing terminology. We will talk about calculation issues for semi-additive and non-additive measures in the "Different Aggregations along Different Dimensions (Semi-Additive Measures)" section.

NOTE
We will use MDX functions and operators in this chapter without describing them in detail. If you want to pick up details on them, read their descriptions in Appendix A. We'll encourage you right now to start reading the function reference just to get an idea of what the functions available to you are.

If you want to find a way to solve a calculation problem immediately, here is an outline of the topics in this chapter:

- Many kinds of ratios, averages, percentages, and allocations
  - Simple ratios between levels in a hierarchy
  - Ratio to parent
  - Ratio to ancestor
  - Ratio to [All]
  - Percentage contribution to parent/ancestor/All
  - Handling divide-by-zero
  - Basic allocations
  - Proportional allocation of one quantity based on the ratios of another
  - Unweighted allocations down the hierarchy
  - Averages
  - Simple averages
  - Weighted averages

- Time-based references and time-series calculations
  - Period-to-period references and calculations
  - Year-ago references and calculations
  - Year-to-date (period-to-date) aggregations
  - Rolling averages
  - 52-week high/low
- Different aggregations along different dimensions (semi-additive measures)
  - Mixing aggregations: sum across non-time, average/min/max along time
  - Mixing aggregations: sum across non-time, opening/closing balance along time
- Using member properties in MDX expressions (calculations and sorting)
- Filling in blanks
  - Carryover of balances for slowly changing values
  - Reporting of last entered balance (as opposed to balance for last time descendant)
  - Finding the last time member for which any data has been entered

Each of these calculations is a fairly generic operation that many applications require, regardless of their analytical domain (finance, manufacturing quality, shipping, consumer behavior). They are also more expressions and types of calculations than they are whole analytical queries. We discuss more sophisticated analytical queries in the next chapter. We will now discuss in order each of the expressions presented in the preceding list.

Many Kinds of Ratios, Averages, Percentages, and Allocations

Ratios are one of the most common calculation requirements in an OLAP system, after sums and differences. Percentages, averages, and allocations are all either alternate names for ratios, alternate representations of a ratio, or based on ratios. We devote this section to a variety of common ratios. We won't deal with the most common ratio (taking the ratio of two measures for some location), because we've already done that in earlier chapters.

Simple Ratios between Levels in a Hierarchy

One very common calculation that MDX beginners need to master is how to calculate the ratio of some member to an aggregate based on that member in order to obtain a "percentage of total." This calculation has several permutations. If the total is found at some member of the hierarchy, then the ratio is very simple and can be put into any calculated member. We'll discuss that case here. If the total is found by aggregating some user-defined selection, then you need to do that work in a query. We discuss that case in Chapter 9, "Advanced Operations and Commands—Drill-Through and Actions." The following is a list of the generic types of these ratios within a hierarchy:

- Ratio to parent
- Ratio to ancestor
- Ratio to [All]
- Percentage contribution to parent/ancestor/All

Each of these types of calculations involves taking the ratio of some measure at one level to the measure's aggregate at a higher level and returning the result to a different measure at the lower-level location. Using a payroll expense cube containing a geography dimension as an example, we can find the following examples.

Ratio to parent:

```
[Measures].[Payroll Total] /
([Measures].[Payroll Total], [Geography].CurrentMember.Parent)
```

Ratio to ancestor:

```
[Measures].[Payroll Total] /
([Measures].[Payroll Total],
  Ancestor ([Geography].CurrentMember, [Geography].[State]))
```

Ratio to [All]:

```
[Measures].[Payroll Total] /
([Measures].[Payroll Total], [All Geography])
```

A calculated measure that uses the appropriate formula will specifically name the measure it is taking the ratio of. For example, the ratio to ancestor expression appears in the following query, which requests the payroll proportions and total payroll for each store in Texas and Louisiana, with the results shown in Figure 3.1:

```
WITH MEMBER [Measures].[State Payroll Proportion] AS
'[Measures].[Payroll Total] / ([Measures].[Payroll Total],
   Ancestor ([Geography].CurrentMember, [Geography].[State]))',
```

```
SOLVE_ORDER = 5
SELECT
{ [Measures].[Payroll Total], [Measures].[State Payroll Proportion] } on
columns,
{ Descendants ([Geography].[State].[TX], [Geography].[Store],
            SELF_AND_BEFORE),
  Descendants ([Geography].[State].[LA], [Geography].[Store],
            SELF_AND_BEFORE)
} on rows
FROM [Overheads]
WHERE [Time].[Year].[1999]
```

This calculation could also be put into a calculated member defined at the server, in which case the WITH MEMBER section of the query would be unnecessary.

Measures

Geography	Payroll Total	State Payroll Proportion
TX	110	100
Laredo	65	59
Store_TX001	30	27
Store_TX002	20	18
Store_TX003	15	14
Dallas	45	41
Store_TX004	25	23
Store_TX005	20	18
LA	125	100
Baton Rouge	30	24
Store_LA001	20	16
Store_LA002	10	8
Shreveport	95	76
Store_LA003	15	12
Store_LA004	50	40
Store_LA005	30	24

Figure 3.1 Results of ratio-to-ancestor query.

You will want to keep in mind where these ratios can be calculated. A calculated member that uses the ratio-to-parent pattern will be valid at every level except the top level in the dimension because there is no parent for the member(s) there. The ratio to ancestor will be valid at every level from the ancestor's level (where the ratio's value will simply be 1, unless the total is 0) down to the leaf level. The ratio to [All] will be valid everywhere in the dimension. It is a special case of ratio to ancestor, but it will be slightly more efficient to phrase this special case as the "ratio to the [All]" member than as the "ancestor of the current member at the All level."

Handling Divide-by-Zero

One issue that almost always pops up when taking ratios is how to handle division by zero. The standard way is to compare the denominator to zero and return NULL, if that is the case. For example, the preceding Payroll Proportion calculation would be re-phrased as the following to handle zeros:

```
'iif (
 ([Measures].[Payroll Total],
   Ancestor ([Geography].CurrentMember, [Geography].[State])) = 0,
 NULL,
 [Measures].[Payroll Total] / ([Measures].[Payroll Total],
   Ancestor ([Geography].CurrentMember, [Geography].[State]))
 )'
```

Basic Allocations

One use of ratios between levels within a hierarchy is to use the ratios to allocate higher-level values like total overhead or sales down to lower levels like individual business units or products. Here, we will discuss two basic types of allocations: allocation of a measure weighted by some proportion of another, and unweighted allocation.

Proportional Allocation of One Quantity Based on Ratios of Another

Given a ratio between a measure and its value at some ancestor, you can perform a proportional allocation of any other measure based on that ratio. The measure being allocated is likely to come from a higher level than the target locations, although it could come from the same level. For example, budgeting models frequently allocate costs from a higher level down, based on head count or anticipated sales. Suppose that you need to allocate an advertising budget to arrive at a calculated budget per store, given your anticipated sales aggregated up a geography dimension. The following calculated measure would perform the allocation of advertising budget based on sales:

```
CREATE MEMBER [Measures].[Allocated Advertising] AS
'([Measures].[Advertising], [Geography].[All Geography]) *
[Measures].[Sales] / ([Measures].[Sales], [All Geography])'
```

At the [All Geography] member, the allocated advertising budget should be equal to the total advertising budget. Assuming that sales has summed evenly up all levels, at each state in the Geography.State level, the allocated advertising budget should be proportional to that state's sales compared to the total organization's sales. At each city, the allocated ad budget should be proportional to that city's sales compared with the cities in that state. That budget should also be proportional to the city's sales compared with the total organization's sales.

Unweighted Allocations Down the Hierarchy

You may also need to allocate values for some measure down a hierarchy, but in proportion to the number of children under a parent, rather than in proportion to some other measure's values. For example, measures that were input by quarter may need to be spread out to days. In this case, the ratio is simply going to be the reciprocal of the number of days in each quarter. In general, to get the ratio, you simply divide 1 by the number of descendants under the ancestor of the current member in that dimension. For example, to allocate from the quarter level of the time dimension down to a lower time level, the ratio would be expressed by the following:

```
(1.0 / Count (Descendants (Ancestor ([Time].CurrentMember, [Time].
[Quarter]), [Time].CurrentMember.Level, SELF), INCLUDEEMPTY))
```

Notice that we use the *Member*.Level operator to get the level of the current member in the time dimension. For clarity, we also explicitly list the default SELF option for Descendants( ).

Averages

Another very frequent task in OLAP applications is to calculate averages. There are a number of types of averages to calculate; we'll look at some simpler ones here. Rolling averages will be treated in their own section later.

Simple Averages

Because Microsoft OLAP Services does not provide the capability to pre-aggregate data by averaging, you will frequently calculate an average by explicitly taking the ratio of a measure that represents a sum with a measure that represents a count. Since the measures often represent the same concept aggregated two different ways, their names will often be related, as in the following expression that you might well use as the formula for a Sales Average calculated measure:

```
[Measures].[Sales Sum] / [Measures].[Item Count]
```

If you need to take a simple average of values associated with a set of cells, you can use the MDX Avg( ) function, as in the following example:

```
WITH
SET [Best5Custs] AS
'TopCount ([Customer].[Individual].Members, 5, [Measures].[Profit])'
MEMBER [Customer].[Avg Over Best] AS 'Avg ([Best5Custs])'
SELECT
{ [Measures].[Sales], [Measures].[Units], [Measures].[Profit] }
on columns,
{ [Products].[Category].Members } on rows
FROM Sales
WHERE ([Customer].[Avg Over Best])
```

This query returns a grid of three measures by N product categories. The sales, units, and profit measures are each averaged over the five best customers in terms of total profit. The mechanics of this query are diagrammed in Figure 3.2. Notice that we left the expression to be averaged by the Avg( ) function unspecified in the [Avg Over Best] calculation. Leaving it unspecified is the equivalent of saying:

```
([Measures].CurrentMember, [Products].CurrentMember , . . . )
```

Weighted Averages

When we calculate weighted averages, we are usually trying to take the average of some ratio (like the price per share of stock) weighted by some quantity of the quotient (like the number of shares traded). What we want to calculate is the average of the product of these two things. As far as the calculation architecture of OLAP Services is concerned, the most efficient overall way to calculate the average of the product would be by performing the multiplication into yet another measure in the fact table, and then summing it and counting it through the implicit aggregations. Assuming that this was not done for us (we might have wanted to precalculate a variety of things that weren't), we can still do it effectively. For example, the expression

```
Avg(
  CrossJoin(
    Descendants ([Industry].CurrentMember, [Industry].[Company], SELF),
    Descendants ([Time].CurrentMember, [Time].[Day], SELF)
```

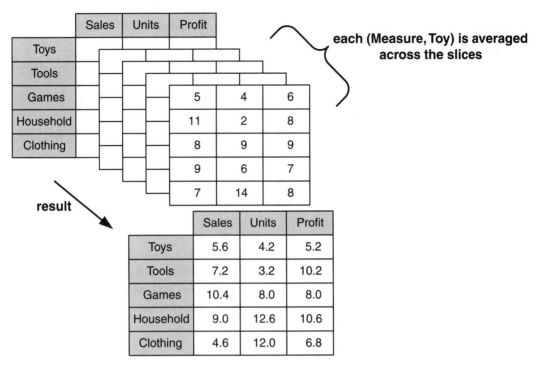

each (Measure, Toy) is averaged across the slices

result

	Sales	Units	Profit
Toys	5.6	4.2	5.2
Tools	7.2	3.2	10.2
Games	10.4	8.0	8.0
Household	9.0	12.6	10.6
Clothing	4.6	12.0	6.8

Figure 3.2 Calculated aggregate member as a slicer.

```
    )
   ,([Measures].[Share Price] * [Measures].[Units Sold])
    )
```

will calculate this weighted average.

A difficulty lurks in formulating the query this way, however. The greater the number of dimensions we are including in our average, the larger the size of the cross-joined set. We can run into performance problems (as well as intelligibility problems) if the number of dimensions being combined is large. Moreover, we should account for all dimensions in the cube or we may accidentally involve aggregate [share price] values in a multiplication, which will probably be an error. So, if you are setting up a database for others to use and some measures, such as prices, are ratios, try to anticipate the ways in which the measures will be used. For example, in Microsoft OLAP/Analysis Services, if the [Units Sold] and [Share Price] can come from the same fact table, then a single base measure can calculate their product, and another regular member can provide a count of transactions, so that the weighted average can be calculated as a simple ratio in the cube.

Time-Based References and Time-Series Calculations

A great many OLAP reports and analyses revolve around time. In this section, we will take a look at the basics of working with the time dimension in terms of referencing members and cells based on time and in terms of time-series calculations. The examples in this section create calculated measures that define time-series calculations. In Chapter 11 "Advanced Applications in Cube Design," we discuss database options and MDX constructs for making time-based calculations even more powerful.

NOTE In all of these examples, we are assuming that time is a single-hierarchy dimension. Many time dimensions will have multiple hierarchies. Multiple time hierarchies will add a layer of complexity that we will not address here, but the section "Multiple Time Hierarchies" in Chapter 11 will deal with the relevant issues.

Period-to-Period References and Calculations

One typical query requirement is to return or use data from a prior period. For example, the following query includes a calculated measure that returns the period-to-period difference in expenses:

```
WITH MEMBER [Measures].[Period Expense Increase] AS
'[Measures].[Expenses]
- ([Measures].[Expenses], [Time].CurrentMember.PrevMember)'
SELECT
{ [Time].[Quarter].Members } on columns,
{ [Measures].[Expenses], [Measures].[Period Expense Increase] } on rows
FROM Costing
```

The way that the calculation is phrased, it does not matter what level the time members in the query belong to. The following is equally valid, and its results are shown in Figure 3.3. Note that the Q2 difference is based on Q1 and Q2 expenses, while each month's difference is based on its expense and the prior month's expense:

```
WITH MEMBER [Measures].[Period Expense Increase] AS
'[Measures].[Expenses]
- ([Measures].[Expenses], [Time].CurrentMember.PrevMember)'
SELECT
{ [Time].[Quarter].[Q1, 1999], [Time].[Quarter].[Q1, 1999].Children,
  [Time].[Quarter].[Q2, 1999], [Time].[Quarter].[Q2, 1999].Children
```

Time

		Q1-1999	Jan-1999	Feb-1999	Mar-1999	Q2-1999	Apr-1999	May-1999	Jun-1999
Measures	Expenses	300	100	110	90	350	80	100	170
	Period Expense Increase			10	-20	50	-10	20	70

Figure 3.3 Result from multi-level prior-period calculation.

```
} on columns,
{ [Measures].[Expenses], [Measures].[Period Expense Increase] } on rows
FROM Costing
```

Year-Ago References and Calculations

Another very common request is for the same period one year ago. This is very easy to phrase in MDX, and in such a way that the query can be run for any time level at or below the year (such as months, quarters, weeks, or days). The following query demonstrates the use of the ParallelPeriod( ) function for just this purpose:

```
WITH MEMBER [Measures].[Year-ago Expense Increase] AS
'[Measures].[Expenses]
- ([Measures].[Expenses],
    ParallelPeriod ([Time].[Year], 1, [Time].CurrentMember))'
SELECT
{ [Time].[Quarter].[Q1, 1999], [Time].[Quarter].[Q1, 1999].Children,
    [Time].[Quarter].[Q1, 2000], [Time].[Quarter].[Q1, 2000].Children
} on columns,
{ [Measures].[Expenses], [Measures].[Year-ago Expense Increase] } on
rows
FROM Costing
```

Our treatment of this topic is not quite complete with respect to Microsoft's OLAP and Analysis Services. Let's assume that January 1999 is the first month in the time dimension. What should the year-ago or period-ago value be when we do a period-to-period difference (or ratio) for January 1999 or Q1 1999? If we don't account for this in the calculated member expression, we'll get a misleading result because Microsoft's OLAP will substitute a value of zero into the overall equation, and we probably want to see an empty difference. We'll rewrite the expression here to deal with it, and we'll explain the topic in more detail in Chapter 5, "MDX Context and Execution." In Analysis Services 2000, we can re-write the period-to-period expression as follows to give us empty results for the beginning of 1999:

```
WITH MEMBER [Measures].[Period Expense Increase] AS
'iif (
  [Time].CurrentMember.PrevMember IS NULL,
  NULL,
  [Measures].[Expenses]
  - ([Measures].[Expenses], [Time].CurrentMember.PrevMember)
)'
SELECT
{ [Time].[Quarter].[Q1, 1999], [Time].[Quarter].[Q1, 1999].Children,
  [Time].[Quarter].[Q2, 1999], [Time].[Quarter].[Q2, 1999].Children
} on columns,
{ [Measures].[Expenses], [Measures].[Period Expense Increase] } on rows
FROM Costing
```

Year-to-Date (Period-to-Date) Aggregations

The calculation of year-to-date totals (or averages) is also a frequent requirement. The examples we have just looked at involved referencing individual members. Year-to-date calculations, by contrast, involve aggregating over a set of time members. We can go about constructing these sets in a couple of different ways.

The PeriodsToDate( ) function provides a direct way of building the set. The function is documented in detail in Appendix A. To calculate a year-to-date total, such as year-to-date expenses, we can create and use the calculated member in the following query:

```
WITH MEMBER [Measures].[YTD Expenses] AS
'Sum (
  PeriodsToDate ( [Time].[Year], [Time].CurrentMember ),
  [Measures].[Expenses]
)'
SELECT
{ [Time].[Quarter].[Q3, 2000], [Time].[Quarter].[Q4, 2000],
  [Time].[Quarter].[Q1, 2001]
} on columns,
{ [Measures].[Expenses], [Measures].[YTD Expenses] } on rows
FROM Costing
```

If the time dimension is tagged as being of Time type and the year level within it is tagged as being of type Year, then you could also use the shorthand

```
'Sum (
  YtoD ([Time].CurrentMember),
  [Measures].[Expenses]
)'
```

or even

```
'Sum (
  YtoD (),
  [Measures].[Expenses]
)'
```

One requirement that comes up for some applications is calculating a running total for all periods to date in the database. That is, instead of year-to-date, the request is for all time-to-date. This is pretty straightforward, although there is no direct MDX primitive for it. We can reference the first member at our current level of the time dimension with either [Time].CurrentMember.Level.Members.Item(0) or OpeningPeriod ([Time].[All Time], [Time].CurrentMember .Level). The first way takes the level of the current time member, gets its members, and selects the first member in it, while the second one simply asks for the opening period at the current member's level across all times. The second way also requires an All level in the time dimension. Using the first way, we could specify:

```
WITH MEMBER [Measures].[All Accumulated Expenses] AS
'Sum (
  { OpeningPeriod ([Time].[All Time], [Time].CurrentMember.Level)
    : [Time].CurrentMember },
  [Measures].[Expenses]
)'
SELECT
{ [Time].[Quarter].[Q3, 2000], [Time].[Quarter].[Q4, 2000],
  [Time].[Quarter].[Q1, 2001]
} on columns,
{ [Measures].[Expenses], [Measures].[All Accumulated Expenses] } on rows
FROM Costing
```

The most direct way, if the time dimension has an All level, is simply to use PeriodsToDate( ) with the [Time].[(All)] level:

```
WITH MEMBER [Measures].[All Accumulated Expenses] AS
'Sum (
  PeriodsToDate ( [Time].[(All)], [Time].CurrentMember ),
  [Measures].[Expenses]
)'
SELECT
{ [Time].[Quarter].[Q3, 2000], [Time].[Quarter].[Q4, 2000],
  [Time].[Quarter].[Q1, 2001]
} on columns,
{ [Measures].[Expenses], [Measures].[All Accumulated Expenses] } on rows
FROM Costing
```

If you have no All level in the time dimension, then you must use {[Time].CurrentMember.Level.Members.Item(0) : [Time].CurrentMember } to define the set over which you are aggregating.

Rolling Averages and 52-week High/low

These two calculations are part of a general class of calculations that we will call *moving aggregates*, in which a measure is aggregated over a sliding window of members within a level. (A Pareto, or 80/20 , analysis is related to moving aggregates, but in Pareto, the window is fixed at one end and grows toward the other. We will talk about the techniques for related calculations in the "Pareto Analysis and Cumulative Sums" section of Chapter 4.)

In a moving aggregation, the important technique is to construct a range within the level using endpoints that are relative to the current member. MDX gives us several functions and operators to construct these with: Dimension.CurrentMember lets us reference the current member; the colon (:) implies a range between two endpoints; and .Lag( ), .Lead( ), PrevMember( ), NextMember( ), Cousin( ), and ParallelPeriod( ) all let us reference members that are related to the current member. Note that to use these MDX member-referencing operators and functions, we assume that the ordering of members within the hierarchy corresponds with the ordering our sliding window will follow. For the time dimension, this will be generally true.

Let's go through some examples. Consider the following two expressions:

```
Avg ( { [Time].CurrentMember.Lag(5) : [Time].CurrentMember },
     Measures.[Volume Traded])
Avg (LastPeriods (6, [Time].CurrentMember),
     [Measures].[Volume Traded])
```

These expressions easily take the rolling average over a six-period time range: from the current time through the time five units back (0, 1, 2, 3, 4, and 5 units away makes six periods altogether). The expression

```
Avg( {[Time].CurrentMember.PrevMember, [Time].CurrentMember,}
     [Measures].[Volume Traded])
```

takes the average of the current period and the prior period.

Notice that each of these three expressions is taking either a six-period or two-period average, not a six-month or two-day average. The level at which these averages are being calculated is determined by the context they are being evaluated at. If the first expression we gave is being calculated for a month-level cell, then it will create a six-month average, and if it is being calculated for a year-level cell, it will create a six-year average.

We can control that behavior in a couple of ways. If the measure being calculated truly needs to be a six-month average, we can control the function so it is only evaluated at the month level (read the section titled "One Formula Calculating Different Things in Different Places" in Chapter 4, "Advanced MDX Application Topics"). If the measure really means "Average over the last half-year's worth of data at this level," then we can use the ParallelPeriod( ) or Cousin( ) functions to set this up for multiple levels at the same time.

If we have a half-year level in our database, we can be direct, as with the following two expressions:

```
Avg( { ParallelPeriod ([Time].[HalfYear], 1, [Time].CurrentMember) :
[Time].CurrentMember }, [Measures].[Volume Traded])
Avg( {ParallelPeriod ( [Time].[HalfYear]) : [Time].CurrentMember },
[Measures].[Volume Traded])
```

The second of these examples is terse but adequate, in that the 1 and Time.CurrentMember are the default arguments for ParallelPeriod. If we don't have a half-year level, but we do have quarters, then we can be a little less direct:

```
Avg( { ParallelPeriod ([Time].[Quarter], 2, [Time].CurrentMember) :
Time.CurrentMember }, [Measures].[Volume Traded])
```

This works as well because two quarters create the same distance as one half-year. A 52-period high can be computed at the week level with the following:

```
Max ({ [Time].Lag(51) : [Time] }, [Measures].[Share Price])
Max ({ LastPeriods (52, [Time]) }, [Measures].[Share Price])
```

If your calendar uses years and weeks, you may have some 53-week years to deal with inconsistencies between weeks and years. ParallelPeriod( ) will not work when you are looking for the fifty-third week of one year in a parallel year that has only 52 weeks, so you wouldn't want to use it for that purpose.

Note as well in the "Invalid Locations" discussion of Chapter 5 "MDX Context and Execution," that when there is no time period 52 weeks ago or two quarters ago, we will get ranges of time members in our sets that may or may not be what we want.

Different Aggregations along Different Dimensions (Semi-Additive Measures)

In this section, we will discuss aggregating along the time dimension using a different function than along the other dimensions. We will discuss two basic cases: taking the average, min, or max along time, and taking the opening or closing balance along time. In the data warehousing community, the term "semi-additive" measure refers to a measure that sums along one set of dimensions, but not along others.

Mixing Aggregations: Sum across Non-time, Average/Min/Max along Time

Depending on the data you are aggregating, cases may arise when you want the measures to aggregate according to different techniques in different dimensions. For example, measures that represent populations, including both people and inventory, will typically sum in all dimensions except time and they will aggregate across time by average, MIN, or MAX.

OLAP Services's built-in SUM, COUNT, MIN, and MAX aggregations for base measures aggregate along all dimensions equally. To take an average over the time dimension of sums over the non-time dimensions, we take the average of the pre-calculated sums over the averaging period. We must be careful to define the averaging period as being the span of time members from the time level at which the data entered the cube. Otherwise, we will be dividing by either too many time periods or too few. To take the MIN or MAX over the time of sums over non-times, we simply need to take the MIN or MAX over the time period. We can do each of these by using the Descendants( ) function, which will return the appropriate set.

For many applications, we will discover that the measure that we want to sum and then average will already be implicitly summed up to the current level. In this case, we can simply divide the sum we find by the number of time periods over which the data entered the cube. For example, in a human resources-related cube, our Headcount measure represents a population. Assuming that the head count number is input at the week level of time, in order to calculate the average and maximum aggregate head counts for the enterprise, we would need to use the following query:

```
WITH
MEMBER [Measures].[Aggregated Headcount] AS
'[Measures].[Headcount] / Count (Descendants ([Time].CurrentMember,
[Time].[Week], SELF)'
MEMBER [Measures].[Max Headcount] AS
'Max (Descendants ([Time].CurrentMember, [Time].[Week], SELF),
[Measures].[HeadCount])'
   . . .
```

Mixing Aggregations: Sum across Non-time, Opening/Closing Balance along Time

For inventory balances, we are frequently also interested in opening and closing amounts in any time period. This can be expressed straightforwardly in

MDX. The OpeningPeriod( ) and ClosingPeriod( ) functions give us direct references to the appropriate members. For example, the following defines a measure that represents the closing inventory balance for any time period:

```
CREATE MEMBER [InventoryCube].[Measures].[Closing Balance] AS
'([Measures].[Inventory],
  ClosingPeriod ([Time].[Day], [Time].CurrentMember)
)'
```

From whatever time member we are at in any time level, we can find the last day-level member that corresponds to that time in the hierarchy, and the value is taken from that member. Since this is not really an aggregation function (it selects from a single member, not over a range), it executes quickly, even though it is not pre-aggregated.

If you are looking to calculate the last balance found in a time range in which not all of the data has been filled in (that is, the last balance so far in the quarter since we only have data for October and November), look ahead to the section "Carryover of Balances for Slowly Changing Values" for techniques on carrying over balances for slowly changing values.

Using Member Properties in MDX Expressions (Calculations and Sorting)

Member properties in a dimension are often used as the basis for selecting members and sorting them in queries, as well as for simply displaying alongside query results. You may be interested in sorting a set of customers by the date they first placed orders, or sorting stores by their associated zip/postal code rather than their name.

In order to reference member properties in an OLAP/Analysis Services MDX expression, including for filtering and sorting, as well as for other cell calculations, you need to make use of the .Properties( ) function, as opposed to using the standard MDX member property syntax. Through that, you can use the values of member properties generally as though they were values of cells, although you need to remember that .Properties( ) returns strings regardless of the underlying type of the member property. For example, if store square footage is a numerical member property and sales is a measure in a cube, the expression that calculates sales per square foot is:

```
[Measures].[Sales] / Val([Store].CurrentMember.Properties ("Store Sq
Ft"))
```

We might also sort our stores by square footage in a query; the following query uses the same member property to sort on:

```
SELECT
{ Measures.Sales, Measures.[Sales per Square Foot] } on columns,
{ Order (
  [Store].[Store].Members,
  Val ([Store].CurrentMember.Properties ("Store Sq Ft")),
  BDESC
) } DIMENSION PROPERTIES [Store].[Store].[Store Sq Ft] on rows
FROM Sales
```

In regular OLAP/Analysis Services dimensions, member properties are defined for a single level. Sometimes, this causes problems for a query if the set of members/tuples in the query includes members from other levels. For example, let's alter the previous query to request stores and cities and to simply request the square footage:

```
WITH MEMBER [Measures].[Square Feet] AS
'Val ([Store].CurrentMember.Properties ("Store Sq Ft"))'
SELECT
{ Measures.Sales, Measures.[Sales per Square Foot] } on columns,
{ Descendants (
    [Store].[City].[Dallas, TX],
    [Store].[Store],
    SELF_AND_BEFORE
) } on rows
FROM Sales
```

The results for this are represented in Figure 3.4. Note that a "#ERR" is showing in the ([Dallas, TX], [Square Feet]) cell, which is an attempt to reference the cell value results in an error because there is no property on the [Store] dimension named "Store Sq Ft" at the city level.

If a query simply requests the value of a member property to be a new cell value (usually in the measures dimension), then the query will succeed and simply have cells for which data cannot be retrieved. However, if a query uses those member property values for another purpose, such as sorting, then the query

Difference between Val() and CDbl() with Member Properties

For converting a string into a number, we could use either Val() or CDbl(). When .Properties() returns a string form of a number, these two functions will return essentially the same value. However, there is a big difference if the string is empty or can't be found. Val() will return an error, causing the whole cell calculation to result in an error. CDbl() will return -2,147,467,259, which will not be an error, but is not a number we really want.

Measures

Geography	Sales	Sales per Square Foot
Dallas	1500	#ERR
Store_TX004	850	3.1
Store_TX005	650	2.5

Figure 3.4 Results of member property request at multiple levels.

will fail in its entirety. For example, the following query attempts to sort the [Store] members of the previous query by the store square footage. Attempting to execute the query will fail, though:

```
SELECT
{ [Measures].[Sales], [Measures].[Sales per Square Foot] } on columns,
{ Order (
  Descendants (
    [Store].[City].[Dallas, TX],
    [Store].[Store],
    SELF_AND_BEFORE
  ),
  Val ([Store].CurrentMember.Properties ("Store Sq Ft")),
  DESC
) } on rows
FROM Sales
```

Also, you should be aware that in Analysis Services, member properties cannot be defined for a server-defined All level, so accessing a property there will fail too. (This is one reason to provide an explicit All level in your database.)

If you run into a case where you need to sort a multi-level set by a member property, then you should include a test for the level the member is at. For example, say that you only need to perform a simple hierarchical ordering by the store square footage. When you do not break the hierarchy in a sort, members will sort into hierarchical order if there is nothing else to distinguish them. We can include a test for the appropriate level into the Order() clause as follows to make the query work:

```
SELECT
{ [Measures].[Sales], [Measures].[Sales per Square Foot] } on columns,
{ Order (
  Descendants (
```

```
      [Store].[City].[Dallas, TX],
      [Store].[Store],
      SELF_AND_BEFORE
    ),
    iif (
      [Store].CurrentMember.Level IS [Store].[Store],
      Val ([Store].CurrentMember.Properties ("Store Sq Ft")),
      NULL
    ),
    DESC
  ) } on rows
FROM Sales
```

TIP

The [All] member defined by Microsoft OLAP/Analysis Server never has database member properties associated with it. For correct queries, you either need to include MDX logic that handles a reference to the [All] member, or you need to define an All member in your dimension table(s) with which you can associate member properties.

Similar constraints hold for filtering members. For example, if you are trying to filter out of a set the members that have a certain property value (retaining all of the others), of course the members at the higher levels don't have the wrong property value. You would need to compose the filter expression to retain these members or to filter them out as well so the error result of Val( ) doesn't cause the whole query to fail:

```
Filter (
  Descendants (
    [Store].[City].[Dallas, TX],
    [Store].[Store],
    SELF_AND_BEFORE
  ),
  iif (
    [Store].CurrentMember.Level IS [Store].[Store],
    Val ([Store].CurrentMember.Properties ("Store Sq Ft")) < 250,
    1  /* this value will function as a TRUE value */
  )
)
```

One thing that we have not yet addressed is what [Measures].[Sales per Square Foot] means at higher levels. Ideally, if we care about this, we should think about making [Square Feet] a measure of a one-dimensional cube (dimensioned by Store) and then combining it with sales information in a virtual cube.

Remember that member properties are defined for a particular level, but when you reference them through the .Properties( ) function, only the name is of interest, not the unique name. This means that if the same property name is in

Database Design Tip

If you find yourself using member properties as values in calculations in Microsoft OLAP/Analysis Services, consider turning the member property into a measure of a one-dimensional cube and joining it in a virtual cube to the cubes in which you are using it to calculate. For example, we could have created a cube consisting of a single [Store Sq Ft] measure and just the Store dimension, and made a virtual cube with it and the Sales cube our examples were using. Then, we'd have no data conversion issues, and we'd have automatic aggregation of city-level and state-level square footage as well.

two or more levels, all of them will return a result when referenced through the .Properties( ) function. In the case of parent-child dimensions, a member property is defined for every apparent level (except perhaps the All level, depending on the dimension definition), because internally, all parent-child members are stored in one database level.

Filling in Blanks

Occasions will arise when you need to look up the most recently entered value for a non-time dimensional slice, such as the size of the most recent purchase made by a customer. The following section explains techniques for creating a carryover of balances and reporting the last entered balance.

Carryover of Balances for Slowly Changing Values and Reporting of Last Entered Balance

Sometimes records in a fact table represent the attainment of a certain state, such as an account balance or a salary level. Rather than posting these records every time period, these records will only appear when the state is attained. Your application would like to use the value that is relevant for the time period of evaluation, yet the last record for that kind of balance may have been posted that month, one time period ago, two time periods ago, or more.

You can get around this problem within Microsoft OLAP Services, but it may be worth your time to perform the logic in SQL so a value actually exists for each month. This is because whenever the slowly changing value is used as the input for a calculation (especially one that is then aggregated), the calculations will be performed in a cache at run time. When the calculation is then aggregated, as a calculation involving a tax rate, price, or salary would be, the performance of the query may be quite bad.

Two very different methods can be used to perform the reference for balance carryover for slowly changing values: by a recursive calculated member function and by using set expressions. The most practical method in terms of calculation speed is the recursive function. (We do not know whether to recommend recursive functions as a general style because we do not know how deep the stack that the recursion relies on is. It seems to be deep enough for all applications that we have tried.) The set expression technique is instructive for examining issues in expression construction, however, but let's look at the recursive calculation first.

Our goal is to find the most recent value for a cell if one is not available in the current cell. This means we need to test whether the current cell is empty or not, and if it is empty, we need to check the previous cell. To efficiently reference the previous cell, we should put this calculation into its own calculated measure that searches the last found value of the measure we are interested in. A calculated member that almost does this to our liking is as follows:

```
WITH MEMBER [Measures].[Last Update of Price] AS
'iif (NOT IsEmpty ([Measures].[Price]),
  [Measures].[Price],
  ([Measures].[Last Update of Price], [Time].PrevMember)
)'
 . . .
```

The reason this calculated member is almost but not quite adequate is that if the value for [Price] at the first time member along this level were itself empty, the formula would reference the value for a non-existent member. This would make the cell reference for [Measures].[Price] empty and trigger a recursive reference for another non-existent cell from another non-existent member. Since MDX does not intrinsically distinguish between invalid locations and empty cells, we need to wire the appropriate logic into the expression. We can do this by testing whether the time member itself exists using the Microsoft-specific IS operator, as in the following expression:

```
WITH MEMBER [Measures].[Last Update of Price] AS
'iif ( NOT IsEmpty ([Measures].[Price]),
  [Measures].[Price],
  iif ( [Time].PrevMember IS NULL,
    NULL,
    ([Measures].[Last Update of Price], [Time].PrevMember)
  )
)'
 . . .
```

Since we expect that some value will usually be found before the searching operation runs off the edge of the dimension, we place the clause that tests for the edge of the dimension after the test for a valid cell value. Either way, [Last Update of Price] now returns values corresponding to the most recent change of price at the level which the measure is requested.

Now, let us see how we would express this using set expressions. A set-based strategy would be to (1) filter out all empty cells and then (2) isolate the last one. The following is a search expression that makes no assumptions about where data can be found and performs those two steps:

```
Tail(
  Filter( PeriodsToDate([Time].[All]),
    NOT IsEmpty ([Measures].[Price])
  )
  , 1
)
```

If you are assured that every N time period will contain one record, then you can search through that many periods with .Lag( ) or LastPeriods( ), as with:

```
Tail(
  Filter( LastPeriods (12, [Time].CurrentMember),
    NOT IsEmpty([Measures].[Price])
  )
  , 1
)
```

Since each of these options returns a set of one tuple, you will need to do something to turn it into a single value. The .Item( ) function will extract this one tuple, which expands our expression. The full member definition for [Last Update of Price] becomes the following:

```
WITH MEMBER [Measures].[Last Update of Price] AS
'Tail(
  Filter( PeriodsToDate([Time].[All]),
    NOT IsEmpty([Measures].[Price])
  )
  , 1
).Item (0)'
  . . .
```

Regardless of how we defined it, using our last found value in queries is straightforward. Using it to calculate further values is also straightforward, but possibly costly. Let us assume that we have an adequate [Last Update of Price] measure. Using it to compute, say, [Dollars Sold] AS '[Units Sold] * [Last Update of Price]' will almost certainly require that we aggregate it. Performing aggregations of leaf-level cells in MDX also can be expensive if the number of leaf-level cells being aggregated to solve our query is high. The aggregation function will need to incorporate potentially all leaf-level cells, which will be expensive with one or more large dimensions:

```
WITH MEMBER [Measures].[Dollars Sold] AS
'Sum (Descendants ([Time].CurrentMember, [Time].[Month],
  Sum (Descendants ([Geography].CurrentMember, [Geography].[Store],
    Sum (Descendants ([Products].CurrentMember, [Products].[SKU]),
      ([Measures][Units Sold] * [Measures][Last Update of Price])
 )))'
 . . .
```

This assumes that sales only vary by time, geography, and product. If sales vary by other dimensions, then those dimensions must all have aggregations in the formula for Dollars Sold as well.

Note that the difficulty with these carryover calculations is more in tractability than logic. OLAP Services provides a much more convenient environment for expressing the logic of [Last update of price] than SQL. And in your specific environment, the system that feeds you transaction data may currently only track changes to price (or salary, tax rate, and so on). However, the larger the number of dimensions involved in calculations that use this value and the larger the number of members in these dimensions, the greater the challenge of maintaining them and the greater the resources required to calculate them. Furthermore, other applications in your overall decision-support environment may well benefit from having these values explicitly maintained at every time period. For example, data mining tools tend to have very weak dimensional logic, and their capability to discover patterns based on rates or balances over time will be enhanced if the rates or balances are explicit in the database.

Finding the Last Time Member for Which Any Data Has Been Entered

An issue related to reporting the last entered balance is determining the last time period for which data is actually available. A cube may use a time dimension with months for the entire year for budgeting purposes, but while the year is in progress, the last month for which data is available will not be the last month for the year. One solution for this is to use an external function to retrieve the last time period for which that data was stored from an external source. (We discuss this use for an external function in Chapter 8, "Building Queries in MDX.")

Another plausible solution, entirely in MDX, would be to scan the leaf level of the time dimension for the last non-empty time member at the All level of every other dimension. Once the cube has been processed, at every time member for which data has been entered, there will exist an aggregate value at the intersection of that time member with the All member for every other dimension. So, requesting the last time member for which there is an all-product, all-store, all-customer (and so on) sales value present would give you the last time member for which you have data. An expression that returned that time member could be used in a query, in a CREATE SET or WITH SET statement, or as the expression for a default member in an Analysis Services time dimension.

The following Analysis Services CREATE SET expression will capture the last time member for which any data exists, across all levels of the time dimension, assuming that [Time].[Day] is the leaf level:

```
CREATE SET [Cube1].[Last Time Periods] AS
'Ascendants (
  Filter (
    [Time].[Day].Members,
    Not IsEmpty ([Measures].[Sales])
  ).Item (
    Filter (
      [Time].[Day].Members,
      Not IsEmpty ([Measures].[Sales])
    ).Count - 1
  ).Item (0)
)'
```

First, this filters the set of days based on whether any recorded sales value existed at the default members of each dimension. (If the default member in a dimension might not be the All member, then we should add a reference to the All member in the IsEmpty( ) tuple reference.) We want to select the last member in this set, and since we have no shorthand way to do this, we need to obtain the count of that set (which means repeating the Filter( ) expression). We subtract one from the count since .Item( ) uses a zero-based index. Finally, since the Ascendants( ) function takes a time member, and the first .Item( ) function returns a tuple, we use .Item(0) to reduce the tuple to a member.

As an alternative, to demonstrate another way of approaching the problem of finding the last tuple in a set, we present the following formulation:

```
CREATE SET [Cube1].[Last Time Periods] AS
'Ascendants (
  Order (
    Filter (
      [Time].[Day].Members,
      Not IsEmpty ([Measures].[Sales])
    ),
    CLng([Time].CurrentMember.Properties ("ID")),
    DESC
  ).Item (0).Item (0)
)'
```

We'd like to find the last member of the set of non-empty days. We can directly obtain .Item(0), which is the first member. If we can reverse the set, we can take the .Item (0) of the reversed set. Every member has an associated ID property in OLAP/Analysis Services, and this property can be used to sort on. We simply perform a descending sort on this property, and the set is now in reverse order from the database order. (Using Hierarchize (. . . , POST) would not perform the same operation.) We can now take .Item(0) of this reversed set to get the last day-tuple with data and its .Item(0) to get the last day-member.

Which of these two ways is preferable? In the first formulation, we evaluate a set twice, which sometimes will be expensive, and in this case is not. In the second formulation, we evaluate a set once and then sort it. Whether sorting is expensive or not depends on the size of the set and what you are sorting on. In most databases, either of these will perform well since the size of the time dimension is usually pretty small (1,500 members covers five years to the day level). We'd probably opt for the first way in this case.

Summary

In this chapter, we have explored the most frequent types of calculations and uses for MDX. Virtually every application of Analysis Services will use one or more of the types of calculations and set expressions that we have explored here. Additionally, we explained the techniques of applying an MDX construct that you can use much more widely than in the examples here. In the next chapter, we will explore more advanced uses of MDX that many applications will require as well.

CHAPTER 4

Advanced MDX Application Topics

N ow that we have seen a variety of common operations expressed in MDX, let us turn our attention to more advanced expressions and queries. This chapter continues from the last chapter, expanding the scope of topics. In this chapter, we're going to work through some more advanced concepts and techniques. Many of these come from assistance the author has given to other MDX users over the last two years, so if they seem esoteric at first, remember that MDX has many different applications!

The expressions and queries in this chapter are oriented more toward the composition of whole analytical queries, and the principles that go into constructing them are useful for constructing all manner of sophisticated analyses, even if the particular examples we present in this section do not address the applications you are going to build.

The types of expressions and queries we are going to explore here are:

- Using Generate( ) to turn tuple operations into set operations
- Calculating dates and date arithmetic
- Report totals-to-parent, totals-to-ancestor, and percentage contribution to report totals
- Hierarchical sorting that skips levels in the hierarchy
- Pareto analysis and cumulative sums

- Sorting on multiple criteria

- Reporting on ranks (and ranks from another time period)

- Building a set that sums backward in time

- Drilling down from virtual dimensions

- One formula calculating different things in different places (also called "formula application ranges")

- Logical aggregations (ForAny, ForEach, ForNone)

- Including all tuples with tied ranking in sets

After we work through these expressions and queries, we will apply the same principles for using MDX we discuss here in a complete series of analytical queries.

Using Generate() to Turn Tuple Operations into Set Operations

How do I get the descendants / ancestors / children / and so on from a set of members?

Most of the MDX functions and operators that return members based on hierarchical references (such Descendants( ), Ancestor( ), and the like) only work on a single member. However, you may find that you need to take the descendants or ancestors for a set of members. The way to accomplish this is to use Generate( ) around the function or operator to get it to return the set that you want.

For example, say that you want to take the average of a measure over a set of day-level descendants for a set of quarters or months that the user has chosen. The following query is tempting but will not work:

```
WITH
SET InterestingMonths AS
'LastPeriods (3, [Time].[Month].[Apr 2000])'
MEMBER [Time].[AverageVal] AS
'Average (
  Descendants (
    [InterestingMonths],    // problem!
    [Time].[Day]
  )
)', SOLVE_ORDER = 10
SELECT ...
```

Instead, we need to define [Time].[AverageVal] as

```
'Average (
  Generate (
    [InterestingMonths],
    Descendants (
      [Time].CurrentMember,
      [Time].[Day]
    )
  )
)', SOLVE_ORDER = 10
```

which loops over each given time period (be it a month, a quarter, or even a day) and produces the related day members. We'll see another example of this use of Generate( ) in the Report Totals-to-Ancestor section later in this chapter.

Calculating Dates/Date Arithmetic

Sometimes, an application calls for calculating values based on dates. Perhaps you need to calculate the number of days between two dates, or the number of days between a date-valued measure or member property and a day member in a cube. Perhaps you need to calculate the number of weekdays between two day-level members (or in a month, which works out to nearly the same thing). Or, perhaps you need to calculate an expected date for something. SQL has a fairly rigorous definition of dates and a set of date calculation functions built in. Microsoft's OLAP/Analysis Services does not contain a notion of a date/time data type, and MDX does not provide much by itself, but we can leverage external functions and MDX capabilities to do a lot of what we need.

As usual, these calculations can be implemented in more than one way. Depending on your database design, your MDX will look different.

NOTE All of the examples here are assuming a U.S. locale for constructing and parsing text representations of date values. If you are implementing in Europe, Canada or elsewhere, you will need to adjust for our assumptions.

If you are simply trying to calculate the number of days between two day-level members, and every day in the calendar has a corresponding day in the database, then you just need to count the members.

```
{ First_Day : Last_Day }.Count
```

is a brief expression that performs the count of the days (and you could subtract one from it to get the number of days in between the first and last days).

Other types of date-related calculations can rely on VBA or Excel functions. For example, let's say that you are trying to count the weeks between two dates. The VBA DateDiff( ) function can directly calculate this number, so you only need to pass the two dates into it. Assuming that the datestamp for the day members is stored as the DateStamp member property, you will also need the VBA CDate( ) function to convert it from a string into an input for DateDiff ( ). You can simply define the member (in the WITH clause of a query) as:

```
MEMBER [Measures].[WeeksBetween] AS
'VBA!DateDiff (
  "w",  // this tells it to calculate weeks
  CDate ([Time].[Day1].Properties ("DateStamp")),
  CDate ([Time].[Day2].Properties ("DateStamp"))
)'
```

(The VBA! prefix makes explicit which library the DateDiff( ) function is being called from; we discuss this notation in Chapter 7 "Extending MDX Through External Functions") This will only produce one number. To count the number of weeks between a particular day and each day returned in a query, define the member as:

```
MEMBER [Measures].[WeeksBetween] AS
'VBA!DateDiff (
  "w",
  CDate ([Time].[Day1].Properties ("DateStamp")),
  CDate ([Time].CurrentMember.Properties ("DateStamp"))
)'
```

Let's say that the starting date is a member property of the customer dimension that refers to the date the customer enrolled with our organization, named [Date Enrolled]. Then, for each customer we could get the number of weeks the customer has been enrolled. The [Time].[Day1].Properties("DateStamp") in these expressions would be replaced by [Customer].CurrentMember.Properties (" Date Enrolled"). If we have unique names across all levels of our time dimension in Analysis Services and the format of the string stored in [Date Enrolled] matches the format of our time member names (that is, "May 01, 2000"), we could substitute StrToMember ("[Time].[" + [Customer].CurrentMember.Properties ("Date Enrolled") + "]") in for the [Time].[Day1] of the preceding examples.

TIP Using unique names across the members of a time dimension (for example, [2001], [Q2, 2001], [May 2001], and [May 11, 2001]) makes it easy to perform date translations in MDX.

Another variation on this is when you are forming a query that involves a set of days from the time dimension, perhaps not every day but some days (for example, December 4, 5, 6, 9, and 10, 1999). If you want to find out how many calendar days are between the first and the last day members in the query, then you need to extract those members and plug them into the kinds of expressions that we have been looking at.

Let's assume that you simply need to calculate a time member that returns the span of days represented by the set. The VBA DateDiff() function comes in handy in this example:

```
WITH
SET [Times] AS
'{ [Dec 04, 1999], [Dec 05, 1999], [Dec 06, 1999], [Dec 09, 1999], [Dec
10, 1999] }'
MEMBER [Time].[DaysInQuery] AS
'VBA!DateDiff  (
  "d",
  CDate (
    [Times].Item(0).Item(0).Properties ("DateStamp")
  ),
  CDate (
    [Times].Item ([Times].Count - 1).Item(0).Properties ("DateStamp")
  )
)'
```

To calculate a date in the future, you once again might want to look at the VBA functions. For example, given a date value and a calculated measure that yields a number of days, you can use the VBA DateAdd () function to add the two together. (The result might be converted to a string and returned to the client as a raw value, or it might be used as an argument to the Members() function to look up a time member for further work.)

If your time dimension is broken up so that years are in one dimension and quarters/months/days are in another, then you need to rely on different techniques. This is because your day members won't necessarily have a timestamp that corresponds to a particular year as opposed to a generic year like 1900. For example, in order to count the number of days between a customer's enrollment date and a particular date in the cube, you will need to combine the day-level datestamp with the year-level year value in some way. Let's say that you have datestamps for days that are days in 1900 (Jan-01-1900 for January 1, and so on). The VBA DateAdd() function can add a number of years to the date value, so you could combine the year number from the year dimension with the day value in the day/month/quarter dimension to arrive at the date value to work with.

Combining the strings that form the member names is the easiest technique for this example and avoids problems with datestamps and leap years. For example

```
MEMBER Measures.WeekDaysBetween AS
'VBA!DateDiff (
  "d",
  CDate ([Customer].CurrentMember.Properties ("EnrollDate")),
  CDate ([Time].CurrentMember.Name + "/" + [Year].CurrentMember.Name)
)'
```

would construct the name and convert to a date.

Report Totals-to-Parent, Percentage Contribution to Report Totals

Some reports need to provide a subset of children or a subset of descendants for a member, along with a total of those children or descendants. For example, for a group of interesting customers within a sales region, we want to see summary values for them at the city and state level. In addition to seeing the summary values, we want to see the influence of each of them as a percentage of all the interesting customers in that group. OLAP Services provides intrinsic aggregation of all children to their parents (and all descendants to their ancestors), but this may include many children and descendants that are not part of the query. (In a query of this sort, in MDX we are really creating a proxy set of levels and ancestor members whose names are the same as the database's, but who represent a different and interesting subset of the original dimension.)

NOTE

You can set a connection property when the client connects to the server (Default MDX Visual Mode) that can automatically set every query to use a VisualTotals aggregation for parent members. We describe this in some detail in Appendix B.

VisualTotals( ) is a Microsoft OLAP/Analysis Services-specific function that will give us the report total to a parent member, which makes some of this process easy when only parents and children are involved. In essence, VisualTotals( ) returns a set that includes a new calculated member as a part of it, defined within VisualTotals( ). For example, the query

```
SELECT
{ [Measures].[Sales], [Measures].[Costs] } on columns,
{ [Customer].[Fargo, ND],
  VisualTotals ( {
    [Customer].[Fargo, ND],
```

```
     [Customer].[Fargo, ND].[C#4521772],
     [Customer].[Fargo, ND].[C#2329384],
     [Customer].[Fargo, ND].[C#3847321]
     }, "Total in *"
  )
} on rows
FROM Shipments
```

would generate a straightforward report of three customers in Fargo, North Dakota, and their total sales and costs, along with the database total for Fargo, North Dakota, for contrast. The result would appear as shown in Figure 4.1. This approach is expedient when we only want the total values for children values, grouped according to their hierarchy. VisualTotals( ) also let us total up descendants farther away than children and in fact enable us to use descendants at multiple levels without double-counting their results. Using VisualTotals( ) is very convenient because it does not require us to devote any logic to the creation of calculated members:

```
WITH
SET [InterestingCustomers] AS ' {
[Customer].[Fargo, ND].[C#4521772],
[Customer].[Fargo, ND].[C#2329384],
[Customer].[Fargo, ND].[C#3847321]
}'
MEMBER [Customer].[Explicit Total in Fargo, ND] AS
'Aggregate ( [InterestingCustomers] )'
SELECT
{ [Measures].[Sales], [Measures].[Costs] } on columns,
{ [Customer].[Fargo, ND], [Customer].[Explicit Total in Fargo, ND],
[InterestingCustomers] } on rows
FROM Shipments
```

However, when we wish to calculate percentage-of-total contributions for each customer in our [InterestingCustomers] set, we do need to create calculated

	Sales	Costs
Fargo, ND	25,000	18,000
Total in Fargo, ND	9,000	8,850
C#4521772	6,000	7,000
C#2329384	2,000	1,000
C#3847321	1,000	850

Figure 4.1 Report totals versus VisualTotals.

members. This is because the member total created by VisualTotals does not have a name that we can reference in our query. When the query is parsed, the name has not yet been generated, and though we could form the expression (sales / [Total in Fargo, ND]), the MDX parser will not know what member it corresponds to because it will not exist until later.

The percentage-to-total calculation does not belong in the customer dimension. It is best suited to the measures dimension, on a measure-by-measure basis. For example, consider the following query:

```
WITH
SET [InterestingCustomers] AS
'{
  [Customer].[Fargo, ND].[C#4521772],
  [Customer].[Fargo, ND].[C#2329384],
  [Customer].[Fargo, ND].[C#3847321]
}'
MEMBER [Customer].[Explicit Total in Fargo, ND] AS
'Aggregate ( [InterestingCustomers])'
MEMBER [Measures].[Percent to Report Sales Total] AS
'Sales / (Sales, [Customer].[Explicit Total in Fargo, ND])'
SELECT
{ [Measures].[Sales], [Measures].[Costs],
  [Measures].[Percent to Report Sales Total] } on columns,
{ [Customer].[Fargo, ND], [Customer].[Explicit Total in Fargo, ND],
[InterestingCustomers] } on rows
FROM Shipments
```

We can use this approach of creating a named set, a calculated member on the same dimension, and one or more calculated measures for any set of members that aggregate into one member only. More difficult, however, is when we wish to see a set of descendants and their contributions to ancestors for more than one ancestor. For example, we may have a set of interesting customers in North Dakota, South Dakota, Minnesota, and Wisconsin. Our last approach would run into a few complications when we try to extend it. The [Percent to Report Sales Total] measure hardwires the Fargo, North Dakota, ancestor member within it. We would need to add a separate percentage measure for each ancestor, which is an ugly solution. It would create a set of four measures, each of which would only have a valid intersection with one of the four state-level members, something we would prefer to avoid. In addition, we would need to do other things like generate multiple sets of interesting customers, one for each Explicit Total pseudo-parent.

We can avoid this ugliness if we create a new calculated report total measure and use some of the set manipulation functions provided in MDX. Let's say that we have a set of interesting customers in three different states:

```
SET [InterestingCustomers] AS ' {
  [Customer].[Fargo, ND].[C#4521772], [Customer].[Fargo,
```

```
ND].[C#2329384],
   [Customer].[Pierre, SD].[C#8212633], [Customer].[Pierre,
SD].[C#1012233],
   [Customer].[Hibbing, MN].[C#71236931], [Customer].[St. Cloud,
MN].[C#3492945],
}'
```

Let's also say we wish to get the sum of sales and costs within each of these customers' states, along with the percentage contribution of each customer to that total. We do need to include the ancestor members within the query. If we are starting only with a set of customers, we can do that with Generate( ) (because Ancestor( ) only works on members, not on sets). A hierarchically ordered set to be used as one axis of the query could be obtained from an arbitrary set of customers with the following query:

```
SET [rowset] AS 'Hierarchize (
   [InterestingCustomers],
   Generate (
     [InterestingCustomers],
     { Ancestor([Customer].CurrentMember, [Customer].[State]) }
))'
```

The real heart of the query is in the calculated measures that compute the report total of the sales and cost measures. Each is similar. The one for sales looks like this:

```
MEMBER [Measures].[Report Total Sales] AS 'Sum (
   Intersect ([InterestingCustomers],
Descendants ([Customer].CurrentMember, [Customer].[Individual Customer])
   ),
   [Measures].[Sales])'
```

At each customer member, we take the individual customer(s) that corresponds to that customer member. Intersecting that with our customers of interest gives us only the interesting individual customers that are under our customer member. (Or it will give us the interesting customer back, if one of the customers is our current member.) For each state-level member, the sum over that set gives us the report total sales for the interesting customers within that state.

Because we are using real state-level members to organize our report total sales, we can simply take the ratio of individual customer sales to the ancestor's Report Total Sales to obtain our percentage of total, as in the following code:

```
MEMBER [Measures].[Sales Percent of Report Total] AS '[Measures].[Sales]
   / ([Measures].[Report Total Sales], Ancestor ([Customer],
[Customer].[State])'
```

So, the whole query rolled together would be as follows (excluding the details of the individual customers), with the query's result shown in Figure 4.2.

	Report Total Sales	Report Total Costs	Sales Pct Of Report Total	Cost Pct of Report Total
MN	15,500	10,500	100.00%	100.00%
C#3492945	3,500	4,500	22.58%	42.86%
C#7123693	12,000	6,000	77.42%	57.14%
ND	8,000	8,000	100.00%	100.00%
C#2329384	2,000	1,000	25.00%	12.5%
C#4521772	6,000	7,000	75.00%	87.5%
SD	10,300	6,500	100.00%	100.00%
C#1012233	5,800	3,000	56.31%	46.15%
C#8212633	4,500	3,500	39.69%	53.85%

Figure 4.2   Full report totals and percent total results.

```
WITH
SET [InterestingCustomers] AS '. . .'
SET [Rowset] AS 'Hierarchize ([InterestingCustomers],
  Generate ([InterestingCustomers],
    { Ancestor([Customer].CurrentMember,
[Customer].[State]) } ))'
MEMBER [Measures].[Report Total Sales] AS 'Sum (
Intersect ([InterestingCustomers],
  Descendants ([Customer].CurrentMember,
    [Customer].[Individual Customer])), [Measures].[Sales])'
MEMBER [Measures].[Report Total Costs] AS 'Sum (
Intersect ([InterestingCustomers],
  Descendants ([Customer].CurrentMember,
    [Customer].[Individual Customer])), [Measures].[Costs])'
MEMBER [Measures].[Sales Percent of Report Total] AS '[Measures].[Sales]
/ ([Measures].[Report Total Sales], Ancestor ([Customer],
[Customer].[State])', FORMAT_STRING = '#.00%'
MEMBER [Measures].[Cost Percent of Report Total] AS '[Measures].[Costs]
/ ([Measures].[Report Total Sales], Ancestor ([Customer],
[Customer].[State])', FORMAT_STRING = '#.00%'
SELECT
{ [Measures].[Report Total Sales], [Measures].[Report Total Costs],
[Measures].[Sales Percent of Report Total], [Cost Percent of Report
Total] } on columns,
{ [Rowset] } on rows
FROM Shipments
```

Hierarchical Sorting That Skips Levels in the Hierarchy

The hierarchical sorting provided by the Order( ) function is very convenient when we wish to display data sorted within all hierarchical relationships. Sometimes, however, we may wish to sort by hierarchical relationships but not use all levels in the hierarchy. For example, we may use a geography dimension in a cube that has levels of state, city, and store. If we sort our geography members hierarchically by profit per unit, we will get each store sorted per city and each city sorted per state, whether or not those intermediate levels are in the report. How, in a report, can we sort each store per state, leaving out the cities?

The answer is to break apart the sorting so we are sorting the cities within each state independently. The Generate( ) function provides us with the iterative framework we need to do this. The first set can be our set of states, and the second set can be an expression that sorts the descendants of the current member of the first set:

```
Generate(
  { [Geography].[State].Members },    // for each state
  Order(      // sort its stores
    { Descendants( [Geography].CurrentMember, [Geography].[Store],
    SELF) },
    [Measures].[Profit Per Unit],
    BDESC
  ) }
)
```

It is important, of course, to specify BDESC or BASC rather than ASC or DESC. In a report where we wish to hierarchically represent the states with the stores, we can add them into the second set for Generate( ):

```
Generate(
  { [Geography].[State].Members },  // for each state
  { [Geography].CurrentMember,   // add the state
    Order(                       // and its sorted stores
      { Descendants( [Geography].CurrentMember, [Geography].[Store],
SELF) },
      [Measures].[Profit Per Unit],
      BDESC
    )
  }
)
```

As an aside, the default hierarchical ordering always places parents before children, whether the sorting is ascending or descending. We can use the same sort of construct we just gave to put our states after their children, in a typical subtotal format:

```
Generate(
  { [Geography].[State].Members },   // for each state
  { Order(                           // add its sorted stores
    {Descendants([Geography].CurrentMember, [Geography].[Store], SELF)},
    [Measures].[Profit Per Unit],
    BDESC
    ),
    [Geography].CurrentMember        // and add in the state
  }
)
```

Pareto Analysis and Cumulative Sums

When you query for parents and children, you can use Order( ) with ASC or DESC to preserve the hierarchy while sorting. For example, given the store and employee count data values shown in Figure 4.3, the following set expression results in the ordering of stores shown in Figure 4.4:

```
Order(
  {[Store].[California],
   [Store].[California].Children,
   [Store].[Nevada],
   [Store].[Nevada].Children
  },
   [Measures].[Employee Count],
   DESC
  )
```

Now, let's say that for each of the children, we want the cumulative sum as we go from the first child in this ordering to the last child. This will essentially give us a Pareto analysis within each state. If we used the following expression,

```
[Measures].[Cum Employee Count] AS
'Sum ( { [Employee].FirstSibling : [Employee].CurrentMember},
  [Measures].[Employee Count])'
```

our results will be quite wrong. This is so because .FirstSibling is not relative to this ordering, even though .CurrentMember will be.

To get the cumulative sum for each of the children as we go from the first child in this ordering to the last, we must re-create the range of ordered children within our calculated member. We also need to find our current tuple within the range, using Rank( ), and we need to create a range from the first tuple in the set to the referent child's tuple, using Head( ). The following expression gives us the proper ordering of members:

Store	Associated Employee Count
California	124
Sacramento	49
Los Angeles	72
Ukiah	3
Nevada	129
Reno	55
Las Vegas	62
Tahoe	12

Figure 4.3 Store and employee count data values.

Store	Associated Employee Count
Nevada	129
Las Vegas	62
Reno	55
Tahoe	12
California	124
Los Angeles	72
Sacramento	49
Ukiah	3

Figure 4.4 Store and employee count data results.

```
Order ( {[Employee].Parent.Children}, [Measures].[Employee Count], DESC)
```

We obtain the ranking of any tuple in that set with

```
Rank ([Store], Set)
```

The Rank( ) term gives us the rank of the current store member within that set to use as our cutoff point for aggregating. In addition, the expression

```
Head( Set, Index)
```

gives us the subset to aggregate. We must use the set once to get the members to aggregate over and another time to get them to rank over. Rolling it all together, we get

```
MEMBER [Measures].[Cum Employee Count] AS '
Sum (
  Head(
    Order( {[Store].Parent.Children}, [Measures].[Employee Count],
BDESC),
    Rank (
      [Store],
      Order( {[Store].Parent.Children}, [Measures].[Employee Count],
BDESC)
    )
  ),
  [Measures].[Employee Count]
)'
```

A sample complete query would look like the following, with its results shown in Figure 4.5:

```
WITH
MEMBER [Measures].[Cum Employee Count] AS '. . .'
SELECT
{ [Measures].[Employee Count], [Measures].[Cum Employee Count] } on
columns,
{ [Store].[Nevada], [Store].[Nevada].Children, [Store].[California],
[Store].[California].Children} on rows
FROM [Employee Cube]
```

Store	Employee Count	Cum. Employee Count
Nevada	129	129
Las Vegas	62	62
Reno	55	117
Tahoe	12	129
California	124	253
Los Angeles	72	72
Sacramento	49	121
Ukiah	3	124

Figure 4.5 Cumulative employee counts.

The exact results for Nevada and California are dependent on the contents of their siblings, of course. If you want to only return results for [Cum Employee Count] at the city level and omit cumulative counts at higher levels, use the techniques we discuss for "One Formula Calculating Different Things in Different Places" later in this section.

For comprehensibility if nothing else, it would be highly desirable to abstract the Order(. . .) clause into one definition and two uses. Although for each store member the set could be different (because it will be evaluated for the children of multiple parents), within the sum it doesn't change. However, named sets are evaluated at the time they are parsed, not each time they are referenced, so we cannot use them. Microsoft does allow an alias to be used when the set is constructed that we can use for referencing it later on. We can make this a little easier on our eyes through the following re-phrasing:

```
MEMBER [Measures].[Cum Employee Count] AS '
Sum (
  Head(
    Order(
      {[Store].Parent.Children},
      [Measures].[Employee Count],
      BDESC
    ) AS OrdSet,    // create an alias for the set
    Rank (
      [Store],
      OrdSet        // use it here
    )
  ),
  [Measures].[Employee Count]
)'
```

Note that we have added an alias to the set through the use of "AS OrdSet". We can then refer to OrdSet later on in the expression.

If constructing, maintaining, and executing this sort of MDX is less onerous to you than maintaining code in an ActiveX Automation language, then you can certainly do it in MDX. If you would rather maintain Automation-related code, then a UDF is the way to go. For example, with the following query you could call a UDF named PartialSum to take an ordered set of stores, an ordered set of values, and the name of the store to stop summing at

```
WITH
MEMBER [Measures].[StoreUniqueName] AS '[Store].UniqueName', VISIBLE =
'0'
MEMBER [Measures].[CumSum] AS
'PartialSum (
  SetToArray (Order( {[Store].Parent.Children}, [Measures].[Employee
Count], DESC), [Measures].[StoreUniqueName]),
```

```
    SetToArray (Order( {[Store].Parent.Children}, [Measures].[Employee
  Count], DESC), [Measures].[Employee Count]),
    [Measures].[StoreUniqueName]
  )'
  . . .
```

Notice that you need to create a dummy measure that contains the name of the current store member (which we called [Measures].[StoreUniqueName] in the example). The first release of Microsoft OLAP Services generates a parser error if you try to access the unique name directly in SetToArray( ). The same is true in Analysis Services, but at least we can hide the calculated member from the client application by setting its (Microsoft-specific) HIDDEN property to True.

Sorting on Multiple Criteria

In MDX, sorting a set of tuples based on one criterion is directly supported through the Order( ) function. Somewhat surprisingly, it doesn't support multiple criteria for sorting. Frequently, the default database ordering for dimensions provides the necessary primary and secondary sorting that a report needs with data providing the last level of sorting needed. (To see how this works in full detail, take a look at the description of the Order( ) function in Appendix A.) However, at times, you may need to sort based on more than one criterion. Although somewhat awkward, it is possible.

For example, let's say that you need to sort a set of policyholders primarily by age and secondarily by total claims to date per customer. In this example, age is stored as a member property named [P Age] and is measured in whole years, whereas claims to date is represented by a calculated measure named [Measures].[Claims To Date]. We can directly use Order( ) to sort policy holders by age or by claims to date, but we need to resort to cleverness to sort by both of these. The trick is to combine the two numbers (age and claims) into a single number that can sort appropriately. How can we do this?

The answer is to scale the age value up by some amount and add the claims value to it. For example, if two policy holders have an age of 75 and one has claims to date of 300 and another of 3,000, we can get these in increasing order by multiplying the 75 by 10,000 and adding 300 and 3,000 to it; the numbers 750,300 and 753,000 will sort in correct order. (We are assuming ascending sorts in both criteria; you can apply the techniques we describe for mixed ascending and descending sorts as well.) All we need to figure out is what the right scaling factor is. For a wide range of queries, you can probably get by with an educated guess. (For example, if you were to sort on claims to date first and age second, you could safely multiply the age by 1,000.) If you can't make a guess based on knowledge of the data, the right scaling factor is the absolute value of the difference between the max value and the min value across all values. For example, claims values could range from zero to millions of U.S. dollars. We could assume that multiplying age by 1,000,000,000 is safe, but it might not be for too long. In this case, because claims won't go below zero, we can take the all-time, all-policy holder sum of [Claims to Date] as our scale factor; it is larger than necessary but also faster to calculate than the Min( ) or Max( ) across the database (unless we actually added Min and Max measures to the cube). The following query orders the policyholders primarily in terms of descending age, secondarily in terms of descending claims to date:

```
WITH
...
MEMBER [Measures].[P Age] AS
'Val ([Policy Holder].CurrentMember.Properties ("P Age"))'
MEMBER [Measures].[Claims Scale] AS
'([Measures].[Claims To Date], [Policy Holder].[All Policy Holder])'
  // Add other [All] members to the Claims Scale tuple as necessary
SET [Ordered Policy Holders] AS
'Order (
  { Selected Policy Holder Members },
  ([Measures].[P Age] * [Measures].[Claims Scale])
    + [Measures].[Claims To Date]),
  BDESC
)'
SELECT
{ [Measures].[Claims To Date], [Measures].[Policy Cost] } on columns,
{ [Ordered Policy Holders] }
DIMENSION PROPERTIES [Policy Holder].[P Age]
on rows
FROM [Claims Analysis]
WHERE ( [Time].[Q4 2001] )
```

If you need to sort based on multiple string criteria, you can do this by concatenating the strings together. If the strings have different lengths, you can use the VBA Space( ) function to add spaces to the end of the primary sort string (and the Len( ) function to help you figure out how many spaces to add) before appending the second string to sort by. If you need to sort based on a mixture of strings and numbers, you will need to convert the numbers to strings and sort based on the resulting string. This means that you should use the VBA FormatNumber( ) function to format the numbers to an equal number of digits before and after the decimal place.

Reporting on Ranks

Although the various ranking filter functions (TopCount( ), BottomCount( ), TopSum( ), and so on) return members in their ranking order, sometimes a report needs to return the actual rank number (1, 2, 3, and so on). Furthermore, rank numbers may be necessary sometimes because the members are being returned in another order. For example, salespeople may be ranked both for this year and last year, or the top 10 suppliers in terms of delivery times could have their cost rankings reported as a measure.

Let's examine the case of looking at the top 10 suppliers in terms of delivery time (shorter time is better) and their cost rankings. The [Cost Ranking] will be a calculated member in the query. MDX offers us the Rank( ) function, which returns the index that a tuple has in a set. This is suited to our purpose because we can sort our suppliers by costs and use that as the set. Rank counts from one, so the first one will be our #1-costing supplier. We don't want to sort the suppliers over and over again, so we'll define a named set to hold the sorted suppliers. Notice that we sort in descending order so the highest-cost supplier is at position #1, and we break the hierarchy so that the order is meaningful:

```
WITH
SET [Cost-Ordered Suppliers] AS
'Order (
  [Supplier].[Supplier].Members,
  ([Measures].[Total Cost], [Time].[2000]),
  BDESC
)'
MEMBER [Measures].[Cost Ranking] AS
'Rank (
  [Cost-Ordered Suppliers] ,
  [Supplier].CurrentMember
)'
SELECT
{ [Measures].[Total Cost], [Measures].[Cost Ranking] } on columns,
{ BottomCount (
  [Supplier].[Supplier].Members,
  10,
  [Measures].[Delivery Time]
) } on rows
FROM [Purchasing]
WHERE [Time].[Year].[2000]
```

We chose BottomCount( ) instead of TopCount( ) because the business problem wanted the top performers, which is opposite of those that have the top times. The supplier with the lowest time appears first in the list.

Note that the cost ranking returned from this query for each supplier is that supplier's rank among all suppliers in the database, not among the set of 10. If we only wanted to take the cost ranking among the 10, then we would re-phrase the query like so:

```
WITH
SET [Delivery-Ordered Suppliers] AS
```

```
'BottomCount (
  [Supplier].[Supplier].Members,
  10,
  ([Measures].[Delivery Time], [Time].[Year].[2000])
)'
MEMBER [Measures].[Cost Ranking] AS
'Rank (
  [Delivery-Ordered Suppliers],  // our 10 suppliers
  [Supplier].CurrentMember
)'
SELECT
{ [Measures].[Total Cost], [Measures].[Cost Ranking] } on columns,
{ [Delivery-Ordered Suppliers] } on rows
FROM [Purchasing]
WHERE [Time].[Year].[2000]
```

Now, let's tackle a more demanding yet very real-life query. Let's say that we need to generate a report which lists the top 10 salespeople according to the year-to-date units sold, their ranking number according to those units, their previous year's rank, and the difference in units sold between year-to-date and the previous year's YTD.

We will need to derive the year-to-date units sold to calculate this. We're also going to take the ranking of our 10 salespeople within an ordered set of all salespeople, so we should name that ordered set. Let's assume that our time dimension is marked as being a time dimension and that the year level in it is tagged as being a year-typed level, so that we can make use of the YTD( ) function as well:

```
WITH
// define our year-to-date units count
MEMBER [Measures].[YTD Units Count] AS
'Sum(YTD(), [Measures].[Units Sold])'
// define a set of ordered salespeople for repeated references
// break the hierarchy, and put the top-valued ones first in the list
SET [Last Year Ordered SalesPeople] AS
'Order (
  [SalesPerson].[Individual].Members,
  ([Measures].[YTD Units Count], ParallelPeriod ([Time].[Year],1)),
  BDESC
)'
MEMBER [Measures].[Previous Year Rank] AS
'Rank (
  [Last Year Ordered SalesPeople],
  [SalesPerson].CurrentMember
)'
SET [This Year Top 10 SalesPeople] AS
'TopCount (
  [SalesPerson].[Individual].Members,
  10,
```

```
    [Measures].[YTD Units Count]
  )'
MEMBER [Measures].[This Year Rank] AS
'Rank (
  [This Year Top 10 SalesPeople],
  [SalesPerson].CurrentMember
)'
MEMBER [Measures].[YTD Units Change] as
'[YTD Units Count] -
  ([YTD Units Count], ParallelPeriod ([Time].[Year],1))'
SELECT
{ [Measures].[This Year Rank], [Measures].[YTD Units Count],
  [Measures].[Previous Year Rank], [Measures].[YTD Units Change]
} on columns,
{ [This Year Top 10 SalesPeople] } on rows
FROM Sales
WHERE ([Time].[Month].[Aug. 2000])
```

Note that the WHERE clause defines the date that the year-to-date accumulates all the values to as August 2000.

Building a Set That Sums Backward in Time

How to select a set of times back from some date such that a measure totaled across them reaches some value.

Another challenge that has shown up in constructing queries is building a set of prior time periods such that their sum of a measure is at least greater than a given quantity. One application of this is creating a set that contains the last time periods required to accumulate 500 new customers from a cube where [New Customer Count] is a measure. (This set could then be used to total up advertising and sign-up costs over that time range.)

From a glance at the TopSum( ) function, it seems nearly suited to this need, as it returns a set of tuples based on their overall sum meeting or just exceeding a certain value. However, it sorts all of the tuples first in terms of the value being summed, which scrambles them from the point of view of our goal—we want our set of time periods to be in database order.

There are straightforward solutions to this using either straight MDX or an external function call. Actually, the larger the number of time periods being considered, the more efficient an external function call will be compared to straight MDX. We will consider how to do this in Chapter 7 "Extending MDX Through External Functions."

We can solve this problem with a recursive calculated member that computes the total new customer count backwards in time, which lets us build a named set that contains the time members where the accumulated value does not exceed the threshold of 500. We will look for the set of time periods up to October 2000. This query is shown in Figure 4.6.

Since we do not know in advance how far back in time to go, we take all months prior to the time that we are counting back from.

The named set [Times Until Sum] contains a set that you can use for a result axis or for further filtering and so on. If you need to include the time period whose associated item value causes the sum to become greater than 500, then some additional logic is required. The simplest way would be to add a test for the calculated member that flags when it reflects the sum becoming greater than or equal to 500:

```
SET [Times Until Sum] AS
'Filter (
  [Time].[Month].Item(0) : [Time].[Month].[Oct 2000],
  [Measures].[Accum New Count] < 500
   OR ([Measures].[Accum New Count] >= 500
    AND ([Measures].[Accum New Count],
         [Time].CurrentMember.NextMember) < 500
   )
)'
```

The [Times Until Sum] set is defined only for the course of the query. If you wanted to share the set among queries by using CREATE SET to define a named

```
WITH
MEMBER [Measures].[Accum New Count] AS
'Sum (
   { [Time].CurrentMember : [Time].[Month].[Oct 2000] },
   [Measures].[New Subscribers]
)'
SET [Times Until Sum] AS
'Filter (
   { [Time].[Month].Members.Item(0) : [Time].[Month].[Oct 2000] },
   [Measures].[Accum New Count] <= 500
)'
SELECT
{ [Times Until Sum] } on columns,
{ [Measures].[Advertising Cost], [Measures].[Processing Cost] } on
rows
FROM [Subscriptions]
```

Figure 4.6 Query for counting backwards.

set, you would need to first define the calculated [Accum New Count] member using CREATE MEMBER (or define it at the server).

In terms of efficiency, you should note that [Measures].[Accum New Count] may be calculated up to three times per time member being filtered, with cells for later time periods being recursively referenced through more time members than cells for earlier time periods, so this is even less efficient compared with using an external function. Depending on the number of actual calculations performed, this could be quite tolerable. However, cell calculations in Analysis Services 2000 provide a mechanism for making these more efficient, by calculating the [Accum New Count] in one pass and referencing that pass in Filter( ) statement.

Drilling Down from Virtual Dimensions

The members of a virtual dimension exist in an N − 1 hierarchical relationship with the members of the real level upon which it is based. However, because the virtual dimension is distinct from the real dimension, you cannot directly drill down on it to the underlying real members. This is, however, something that you might wish to allow in an application if a virtual member's slice is interesting to the user. We can always directly drill down on the virtual dimension to the underlying real members because the real dimension exists in a cube with the property's level enabled if the virtual dimension is used in that cube. Furthermore, the name of the member will be identical to the value of the corresponding member property. We simply filter the real dimension based on the property value that was used to create the virtual dimension. The abstract template for this operation is as follows:

```
Filter( Set Of Real Members On Real Dimension, Member.Properties ("Prop-
    ertyName") = Virtual Dimension Member.Name)
```

Notice that we are comparing the member property values to the Name of the virtual member, not to the UniqueName. The unique name has extra information in it (like the name of the virtual dimension) that isn't part of the property. For any particular virtual member, this doesn't give us any extra power. If we know the name of the virtual member, we know the property value to compare it with. (Properties whose values are dates, numbers, and so on, may require a data type conversion because the name is always a text value. Nevertheless, the principle still holds.) Consider the following trivial example. With a product dimension and a virtual dimension whose members are formed out of the product color property, we can select only those products where:

```
Filter ([Products].[SKU].Members, [Product].Properties ("Flavor") =
    [ProductSKU].[Zesty Garlic].Name)
```

However, we can do some powerful things with sets of virtual members when we are filtering on virtual members that are themselves determined in the course of the query. As an example, suppose we want to see the top-selling three flavors of marinara sauce, and for each of these we want to see in a report the product SKUs nested within them. If we simply cross-joined SKUs within flavors, we wouldn't get the association—we would get a grid with an awful lot of empty cells within it. We would once again use Generate( ) to provide the iterative framework. The following query would yield the result shown in Figure 4.7:

```
WITH
SET [Top3flavors] AS 'TopCount ([ProductSku].[ProductSku].Members, 3,
([Measures].[Unit Sales], [Time].[2000], [Store].[All Stores]))'
SET [Flavors and Skus] AS
'Generate (
  [Top3Flavors],
  CrossJoin ({ [ProductSku].CurrentMember } ,
      { [Product].[All Products],
Filter ([Product].[Sku].Members, [Product].Properties ("Flavor") =
[ProductSku].CurrentMember.Name)
    }
  )
)'
```

			Unit Sales	Dollar Sales
All Of This Flavor	Zesty Garlic	All Products	540,000	1,080,000
	Zesty Garlic	SKU 254	223,000	446,000
	Zesty Garlic	SKU 996	205,000	410,000
	Zesty Garlic	SKU 223	112,000	224,000
All Of This Flavor	Tomato Alarm	All Products	350,000	700,000
	Tomato Alarm	SKU 105	180,000	360,000
	Tomato Alarm	SKU 099	50,000	100,000
	Tomato Alarm	SKU 313	120,000	240,000
All Of This Flavor	Pesto Walnut	All Products	315,000	630,000
	Pesto Walnut	SKU 291	120,000	240,000
	Pesto Walnut	SKU 293	195,000	390,000

Figure 4.7 Virtual dimension drill-down report.

```
SELECT
{[Measures].[Unit Sales], Measures.[Dollar Sales] } on columns,
{ [Flavors and SKUs] } on rows
FROM SalesCube
WHERE ([Time].[2000])
```

You may expect that you could use the LinkMember( ) function to provide this drill-down (see Appendix A if you are unfamiliar with it), but actually, you can't. It links one member to another via keys, and each virtual ProductSku member essentially is a parent for a set of products. There is no key in common between ProductSku members and Product members.

One Formula Calculating Different Things in Different Places

We have seen that calculated members create slices across all intersections of all other dimensions. Sometimes, however, we need a calculated member to give a different result depending on where in the hypercube it is being evaluated. How can we make one calculated member return two different things at two different places? The answer is to use a conditional function and the various properties of members, levels, hierarchies, tuples, and sets in a calculated member to test for the location where the members are being evaluated, and then choose the correct formula to use for that place in the cube.

For example, if we wish to create a calculated measure that shows a three-month moving average of sales, but we don't want it to show any values for any level other than month, we can use the Level.Ordinal property to tell us at what level the formula is being evaluated:

```
iif (
   [Time].[CurrentMember].[Level].Ordinal = [Time].[Month].Ordinal,
   Avg( LastPeriods (3, [Time].CurrentMember), [Measures].[Sales]),
   NULL
)
```

Notice that the test for whether or not this formula is being evaluated at the month level is implemented as a test to determine if the level's ordinal (depth from the root level) is equal to the month level's ordinal. In standard MDX, we can test to see if the level's name was "Month," or we can test for a hard-wired depth like 2. However, this seems to capture the best combination of efficiency (comparing numbers instead of strings) and grace (we know what [Time].[Month] refers to, whereas 2 would not be as easily understood). This example has a maintenance issue as well: If the dimension changed and a new level was inserted between the month level and the root, then the 2 would need to be updated to a 3. Using Microsoft's extensions to MDX, we can also use the IS statement to test for equivalence of object identity, as with the following:

```
iif (
  [Time].[CurrentMember].[Level] IS [Time].[Month],
  Avg( LastPeriods (3, [Time].CurrentMember), [Measures].[Sales]),
  NULL
)
```

This formulation should not only be efficient, but will also be graceful to changes in the set of levels in the time dimension (so long as the Month level does not disappear.)

Earlier in this chapter, we showed an example of how to spread quarter-level input values down to lower time levels based on the number of time periods in the quarter. The calculated measure that resulted would only show values at or below the quarter level and result errors above it. We can use the same sort of testing for level ordinals to create one calculated measure that shows aggregated values above the month level and allocated values below the month level:

```
CREATE MEMBER [Competitor Earnings Rate] AS
'iif ([Time].[CurrentMember].[Level].Ordinal < [Time].[Quarter].Ordinal,
  [Measure].[Earnings],
  ([Measure].[Earnings] / Descendants (Ancestor (
    [Time].CurrentMember, [Time].[Quarter]),
    [Time].CurrentMember. Level, SELF).Count)
)'
```

Sometimes, you may find that you need to use a different formula depending upon what member you are evaluating a calculated member at. For example, a multinational corporation may use a slightly different net profit calculation depending upon the country in which it is performing the calculation. For our case, we can use the unique name or the name of a member. The following example demonstrates three different profit formulas, two of which are specific to a single country as exceptions to the general rule:

```
iif ([Geography].CurrentMember IS [Geography]."[Japan]",
  [Sales] - [Deductible Expenses 1],
  iif ( [Geography].CurrentMember IS "[Geography].[Malaysia]",
    [Sales] - [Deductible Expenses 2],
    [Sales] - [Deductible Expenses 3]
  )
)
```

Although the MDX specification provides the CASE ... WHEN ... construct, Microsoft's OLAP products do not support it, so we need to resort to nested IF-THEN logic using iif( ).

If you are using IF-THEN logic to specify a constant value based on member name, you might also think about putting that information into a table and using it either as a member property or as a measure. The less conditional the logic in a formula, the easier it is to comprehend and maintain over time. The numbers that you are specifying might be exceptions to a general rule, for example, commission rates to charge based on product. In that case, the logic of the formula would test for the special commission being empty or not and to use the special commission value if it is present or the default value if the special commission is absent.

Three types of tests you may wish to perform on the current member are

- Is it at a particular member or members?
- Is it at a particular level or levels? Is it at the leaf level?
- Is it at a descendant of a particular member?

To test whether the current member is at a particular level (or above or below a particular level, including the level of an arbitrary named level), compare its level with the target level using IS. Compare the current member's level ordinal to the ordinal of the level you are interested in using level.Ordinal. To test whether the current member is a descendant of a particular member, you can check the name of the current member's ancestor at that level with the target ancestor's name, as with the following expression:

```
Ancestor( [Dimension], Member).UniqueName = Ancestor-Member.UniqueName
```

The six standard functions you can use against the current member or its related information for this purpose are

- Member.Level.Ordinal
- Member.Level.Name
- Member.Level.UniqueName
- Member.Name
- Member.UniqueName
- Member.Properties ("Property Name")

Microsoft extends the set of tests you can use with the following:

- IsAncestor(target-member, source-member)
- IsGeneration(member, generation-number)
- IsLeaf(member)
- IsSibling(member1, member 2)

They work as shown in Table 4.1.

Also, Rank([Dimension].CurrentMember, { member1, member2, . . . memberN }) > 0 can be used to test for whether or not the current member is in the given set. Using IsGeneration( ) is a bit complicated and requires an understanding of how generation numbers are assigned; please refer to its discussion in Appendix A.

Table 4.1 Functions and Operators for Testing the Member or Level at Which a Cell Is Being Calculated

EXTENSION?	EXPRESSION	PURPOSE
	[dimension].Level.Ordinal = Named_Level.Ordinal	tests for being at level
	[dimension].Level.Ordinal > Named_Level.Ordinal	tests for being below level
	[dimension].Level.Ordinal < Named_Level.Ordinal	tests for being above level
	[dimension].Currentmember. Uniquename = [Specific Member]. Uniquename	tests for member equivalence
	[dimension].UniqueName = "Unique Name"	
	[dimension].CurrentMember. Properties("External Property") = Value	tests for arbitrary condition on property; can be applied to this purpose
*	[dimension].CurrentMember IS [member]	Tests for member equivalence
*	[dimension].CurrentMember.Level IS [level]	Tests for being at level
*	IsAncestor ([member], [dimension].CurrentMember)	Tests for current member being descendant of specific member
*	IsLeaf ([dimension]. CurrentMember)	Tests for current member being at the leaf level
*	IsSibling([dimension]. CurrentMember, [Specific Member])	Tests for current member being sibling of target member

When you are testing for member equivalence in Analysis Services, you should favor the dimension.CurrentMember IS [Specific Member] construct. This is because unique names can have many different formats and you are not always in control of the format chosen. We talk about name construction in both Chapter 2 "MDX in More Detail, and Chapter 8 "Building Queries in MDX."

Logical Aggregations

You may want some queries to return a result that is essentially a logical aggregation: Are there any cells at lower levels where some condition is true? Is it true at every cell? True at none? Essentially, these would be logical OR and AND operators that take cell ranges as inputs rather than discrete cells. For example, we could look at a report of states by quarters and see if sales were below some threshold at any related store for any related week.

Although MDX doesn't provide a direct way to do this, we can do it indirectly and get some useful side benefits along the way. We can count the cells for which the condition is true and compare that number with the number of cells in the range. Counting the cells itself is done indirectly too. The Count( ) function only counts cells, but we can sum an expression over the cells, where the expression returns one if the expression is true, and zero otherwise. We know that the condition is true for some location if the sum is greater than zero, and we know it's true everywhere if the sum is equal to the count of cells in the range. Using the rules of logic, we also know it's true everywhere if its opposite condition has a sum of zero. A useful analytical byproduct of this approach is that we can say what percentage of the time the condition is true by taking the ratio of the sum to the count of cells in the range.

For example, the following would be a query to obtain the count of stores per week where the profit was less than half of the year's average for stores in that province of Canada and for all Canada's provinces and cities in 1999:

```
WITH
MEMBER [Measures].[Avg Profit] AS
'[Measures].[Profit] / [Measures].[Units Sold]'
MEMBER [Measures].[Condition Count] AS
'Sum (Descendants ([Geography], [Geography].[Store], SELF),
  Sum (Descendants ([Time], [Time].[Week], SELF),
    iif ([Measures].[Profit] <
        ([Measures].[Avg Profit], Ancestor ([Time], [Time].[Year]),
         Ancestor ([Geography], [Geography].[Province])),
    1, 0)
  ))'
SELECT
CrossJoin ({ [Time].[Quarter].Members }, { [Measures].[Profit],
[Measures].[Condition Count] } ) on columns,
{ Descendants ([Geography].[Canada], [Geography].[City],
SELF_AND_BEFORE) } on rows
FROM Sales
WHERE ([Time].[1999])
```

Including All Tuples with Tied Ranking in Sets

Following from the preceding example, if you're truly trying to be fair to your salespeople and it's possible that two or more are tied for tenth place, then you need to apply more MDX. The trick is simply to add to the set all tuples (salespeople in this case) whose values are equal to the 10th-place salesperson, and unite this filtered set with the ranked set. Because MDX preserves the ordering in the sets when they are united, the final set that is created will be in the correct order:

```
WITH
MEMBER [Measures].[YTD Units Count] AS
'SUM(YTD(), [Measures].[Units Sold])'
SET [Last Year Ordered SalesPeople] AS
'Order (
  [SalesPerson].[Individual].Members,
  ([Measures].[YTD Units Count], ParallelPeriod ([Time].[Year],1)),
  BDESC
)'
MEMBER [Measures].[Previous Year Rank] AS
'Rank (
  [Last Year Ordered SalesPeople],
  [SalesPerson].CurrentMember
)'
SET [This Year Top 10 SalesPeople] AS
'TopCount (
  [SalesPerson].[Individual].Members,
  10,
  [Measures].[YTD Units Count]
)'

/* We add some new set declarations */

// collect all salespeople whose units are equal to the 10th's
SET [This Year Tied SalesPeople] AS
'Filter (
  [SalesPerson].[Individual].Members,
  [Measures].[YTD Units Count] =
    ([Measures].[YTD Units Count],
      [This Year Top 10 SalesPeople].Item (
        [This Year Top 10 SalesPeople].Count - 1
      )
    )
)'

// Put the two sets together, and eliminate the duplicated 10th member
SET [Top Ranked SalesPeople] AS
'Union (
  [This Year Top 10 SalesPeople],
  [This Year Tied SalesPeople]
)'

/* Done adding the set declarations */

MEMBER [Measures].[This Year Rank] AS
'Rank (
```

```
    [This Year Top 10 SalesPeople],
    [SalesPerson].CurrentMember
)'
MEMBER [Measures].[YTD Units Change] as
'[YTD Units Count] -
    ([YTD Units Count], ParallelPeriod ([Time].[Year], 1))'
SELECT
{ [Measures].[This Year Rank], [Measures].[YTD Units Count],
    [Measures].[Previous Year Rank], [Measures].[YTD Units Change]
} on columns,
{ [Top Ranked SalesPeople] } on rows
FROM SALES
WHERE ([Time].[Month].[Aug. 2000])
```

But how do we get the rank numbers right? If three salespeople are in the 10th position, then one of them will be ranked 11th and another 12th. Also, if two of them share the same second-ranked number of units sold, one will have a rank number of 2 and another will have a rank number of 3 (as opposed to both of them having a rank number of 2 or 2.5). In standard MDX, this is quite complicated. We had worked out an example of this for an early draft of this book. However, for those of you that are using Microsoft Analysis Services, a direct solution is actually built in. The Rank( ) function now takes an optional third argument that specifies an ordering value for the set. If it is supplied, Analysis Services uses the values it supplies to determine tied rankings within the set. (Without it, it looks for the position of the tuple within the set, which has no information that can be used to determine ties.) We can modify the definitions of the measures, the text of which we provide in Figure 4.8 and the results of which are shown in Figure 4.9.

We can do the fair ranking in an external function, but the external function will be called once for every [This Year Rank] and once for every [Previous Year Rank]. Only 10 members will be passed into it small for [This Year Rank] and it will only be called 10 times, so for [This Year Rank], performance should be good. For [Previous Year Rank], the entire set of salespeople will be passed into the external function; as that number climbs, the performance feasibility drops and it becomes much more desirable to implement the calculation in some combination of client logic with MDX.

A Sample Analysis

MDX is rich enough to support advanced analytical queries. Indeed, once you have created a database schema for Microsoft OLAP Services and populated it with data, MDX provides many of the tools you need to support complex analyses within queries. We will spend the next several pages rolling up our sleeves and using MDX to explore a useful set of questions related to the topic. What are the important products to our important customers? Although your

```
// . . .

MEMBER [Measures].[Previous Year Rank] AS
'Rank (
  [Last Year Ordered SalesPeople],
  [SalesPerson].CurrentMember,
  ([Measures].[YTD Units Count], ParallelPeriod ([Time].[Year],1))
)'

// . . .

MEMBER [Measures].[This Year Rank] AS
'Rank (
  [This Year Top 10 SalesPeople],
  [SalesPerson].CurrentMember,
  [Measures].[YTD Units Count]
)'

// . . .
```

Figure 4.8 Query that results in fair rankings for this year and last.

Measures

Salesperson	This Year Rank	YTD Units Count	Last Year Rank	YTD Units Change
Nishi Agrawal	1	45,000	4	2,000
Sarah Mayer	2	44,020	1	-100
Pat Bates	3	42,500	6	10,000
Ian Walter	3	42,500	15	22,000
Rama Lahori	5	40,000	3	-4,500
Kate Higgins	6	30,100	9	10,000
Levi Chen	7	22,000	22	6,000
Joe Bergman	7	22,000	16	5,500
Larry Levy	9	16,500	11	2,000
Joanne Luongo	10	15,000	10	-150
Ted Johnson	10	15,000	12	250

Figure 4.9 Results of fair ranking query.

applications may not be related to customers and products, a generalization of the analysis we discuss is "What are the important factors to each of a set of interesting members?" This is a form of data mining, even though we are performing it in an OLAP tool. Within the framework of this analysis, we will explore set construction and the use of the Generate( ) and Extract( ) functions, and make extensive use of named sets.

The dimensions of primary interest in this analysis are customer, product, and time. A familiar simple OLAP query to use as a starting point is "Who are our best customers?" If we are interested in the top 10 customers in terms of total profitability in 2001, we may start with the set defined by the following:

```
TopCount ([Customer].[Individual].Members, 10,
([Measures].[Profit], [Time].[2001]))
```

A query that shows profitability for 2000 and 2001 for these customers is as follows:

```
SELECT
{ [Time].[2000], [Time].[2001] } on columns,
{ TopCount ([Customer].[Individual].Members, 10,
([Measures].[Profit], [Time].[2001])) } on rows
FROM Sales
WHERE ( [Measures].[Profit] )
```

Now, this query is useful in its own right, but we want to go a bit deeper and learn about the products that these customers are buying. We can learn about the top three product brands (in terms of profit) that some customers are buying with the following expression:

```
TopCount ([Product].[Brand].Members, 3, ([Measures].[Profit],
[Time].[2001]))
```

Because this is along a separate dimension, we can put it on a different query axis than the customer dimension, or we can put it on the same axis as the customers with CrossJoin( ). For example:

```
WITH
SET [Top3Prods] AS
'{ TopCount ([Product].[Brand].Members, 3,
([Measures].[Profit], [Time].[2001])) }'
SELECT
{ CrossJoin ([Top3Prods], {[Time].[2000], [Time].[2001]}) } on columns,
{ TopCount ([Customer].[Individual].Members, 10,
([Measures].[Profit], [Time].[2001])) } on rows
FROM Sales
WHERE ( [Measures].[Profit] )
```

However, this still doesn't tell us about the products that these top customers are buying. Regardless of the way products are oriented in the query or whether the product set is evaluated as a named set or within the body of the SELECT clause, the context in which the product set is evaluated is going to be at the All-customer member because that is the default member in the query context. What we want is the set of products that these customers are buying. We can explore a couple of different paths for determining this.

One path is to ask about the top three product categories over the entire set of top 10 customers. To do this, we need to calculate profitability across the top 10 customers. Calculating the top 10 customers from the leaf level of a fairly large dimension takes significant CPU time because of the sorting involved, so we should use a named set to hold the result customer set. We can then sum across that directly or use a calculated member to hold the result:

```
WITH
SET [Top10Custs] AS
'{ TopCount ([Customer].[Individual].Members, 10,
      ([Measures].[Profit], [Time].[2001])) }'
MEMBER [Measures].[Top10profit] AS
'Sum (Top10Custs, [Measures].[Profit])'
SET [Top3Prods] AS
'{ TopCount ([Product].[Brand].Members, 3,
      ([Measures].[Top10profit], [Time].[2001])) }'
SELECT
{ CrossJoin ([Top3Prods], {[Time].[2000], [Time].[2001]}) } on columns,
{ TopCount ([Customer].[Individual].Members, 10,
      ([Measures].[Profit], [Time].[2001])) } on rows
FROM Sales
WHERE ( [Measures].[Profit] )
```

This helps us out. We are now looking at the top three products of the top 10 customers, which gives us a better picture of those products and customers in particular. Although these customers could be a fairly homogeneous group, each of them may be fairly different from the others. (They also may be pretty different from the average customer in terms of product preferences; we will explore that later in this section as well.) In terms of our individual customers' favorite product mixes, we can get even more precise than we have, but the MDX requires a quantum leap in sophistication.

Exploring possibilities that don't give us what we are looking for helps us understand the MDX that gives us what we need. MDX's tuple orientation enables us to take the top N tuples from a set from multiple dimensions. However, taking the top N tuples from a customer-product set, by cross-joining customers and products together, won't give us what we are looking for. We are interested in 10 customers and three products for each customer. However, the top 30 customer-product combinations (TopCount (CrossJoin (. . .), 30, . . .) could be dominated by 30 products sold to the most profitable customer. The top 30 customer-products of the top 10 customers aren't any better. Taking the top three products of the top 10 customers involves somehow breaking it up among the customers, instead of cross-joining customer and product sets. The MDX function that enables us to do this is Generate( ).

If we are going to create a set named Top3ProdsOf10Custs, the basic template for this is going to be:

```
WITH
SET [Top10Custs] AS
'{ TopCount ([Customer].[Individual].Members, 10,
        ([Measures].[Profit], [Time].[2001])) }'
 . . .
SET [Top3ProdsOf10Custs] AS
'{ Generate ([Top10Custs], . . . )}'
```

Within the Generate( ) function, for each tuple in the set Top10Custs we want to find the top three products. The following looks tempting:

```
Generate ([Top10Custs], TopCount ([Product].[Brand].Members, 3,
        ([Measures].[Profit], [Customer].CurrentMember, [Time].[2001])))
```

But even that will not get us there. (The [Customer].CurrentMember is completely superfluous and is only included to clarify our interest in the operation. The current member of a dimension does not need mentioning in this context unless we are going to modify it or access something related to it.) It will get us partway there, but when we put it into a query, the total result (as shown in Figure 4.10) isn't what we want:

```
WITH
SET [Top10Custs] AS
'{ TopCount ([Customer].[Individual].Members, 10,
        ([Measures].[Profit], [Time].[2001])) }'
SET [Top3ProdsOf10Custs] AS
'{ Generate ([Top10Custs], TopCount ([Product].[Brand].Members, 3,
        ([Measures].[Profit], [Time].[2001]))) }'
SELECT
{ [Time].[2000], [Time].[2001]} on columns,
{ [Top3ProdsOf10Custs] } on rows
FROM Sales
WHERE ( [Measures].[Profit] )
```

	2000	2001
Gobi Crab Cakes	25,000	28,400
Silver Scales	24,500	26,900
Poseidon's Platter	21,100	19,000

Figure 4.10 Results of first try.

Our Generate( ) clause returned the right products but no customers. How do we get the customers in? The Generate( ) function returns a set with the dimensionality of the second set, not the first set. We cannot express

```
Generate( [Top10Custs],
 { [Customer].CurrentMember, TopCount ([Product].[Brand].Members, 3,
      ([Measures].[Profit], [Time].[2001]))))
```

because that is syntactically and semantically illegal (we are mixing customer and product members in a single set). Using the following query we can, however, combine the customer member with the product set using the CrossJoin( ) function, which gives us the customer by product tuples that we want:

```
Generate ( [Top10custs],
  CrossJoin (
    {[Customer].CurrentMember },
    TopCount ([Product].[Brand].Members, 3,
      ([Measures].[Profit], [Time].[2001]))
  )
)
```

At last, we have the tuples that we want (see Figure 4.11). Note that in this last version of the query, we needed to reference the current member of the customer dimension in order to have the result set contain both customers and products.

Analytically, this particular result is useful for the fairly arbitrary cutoffs that we chose to define important products for important customers. Importance is defined for this example as importance to our organization (we are looking at

		2000	2001
Hudson Food Dists.	Gobi Crab Cakes	1,200	1,370
Hudson Food Dists.	Silver Scales	1,400	1,250
Hudson Food Dists.	Poseidon's Platter	1,100	1,000
Barbara, Levin Inc.	Gobi Crab Cakes	1,120	990
Barbara, Levin Inc.	Briny Deep	1,040	980
Barbara, Levin Inc.	Silver Scales	1,200	1,300
...	...	...	...

Figure 4.11 Results of desired query.

profitability, not units, revenue, value of long-term contracts, and so on). The thresholds are very arbitrary because we are choosing the top N products and customers. Choosing sets of customers and products based on their percentage contribution to profits, revenues, and the like would be a less arbitrary choice, and these are equally easy. For example, for the set of customers that form our most profitable 10 percent, what are the most profitable 20 percent of the products they each buy? Replacing the TopCount( ) function in our expression with TopPercent( ) gives us the following:

```
SET [Top 10% of Custs] AS
'{ TopPercent ([Customer].[Individual].Members, 10,
      ([Measures].[Profit], [Time].[2001])) }'
SET [Top 20% Prods Of Top 10% Custs] AS
'{ Generate ( [Top 10% of Custs],
    CrossJoin ( { [Customer].CurrentMember },
      TopPercent ([Product].[Brand].Members, 20,
        ([Measures].[Profit], [Time].[2001])
      )
    )
  )
}'
```

This can lead us to several other useful related queries. For example, this expression gives us the products per customer. If our goal is to then focus on the production, distribution, or pricing of these products, we may be interested in removing the specific customers and looking just at the products. Each customer is likely to have products in common with other customers. In fact, it is not immediately obvious how many different products are in this group. The set of customers is unknown in advance of the query. How can we find out the number of products or the set of products?

The answer can be found by using the MDX Extract( ) function, which returns a set of selected dimensionality. We can use it to return the unique set of products from our selected customer by product tuples, as with the following expression:

```
SET [Top 10%'s Top 20 Products] AS
'Extract ([Top 20% Prods Of Top 10% Custs], [Product])'
```

Extract( ) returns only unique tuples, so we don't have to worry about finding duplicates. The products will be in a fairly arbitrary order, and we can sort them further if we want to. We can also take this set and count the tuples to find out how many products make up this group.

If our goal is to understand how these customers are or are not representative of our customers as a whole, we may want to compare the product mix purchased by the top 10 percent of customers with the product mix purchased by the average customer. Which brands that are in the top 20 percent by profitability for our top 10 percent of customers are also in the top 20 percent of profitability for all customers? Which ones are peculiar to the top customers? Which ones, if any, are among the most profitable products for all customers, but not among the most profitable products for our top customers? If we are exploring customers and products by profitability, these are also important questions.

This last set of three questions could be answered in one query, and we will continue our train of thought to create it. We will make one creative leap to put it together. The goal is to create a grouping of products into three different groups: those that correspond to only the top 10 customers, those which correspond to both the top 10 group and across all customers, and those that correspond only across all customers and not within the top 10. These three groups represent customer populations, and we will use three calculated members on the customer dimension to represent these groups. (If no products exist in one of these three groups, we will not have any product-customer group tuples that use that customer group, and that group will not appear in the query result.)

We need to construct two basic sets and then manipulate them to get the third. The first set, of top products for top customers, we have already created as [Important Products]. The second set, of top products across all customers, is similar:

```
SET [Top 20% Prods Across All Custs] AS
'TopPercent ([Product].[Brand].Members, 20,
    ([Measures].[Profit], [Time].[2001]))'
```

The trick now is to create three divisions between those two sets. We need to pool them together before dividing them up, using the following expression:

```
SET [Product Union] AS 'Union ([Top 20% Prods Across All Custs],
[Top 10%'s Top 20 Products])'
```

We could also create the same effect with the following expression:

```
Distinct ({[Top 20% Prods Across All Custs],
    [Top 10%'s Top 20 Products] })
```

Now, we simply create three subsets using set functions in sequence:

```
SET [Top10 Only] AS
'Except ([Product Union], [Top 20% Prods Across All Custs])'
SET [Both Groups] AS
'Intersect ([Top 10%'s Top 20 Products],
    [Top 20% Prods Across All Custs])'
SET [All Customers Only] AS
'Except ([Top 20% Prods Across All Custs], [Product Union])'
```

The last step is to create the calculated members that will group these three subsets. "Calculated members" implies computation; what formula calculates the cells within these sets without altering the contents of the cells?

We know that we want to use some sort of default member for this calculation. These members are on the Customer dimension, so a formula of [Customer]. [All Customer] makes sense. That formula causes the values of each of the products to be taken from the [All Customer] member for whatever measure is being calculated. So, the three calculated members can each have a very simple formula:

```
MEMBER [Customer].[Top 10% Only Group] AS '[Customer].[All Customer]'
MEMBER [Customer].[Top 10% And All Group] AS '[Customer].[All Customer]'
MEMBER [Customer].[All Customers Only Group] AS '[Customer].[All
Customer]'
```

And we can create our final set of tuples for reporting on as follows:

```
SET [Report Tuples] AS '{
  CrossJoin ( { [Customer].[Top 10% Only Group] }, [Top10 Only] ),
  CrossJoin ( { [Customer].[Top 10% And All Group] }, [Both Groups] ),
  CrossJoin ( { [Customer].[All Customers Only Group] }, [All Customers
Only]) }'
```

When we put it all together, it forms the following (long) query, whose results are shown in Figure 4.12:

```
WITH
SET [Top 10% of Custs] AS
'TopPercent ([Customer].[Individual].Members, 10,
     ([Measures].[Profit], [Time].[2001]))'
SET [Top 20% Prods Of Top 10% Custs] AS
'Generate( [Top 10% of Custs],
  CrossJoin (
    {[Customer].CurrentMember},
    TopPercent ([Product].[Brand].Members, 20,
      ([Measures].[Profit], [Time].[2001])
```

		2000	2001
Top 10% Only Group	Gobi Crab Cakes	25,000	28,400
Top 10% Only Group	Silver Scales	24,500	26,900
Top 10% And All Group	Poseidon's Platter	21,100	19,000
Top 10% And All Group	Mako Steak-o	18,300	21,000
All Customers Only Group	Atlantic Trench Mouthfuls	18,100	16,300

Figure 4.12 Results of full query.

```
      )
    )
  )'
SET [Top 10%'s Top 20% Products] AS
  'Extract ([Top 20% Prods Of Top 10% Custs], [Product])'
SET [Top 20% Prods Across All Custs] AS
  'TopPercent ([Product].[Brand].Members, 20,
      ([Measures].[Profit], [Time].[2001]))'
SET [Product Union] AS
  'Union ([Top 20% Prods Across All Custs],
    [Top 10%'s Top 20% Products])'
SET [Top10 Only] AS
  'Except ([Product Union], [Top 20% Prods Across All Custs])'
SET [Both Groups] AS
  'Intersect ([Top 10%'s Top 20% Products],
  [Top 20% Prods Across All Custs])'
SET [All Customers Only] AS
  'Except ([Top 20% Prods Across All Custs], [Product Union])'
MEMBER [Customer].[Top 10% Only Group] AS '[Customer].[All Customer]'
MEMBER [Customer].[Top 10% And All Group] AS '[Customer].[All Customer]'
MEMBER [Customer].[All Customers Only Group] AS '[Customer].[All
Customer]'
SET [Report Tuples] AS '{
  CrossJoin ( { [Customer].[Top 10% Only Group] }, [Top10 Only] ),
  CrossJoin ( { [Customer].[Top 10% And All Group] }, [Both Groups] ),
  CrossJoin ( { [Customer].[All Customers Only Group] }, [All Customers
Only])
}'
SELECT
{ [Time].[2000], [Time].[2001] } on columns,
{ [Report Tuples] } on rows
FROM SalesInfo
WHERE ([Measures].[Profit])
```

Whew! Although this is an involved query, it is not as complex as it would have been if we had tried to perform the same operation in SQL against the original source tables!

Summary

Although we have discussed a number of topics in this chapter, we have used only a fraction of the MDX functions available. It would not be possible to exhaustively cover all applications and MDX techniques in any one book. Hopefully, this chapter has given you all of the conceptual tools you need to understand how MDX functions as a language and how Microsoft OLAP Services and MDX work together so you can construct as sophisticated an application as your situation requires.

CHAPTER 5

MDX Context and Execution

Having explored the basics of MDX queries, we need to turn our attention to the way MDX queries and statements actually get evaluated. Context and interpretation are the two major themes of this chapter. As we examine them, we will look at how MDX is supposed to function in any vendor's implementation and point out a number of concrete aspects of Microsoft's implementation.

Although context isn't everything, it is important. Every portion of every query and action has a particular context within a cube's space, which affects how dimensions that are not explicitly referenced in any step are interpreted. This impacts how you actually compose queries and calculations in MDX. The interpretation of invalid data, missing data (NULLs), and invalid members is another important area that we will cover in this chapter. Cubes that you build will usually have many cells that contain no data, and your queries will need to deal with both invalid data and invalid members.

Every cell that is obtained from a query has a set of properties associated with it. One such property is the type of data that results in a query for that cell, and another is the formatted string version of that value as well as rendering information like the name of the font in which to display it. In this chapter, we will take a look at how the context of calculated members affects these cell properties.

So far, we have hardly discussed the concept of data types in MDX expressions at all, apart from the distinction between numbers, strings, Boolean conditions, and empty cells. In this chapter, we will discuss the specific data types that MDX calculations take on in OLAP Services. The relevance of the data types used in calculations depends on your application, in that you can readily put cells into a calculation and report values out of them and usually get a suitable answer. However, depending on your application, you may need to precisely control the data types that are used. For example, external functions may need to deal with the exact data types of the values passed to them. (Considerations to be taken into account when using external functions are described in Chapter 7, "Extending MDX Through External Functions.")

As in Chapter 2, "MDX in More Detail," as far as Microsoft OLAP/Analysis Services goes, we will generally not make distinctions between the server and the local PivotTable Service, but instead refer simply to OLAP/Analysis Services. Our primary goal in this chapter is to provide guidance on how to construct and use MDX queries and statements and the details of their execution.

Cell Context and Resolution Order in Queries

The process of answering a query involves resolving the sets that comprise each of the axes and the member of the slicer, then filling in the cells at each intersection of members from each axis and the slicer. Resolving the sets that make up each axis will very often require calculations against cells that are formed from base or calculated members. At every point in the preparation of the set of result cells, a context for calculations determines what you need to say to reference the cell data you are interested in using.

Analysis Services 2000 introduces calculation passes for cell calculations and a collection of ways to calculate cells (custom members and custom rollups), which make for a complex set of possibilities. We'll examine them in depth in due course but will start here with the basics.

For example, referring to our earlier typical cube example that has dimensions of measures, time, customers, and products, consider the following query:

```
WITH
MEMBER [Measures].[Margin Percent] AS
'[Measures].[Sales] / ([Measures].[Sales] - [Measures].[Costs])'
SET [GoodBets] AS
'Filter( [Customer].[City].Members,
        [Measures].[Margin Percent] > 0.1)'
SELECT
  { [Measures].[Sales], [Measures].[Margin Percent] } on columns,
  { CrossJoin ([GoodBets], [Product].[Product Category].Members) } on
rows
FROM
```

```
    SalesCube
WHERE
  [Time].[Q1 2000]
```

There's more going on in this query than meets the eye; key things are left unsaid in several places. Let's walk through the parts of this query and explore how a query is answered. Keep in mind its basic skeleton, which is as follows:

```
WITH
  MEMBER
  SET
SELECT
  { axis set 0 } on COLUMNS,
  { axis set 1 } on ROWS
FROM
  cube
WHERE
  slicer
```

The first relevant element in the query is the FROM clause, which names the cube. Naming the cube implies that all of its dimensions will be involved in one way or another in the query. Any dimension that is not explicitly mentioned in the cube will implicitly be referenced in the slicer at the default member. If the logged-in user role or the dimension definition itself has a default member defined for this dimension, then that will be the member implicitly referenced. (We discuss database default members in Chapter 10, "Changing the Cube and Dimension Environment through MDX.") If no default member has been specified, an implicit default member will be used (which will be the All member, or the "first" member in the top level of the dimension if there is no All level). Naming the cube in the WHERE clause therefore implicitly sets the default member of every dimension in the cube, unless it is otherwise modified by some other part of the query. Another way of thinking of this is that in the absence of specified default members, the default tuple for any cell in the cube is as follows:

```
([Customer].DefaultMember, [Time].DefaultMember,
  [Product].DefaultMember, [Measures].DefaultMember)
```

This will frequently be (and for our sample query is) the case:

```
([Customer].[All Customers], [Time].[All Time],
  [Product].[All Products], [Measures].Members.Item(0))
```

The default measure is usually the one that was picked first when the cube was defined.

The next relevant element is the WHERE clause. The slicer specifies a tuple of one member from one or more of the dimensions of the cube. (Although the MDX specification provides for sets from each dimension, this is not implemented by Microsoft.) Dimensions mentioned in the slicer cannot have members on any of the other axes of the result cube. The members that are specified override the implicit default members on those dimensions. For our sample query, the following is now the context:

```
([Customers].[All Customers], [Time].[Q1 2000],
  [Products].[All Products], [Measures].Members.Item(0))
```

The next relevant items are any member and set definitions between the WITH and the SELECT. No calculations will be performed when defining the member [Measures].[Margin Percent]. However, calculations will be performed during the definition of the set [GoodBets]. After the whole MDX statement is parsed, the tuples of each named set that is defined in the WITH . . . section are determined according to the order of the dependencies between them, which will roughly correspond to the order in which they appear (if set A uses the results of set B and set C, OLAP/Analysis Services will resolve sets B and C before set A).

When the set declaration appears, none of the cells have been computed yet. The expression Filter([Customer].[City].Members, [Measures].[Margin Percent] > 0.1) returns a set that is formed out of members from the customer dimension, but it returns them based on the calculated values associated with the cells. The current context to this point is as follows:

```
([Customers].[All Customers], [Time].[Q1 2000],
  [Products].[All Products], [Measures].Members.Item(0))
```

During the evaluation of the Filter() function, the [Customer].[City].Members term overrides the [All Customers] member in the context, and the [Measures].[Margin Percent] overrides the [Measures].Members.Item(0). As a result, the set of cells that will be evaluated and compared with 0.1 can be defined as follows:

```
CrossJoin(  [Customer].[City].Members, { ([Time].[Q1 2000],
  [Products].[All Products], [Measures].[Margin Percent] } ).
```

You can think of this context for the evaluation of cell values as "within the context of the Filter() operator." After the evaluation of cell values within the Filter() context is done, the context returns to ([Customers].[All Customers], [Time].[Q1 2000], [Products].[All Products], [Measures].Arbitrary Measure) and the following set is returned for use within the SELECT clause:

```
{ [Customer].[Tucson, AZ], [Customer].[Laredo, TX],
  [Customer].[Honolulu, HI] }.
```

Once OLAP/Analysis Services has processed all of the set declarations and member definitions, it processes the SELECT clause. Within the SELECT clause, OLAP Services processes the sets for each axis in turn. The process of creating the sets for each axis is similar to the process for creating the set in the

WHERE clause. Across the columns, the set of measure members is spelled out as follows:

```
{ [Measures].[Sales], [Measures].[Margin Percent] }
```

Down the rows, the set of tuples is determined by taking the CrossJoin( ) of our three cities with every member of the product category level. Each axis is independent of the others; the columns do not form an additional context for the rows and vice versa.

Now that OLAP Services has determined the sets for each axis, both in dimensionality and with respect to the exact set of tuples in each, it calculates the cells. Each cell is defined entirely by a member of each of the four dimensions; every one will have its time member set to [Time].[Q1 2000] and will have a different ([Customer], [Product], [Measure]) component.

For each cell in the result set, if more than one of the members defining the cell is a calculated member, OLAP Services will determine the correct formula to use by selecting the formula for the member with the highest associated solve order number. The context for the evaluation of the cell will be the ([Time], [Customer], [Product], [Measure]) tuple that identifies the cell (this is similar to the way the overall query started off with a single cell as its context).

Cell Context in Set Functions

The example in the preceding section showed the cell context that is generated within a Filter( ) expression. This cell context extends to all functions that operate over a set, including aggregation functions. For example, let us alter the sample query to the following, which has some problems that we will address:

```
WITH
MEMBER [Measures].[Costs] AS
'Sum (
  Descendants (
    [Product].CurrentMember,
    [Product].[SKU]
  ),
  [Measures].[Units Manufactured] * [Measures].[Cost Per Unit]
)'
MEMBER [Measures].[Margin Percent] AS
'[Measures].[Sales] / ([Measures].[Sales] - [Measures].[Costs])'
SET [GoodBets] AS
'Filter( [Customer].[City].Members,
         [Measures].[Margin Percent] > 0.1)'
SELECT
  { [Measures].[Sales], [Measures].[Margin Percent] } on columns,
  { CrossJoin ([GoodBets], [Product].[Product Category].Members) } on
rows
```

```
FROM
  SalesCube
WHERE
  [Time].[Q1 2000]
```

In this, we have added an expression to sum up product costs. Within the execution of the Sum( ), the product portion of the context for evaluating [Units Manufactured] * [Cost Per Unit] is set in turn to each [SKU]-level descendant of the current product member. Within the Filter( ) function, the product portion will be the default member of the Product dimension, and when evaluating cells related to [Product Category] members in the SELECT clause, it will be set to the appropriate product category.

However, this does not modify the customer or the time aspects of the units and costs being multiplied and summed. Let us assume that [Cost Per Unit] enters at the month level of the cube and aggregates by simple summation. As we are filtering and reporting on values, we will be getting the [Q1 2000] sum of [Cost Per Unit]. In this case, a quarter-level sum of the costs per time is not useful; we want to access the values from the month level. So, we need to extend the Sum( ) to use month-level values, which would look like the following:

```
MEMBER [Measures].[Costs] AS
'Sum (
  Descendants (
    [Product].CurrentMember,
    [Product].[SKU]
  ),
  Sum (
    Descendants (
      [Time].CurrentMember,
      [Time].[Month]
    ),
    [Measures].[Units Manufactured] * [Measures].[Cost Per Unit]
  )
)'
```

TIP

If you are going to perform sums in MDX over two or more dimensions, then you should create a series of nested sum expressions rather than an MDX expression that performs a sum over a single CrossJoin( ). For example, use Sum([Geography].[State].Members, Sum([Time].[Month].Members, [Measures].[Units Manufactured] * [Measures].[Cost Per Unit])) rather than Sum(CrossJoin ([Geography].[State].Members, [Time].[Month].Members), [Measures].[Units Manufactured] * [Measures].[Units Manufactured] * [Measures].[Cost Per Unit]). Numerically, both of these will lead to the same result, but the sum of sums will be much more efficient. We cover efficiency issues for MDX queries in Chapter 14, "Optimizing MDX," on optimizing queries and expressions.

Infinite Recursion: A "Gotcha"
Related to Calculation Context

When you are defining calculated members, you have to take into account the concept of the current context along the dimension in which the calculated member is placed. This includes the measures dimension, which has a current member just like every other dimension. For example, the following calculated measure definition will not quite work, though it is syntactically correct:

```
MEMBER [Measures].[Avg Sale] AS
'Sum (Descendants ([Geography], [Geography].[City]),
     [Measures].[Sales])
/ Count (Descendants ([Geography], [Geography].[City]),
     EXCLUDEEMPTY)'
```

This may look like a perfectly good definition of an average (dividing a sum by a count), but it will not work. When OLAP Services calculates the [Measures].[Avg Sale] member, although the sum is quite clear, the count cannot be evaluated. When values are being calculated for the count, the current measure is [Measures].[Avg Sale]. When the cells formed by

```
{ Descendants ([Geography], [Geography].[City]) }
```

intersect with the current measure in that context, OLAP Services will go into infinite recursion in its attempt to determine whether the set is empty. To evaluate whether any [Measures].[Avg Sale] cell is empty or not, OLAP Services needs to evaluate it by this formula, which will require recursive reevaluation ad infinitum. If you were going to include empty cells using INCLUDEEMPTY, then it wouldn't really matter which measure you chose; the algorithm employed by Microsoft OLAP Services will just count the cells without testing them, and it will work fine.

The solution to this problem is to be cognizant of the cell context. OLAP/Analysis Services does not flag a potential infinitely recursive calculated member when it is defined, but you will notice it when the cell returns an ERR instead of a value or NULL. OLAP/Analysis Services will also set an appropriate text message inside the error information retrieved by the client for this cell, indicating the presence of infinite recursion. Usually, when you are performing a SUM/COUNT over the same set of non-measure tuples, you are performing the SUM and the COUNT over the same measure. We can remedy this by cross-joining the non-measures tuples with the measure of interest to get the right set of cells.

Stylistically, you may want to consider the equivalence of the following three ways of phrasing the calculation. First,

```
WITH
MEMBER [Measures].[Avg Sale] AS
'Sum (Descendants ([Geography].CurrentMember, [Geography].[City]),
     [Measures].[Sales])
/ Count (
    CrossJoin ( { [Measures].[Sales] },
      Descendants ([Geography].CurrentMember, [Geography].[City])
    ),
   EXCLUDEEMPTY
)'
```

Second,

```
WITH
MEMBER [Measures].[Avg Sale] AS
'Sum (
  CrossJoin ( {[Measures].[Sales]},
    Descendants ([Geography].CurrentMember, [Geography].[City])
  )
)
/ Count (
    CrossJoin ( { [Measures].[Sales] },
      Descendants ([Geography].CurrentMember, [Geography].[City]
    ),
    EXCLUDEEMPTY
)'
```

Third,

```
WITH
SET [CellSet] AS
'CrossJoin ( { [Measures].[Sales] },
   Descendants ([Geography].CurrentMember, [Geography].[City])
)'
MEMBER [Measures].[Avg Sale] AS
'Sum ([CellSet]) / Count ([CellSet], EXCLUDEEMPTY)'
```

The first of these variations simply sums sales over the city members and divides by the count of the non-empty tuples that were formed by cross-joining those tuples with the sales measure. The second variation cross-joins the city members with the sales measure in both the SUM and the COUNT; when the set is summed, the set specification includes the measure whose values are to be summed over the cities. The third variation does the same thing but encapsulates the definition of the set into a named set. This means that the cross-join is only performed once when the query is evaluated.

TIP

If you want to supply a set to a function (for example, an aggregation like Sum( ), Avg( ), Max( ), Correlation( ), and so on) and you want the cells of a specific measure to be used in the function, simply cross-join the measure with the set. Then, even if the current context includes a different measure, your specific measure's cells will be used.

Non-Data: Invalid Numbers, NULLs, and Invalid Members

When performing queries and calculations, we will frequently need to deal with data that isn't valid as well as the empty space in our cubes where data could be but isn't. We may encounter three sorts of non-data when evaluating queries: invalid numbers, NULLs (or empty cells), and invalid member specifications (which we have also seen referred to as NULL members). Let us take a look at each of these.

Invalid Calculations: Divide by Zero and Numerical Errors

Even though the result of a divide-by-zero is not a valid number, Microsoft OLAP Services does not treat it as an empty value. In some instances, you can test for the results of a divide-by-zero, or for a floating-point overflow caused by other means, by comparing the cell value with (1/0). For example,

```
iff (1.0e+40 * 1.0e+40 = (1/0), "Overflowed", "Didn't Overflow")
```

multiplies a very large double-float value by itself and will cause an overflow condition. When performing a comparison, OLAP Services will consider the overflow value as being equal to (1/0), so the expression will always return the string Overflowed. Be aware, however, that this test is dependent upon how the processor of the machine on which OLAP Services is installed handles different types of numeric errors. Different CPUs (different generations of Intel CPUs or the Compaq/Digital Alpha CPU) may return different values, and different causes of overflow may cause different values to appear. In short, you may not be able to effectively test for an overflow condition for any given calculation without using an external function. We discussed how to avoid problems like divide-by-zero in Chapter 3, "MDX In Use."

Note that OLAP Services will never detect overflow in integer calculations. If you add 2,000,000,000 to 2,000,000,000 in a small-integer calculation, you will not get 4,000,000,000 as a result but rather 1,852,516,354. BigInt calculations are extremely unlikely to overflow; if 2,000,000,000 input cells each contribute a value of 2,000,000,000 to a sum, the result will still not overflow. Numerical errors trapped by external function libraries frequently raise an ActiveX Automation error rather than return a bogus value. When this happens, the evaluation of the cell will halt, and it will neither be empty nor have a value of any type.

Semantics of Empty Cells

Given the usual sparseness of data in a multidimensional data set, empty cells are frequently the rule rather than the exception. When you are looking at a data set as a set of cells within a big CrossJoin( ) of all dimensions, you will see a lot more empty cells in the cube than there are NULLs in the underlying fact tables. The reason for this, of course, is because not every consumer, supplier, employee, or factory participated in every type of transaction at every possible time period with every possible geographical location. (In Analysis Services 2000, empty values in fact table measure columns will result in a zero cell value.)

Microsoft OLAP Services has default semantics for handling empty cells in an MDX expression that differ somewhat from the default semantics for handling NULLs in SQL. OLAP/Analysis Services also extends standard MDX with a NULL operator, which can be used to return an empty or NULL value from a formula. (Because MDX has an operator called IsEmpty( ) and OLAP Services has a NULL operator to make a cell empty, no clear terminology is laid out for us to use. We will therefore use both NULL and empty in our discussion here.)

The MDX that OLAP/Analysis Services provides does not, however, provide any operators for determining whether a cell is empty because the underlying table column values were NULL or because rows were not present for that dimensional combination. Also, no standard ways in a dimensional OLAP model are available for an application to signify whether an empty cell could possibly have had a value or not (such as the invalidity of a "how many months pregnant" condition for a male patient, or sales values for a store member in the months before the store actually opened).

According to the OLE DB for OLAP specification of MDX semantics, empty cells are treated almost identically to zero in a numerical context and as an empty string in a string context. That is, in a numerical context, they should add, subtract, multiply, and divide as though they were zero. In an ascending sort, they will sort before zero and after the negative number that has the smallest magnitude. In a string context, concatenating a string with an EMPTY will result in the original string, and empty cells that have a string type will sort immediately before cells that have a real empty string for a value. That is, the following sets of values are sorted according to the MDX specification:

- Numbers: $-10, -1, -0.00001$, NULL, $0, 0.00001, 1, 10$
- Strings: NULL, "", "a," "ab," "z"

NOTE

Microsoft OLAP Services 7.0 and Analysis Services RTM do not adhere to the OLE DB for OLAP specification in treatment of NULLs. When ordering a set, NULL values are treated as if they actually were zero or empty strings. Refer to Chapter 3 for information on how to work around this.

Microsoft OLAP Services does not enable cell values to have a Boolean data type, so there is no need to define a Boolean interpretation of NULL. Since iif( ) must return a numeric or string value, the expression iif([cell] > 5, True, NULL) and [cell2] > 6 will not parse because it treats the result of iif( ) as a Boolean. Thus, in OLAP Services, we don't have to consider the case in which NULL enters into a Boolean expression.

OLAP/Analysis Services interprets NULL cell semantics differently from the OLE DB for OLAP specification in that the result of a calculation that involves empty cells may be NULL or it may not be NULL. A NULL value will be treated as zero when it is combined with a non-NULL value in a calculation, but a calculation that involves only NULL values will be regarded as NULL. Let's use as an example the following calculation:

```
([Measures].[Sales] - [Measures].[Costs]) / [Measures].[Costs]
```

If Sales and Costs are both present, we will get a value in return; if Sales are 10 and Costs are 8, then $(10 - 8)/8 = 0.25$. If Sales is present but Costs is not, the expression would be evaluated as $(10 - 0)/0$, and the floating-point overflow value (with a typical string representation of -1.INF) will be returned. If Costs is present but Sales is not, the expression would be evaluated as $(0 - 8)/8 = -1$. However, if neither costs nor sales are present (if both are NULL), the expression will return an empty value.

In a comparison, a NULL will be equal to zero in all circumstances. That is, the expression iif (NULL = 0, . . . , . . .) will always return the result of the if-true expression. Of course, NULL = NULL is true, and (NULL <> NULL) is always false. Don't fall into the trap of comparing a value with NULL directly, as with iif ([Measures].[Units Sold] = NULL, . . .). The NULL will be silently converted into a zero if the [Units Sold] reference is present. If the [Units Sold] reference is NULL, perhaps a NULL will actually be compared to a NULL (which will result in true). The result will be exactly as if you compared [Units Sold] with zero.

If you include any constants in a expression, the expression will always return a result because any empty cell value will be combined with a non-empty value (the constant) as a result. For example, a growth projection formula of (1.5 * ([Time].[Q2 2001] + [Time].[Q3 2001])) will return zero if the given measure does not have a value at either [Q2 2001] or [Q3 2001]. It will return 1.5 times the sum of the values that are present, if any are. If we break this down into pieces, the expression ([Time].[Q2 2001] + [Time].[Q3 2001]) will have a NULL result if all of the cells are empty, but (1.5 * (EMPTY)) will be treated as 1.5 * 0.

Keep in mind that the Sum( ) of values from cells that are defined as calculated results will be the same whether the cells return zero or NULL. However, if you are calculating averages based on the count of non-empty cells, you will need to pay attention to the averages of calculated members. The result of Avg( ) over an empty set returns a floating-point overflow (divide-by-zero), not a NULL.

You should also note that Microsoft OLAP/Analysis Services only performs the IsEmpty( ) operation on cells. Properties and the results of functions on members like.UniqueName can have no result (see the following section on invalid locations). However, if you attempt to use IsEmpty( ) on these members, it will result in a parser error. Hopefully, this will change in a later version or service release. The workaround for this problem is to declare a calculated member that returns the value of the property or name and then to test whether that value is empty. In Analysis Services, if you are testing for an empty member name, you probably are trying to see if the member itself exists, which you can do with *member* IS NULL as well.

Invalid Locations

Non-information may need to be dealt with in MDX in another way: when invalid tuples or empty sets are specified. These can arise in a variety of ways. Microsoft OLAP Services has a very simple logic for dealing with them, which you will need to account for when you are constructing ranges using the colon (:) operator.

Change in Logic between OLAP Services 7 and Analysis Services 2000

With the release of Analysis Services 2000, the semantics of providing an invalid location on one or both sides of the colon (:) operator has changed.

An empty set or tuple arises whenever you request a member(s) that just aren't there. For example, take a time dimension whose leaf level is months and whose first month is January 2000. Since there are no children to January 2000, the set expression [Time].[Jan 2000].Children will return an empty set. The MDX parser will treat it as a set, and the set can be combined with other sets, as in {[Time].[Jan 2000], [Time].[Jan 2000].Children}. However, the [Jan 2000].Children term will contribute zero members to the resulting set. Similarly, the member expression [Time].[Jan 2000].PrevMember specifies a non-existent member. A set that combined this non-existent member with other members, such as { [Time].[Jan 2000], [Time].[Jan 2000].PrevMember } will only result in the members that were actually present in the dimension meta data ({[[Time].[Jan 2000]]}, in this case). If the geography dimension had [City] as its leaf level, then the tuple specification ([Geography].[Atlanta GA].FirstChild, [Time].[Jan 2000].PrevMember) would result in an invalid tuple (as would ([Geography].[Atlanta GA], [Time].[Jan 2000].PrevMember). This is because if only one member in a tuple specification is invalid, the entire tuple is.

References to invalid members, tuples, or sets can occur in queries for a variety of reasons. Only valid locations can return results, however, so you will not get valid values back from invalid locations—only NULL. Invalid locations can spring up in two contexts: when a set is being specified and when a tuple is being specified. We've just talked about the case in which a tuple is being specified; let's take a look at sets next.

When a set is being specified, it will ultimately form the range over which a set of values will be evaluated. This is true whether the set is the axis of a query, is a set created by CREATE SET or WITH SET, or is specified in a calculated member as input to an aggregation function. As the set specification is evaluated, valid tuples are included, and invalid ones will not appear. If the set specifies one valid member and 100 invalid members, only one member will be in the final set, and all values (cell or property) that are evaluated relative to that will be related to the one member. Thus, OLAP/Analysis Services prevents invalid member references (which will lead to invalid tuples) from contributing empty cell values to calculations like Count( ) and Avg( ).

It is important to understand the behavior of invalid members when they are used with the colon operator (:) provided by Microsoft OLAP/Analysis Services. (This behavior has changed between releases.) Common usage of MDX functions like .Lag( ), .Lead( ), Cousin( ), and ParallelPeriod( ) will frequently result in an invalid member. Part of the utility of Cousin( ) and ParallelPeriod( ) is that comparable ranges from multiple levels can be specified with one simple operator. The set of time members described by {ParallelPeriod ([Time].[Year], 1) : [Time].CurrentMember} provides us with the last year's worth of members at the level of the current time member, regardless of whether it is month, quarter, or day. The byproduct of constructing ranges like this is that some ranges may not mean what you want them to mean. What does it mean when the current time member is already in the first year, so there is no parallel period a year ago?

In OLAP Services 7, when you specify a range in MDX in which one member is valid and the other is not, the resulting range extends to the edge of the database's ordering of members on the level of the valid member. For example, consider a time level that has the 12 months January through December in calendar order. The range { [March] : [January].PrevMember } specified a valid member on the left and an invalid member on the right. The set that resulted would be { [March] : [December] }.

In Analysis Services 2000, when an invalid location is specified on either or both sides of the colon (:), an error occurs when the query is executed. On the one hand, this prevents surprising results to a query. On the other hand, it means that you should make sure that an invalid location cannot end up on either side of the colon.

You can use iif( ) to test indirectly for the existence or non-existence of members or you can use other indirect means. A direct test would be asking whether the member itself is empty. OLAP Services 7 offers no direct way to do this, but Analysis Services 2000 introduces a way.

An indirect test would be to test the count of tuples from one member in a dimension back to the edge of the dimension. For example, if you want to calculate a six-month moving average only where at least six months exist over which to calculate it, you can count the number of tuples stretching from the current member backwards and only return the average if there are six of them, as the following expression does:

```
iif (
  LastPeriods (6, [Time].CurrentMember).Count >= 6,
  Avg(LastPeriods (6, [Time].CurrentMember),
    [Measures].[Volume Traded]),
  NULL
)
```

A direct test would involve comparing the member with NULL using the Microsoft-specific IS operator.

```
iif (
  Not ([Time].CurrentMember.Lag(5) IS NULL),
  Avg({[Time].CurrentMember.Lag(5) : [Time].CurrentMember },
    [Measures].[Volume Traded]),
  NULL
)
```

For some reason, OLAP/Analysis Services requires that the argument to the IsEmpty( ) function be a cell, not an expression and not a tuple (though the MDX specification requires that any expression be allowed to be used there). An alternative approach is to compare the name to an empty string, although you have to beware of empty member names (hopefully, you don't have any in your time dimension):

```
iif (
  [Time].Lag(5).UniqueName <> "",
  Avg([Time].Lag(5) : [Time],
      [Measures].[Volume Traded]),
  NULL
)
```

Alternatively, if using IsEmpty( ) appeals to you more, you can define a cell expression that returns the following unique name. Note that because Microsoft's IsEmpty( ) cannot take a tuple, we need to create a measure reference that contains its own .Lag(5):

```
WITH
MEMBER [Measures].[Time-name] AS '[Time].UniqueName'
MEMBER [Measures].[Time-name-lag5] AS
  '([Measures].[Time-Name], [Time].Lag (5))'
MEMBER [Measures].[Rolling Avg Volume] AS
  'Iif ( Not IsEmpty( [Measures].[Time-name-lag5] ), . . . , . . . )'
. . .
```

Precedence of Cell Properties in Calculations

Another aspect of context that we have not yet talked about is that of a single cell and the calculation chosen as having precedence for that cell. We introduced precedence issues and solve order numbers in Chapter 2. When a calculated member is used to define the value of a cell, it defines the values for every aspect of that cell. Not only does that include the raw numerical quantity for the cell, but all associated properties for that cell as well. In combination with the data types of the cells that go into calculating the cell, the formula itself will determine the data type of the raw value that is returned to the client or passed to an external function. The other properties of a cell, including textual display formatting and font-rendering information, will be those that are also defined for the calculated member. In the following sections, we explore each of these areas.

Precedence of Display Formatting

Let's revisit the trivial query introduced at the beginning of Chapter 1, "A First Introduction to MDX," this time with formatting applied. Assuming that our sales and costs are formatted to return zero decimal places, we will see the results shown in Figure 5.1 if we ask for a June-to-July difference to two decimal places and that Margin Pct be formatted as a percentage to one decimal place:

```
WITH
MEMBER [Measures].[Margin Pct] AS
'([Measures].[Sales] - [Measures].[Costs]) / [Measures].[Costs]',
SOLVE_ORDER = 1, FORMAT_STRING = '#.0%'
MEMBER [Time].[June to July] AS
'[Time].[July 2001] - [Time].[June 2001]',
SOLVE_ORDER = 2, FORMAT_STRING = '#.00'
SELECT
  { [Measures].[Sales], [Measures].[Costs], [Measures].[Margin Percent]
} on columns,
  { [Time].[June 2001], [Time].[July 2001], [Time].[June to July]} on
rows
FROM TrivialCube
WHERE ( [Stores].[Downtown] )
CELL PROPERTIES [FORMATTED_VALUE]
```

As you can see from Figure 5.1, the cell formatting defined in the calculated member that calculates the cell is the formatting that is applied to the value of the cell. The PivotTable Service itself takes on the chore of performing the formatting, so your clients will not need to devote any logic to this task. Font choice, size, style, and color information can also be specified by the calculated member; whether this information is used is up to the client application.

Data Types from Calculated Cells

It is a simple matter to describe the rules for the data types that are returned for calculations involving valid data and that return a valid result. The data type for

		Measures		
		Sales	Costs	Margin Pct.
	June-2001	1,200	1,000	20.0%
Time	July-2001	1,300	1,050	23.8%
	June to July Difference	100.00	50.00	3.8%

Figure 5.1 Overlapping calculated members with cell formatting.

the result of a calculated member depends on the formula as well as the types of cells it uses as inputs. The following rules are used in MDX calculations in Analysis Services 2000:

- Two integers added, subtracted, or multiplied together result in an integer. If one integer is BigInt-sized, then the result will be BigInt size.

- An integer added to, subtracted from, or multiplied by a floating-point number in any way results in a floating-point number. The result will be the size of the floating-point number (single-float or double-float).

- Any number divided by any other number results in a double-float result.

- The data type of the value returned by Count( ), Rank( ), or .Ordinal is a 32-bit integer.

- The data type of the value that is returned by Max( ) and Min( ) is the largest type of any of its inputs (the maximum of an integer and a single float is a single float, even if the integer is the larger of the numbers; the maximum of a double float and any other type is a double float).

- The Sum( ) of an empty set or of a set of entirely empty cells is an empty value. The Avg( ) of an empty set or a set of entirely empty cells is a divide-by-zero overflow.

- Any values calculated by an aggregation operator other than those listed in the preceding rules (including Sum( ), Max( ), and so on) are returned as a double float. All values that are input to the aggregation operator are converted to a double float prior to aggregation, so if you take the sum of a large number of integers, the aggregation operator will not overflow as the sum passes the 2,147,483,647 limit on a 32-bit integer.

- In an external function, a calculation that results in an error will cause a variant containing an Error value (vbError) to be created.

Strings have no conversion rules. They may be concatenated with other strings within Microsoft OLAP Services, but otherwise they are simply passed into functions and/or returned from functions. Although a Boolean result cannot be used in a context that expects a number, calculated members can be defined with a formula that just performs a logical operation, as follows:

```
CREATE MEMBER [AccountCube].[Measures].[Indebted] AS '[Measures].[Bor-
rowed] > [Measures].[Assets]'
```

Microsoft OLAP Services will convert the Boolean result into a 32-bit integer, with a true result represented by 1 and a false by 0.

Thus, even though a measure may have a defined data type, if the formula of some calculated member has precedence at a cell, the data type returned for the cell is defined by the calculation. For example, suppose an inventory units measure is defined as having an integer type and the following scenario variance member is used:

```
[Scenario].[Budget Pct. Variance] AS
  '([Scenario].[Actual] / [Scenario].[Budget]) -1'
```

In this case, the result of any ([Scenario].[Budget Pct. Variance], [Measures].[Inventory Units]) tuple is going to be a double float (unless yet another calculation has precedence for that cell).

Cube Context in Actions

Although an action is not executed from an MDX query (instead, it is invoked by manipulating data structures), it executes in a context as though it were a single-cell query, and in fact is basically a single-cell text query. The default context for the action is the default member for the user/role in each dimension. Although actions can be defined over more scopes, if the scope is a member, a tuple, or a set, then the member, tuple, or set provided by the client can affect the query context for the action. In the case of member or tuple, the context members of the listed dimensions are set to the member(s) provided by the client when the action is invoked. In the case of a set-scoped action, the context is not directly affected by invoking the action, but the set can be referenced by the action itself and use its contents in set functions and tuples.

Execution When Defining Calculations, Actions, and Executing Other DDL Commands

In Microsoft Analysis Services, when a client opens a cube using a role, all commands defined for that cube and that role are executed in the client session by the PivotTable Service. This is how calculated members, named sets, cell calculations, and actions all come to be defined for that session. Figure 5.2 illustrates this activity.

One thing that gets lost in the Analysis Manager interface is the importance of the total ordering of definitions among these calculations. For example, if a named set definition or a cell calculation requires a calculated member in order to execute, then the command that creates the calculated member needs to come first in the list of commands sent from the server. Similarly, if an action references a named set or a calculated member, then the action's definition must follow the set or member.

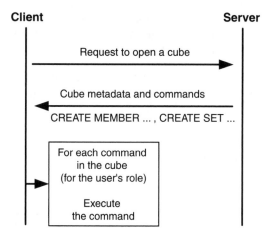

Figure 5.2 Commands transferred to PTS upon connection.

The following DDL statements can be executed via COMMAND objects stored at the server:

ALTER CUBE

CREATE ACTION

CREATE CACHE

CREATE CELL CALCULATION

CREATE MEMBER

CREATE SET

DROP ACTION

DROP CELL CALCULATION

DROP MEMBER

DROP SET

DROP LIBRARY

USE LIBRARY

The virtual cube version of the CREATE CUBE statement will be executed but will not have any effect. (The REFRESH CUBE and UPDATE CUBE statements could also be executed but are unlikely to serve any purpose.)

When a named set is created, the members of the set are resolved right then. There is no way to define a named set so that the actual members are determined at the time a query uses it as though it were a sort of macro (except by defining it in a WITH clause). Because there is no way to specify WITH clauses or slicers in a CREATE SET statement, the context for the CREATE SET is simply the current default members from each dimension.

Ordinarily, you won't include any DROP commands in the list of commands, although it is conceivable that you define a calculated member only in order to create a named set (or vice versa) and then drop it afterwards.

Interaction between Global, Session, and Query-Specific Calculations

In Analysis Services, calculated members, named sets, and cell calculations can be defined both at session scope via CREATE and at query scope via WITH. It is not an error to define one of these entities in a WITH clause that has the same name as the one defined at the server. That is, if the cube [Sales] has a named set [Fast Cars] defined at the server, you can build a query that starts with

```
WITH
SET [Fast Cars] AS '...'
```

and no error occurs. If the entity being redefined is a set, then any reference to that set in the query will use the new definition. If the entity is a cell calculation or a calculated member, then the definition is added alongside the pre-existing definition and both will be present for the course of the query.

This behavior can be applied for certain types of queries. If you are building queries on the fly in response to user actions, you can rely on a server-side calculated member or named set being present in the query, and you can put a WITH clause in the query that creates a new version if required. If you issued the statements

```
DROP SET [Sales].[Fast Cars]
CREATE SET [Sales].[Fast Cars] AS '...'
```

then you would redefine (for the client session) what the default set was, but if you simply chose to build

```
WITH SET [Fast Cars] AS '...'
```

when necessary you would retain the server-side default while retaining the query text that refers to [Fast Cars].

When a CREATE CELL CALCULATION, SET, or MEMBER is executed, if it refers to a specific named set, then the definition of the cell calculation, set, or member is fixed at that moment in time. For example, suppose that you executed the command

```
CREATE MEMBER [Sales].[Car].[Fast Car Total] AS
' Sum ([Fast Cars] )', SOLVE_ORDER = 1
```

If the set [Fast Cars] consists of the set {[Porsche], [Lotus], [Turbo Yugo]}, then the member [Fast Cars Total] will sum up measure values for these three cars. Now consider the following query:

```
WITH
SET [Fast Cars] AS
'{[Porsche], [Lotus], [Corvette], [Audi]}'
SELECT
{ [Measures].[Units Sold] } on columns,
{ [Fast Cars], [Car].[Fast Car Total] } on rows
FROM [Sales]
```

The [Fast Car Total] member returned in the report will be the sum of {[Porsche], [Lotus], [Turbo Yugo]}, while the car members listed on the rows will be {[Porsche], [Lotus], [Corvette], [Audi]}. This reflects the binding of the [Fast Car Total] to the particular session-level set, which still exists even though it is not visible in the query. Similarly, a set or cell calculation that includes a session-level calculated member will return the results of its calculation, even though a query may redefine the calculated member to have a new definition.

In the Analysis Services RTM version, however, if you define a calculated member in a WITH clause that has the same name as a calculated member created via CREATE MEMBER and you request that member to be returned, you will get both versions. Consider the following:

```
CREATE MEMBER [Sales].[Measures].[Profit] AS '[Measures].[Sales] -
[Measures].[Direct Costs]'

WITH
MEMBER [Measures].[Profit] AS '[Measures].[Sales] -
([Measures].[Indirect Costs] + [Measures].[Direct Costs])'
SELECT
{ [Measures].[Sales], [Measures].[Direct Costs], [Measures].[Profit] }
on columns
FROM [Sales]
WHERE ([Time].[Q3, 2001], [Customer].[Vancouver, BC] )
```

The resulting cellset will look like that shown in Figure 5.3.

Measures

Sales	Direct Costs	Profit	Profit
4,000	1,000	2,200	3,000

Figure 5.3 Query result showing the results of multiple member definitions.

Also, if you create a session-level named set that references a calculated member, but you redefine the calculated member in the WITH clause of the query, the member that gets used in the set is the newly defined calculated member, not the session-level calculated member.

NOTE
This behavior reflects a change in MDX semantics between Analysis Services 2000 and OLAP Services 7.0. As Microsoft does not document any semantics, there is no guarantee that they won't change again.

Summary

In this chapter, we looked at context in a query, the properties that are affected by the cell-by-cell calculation of members within a query, and the way in which OLAP Services handles missing and invalid data in a query. Combined with the base of MDX knowledge we have gained so far, these factors enable us to begin understanding all aspects of a query that are relevant to a client.

CHAPTER 6

The Many Ways To Calculate in Microsoft Analysis Services

M icrosoft Analysis Services provides six (!) separate ways of calculating a cell, and not much guidance on which one to choose for your application. In this chapter, we describe all of the different ways and describe the mechanics of how they interact. We also provide a few simple tips to keep in mind when applying them.

The six ways to calculate a cell are the following:

1. Intrinsic aggregation for a measure
2. Rollup by custom unary rollup operator
3. Custom member formula
4. Rollup by custom rollup formula
5. Calculated member
6. Cell calculation

We have described calculated members in some detail already as they are part of standard MDX and useful in almost every application. We haven't discussed the intrinsic aggregation for a measure very much, but then again it's simple enough almost to take for granted. (It's also something that you don't have any control over in MDX, except when creating a local cube using Microsoft's CRE-ATE CUBE statement.) We'll discuss the custom rollups in some depth in this chapter. The custom member formulas and custom rollup formulas are MDX expressions, whereas the unary rollup operators are a simplified (and non-MDX) way of specifying calculations within a hierarchy. The application designer and DBA ordinarily set up the various custom rollups (they live on the server). However, if they are in a write-enabled parent-child dimension, they can be modified using the ALTER CUBE UPDATE DIMENSION command (described in Chapter 10, "Changing the Cube and Dimension Environment through MDX"). Cell calculations are a way of layering calculation specifications over cell regions of a cube, and provide another way to accomplish calculations without adding new members.

Overview of Calculation Mechanisms

Before looking at how all of the ways to calculate interact with each other, let's set the stage by looking at each of them individually. We will briefly describe how each technique works on its own and how it is created and edited. For calculated members and cell calculations, we will also look at the syntax used to create them.

Intrinsic Aggregation for a Measure

If a cell has no other calculations applied to it, it is calculated by simple, intrinsic aggregation. In Microsoft's Analysis Services, every base measure of every regular cube has an aggregation function associated with it, which can be SUM, COUNT, MIN, MAX, or DISTINCT COUNT; if two or more fact records are associated with a particular cell, then the column associated with that measure is aggregated by that function and the results appear in that cell. In a parent-child hierarchy, it is possible for a parent member to aggregate records for itself, and also to incorporate the aggregates for its descendants in the hierarchy, but the data is still aggregated by the built-in function. Thus, even leaf-level cells are essentially aggregated (and you cannot tell without drilling through to the fact records whether a leaf cell was in fact atomic or if it was an aggregation of two or more records).

Rollup by Unary Operator

A level of a dimension can use a column of the underlying dimension table to specify rollup operators, which provide a simple technique for specifying calculations within the hierarchy. The syntax is borrowed from Hyperion Software's Essbase server, and will be familiar to everyone who has built a system from that product. Every child member under a parent can have a single-character operator associated with it. The cell associated with the parent member forms an accumulator for the results; based on the symbol associated with each child member, the value associated with the child is combined with the accumulated value to that point using the operator. The operators are as follows:

OPERATOR	DOES
+	adds the child's data value to the accumulated value
−	subtracts the child's data value from the accumulated value
*	multiplies the accumulated value by the child's value
/	divides the accumulated value by the child's value
%	divides the accumulated value by the child's value and then multiplies by 100
~	the child's value is ignored (contributes NULL to the accumulated value)

The child members and their operators are applied in database order (according to the member ordering per level specified at the server). The first operator applied must be +, −, or ~; no value is in the accumulator before the first operator is applied, and no default value of 1 or 0 is assumed if the *, /, or % operator is used first. If all child operators used are ~, the parent's value will be NULL or empty. Typically, the ~ is used for members that function as placeholders in the hierarchy, serving to organize other members. For example, in a dimension of financial accounts, the hierarchy of accounts that make up the proper P&L may all connect to each other using + and −, whereas a separate subtree of the dimension that holds important ratios would have each of its members using the ~ operator to prevent spurious calculations further up. If the parent member has associated fact data from a fact table that has been aggregated to it, that data is overridden by the results of the rollup operators. Figure 6.1 shows a sample outline of members, operators, and calculated results.

Rollup operators cannot be specified for the measures dimension because you cannot specify hierarchy or member properties for measures. However, a cube that uses rollup operators usually has just one measure named something like "Amount" or "Value," whereas another dimension named "Accounts" or "Indicators" functions as the measures dimension.

In the absence of any other specified calculations, rollup operators cut across all measures in cubes that use the dimension. This includes all measures in any virtual cubes that incorporate the dimension. Where rollup operators are used on two or more dimensions, dimension ordering in the cube determines how the rollups are applied to calculate a cell. (We'll talk about that in the "How the Types of Calculations Interact" section further along in this chapter.)

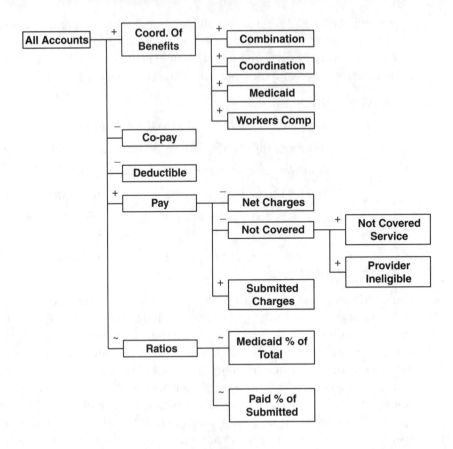

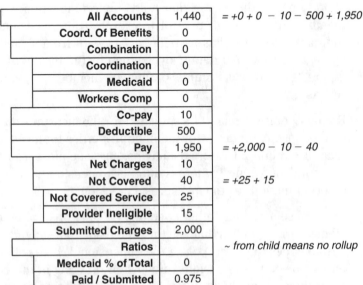

All Accounts	1,440	= +0 + 0 − 10 − 500 + 1,950
Coord. Of Benefits	0	
Combination	0	
Coordination	0	
Medicaid	0	
Workers Comp	0	
Co-pay	10	
Deductible	500	
Pay	1,950	= +2,000 − 10 − 40
Net Charges	10	
Not Covered	40	= +25 + 15
Not Covered Service	25	
Provider Ineligible	15	
Submitted Charges	2,000	
Ratios		~ from child means no rollup
Medicaid % of Total	0	
Paid / Submitted	0.975	

Figure 6.1 Effect of rolling up by unary operators.

NOTE

The RollupChildren( ) function in Analysis Services provides a way to explicitly roll up children using particular unary operators through MDX as well. Because that is an MDX function, it executes as part of one of the other calculation forms (custom member formula, custom rollup, calculated member, and cell calculation). However, the rules for combining the child members using unary operators in this function follow the rules described here. We discuss RollupChildren( ) in Appendix A.

Custom Member Formula

A custom member formula is an MDX formula that is associated with a regular member of a dimension. Like a custom rollup, they are typically used with parent-child dimensions but may also be used in any dimension. They are similar in some ways to a calculated member and different in others. The formula is ultimately stored in a column of a dimension table and may be altered in a write-enabled dimension by the ALTER CUBE UPDATE DIMENSION command.

A custom member formula is like a calculated member in that it is an MDX expression (for example, [Accounts].[Profit]/[Accounts].[HeadCount]), and intersects all members of all other dimensions. Unlike a calculated member, and like a custom rollup, it intersects all members of all other dimensions in every cube that the dimension appears. If the custom member formula is intended for use in calculating values for some measures but not others, you need to craft its formula or other calculations accordingly using Iif( ) to distinguish between the measures.

Unlike a calculated member, the member that holds a custom member formula can have children as well as a parent, and is considered a regular member by OLE DB for OLAP. Actually, the member itself is a regular member; it just happens to have this formula associated with it. Data can be entered for it and aggregated from fact tables, but at the member itself, the calculation overrides the intrinsic aggregation.

A custom formula can even be specified for the All member of a dimension through the All Member Formula property. You can think of this as a custom rollup formula or a custom member formula; the two are essentially equivalent at the All level.

Rollup by Custom Rollup Formula

A custom rollup formula is an MDX formula that is associated with an entire level of a dimension. (This is a level in the DSO sense of levels, so in a parent-child dimension the entire hierarchy except for any server-defined All level will share one formula if specified.) It is specified by the database designer or DBA and stored in the OLAP repository (which is outside the scope of this book), as opposed to in a column of a dimension table. This formula cannot be altered by an MDX command, even in a write-enabled dimension.

Like the other "custom" calculations, a custom rollup formula defined for a level in a shared dimension intersects with all measures and all members of all other dimensions in every cube that uses the level it is associated with. This means that if the level is included in a virtual cube or more than one regular cube, care must be taken with all of the calculations if different measures are to be calculated differently. A custom rollup formula can also be assigned to a level of a dimension within a specific cube, in which case it will intersect all measures in that cube but not be active in any other cube. Unlike the other custom calculations, it is not associated with a particular member. This generally means that the formula used in a custom rollup formula will have some reference to .CurrentMember. For example, a custom rollup function for the leaf level of a product dimension in a cost forecasting cube may have the formula LookupCube ("Production ", " ([Stage].[All Stage], Time.DefaultMember, " + [Product].CurrentMember.Unique-Name + ")").

A level that has a custom rollup formula can be used as the leaf level for a cube, and data can also be aggregated to a level that has a custom rollup formula. The custom rollup formula overrides the ability to retrieve any aggregated cell data for this level unless the .Ignore function is used. For example, the custom rollup formula in Figure 6.2 indicates to return the minimum value from the indicator's children, except for descendants of [Primary Indicators] where it is to return the data value associated with the member itself.

Like the other custom calculations, if a custom rollup on one dimension intersects custom rollups or custom calculations in another dimension, the prece-

```
Iif (
  IsAncestor (
    [Indicators].[Primary Indicators],
    [Indicators].CurrentMember
  ),
  [Indicators].Ignore,   /* indicates to retrieve data with no more
calculation within the Indicators dimension */
  Min (
    [Indicators].CurrentMember.Children
  )
)
```

Figure 6.2 Slightly sophisticated custom rollup formula.

dence between the calculations is determined by the order of the dimensions within the cube. We'll discuss how this works later in the chapter.

Calculated Member

A calculated member is a member defined by a command and associated with an MDX formula. As such, it is treated differently than regular members by certain meta data functions. Although a calculated member can be defined to appear as a child of a non-leaf regular member, a calculated member cannot itself have children.

Calculated members can be created with the CREATE MEMBER statement and dropped by DROP MEMBER. They can be defined either by the database designer/DBA at the server or during the course of a session. The formula associated with a calculated member cannot be modified without dropping and re-creating the member (and, in the process, invalidating every calculation that references it). Query-specific calculated members can be defined using the WITH MEMBER construct.

Unlike the custom calculations, a calculated member is only defined in a single cube. Two different cubes that have a calculated member with the same name can have the same definition for the calculated member, or two different definitions. Calculated members can, of course, be defined in the measures dimension as well as in other dimensions.

Unlike the custom calculations, and like cell calculations, a calculated member also can influence the formatting of cell values. A calculated member can hold a format string, font, and color information for use in representing cells that were directly calculated by the member. Calculated members can be assigned a specific solve order number, which gives their creator fine-grained control over their precedence with intersecting calculated members and cell calculations.

Defining a Calculated Member

The general syntax for defining a calculated member at a session or global level is as follows:

```
CREATE MEMBER cube-member-name AS 'expression' [, optional-property . .
. ]
```

The general syntax for defining a calculated member within the context of a query is as follows:

```
WITH MEMBER member-name AS 'expression' [, optional-property . . . ]
```

The OLE DB for OLAP specification also specifies an ALTER MEMBER construct, but this is not implemented in Microsoft's OLAP/Analysis Services.

The CREATE MEMBER statement is a client-side DDL statement that defines a new calculated member. The calculated member is defined within the context of a particular cube, so the name of the member must also be qualified with the name of the cube. (In a Microsoft DSO Command stored at a Microsoft OLAP server or in a CREATE CUBE command, the token CURRENTCUBE can also be used to indicate the cube that the CREATE MEMBER statement is associated with.) Like any other calculated member, the expression may reference any MDX function, including user-defined functions (UDFs). It may also reference any other members, whether created with the CREATE MEMBER statement or not. Members created through the CREATE MEMBER statement are accessible in member-related meta data through OLE DB for OLAP.

Following the expression itself, one or more optional properties may be defined. The properties that you may define are as follows:

```
SOLVE_ORDER = positive-integer-number
FORMAT_STRING = 'Microsoft-Office-cell-format'
FORE_COLOR = 'color-code'
BACK_COLOR = 'color-code'
FONT_NAME = 'font-name'
FONT_SIZE = 'font-size'
FONT_FLAGS = 'font-flags'
VISIBLE = 'number'    (Microsoft-specific)
NON_EMPTY_BEHAVIOR = 'measure name' (Microsoft specific)
```

For example, the statement

```
CREATE MEMBER [Production].[Measures].[Avg Failure Cost] as '[Mea-
sures].[Failure Cost Sum Per Incident] / [Measures].[Failure Incident
Count]', SOLVE_ORDER = 10, FORMAT_STRING = '#.##'
```

creates the calculated measure [Avg Failure Cost] as the ratio of total failure incident cost to count of incidents, specifies its SOLVE_ORDER number as 10, and indicates that wherever this formula is used to calculate cells, the result should be formatted with two decimal places.

NOTE

Microsoft's documentation for Analysis Services 2000 indicates that SOLVE_ORDER is to be spelled "SOLVEORDER." In fact, Analysis Services accepts both spellings. However, SOLVE_ORDER is standard MDX, and SOLVEORDER is proprietary to Microsoft and inconsistent with their general practice of separating words in these codes with the underbar (_) character.

The SOLVE_ORDER property is used when a value is calculated for a cell that is related to a calculated member. The FORMAT_STRING property, if provided, is used to format the data values into character strings. The VISIBLE flag controls whether the calculated member is visible to the query through .AllMembers and AddCalculatedMembers( ); a zero value means the member is hidden and a non-zero value means the member is visible.

The NON_EMPTY_BEHAVIOR property contains the name of a base measure to use to determine whether or not to attempt calculation of the calculated member. If the named measure is empty at the same non-measures intersection, then the calculated member will be NULL. (This can dramatically speed up complex calculations and NON EMPTY queries against sparse data.) Note that only the measure name is used, not its unique name. For example, you would use 'Unit Sales' instead of '[Measures].[Unit Sales]'.

The default is for the member to be visible. The other properties are specified and stored as character strings and are provided to the client in response to queries that explicitly reference cell properties. The OLE DB data types of these properties as they are delivered back to the client are as follows:

PROPERTY	TYPE
FORMAT_STRING	DBTYPE_WSTR
FORE_COLOR	DBTYPE_UI4
BACK_COLOR	DBTYPE_UI4
FONT_NAME	DBTYPE_WSTR
FONT_SIZE	DBTYPE_UI2
FONT_FLAGS	DBTYPE_I4

For more information on creating programs that use cell properties, refer to the developer's documentation for OLE DB for OLAP.

Within a CREATE MEMBER statement, the SESSION keyword is supported to make explicit the fact that the created member is valid for the OLE DB session in which the statement was issued. In Microsoft's OLAP/Analysis Services, there is no difference between using SESSION or leaving it out. For example, the expression

```
CREATE SESSION MEMBER [Production].[Measures].[Failure rate] AS
' . . .'
```

explicitly creates the member within the scope of that single session, whereas

```
CREATE MEMBER [Production].[Measures].[Failure rate] AS
' . . .'
```

implicitly creates the member within the session.

The only difference between WITH MEMBER and CREATE MEMBER is that the scope of a member created with WITH MEMBER is limited to the query that contains the WITH MEMBER statement. A member created by WITH MEMBER is invisible to any other query in any other session, and it is not accessible as part of the OLE DB for OLAP meta data.

Multiple members may be defined in one CREATE MEMBER statement. After the CREATE and optional session scope identifier, each member's definition is listed in order. For example, the following expression creates two members in the Production cube:

```
CREATE
MEMBER [Production].[Measures].[Failure rate] AS ' . . . ', SOLVE_ORDER
= 10, FORMATSTRING = '#.##'
      MEMBER [Production].[Scenarios].[VarianceOverTrials] AS '. . . ',
SOLVE_ORDER = 20, FORMATSTRING = '#.##%', FONT_NAME = 'Times New Roman'
```

Note that you do not separate the different MEMBER definitions with commas.

You cannot define a calculated member to have the same unique name as another member in the cube, either base or calculated. If you want to redefine a calculated member, use DROP MEMBER to discard it first and then execute CREATE MEMBER. Also, note that you can use WITH MEMBER to create a member whose name is identical to a member created with CREATE MEMBER. If you request all calculated members in their scope with AddCalculatedMembers( ), you will get both of them; if you request a member by that specific name, you will only get the results of the WITH MEMBER definition. See Chapter 5 for more details.

Dropping a Calculated Member

The general syntax for dropping a calculated member is as follows:

```
DROP MEMBER cube-member-name [,cube-member-name . . . ]
```

The DROP MEMBER statement removes one or more calculated cube members and all associated definitions. When more than one calculated member is to be dropped, each name is separated by a comma. When a calculated member is dropped, it disappears from the member-related meta data accessible through OLE DB for OLAP. For example, the following statement drops the two named members:

```
DROP MEMBER
    [Production].[Measures].[Failure Rate],
    [Production].[Scenarios].[Variance Over Trials]
```

You may drop members whose CREATE MEMBER statements were part of the database (stored at the server). You may also drop members that have other calculated members defined on them, and no warning is issued. The definitions of the dependent calculated members remain, but they are internally invalid and return a #ERR cell value when they are included in a query. In Microsoft's OLAP/Analysis Services, it is not ever possible to return the dependent members to a valid state, even by re-creating the dropped input member.

Cell Calculation

A cell calculation is a definition of a pass or set of passes of calculations for the cells in a region of a cube. (We sometimes find it easier to conceive of it in terms of calculation *layers*.) When you have multiple cell calculations defined for a cube, they can be arranged in different sets of passes, which helps you organize which ones ultimately get executed for each cell of a query. Cell calculations interact with all other types of calculations in a cube, including calculated members, custom rollups, and custom member formulas. All of these types of calculations are performed in cell calculation passes as well. Cell calculations can calculate values for cells that would otherwise be calculated by one of these other techniques in the cell calculation's absence. For example, the value for a cell related to a calculated member or custom member formula may actually be calculated by a cell calculation if you desire to override the member's formula. In order to understand how cell calculations function, we need to spend a little time working through calculation passes.

NOTE

Beyond a very simplistic level, to understand what cell calculations are doing you need to understand how calculation passes function and how all the ways to calculate in a Microsoft OLAP system combine on each calculation pass. The best teaching and explaining makes many a topic straightforward, but in the end we don't think this aspect of Microsoft's OLAP will ever truly be straightforward. We'll explain it as best as we can.

Cell calculations can be created with the CREATE CELL CALCULATION statement and dropped by DROP CELL CALCULATION. They can be defined either by the database designer/DBA at the server or during the course of a session. The formula associated with a cell calculation cannot be modified without dropping and re-creating the cell calculation, but because cell calculations are not referred to by name, this does not invalidate any dependents. Query-specific cell calculations can be created using the WITH CELL CALCULATION construct.

Unlike the custom calculations, and like calculated members, a cell calculation also can influence the formatting of cell values. A cell calculation can hold a format string, font, and color information for use in representing cells that were directly calculated by the cell calculation. Cell calculations can be defined to be in effect over a certain range of calculation passes; different cell calculations that overlap in cell space can be organized to contribute to each other. In addition, each cell calculation can be assigned a specific solve order number, which gives their creator fine-grained control over their precedence with intersecting calculated members and cell calculations within each calculation pass.

Calculation passes are a significant source of flexibility and complexity; we will discuss calculation passes in detail further along.

Defining a Cell Calculation

The general syntax for defining a cell calculation is

```
CREATE CELL CALCULATION Cube.CellCalcName
FOR '( dimset [, dimset ...] )' AS 'formula'
[ CONDITION = 'MDX_Condition_Formula' ]
[ , DISABLED = {TRUE | FALSE} ]
[ , DESCRIPTION = 'description string' ]
[ , CALCULATION_PASS_NUMBER = number ]
[ , CALCULATION_PASS_DEPTH = number ]
```

or (the ALTER CUBE variation):

```
ALTER CUBE Cube
CREATE CELL CALCULATION Name
FOR '( dimset [, dimset ...] )' AS 'formula'
[ CONDITION = 'MDX_Condition_Formula' ]
[ , DISABLED = {TRUE | FALSE} ]
[ , DESCRIPTION = 'description string' ]
[ , CALCULATION_PASS_NUMBER = number ]
[ , CALCULATION_PASS_DEPTH = number ]
```

A cell calculation can also be defined for a query in the WITH section of the query in a manner analogous to creating a calculated member or named set for the query.

The CREATE CELL CALCULATION statement is a client-side DDL statement that defines a new cell calculation. The cell calculation is defined within the context of a particular cube, so the name of the calculation must also be qualified with the name of the cube. (In a Microsoft DSO Command stored at a Microsoft OLAP server or in a CREATE CUBE command, the token CURRENTCUBE can also be used to indicate the cube that the CREATE CELL CALCULATION statement is associated with.) Microsoft extends the standard OLE DB for OLAP schema rowsets with a CELL FORMULAS schema rowset, so a client can obtain limited meta data about the cell calculations defined.

For each cell calculation, the following properties available for calculated members can also be used (separated by commas as the other cell calculation properties are):

```
SOLVE_ORDER = positive-integer-number
FORMAT_STRING = 'Microsoft-Office-cell-format'
FORE_COLOR = 'color-code'
BACK_COLOR = 'color-code'
FONT_NAME = 'font-name'
FONT_SIZE = 'font-size'
FONT_FLAGS = 'font-flags'
```

Note that cell calculations have a SOLVE_ORDER property; this is very important to include when using cell calculations along with calculated members.

Each *Dimset* can resolve into a set of members from one dimension, with the following restriction. Each dimension's expression must have one and only one of the following:

- No members
- One member
- A set consisting of one entire level
- A set of all descendants of a particular member at a particular level
- A set of all descendants of a particular member
- All members in a dimension

The region of the cube over which the cell calculation is in effect is the cross-join of the individual DimSets. If a dimension is not specified (which could happen if a dimension's expression has no members), then the cell calculation ranges over all members of the dimension. If any ancestor members to the region are in one or more level-based dimensions (not parent-child dimensions!), then the results of the cell calculation are aggregated from the highest levels of the calculated cell region to the higher-level cells. If the members have associated rollup operators, then the rollup operators are applied to the results of the cell calculations.

To specify a set consisting of one member, you can simply name the member (enclosed by { }). The member can be a calculated member or a regular member. In addition to naming the member, you can reference a single member-set constructed from a wide variety of means. For example, the following four expressions are all perfectly fine:

```
{ [Accounts].[Interest Rate] }
{ [Named Set 1].Item (0) }
{ Tail ([Named Set 1]).Item (0) }
StrToSet ("{[Accounts].[Interest Rate]}")
```

One of the few restrictions that we have noted in building these expressions is that if you are using a named set, it must have been created by CREATE SET at the session level and not by WITH SET within a query.

To specify a set consisting of one level in a level-based dimension, you must use the *level*.Members construct. This won't ordinarily include the calculated members assigned to that level; to do that, you need to use *level*.AllMembers. In a parent-child or ragged hierarchy, if you want to specify all leaf-level members, you need to use the Descendants (*member*, *level*, LEAVES) construct using the All member or the root member of the hierarchy for the starting member. (If you leave out the LEAVES option, all leaf-level members not at that depth will be excluded; see Appendix A for a full description of the options for Descendants( )). For example, in a parent-child dimension that has four apparent levels, if you want to specify a cell calculation for all of the leaf-level members only, you would use

```
WITH
CELL CALCULATION LeafCalcs FOR
'( Descendants ( [Accounts].[All Accounts], [Accounts].[Level 04],
LEAVES) )'
...
SELECT ...
```

If you use Descendants( ) coupled with a depth value instead of a named level, you will get a parse error instead.

To obtain a set of all descendants of a particular member at a level, use the Descendants(*member*, *level*) construct. For example, the following sets up a cell calculation at the Assembly-level descendants of facility [South Bend 45]:

```
WITH
CELL CALCULATION Assumptions_01 FOR
'( Descendants ( [Facility].[South Bend 45], [Facility].[Assembly]) )'
...
SELECT ...
```

To include all members of a dimension, you can either not reference the dimension in the *dimset* section of the cell calculation definition, or you can reference *Dimension*.Members. One reason to reference the dimension's members is to include calculated members, which by default are not included. In this case, you would reference *Dimension*.AllMembers.

The condition specified in the CONDITION clause can be used for both dimension and cell data conditions. For example, if a cell calculation is to apply to every member in a level where some member property is "true," then the condition could state `'Project.CurrentMember.Properties ("Requires Travel") = "1"'`. If a cell calculation is to apply to every cell in a region where the associated [Measure].[Reserve] value is negative, then the condition could state `' [Measures].[Reserve] < 0'`.

Given the constraints on calculation regions and the flexibility of the conditions, more than one way to compose equivalent cell calculations is available. For example, if a calculation applies to more than one member of a level, you could compose one cell calculation per member and give them the same pass number and depth, or you could create one cell calculation for the level and use the condition to filter only the members that the calculation is for. In terms of efficiency, not much difference should be between these. Maintenance issues are more different (for example, how many cell calculations are you managing, might the target member set change, and so on).

Let's put all these together into a complete definition. For example, let's say that we have a Production Cost member that combines production labor cost, production overhead cost, and material costs. We also have a Service Cost member that combines services labor and services overhead. However, for our "service" products, we really want the material costs to be assigned away from the Pro-

```
CREATE CELL CALCULATION CPI.ServiceMaterialAdjustment_Production
FOR '( {[Accounts].[Production Cost]},
  Descendants ( [Products].[Service Products] ) )'
AS
'CalculationPassValue (
 [Accounts].[Production Cost],
  -1,        // take the value from the previous pass
  RELATIVE
)
- CalculationPassValue (
  [Accounts].[Material Cost],
  -1,        // take the value from the previous pass
  RELATIVE
)'
, CALCULATION_PASS_NUMBER = 10

CREATE CELL CALCULATION CPI.ServiceMaterialAdjustment_Service
FOR '( {[Accounts]. [Service Cost]},
  Descendants ([Products].[Service Products] ) )'
AS
'CalculationPassValue (
  [Accounts].[Service Cost],
  -1,        // take the value from the previous pass
  RELATIVE
)
+ CalculationPassValue (
  [Accounts].[Material Cost],
  -1,        // take the value from the previous pass
  RELATIVE
)'
, CALCULATION_PASS_NUMBER = 10
```

Figure 6.3 Cell calculation example.

duction Cost and into the Service Cost member. The cell calculations shown in
Figure 6.3 exclude material costs from the [Production Cost] member (assuming they were already added in) and add them to the [Service Cost] member
where the product category is [Service]:

Dropping a Cell Calculation

A cell calculation can be dropped with one of the two statements:

```
DROP CELL CALCULATION CubeName.CellCalcName
```

```
ALTER CUBE CubeName DROP CELL CALCULATION CellCalcName
```

Although not documented by Microsoft, multiple cell calculations can be dropped by separating their names with commas.

For example, the following statement drops the cell calculations that we just created:

```
DROP CELL CALCULATION
    CPI.ServiceMaterialAdjustment_Production,
    CPI.ServiceMaterialAdjustment_Service
```

How Types of Calculations Interact

Essentially, three different orderings of calculations are available in a cube, of which you have fine-grained control over two. Calculated members and cell calculations have a specified solve order, and a wide range of solve order numbers can be used. Pass number can also be used with cell calculations, and referred to by other calculations. The third kind of ordering is the order of dimensions in a cube, which determines the order in which custom calculations take place. Dimension ordering is much simpler and more rigid than the other kinds of calculation ordering; it is a bit like solve order except that all custom calculations take place at a special, fixed solve orders within the solve order scheme (solve order −5119, the use of which is a bit esoteric for most applications). (By saying "unless otherwise specified," Microsoft documentation indicates that there may be a way to adjust the solve order for custom calculations, perhaps in the future, but there is no way to do this in the RTM of Analysis Services.)

Interaction without Any Cell Calculations

The simplest case to consider is custom calculations and calculated members in the absence of any cell calculations. We took a beginning look at this in Chapter 5, "MDX Context and Execution," although our focus was on how an overall query is set up and how the data types for any given cell combine in a function. The rules for combining data types are the same when custom calculations are considered, but custom calculations introduce wrinkles in picking what calculation to perform.

Precedence of Custom Rollup Formulas and Custom Member Formulas on Multiple Dimensions

For any given cell, if it is not associated with a calculated member but a custom calculation (rollup or member) is on it from any dimension, the cell is calculated according to the formula of the custom calculation. If custom rollups are on two or more dimensions, the rollup from the dimension that appears "earlier" in the list of dimensions for the cube is used to calculate the cell. With custom rollup formulas and custom member formulas as a whole stuck at solve order -5119, in a four-dimensional cube you can consider the first dimension to have solve order -5119, the second dimension to have solve order -5119.25, and so on. (Somewhere above -5120 and below -5118.) Calculated members typically have a higher solve order number than custom rollups, so if a cell is associated with a calculated member, then it is calculated by the calculated member. Typically speaking, as far as calculated members are concerned, the results of a custom calculation appear as if they were directly retrieved from the database.

NOTE Although you can specify cell formatting information for custom member formulas, you cannot specify a SOLVE_ORDER in the custom member cell properties.

Within a single dimension, although frequently only one custom calculation is available for a member, it is conceivable that two different types of custom calculations could be available. (A DSO level can use either custom rollup operators or a custom rollup formula, and in addition one or more members may have custom member formulas.) If a member has a custom member formula, then it is used; otherwise, the custom rollup is used. If a member has a custom rollup formula on its level and its children have rollup operators defined, the rollup formula is used.

TIP If you are incorporating any kind of custom rollups in a dimension, consider the order of dimensions and other custom rollups in all of the cubes that the dimension will be used.

Precedence of Custom Rollup Operators on Multiple Dimensions

The documentation for Analysis Services 2000, RTM, indicates that all custom rollups are applied in the order in which dimensions appear in the cube. This would lead one to believe that if two or more dimensions have rollup operators on them, these operators would be applied in dimension order. Our own work with the RTM version indicates that this is not the case. (The behavior we are about to describe is not clearly documented by Microsoft, and a subsequent service pack may alter the behavior.)

When a cell is defined by two intersecting regular members that each have rollup operators defined for their children, the actual cell calculation that takes place depends on what the rollup operators are. If the rollup operators involved are only + and −, or only *, /, and %, then it does not really matter. However, if the two members have child rollups between them that involve a mixture of + or − with *, /, or %, then the operators are chosen by an assumed precedence (which may or may not be what you want). The following rules are followed in the RTM version of Analysis Services:

- If the children from each dimension contain only + and −, then precedence does not matter.

- If the children after the first child contain only * and /, then precedence does not matter. (The first child that does not have ~ must have either + or −; subsequent children can have any valid operator.)

- A member that has child operators of *, /, or % takes precedence over a member whose children contain purely + and − operators.

- Dimension precedence is used when child operators contain a mixture of + or − with * and / on each of the dimensions (each dimension's children contain a mixture).

For many applications, it would be preferable if a + or − took precedence over *, so that sums of products (like a summation of units * price) would be taken. We do not know whether a service pack will alter the functionality to include that capability.

Cell Calculation Passes

Every cell calculation has an associated *pass number*, which is part of arranging the cell calculations into different passes. Like solve orders, pass numbers help to order calculations when more than one calculation (of any kind) could provide the value for a cell. Like solve orders, higher numbers are essentially calculated after lower numbers (potentially overruling a result provided by a calculation with a lower number). The pass numbers for a cube and query start at zero, although the lowest pass number that a defined cell calculation can use is 1. If you don't specify a pass number, then 1 is the default. (Calculation pass 0 is reserved for calculations that take place prior to any cell calculation.) Unlike solve order, which is used to choose a formula as the "winner" to calculate a cell once, passes may end up calculating the value for a cell multiple times.

Every cell calculation also has an associated *pass depth*, which determines the number of passes (starting from the pass number and working toward lower numbers) in which its formula is in effect. A pass depth of 1 (the default) means that the calculation is only in effect during its stated pass. A pass depth greater than 1 means that it is in effect from the stated pass back by one less than the given number of steps. For example, a pass number of 9 and a pass depth of 3 means that the calculation will be in effect in passes 7, 8, and 9.

There is no way to declare that a cell calculation is to occupy a set of passes after or before another cell calculation, except by keeping control over the pass numbers.

When a query is executed, the passes required for each cell are determined. One pass will be performed for the highest pass number defined across all cell calculations. For example, if there are three cell calculations defined on a cube with pass numbers 5, 10, and 15, then a pass 15 is performed on every cell in a query (regardless of whether the cells accessed by the query fall into the subcubes for the cell calcs or not). This does not mean that 3 or even 15 passes will be performed for any cell, but that even if only one pass is performed for a cell (for example, to simply retrieve a pre-aggregated value from MOLAP storage), it will occur at pass 15. Depending on the mix of defined calculations that overlap at that cell, other passes may take place. The solve order values for these calculations partly determines the order, and if two separate cell calcs share the same, highest solve order number, then the calc that was defined last wins.

Although calculation passes are only assigned to cell calculations, all other calculations will take place at any calculation pass deemed necessary to compute a cell. Thus, a calculated member, custom member or custom rollup may be calculated in any (or every) pass for each cell. So, in each pass you define for a cell calculation, all other calculations may be executed as well. The solve order numbers for custom members and custom rollups are far below zero and are fixed, so ordinarily they will not win out over a cell calc or calculated member for computing a cell, but a calculated member may have a solve order higher than a cell calc, which will cause the calculated member formula to compute the cell's value.

Any MDX calculation (custom or otherwise) may refer to data values calculated in earlier passes through use of the CalculationPassNumber( ) function. (This function is described in Appendix B and we will use it here without further description.) This allows each to have a definition that refers to earlier passes, and even be recursive through the passes. In the case of a calculation for a cell that otherwise is not the target of a cell calculation, the cell is evaluated for the highest-numbered pass number among all cell calculations defined in the cube. (For example, if a cube has 3 cell calculations defined and the highest pass number among them is 5, then any cell being calculated for the cube starts off at pass number 5). As a cell is calculated (by any means), if it references a value at a lower pass number, then that value and pass is calculated (so passes are calculated from highest to lowest). In other words, a calculated member [Forecast Factor] whose definition reads

```
iif (
  CalculationPassNumber( ) > 1,
  1.1 * CalculationPassValue (
    [Measures].[Forecast Factor],
```

```
    -1,
    RELATIVE
  ),
  1
)
```

and that is executed starting at pass 5 will cause pass 4 to be executed, which will cause pass 3 to be executed, and so on down to pass 1 (at which pass it results in 1, and the value returned from pass 5 is 1.4641). Figure 6.4 illustrates this recursive process.

In the case of a cell in a cell calc that references earlier passes of cell calculations, the earlier passes are calculated first and then the later passes. A pair of cell calculations that were defined as

```
CREATE CELL CALCULATION [Fcst].[A1]
FOR '({[Measures].[Forecast Factor]})'
AS
'1.1 * CalculationPassValue (
  [Measures].[Forecast Factor],
  -1,
  RELATIVE
)'
, CALCULATION_PASS_NUMBER = 5
, CALCULATION_PASS_DEPTH = 2
```

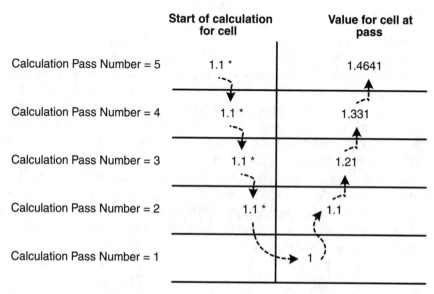

Figure 6.4 Earlier calculation passes invoked from later passes.

```
CREATE CELL CALCULATION [Fcst].[A2]
FOR '({[Measures].[Forecast Factor]})'
AS
'1'
, CALCULATION_PASS_NUMBER = 3
, CALCULATION_PASS_DEPTH = 1
```

would first generate a 1 for [Measures].[Forecast Factor] at pass 3, then create a 1.1 for [Measures].[Forecast Factor] at pass 4, and finally create 1.21 as the value for [Measures].[Forecast Factor] at pass 5. This is diagrammed in Figure 6.5.

Note that in the case of a calculated member referencing calculation passes, the execution of the calculated member at pass 5 is what caused earlier passes to be executed, and passes were executed in the order that they were requested by the recursive definition. In the case of the cell calculation referencing earlier passes, the calculation passes are produced from earlier to later in order.

Only the passes actually required are calculated for each cell. For example, consider the following skeletal cell calc definition,

```
CREATE CELL CALCULATION Budgeting.Layer5
FOR '( { [Measures].[Adjustment] } )'
AS
'Measures.[Amount]
+ CalculationPassValue (
   Measures.[Amount],
   1,
   ABSOLUTE
)'
, CALCULATION_PASS_NUMBER = 10
, CALCULATION_PASS_DEPTH = 8
```

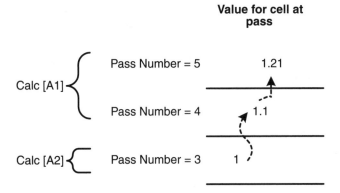

Figure 6.5 Calculation passes invoked in order.

in which a cell calculation for the measure [Adjustment] is defined to start at pass 10 and run back to pass 3, and which results in the value of the measure [Amount] at the current pass plus the value of [Amount] from pass 1. In the absence of other computations actually referencing the values of [Adjustment] between passes 9 and 3, Analysis Services only calculates the value of [Adjustment] from [Amount] at pass 10 and [Amount] at pass 1 and adds those two values together. If some other computation references the value of [Adjustment] at, say, pass 5, then [Adjustment] for pass 5 would be calculated from [Amount] at pass 5 and the value of [Amount] at pass 1. (The value for [Amount] at pass 1 would be cached from the first time it was referenced, so it would only be calculated once.)

While we are on the topic, consider again the definition for the preceding Budgeting.Layer5 cell calculation. If another cell calculation is in the cube whose calculation pass is, say, 20, and which does not calculate a value for the [Adjustment] measure, then Budgeting.Layer5 is calculated at passes 20 and 1 instead of 10 and 1. If another calculation references the value at pass 10, then this makes no material difference; the value of the cell at pass 20 is the same as at pass 10 because no other calculations get in the way, so no other calculation pass is executed. However, let us consider the case that some other calculations may intersect this cell. If some calculation references the value of [Adjustment] at a pass above 10, then the results depend on any other intersecting calculations. For example, if a calculated member intersects [Adjustment], the value for [Adjustment] at pass 15 will be determined by the calculated member. (Like we said, constructing and maintaining calculations in the face of calculation passes can get complicated!)

TIP

One thing to be aware of and guard against when using cell calculations and calculated members is that infinite recursion can occur. If a cell calculation refers to a calculated member in its formula (directly or indirectly) and the calculated member itself draws data from the cell being calculated at the same calculation pass, then an infinite recursion error will occur. The key to breaking out of this recursion is for the calculated member to draw its data from some other calculation pass. This could be accomplished by the calculated member itself referring to data at a particular pass, or by the cell calculation formula referring to the calculated member at a different pass.

Using Solve Order to Determine the Formula in a Pass

For any cell referenced by a query, at least one calculation pass (pass 0) and perhaps more will be executed. Within each pass, solve orders for the potentially applicable formulas are resolved to determine what formula actually calculates the cell. Cell calculations, calculated members, and all custom rollups each have their own solve order. (In fact, data retrieval from intrinsic aggregations has its own solve order as well). The type of calculation does not matter; ultimately, it's the solve order number that makes the difference. In the case of a tied solve order, the order of definition decides which calculation is applied.

When defining a set of calculations on a cube, then, it is very important to understand global solve orders. Consider the definition of a calculated member and a cell calculation in Figure 6.6. The intent is to round the total time per call to the nearest two units (using the Excel Round() function).

Because no solve order is specified for the cell calculation, the default solve order of 0 is assumed. Now, consider what happens when a [Time Per Call] member is calculated at pass 1. Consider these two formulas: the cell calculation and the calculated member. The calculated member has the higher solve order, so the calculated member wins and the cell calculation is ignored.

Suppose, however, that we redefine the [Calls].[Rounding] cell calculation to have SOLVE_ORDER = 15. Now, at pass 1, the cell calculation will perform the rounding against the [Time Per Call] value from pass 0. At pass 0, the only formula to consider is the [Measures].[Time Per Call], so that will be calculated as the ratio.

Why did we define the ratio as being at solve order 10? Perhaps the application allows a user to select a set of call center operators to calculate the total call

```
CREATE MEMBER [Calls].[Measures].[Time Per Call] AS
'[Measures].[Total Call Time] / [Measures].[Count of Calls]'
, SOLVE_ORDER = 10

CREATE CELL CALCULATION [Calls].[Rounding]
FOR '({[Measures].[Time Per Call]})' AS
'CalculationPassValue (
  Excel!Round(
    [Measures].[Time Per Call],
    2
  )
  , 0
  , ABSOLUTE
)'
, CALCULATION_PASS_NUMBER = 1
```

Figure 6.6 System of calculated member and cell calculation.

time, count of calls, and time per call as a group. The sum of total call time and sum of count of calls needs to occur at a lower solve order than the ratio. As described in Chapter 8, "Building Queries in MDX," defining key ratios at a higher solve order like 10 allows us space in our global solve order list to insert other, possibly unforeseen calculations earlier in the list. For example, we could use this in the following query:

```
WITH
SET [Interesting Operators] AS
'{ [John], [Suzie], [Harold] }'
MEMBER [Operators].[Total] AS 'Sum ( [Interesting Operators] )'
, SOLVE_ORDER = 0
SELECT
{ [Measures].AllMembers } on columns,
{ [Interesting Operators], [Operators].[Total] } on rows
FROM [Calls]
```

By the same token, custom rollups are themselves calculated at each pass as well. Because they are stuck at a low solve order (−5119), unless you define a cell calculation or calculated member with a lower solve order number they will not themselves calculate the value of a cell that is a target of a cell calculation or calculated member. They will, however, provide data to a cell calc or calculated member at any pass.

Given the lack of control over solve order in custom member formulas, this is sometimes helpful and sometimes a problem. For example, consider the [Time Per Call] formula in Figure 6.5. If this were implemented as a custom member formula, our original solve order issue with the cell calculation would disappear. However, if we wanted to support summaries of user-defined subsets as in the most recent query, we would need to assign a solve order of < -5119 to the [Operators].[Total] member in order to ensure that we are taking the ratio of the sums instead of the sum of the ratios. If we do that, though, we'll have problems using the results of any custom rollups from any other dimensions.

Calculated Members Not Themselves Aggregated

A cell calculated by a calculated member is not aggregated by the intrinsic aggregation machinery, which sort of makes sense because calculated members aren't considered part of any hierarchy. A calculated measure has no intrinsic aggregation function specified for it, either. (A calculated member can, of course, contain its own aggregation logic to perform aggregation along one or more dimensions if desired.)

Intrinsic Aggregation of Custom Rollups, Custom Members, and Calculated Cell Results

If the parent of a member with a custom formula does not itself have any formulas applied, then the result of the custom formula is aggregated to the parent as if it were drawn from the underlying fact table(s). This is handy when the custom member formula involves only addition or subtraction. It is also frequently useful when the custom member calculation involves multiplication of a rate and some units (like units and price), as the results are automatically summed up the hierarchy instead of requiring additional MDX. This can be a source of problems if the custom member formula is a ratio, however, and you do not want to sum the ratio with other values.

Although custom rollups take precedence over intrinsic aggregation in dimension other than the dimension the custom rollup is defined in, cells calculated by a custom rollup formula at a level below the top level in their dimension are aggregated up the rest of their dimension if no other calculations take place. For example, if a custom rollup function at the month level of a time dimension retrieves related data from another cube, then the quarter-level members and the year-level members in that time dimension will have the appropriate aggregates calculated from the month-level values on the fly. If an indicator level used the formula of Figure 6.2, the parent members that weren't descendants of [Indicator].[Primary Indicators] would aggregate up (probably with sum) the values returned from the custom rollup, even though those values were themselves derived from a minimum aggregation.

Similarly, if a cell calculation region does not include the top-most level in one or more dimensions, the calculated cells at in the region that have parent members outside the region will have their results aggregated to the parent member. Consider the extremely simple cell calculation in the query of Figure 6.7. The result of the query is simply that months whose measure values are less than 100 are not included in total. If the raw cell values for [Jan. 2001], [Feb. 2001], and [Mar. 2001] are 50, 200, and 300, then the raw value for [Q1, 2001] is 550. However, the results of the cell calculations from the months are aggregated to the quarter, so the result of the query for [Q1, 2001] is 500. The process is diagrammed in Figure 6.7.

```
WITH
CELL CALCULATION Calc1
FOR '( {[Time].[Month].Members} )'
AS 'NULL',
CONDITION = 'Measures.CurrentMember.Value < 100'
```

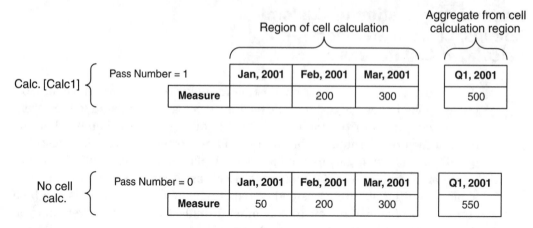

Figure 6.7 Query with cell calculation that is rolled up.

```
SELECT
{ [Time].[Jan, 2001], [Time].[Feb. 2001], [Time].[Mar. 2001],
   [Time].[Q1, 2001]
} on columns
FROM [Cube]
```

Tips on Using the Different Calculation Techniques

In accounting dimensions, custom rollup operators typically are used to combine accounts. A parent-child dimension is the ordinary way to implement an accounting dimension. Most accounting lines are combined with +, and a few with − or ~. Key ratios may be implemented either by the / rollup operator or by custom member formulas. These usually do not present a difficulty when combined with other dimensions such as time, product, branch office, and so on. Lines that roll up to their parent using the * operator or that have custom formulas which perform multiplication need to be looked at carefully in conjunction with the entire set of dimensions and calculations that they will be used in. At aggregate levels of the other dimensions, the results may be the product of sums rather than the sum of products.

Custom member formulas and calculated members need to be considered carefully. Custom member formulas can be more easily managed because they are stored once for all cubes and are stored in the dimension table, but are wholly inflexible with regard to solve order. Therefore, aggregates of user-defined selections are more difficult to work with unless great care is taken with all calculations and solve orders.

The results of a calculated member are not aggregated up the hierarchies of any dimensions, but the results of all other calculations are. This makes the other ways of calculating suitable for specifying complex calculations for a low level that must be aggregated up the hierarchies.

Only intrinsic aggregations may be precalculated and stored. This means that a complex calculation at the leaf levels, which is aggregated up to a high level in several dimensions, may be slow to calculate.

Summary

In this chapter, we have worked through the different kinds of calculations that are available through Microsoft Analysis Services. Given the number of different types of calculation techniques and the subtle differences between them, we have worked through their individual operation and their combined operations so as to understand the impact of choosing one technique or another. These ways all provide different techniques to get the result values that you want. Choosing among them requires an understanding of application usage and maintenance requirements as well as calculation needs.

CHAPTER 7

Extending MDX through External Functions

In this chapter, we will discuss how to create libraries of external functions for use with MDX and illustrate possible applications for these libraries. With the advent of OLE DB for OLAP 2.0, external functions have become part of the standard, instead of a Microsoft extension to it. Libraries of external functions are invaluable because while even Microsoft Analysis Services implements a rich subset of the full MDX specification and adds a number of its own functions and operators on top of it, MDX fails to cover all of the analysis functionality that a typical application will need.

For example, simple operations, like rounding a value to a specified number of decimal places, are not present as primitives in the language. Calculations that require iterating over sets of cell values may also be more easily expressed as an external function, since MDX is declarative and has very limited facilities for iteration.

Through the use of libraries of external functions, any calculation you can express as a function call (within certain limits) can be used in MDX. This feature can be applied in many practical ways in any kind of application, in any sort of calculated member or named set.

Before we get started, let's clarify our terminology. Microsoft's Analysis Services documentation refers to what we call external functions as user-defined functions (UDFs). We use the term external functions because, for example, the function libraries for Excel and Visual Basic for Applications (VBA) fill in a large number of MDX gaps right out of the box, and yet they don't count as "user-defined." You may also purchase libraries from third parties or perhaps distribute libraries you create to others.

In this chapter, we will discuss how external functions are referenced in an MDX expression, what kinds of data they can accept and return, how to construct them (using Visual Basic as the example language), and the special MDX extension functions provided by Analysis Services that are particularly useful in conjunction with external functions. The chapter is organized into the following sections:

- Overview of using external functions with MDX
- Argument and return-type details
- MDX functions for use with external functions
- Additional considerations for external functions
- Loading and using libraries

We will illustrate these topics with several examples along the way. In Chapter 4, "Advanced MDX Application Topics," we described MDX calculations that would be less cumbersome if they were contained in an external function. In this chapter, we will explain how those calculations are implemented and provide additional examples.

Overview of Using External Functions with MDX

External functions and MDX operations work together. External functions are called almost as if they were built-in functions. Let's begin with a simple example to lay the groundwork for an understanding of how MDX and external functions interact. Suppose you are writing MDX expressions that require numerous percentage difference calculations. For example, you need to calculate Profit Percentage as `([Measures].[Sales] - Measures].[Cost])/[Measures].[Cost]`, and you need to calculate Scenario Percentage Variance as `([Scenario].[Actual] - [Scenario].[Forecast])/[Scenario].[Forecast]`. If you are working on a scenario analysis cube that is comparing the relative accuracy of 12 different forecasts to actual results, you may feel like encapsulating this in a single function that we'll call PctDiff(). We would use this function in expressions like `PctDiff ([Measures].[Sales], [Measures].[Cost])` and `PctDiff([Scenario].[Actual], [Scenario].[Forecast])`.

Calling external functions in Microsoft Analysis Services is usually done in just this format: the name of the function, an opening parenthesis, each argument in order separated by commas, and then a closing parenthesis. (If the external function has no arguments, then use an empty pair of parentheses. For example, the bare name PctDiff would be treated like a member or set name, while PctDiff( ) would be treated like a function.)

For example, using our PctDiff( ) function, the complete syntax for creating our Scenario Percentage Variance member in a cube named Scenario Analysis would be as follows:

```
CREATE MEMBER [Scenario Analysis].[Scenario].[Scenario Pct Variance]
AS 'PctDiff([Scenario].[Actual], [Scenario].[Forecast])'
```

For Analysis Services to use external functions, they must come packaged in libraries of functions that are accessible through ActiveX Automation. More than one external function can reside in a library. Since external functions are by definition not a part of Analysis Services, you need to make it aware of them. With the exception of the Excel and VBA libraries, which are automatically loaded when your PivotTable Service starts up, you must tell Analysis Services to load the library or libraries that contain the functions before you use them. The basic MDX statement for loading a library is USE LIBRARY "library-name." We will explain this in greater detail later in the chapter.

The easiest way to create an external function in Visual Basic (version 5.0 and higher) is to simply create, in an ActiveX DLL or other ActiveX library/executable type, a class with GlobalMultiuse instancing and then add public functions to it. For example, our PctDiff( ) function would be created with the following:

```
Public Function PctDiff (ByVal A As Double, ByVal B As Double)
As Double
PctDiff = (A - B) / B
End Function
```

This declares the function as taking two double-typed arguments and returning a double result, which is what we want. The key features of the class are that it must be global (not hidden or restricted) and that the functions to be used must all be public.

We have included a sample function library and the Visual Basic 6.0 project that generates the library on the CD-ROM accompanying this book.

External functions are useful both for calculating cell values and defining named sets. Although you can use the results of any external function as a cell value, you can also use a string result to completely specify or partly specify a set by using the StrToSet( ), StrToTuple( ), and Members( ) functions. Some of the useful applications of external functions involve defining sets and tuples, such as slicers for queries.

Argument and Return-Type Details

You can pass numbers, strings, and arrays of numbers or strings into external functions, and they can return either numbers or strings. The arguments for an external function can be declared to be number types, strings, arrays of numbers or strings, or variant types. If the type is specifically declared in the function signature (like double, integer, or string), the value passed from Microsoft Analysis Services for that argument will be coerced into that type when the function is called. For example, if our PctDiff( ) function takes two arguments of type double, and it is called with the value of an integer-type measure at some cell, then the integer will be changed into a double. If it is called with a string, such as a property value (which must be a string in Analysis Services), the first digit of the string will be converted into a number when the function is called. (You can use the Val( ) function, which is part of the VBA library, to convert the string into a number first. For example, PctDiff(Val("20"), Val("15")) returns 0.333).

If the argument is a variant type, Analysis Services passes the argument as its own internal type for the value. Depending on the actual type of the cell, the value that is received by the external function may be a 32-bit integer, a 64-bit integer, a single or double float, or a string. An empty cell passed to an external function will be received by the external function as an empty variant.

The return type of an external function is a little more restricted in scope. You can declare the return type to be a number, a string, or a variant. If you declare the type to be a variant, you can only return numbers from it, not strings or arrays. Also, in Analysis Services 2000, if an external function returns an empty variant, the PivotTable Service will return an error condition for the calculation.

Passing Arrays of Values to External Functions

You can pass arbitrary-size arrays of values into external functions through the MDX extension function SetToArray( ). Although the documentation for Microsoft Analysis Services indicates that SetToArray( ) only creates arrays of numbers, it will in fact create sets of strings as well, which makes it useful for scanning sets of member names and property values as well as for processing a set of numbers. SetToArray( ) is useful for creating all kinds of custom aggregator functions. For each tuple in the set that is passed to SetToArray( ), Analysis Services will place a value in the array at the corresponding location in the array, so there will be one value in the array for each tuple in the set (with one exception case that we will describe later in this section) in the same order.

For example, consider the issues we examined in Chapter 4, regarding the construction of cumulative sums of members for Pareto analysis. We proposed an external function, PartialSum( ), to perform this task. As envisioned there, PartialSum( ) takes three arguments: an array of values to sum across, an array of names corresponding to the values, and the name of the tuple at which summing should stop. In VB, we could code the function like this:

```
Public Function PartialSum (ByRef ArgVals() As Double, ByRef ArgNames()
As String, ByVal StopAt As String) As Double
Dim Start As Integer
Dim Finish As Integer
Dim i As Integer

Start = LBound(ArgVals, 1)   ' for safety
Finish = UBound(ArgVals, 1)

' initialize working sum to zero
PartialSum = 0
For i = Start To Finish
    ' add value for this tuple
    PartialSum = PartialSum + ArgVals(i)
    ' leave if we have encountered the stopping point
    If ArgVals(i) = StopAt Then Return
Next i

' If we get here, there is a problem
' leave the next two commented out in order to simply return the sum we
got
' PartialSum = 0
Err.Raise 9999

End Function
```

The function takes the lower and upper bounds of the array and loops through the argument value array, adding each value into the sum. (Although the documentation for Analysis Services does not discuss the lower-bound number for the array—does the array numbering start at 0, 1, or something else?—the numbering consistently starts at 0.) At each cycle through the loop, the function tests whether the current argument name is equal to the name at which the loop should stop, and when that condition is met, the function returns the value. If the function does not encounter the name to stop at in the array of names, we have three possible choices: return the total across the entire set, return zero, or raise an error.

We have chosen the most conservative approach in the code (to raise an error), but the other two outcomes may make sense for your applications as well. We could then call this function in a query to generate cumulative sums, as with the following simple query, which would yield the result shown in Figure 7.1 as a spreadsheet grid and as a graph:

```
WITH
MEMBER [Measures].[Geog. Name] AS '[Geography].CurrentMember.UniqueName'
SET [Ordered States] AS 'Order ([Geography].[State].Members,
[Measures].[Profit], BDESC)'
MEMBER [Measures].[Cum Profit] AS
'PartialSum (
    SetToArray ([Ordered States], [Geography], [Measures].[Profit]),
    SetToArray ([Ordered States], [Geography], [Measures].[Geog. Name]),
    [Geography].CurrentMember.UniqueName
)'
SELECT
{ [Ordered States] } on columns,
{ [Measures].[Profit], [Measures].[Cum Profit] } on rows
FROM
[Sales Cube]
```

Microsoft OLAP/Analysis Services makes every value of the array have the same type. That is, arrays passed to functions can be of numbers or of text, but

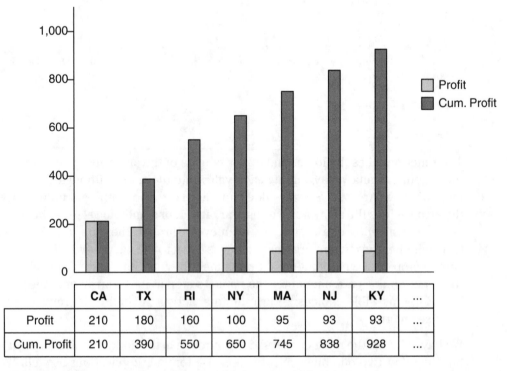

	CA	TX	RI	NY	MA	NJ	KY	...
Profit	210	180	160	100	95	93	93	...
Cum. Profit	210	390	550	650	745	838	928	...

Figure 7.1 Result of cumulative sum query using external function.

Analysis Services cannot pass arrays of variants to an external function. If Analysis Services could pass variants, then we might be able to pass in a single two-dimensional array containing pairs of "(name, value)" and simplify our MDX a bit more. But the function is still handy enough as it is.

Notice that we passed the string array in by first declaring a measure to simply return the unique name of the current geography member and then using that as the value expression for SetToArray( ). Analysis Services generates a parser error if you try to use any value expression that is not the value of a cell here, so we need to make sure to make it a cell value.

Because arrays are passed in COM variant types, we can think about accepting arrays through variant arguments. If we declare our array input to be of variant type, then we must understand how Microsoft Analysis Services prepares the array in its native type. Recall from Chapter 5, "MDX Context and Execution," how the data type for each cell is determined independently of the type of any other cell. When Analysis Services creates the array, it chooses the data type of the first value that it places into the array as the type for the array. If that value is a double, then the variant will contain an array of double-typed values. If that value is an integer, then the variant will contain an array of integer-typed values, and so on. If the first value is an empty cell, then an empty variant is passed, rather than an array whose first element is zero. (Because the variant cannot itself contain an array of variants, no empty argument can be passed in an array.) Any value after the first value that is empty in Analysis Services will have a zero placed in the corresponding array position. Given the issues that handling the array data types entails, you may want to declare your array arguments as being arrays of a specific type.

Raising an error is one of the options that we listed in the code for Partial-Sum( )when the stop-at name is not found. If your external function raises an error, then Analysis Services will immediately stop evaluating the formula and return an error condition for the cell instead of a value for it. A well-constructed client will somehow feed this information back to the user to let him or her know that something went wrong when the cell was calculated, in the same way that cell data errors flagged by Analysis Services are processed.

If you are paying attention to run-time performance (and that is a good idea), you may have already seen how the SetToArray( ) function can be made more efficient. Although a member's unique name will uniquely identify the member within the dimension, the member also has an intrinsic integer ID property. Having Analysis Services construct the array of integers is likely to be a little faster, and it will certainly be faster for our external function to test each of them to see if they are the last one to be processed. We can rewrite our function as follows:

```
Public Function PartialSum (ByRef ArgVals() As Double, ByRef ArgIDs() As
Long, ByVal StopAt As Long) As Double
```

```
Dim Start As Long
Dim Finish As Long
Dim i As Long

Start = LBound(ArgVals, 1)   ' for safety
Finish = UBound(ArgVals, 1)

' initialize working sum to zero
PartialSum = 0
For i = Start To Finish
    ' add value for this tuple
    PartialSum = PartialSum + ArgVals(i)
    ' leave if we have encountered the stopping point
    If ArgIDs(i) = StopAt Then Return
Next i

' If we get here, there is a problem
' leave the next two commented out in order to simply return the sum we
got
' PartialSum = 0
Err.Raise 9999

End Function
```

Our function would be used in our sample query as follows:

```
WITH
MEMBER [Measures].[Geog. ID] AS
'CLng ([Geography].CurrentMember.Properties("ID"))'
SET [Ordered States] AS 'Order ([Geography].[State].Members,
[Measures].[Profit], BDESC)'
MEMBER [Measures].[Cum Profit] AS
'PartialSum (
    SetToArray ([Ordered States], [Geography], [Measures].[Profit]),
    SetToArray ([Ordered States], [Geography], [Measures].[Geog. ID]),
    CLng([Measures].[Geog. ID])
)'
SELECT
{ [Ordered States] } on columns,
{ [Measures].[Profit], [Measures].[Cum Profit] } on rows
FROM
[Sales Cube]
```

One subtle point to note regarding SetToArray( ) is how Microsoft Analysis Services constructs the array. Recall from Chapter 5 how an invalid tuple specification in a set specification ends up contributing no tuple to the set. For example, if a time dimension's month level starts with January 2000, then the set specification {[Time].[Jan 2000], [Time].[Jan 2000].PrevMember, [Time].[Jan 2000].NextMember} will result in a set of only two tuples (for January and February). When this set is used to materialize an array that is passed to an external function via SetToArray( ), the set will only contain two values as a result. If you construct your sets using functions like .PrevMember, Cousin( ), ParallelPeriod( ), SetToArray( ), LastPeriods( ), and the like, you will need to code your external functions to take this into account.

MDX Functions for Use with External Functions

In addition to SetToArray( ), which can only be used with external functions, a number of functions specific to Analysis Services's implementation of MDX are most useful in combination with external functions. We list them in Table 7.1 and describe their utilities in the following paragraphs. All functions are marked by an asterisk (*) because they are Analysis Services extensions to the MDX specification. We will discuss most of these functions in this section. We leave the application of the Dimensions( ) and Levels( ) functions to your imagination and application requirements.

SetToStr( ), TupleToStr( )

SetToStr( ) converts the given set specification into a string. It does not convert the values associated with the set's tuples into a string. The format of the string

Table 7.1 MDX Functions Useful with External Functions

EXTENSION	RETURNS	SYNOPSIS
*	string	SetToStr (Set)
*	string	TupleToStr (Tuple)
*	set	StrToSet (String expression)
*	set	NameToSet (String expression)
*	tuple	StrToTuple (String expression)
*	string, number	StrToValue (String expression)
*	member	Members (String expression)
*	member	StrToMember (String expression)
*	string	MemberToStr (Member)
*	dimension	Dimensions (String expression)
*	level	Levels (String expression)

is simple and is fully described in Appendix A. We could well have written PartialSum( ) so that it uses SetToStr( ) instead of an array of strings or member IDs. An external function that uses SetToStr( ) might be easier to write and might run faster if it uses SetToArray( ) instead of SetToStr( ) because the string will need to be parsed in the external function if the tuples are to be processed there. TupleToStr( ) is similar except that it converts only a single tuple to a string.

Members( ), StrToSet( ), StrToTuple( )

Suppose that we want to create an MDX query that always requested data for the current day, for example, by using it as a slicer in the query. If we are generating the query dynamically, we can create an MDX expression every time the query is accessed, which puts the current date into the slicer. However, we can get the same effect through a completely static query by using an external function that returns name of the current month. For example, a query that always returned the year-to-date sales through the current month might be written as follows:

```
WITH
MEMBER [Measures].[Sales YTD] AS
'Sum (PeriodsToDate ([Time].[Year], Members (OurCurDate())),
     [Measures].[Sales])'
SELECT
{ [Products].[Division].Members } on columns,
{ [Geography].[Regions].Members } on rows
FROM
[Sales Tracking]
WHERE ([Measures].[Sales YTD])
```

The logic that makes this query tick can be included in a single VB function that is 17 lines long, including white space. Assuming that the levels of the time dimension are [All], [Year], [Quarter], and [Month], the following VB code would return the appropriate name (assuming default time member names are used):

```
Public Function OurCurDate() As String
Dim TheDate As Date


TheDate = Date

' e.g. "[Time].[All Time].[1999].[Quarter 1].[February].[Feb 01, 1999]"
OurCurDate = "[Time].[All Time].[" & _
             DatePart("yyyy", TheDate) & _
         "].[" & _
           "Quarter " & Format(DatePart("q", TheDate)) & _
         "].[" & _
```

```
            Format(TheDate, "mmmm") & _
        "].[" & _
            Format(TheDate, "mmm dd, yyyy") & _
        "]"

    End Function
```

If we are using Microsoft Analysis Services and the names for the day level are unique (which we generally advocate), this function can be much simpler because we don't need to list the parents in order to create the unique name. We can just use the name of the day, as follows:

```
    Public Function OurCurDate() As String
    Dim TheDate As Date

    TheDate = Date

    ' e.g. "[Time].[Feb 01, 1999]"
    OurCurDate = "[Time].[" &
                Format(TheDate, "mmm dd, yyyy") & _
                "]"

    End Function
```

We must take care that the name logic is in synch with the name logic of the dimension. For example, if we change the way the quarters are named so that Q1 of 1999 is renamed from [Quarter 1] to [Q1, 1999], then we need to update the function. (If we were generating MDX dynamically to insert the current month, we would need to update its code generator too, so there is no great need to keep the naming principles in synch).

The major difference between Members( ) and StrToTuple( ) is simply that Members( ) returns a single member, while StrToTuple( ) returns a tuple of arbitrary dimensionality. You could, of course, construct a tuple using multiple calls to Members( ). For example,

```
    (Members(MemberF1()), Members(MemberF2()))
```

specifies a tuple that combines the member whose name is returned by MemberF1( ) with the member whose name is returned by MemberF2( ).

StrToSet( ) returns an actual set, so it would be used in contexts where StrToTuple( ) and Members( ) cannot be used. You could, of course, express one-tuple sets as { StrToTuple(. . .) } or { Members(. . .) }. For example, the statement

```
    CREATE SET [Production].[ProductsToAnalyze] AS
    'StrToSet( MyEFThatReturnsAProductSetString( . . . ))'
```

will generate a named set within the context of the production cube that you can use in any number of subsequent queries.

External Procedures (Void-Returning Functions)

Microsoft's Analysis Services provides a Call function in its MDX that enables a void function (a procedure to you Visual Basic developers) to be executed. It's a pretty simple mechanism; the Call can only be executed in a cell context (in an action or a calculated member) and will return an empty cell value. Although Call returns an empty cell value, you can't combine that empty value in an expression. That is, you have to say something like

```
'Call MyProc ([Customer].CurrentMember.Properties ("key"))'
```

and cannot say something like

```
'5 + (Call MyProc ())'
```

The point of such a routine would be either to poke data into the function and have it do useful work like email the values of its arguments to your manager, or to set up some information in a global context that would be accessed by subsequent calls to other external functions. We'll leave the applications to your imagination.

External Function Example: Time Span until Sum

In Chapter 4, we worked through the MDX required to determine how the time span required to accumulate a particular quantity (in that case, number of subscribers). The goal was to get the set of times, as opposed to simply counting how many times there were. Let's look at how to implement this operation in an external function.

First, we should understand what the function will return and how it will be called. In the example of Chapter 5, we were interested in a set of members, so let's have this function return a string containing a set specification. In our query, we'll turn this into a set of members using StrToSet( ), calling it with something like StrToSet (TimeSpanUntilSum (. . .)). It needs to take an array of cell values to figure out the sums. However, it only needs to take one time member name (the latest time member's name), since it can return a string like [Time].[Feb 2000].lag(5) : [Time].[Feb 2000]. (This string assumes that the members are in database order; we'd construct the function differently if this might not be the case.) So, we can pass it just as an array of cell values and the time member name, and call it like

```
SET [Times Until Sum] AS
'StrToSet (
  TimeSpanUntilSum (
    SetToArray (
      {[Time].[Month].Members.Item(0) : [Time].[Month].[Oct 2000]},
      [Measures].[New Customer Count]
    ),
    "[Time].[Month].[Oct 2000]",
    500  // the sum we want to arrive at
  )
)'
```

What would the code for this function look like? It's pretty straightforward in any language; we'll provide a VB implementation here:

```
Public Function TimeSpanUntilSum (ArgVals() As Double, ByVal LastName As
String, ByVal SumTo As Double) As String


Dim i As Integer
Dim RunSum As Double

For i = UBound(ArgVals) to LBound(ArgVals) Step -1
  RunSum = RunSum + ArgVals(i)
  If RunSum >= SumTo Then
    Goto Done
  End If
Next i

Done:

TimeSpanUntilSum = "{" & LastName & ".Lag(" & UBound(ArgVals) - i _
                & ") : " & LastName & "}"

End Function
```

Guess what? This tends to run faster than the plain MDX version, and the more time members, the greater the difference. The more members you have in the time dimension, the more the plain MDX version creates redundant sums. Also, you don't need to create a different calculated measure definition every time you want to run this, whereas you did need to put the ending time member name in the plain MDX's calculated member definition each time you wanted to run it for a new time member. You can also adjust the threshold from 500 to 50,000 without altering any logic.

Additional Considerations for External Functions

Although the calling interface between an external function and Microsoft Analysis Services is fairly restricted, the external function has only a few limits on it what it can do while it is executing. It may open and read files, read the registry, put up dialogs, interact with other programs, and so on. (One restriction to note: while the external function is executing, the OLE DB for OLAP session that is executing the MDX query or statement that calls the external function is blocked. This means that the external function cannot itself call back into Analysis Services on the same session.) A custom browser could expose a global class containing functions that, when called, reference cached metadata, user preferences, real-time data feeds, and so on. These will all be very application-specific, so we will not attempt to go through all of the possibilities here, but you may find that they make a great deal of sense for your own application. Keep in mind that it may not be appropriate for an external function to interact with the production computing environment (for example, popping up a dialog on a Web server). Also, since the functions are global, it is difficult for the function library itself to maintain internal or session state in a stateless Web server environment.

One interesting use of an external function is to have an application combine its specific calculations with cube data in MDX queries. Your application may need to perform some amount of data processing that would be inconvenient in MDX queries and it would then combine the results with data in an Analysis Services cube. One way to perform the combining of the results would be to feed them into a fact table and process a cube that provides additional calculations on them. If the scale of the calculations is small enough (in terms of number of cells calculated and their suitability to calculation in a client's session), it may make sense to have your application read its input data through MDX, perform its calculations, and then expose its results to further MDX calculations through an external function that references the results. Candidates for this approach would be any calculations that require iterative methods on the data from Analysis Services and return results that map to cells in the database.

Loading and Using Libraries

Libraries must be loaded by executing the USE LIBRARY statement (an extension to MDX). Like CREATE MEMBER and CREATE SET statements, this statement may be executed on the fly at the client or may be stored in a command object at the server and invoked when you connect to a database or cube. When you register a function library at the server through the OLAP Manager's calculated member builder, a USE LIBRARY statement for the library you choose gets saved in such an object.

USE LIBRARY Syntax

The USE LIBRARY statement takes the form

```
USE LIBRARY [library-spec [, library-spec . . .]].
```

The USE LIBRARY statement controls the loading and unloading of external function libraries. Zero, one, or more than one library path may be listed as arguments to the command, separated by commas. Each library spec is a string that contains either the directory path and name of the file that contains the function library's type library or a class name that appears in the system registry and identifies the type library and location of the executable code (.DLL, .OCX, .EXE). Executable files (.EXE or .DLL), ActiveX controls (.OCX), and type library files (.DLL, .OLB, .TLB) files are candidates. Analysis Services must find the type library of the function library to understand the functions, and these files all contain enough information for Analysis Services to find the type library information. You can specify the name of the class directly as well.

When one or more libraries are listed in the command, the specified files are examined and their applicable functions are loaded. If the same function name exists in two or more files (either in the same statement or from one USE LIBRARY command to another) and that function name is used in an MDX expression, the first function with that name that was loaded is the version Analysis Services calls. For example, the following statement loads two external function libraries from DLLs:

```
USE LIBRARY
"D:\AppSystems\Bin\StatFunctions01.DLL",
"D:\AppSystems\Bin\FinanceFunctions02.DLL"
```

The following loads a library based on class name:

```
USE LIBRARY "EFStatsPackage.FunctionsClass1"
```

If USE LIBRARY is called without any library pathnames being listed, then all function libraries that are currently loaded become unloaded. There is no way to selectively unload libraries.

Note that if the Safety Options connection parameter is set to 3, the library or libraries listed will not load. See Appendix A for more details.

Loading and Using Libraries and Distribution Issues

It is important to remember that any function libraries that you use for MDX need to be available on the client machine. If queries are executed on a Web server, then the function libraries only need to be installed on the Web server. If you are using Microsoft's Office 2000 Web Components (OWC), you should keep in mind that the queries are actually executed on the client even though they were configured on a Web page.

Using the name of the file that contains the function class is a simple way to identify and load the library on a given machine. When you are creating a USE LIBRARY statement that may be executed on multiple client machines, you will run into the issue of exactly where the file has been installed. For example, it may have been installed to a directory on the C:\ drive of one machine and the D:\ drive of another machine. When this becomes an issue, the easiest solution is to obtain the class name and reference that is used in the USE LIBRARY statement. This is the technique that the OLAP Manager uses when it registers function libraries.

Remember that if you are distributing ActiveX DLL components to client machines, you must register them with COM on the client by running RegSvr32 and make the library available on that machine.

Microsoft Analysis Services introduces connection properties that enable or direct the PivotTable Service to check function libraries for safety. When a function library is signed as being *safe*, the OLAP system will trust that executing a function in it won't cause a security breach. Whether or not you need to deal with this depends on whether you are looking to distribute your libraries to others and your assessment of your own security risks. As far as Analysis Services is concerned, safety is determined by the presence of two registry entries on the computer on which the library is installed. When your library is registered on a computer, it will have its GUID placed as a key under the HKEY_CLASSES_ROOT\CLSID key. In the ImplementedCategories subkey under your library's key, ensure that the following two GUIDs are present as subkeys of ImplementedCategories: {7DD95802-9882-11CF-9FA9-00AA006C42 C4} and {7DD95801-9882-11CF-9FA9-00AA006C42C4}. The following snippet of a .REG file identifies the two keys:

```
REGEDIT4

[HKEY_CLASSES_ROOT\CLSID\{20048BB3-DB68-11CF-9CAF-00AA006CB425}\
Implemented Categories]

[HKEY_CLASSES_ROOT\CLSID\{20048BB3-DB68-11CF-9CAF-00AA006CB425}\
Implemented Categories\{7DD95801-9882-11CF-9FA9-00AA006C42C4}]
```

```
[HKEY_CLASSES_ROOT\CLSID\{20048BB3-DB68-11CF-9CAF-00AA006CB425}\
Implemented Categories\{7DD95802-9882-11CF-9FA9-00AA006C42C4}]
```

Look for further information on safety and the signing of libraries at http://msdn.microsoft.com/workshop/components/activex/signmark.asp.

Disambiguating Duplicated Function Names

Nothing can prevent you from loading two or more function libraries that each contain a function with the same name. Even when a single USE LIBRARY statement references multiple libraries, they are always loaded one at a time, so a clear ordering takes place in terms of which library was loaded before or after which other library. When a function name is found in two or more libraries, the version that was loaded first is the one that is called if the function is simply called by name. For example, if library A and library B both contain a PctDiff( ) function and library B is loaded before library A, then the formula PctDiff ([Time], [Time].PrevMember) will invoke library B's implementation.

You can explicitly qualify the name of the function in order to pick out the exact version that you want to call, however. The syntax for this is to prefix the name of the function with the class ID of the library. If the class ID of library A is EFStatsPackage.FunctionsClass and the class ID of library B is EFFinancialPackage.FunctionsClass, then the formula

```
'EFStatsPackage!FunctionsClass!PctDiff ([Time], [Time].PrevMember)'
```

will call the version of PctDiff( ) that resides in EFStatsPackage.FunctionsClass (our library A).

Class Names Generated in Visual Basic

Remember that when you create a class in Visual Basic, VB will prepend an underscore to the name of the class. If you create a VB project named EFStatsPackage, create within it a class called FunctionsClass, and add a function named PctDiff( ) to that class, you would refer to the specific function within that class by EFStatsPackage!_FunctionsClass!PctDiff (. . .), not by EFStatsPackage!FunctionsClass!PctDiff (. . .).

Summary

Although we cannot extend the calculation capability of Microsoft Analysis Services to include anything, we can create an ActiveX function interface that makes it possible to directly satisfy application requirements that Analysis Services by itself cannot. In this chapter, we covered the mechanisms that are used to call into and receive results from an external function as well as how to register them for use with Analysis Services. We also looked at a set of examples to illustrate situations that these mechanisms can be applied in as well as how to implement them, so you can write your own with confidence. Many applications may have no need for them at all, but you may find they are the perfect technique for implementing the functionality your particular application needs.

CHAPTER 8

Building Queries in MDX

In Chapter 2, "MDX in More Detail" and Chapter 3, "MDX in Use," we used MDX queries as a framework for understanding MDX and its construction. For some applications, those chapters may tell you all you need to know. However, a number of other detail issues arise in composing and leveraging queries, and we will devote this chapter to them:

- Thinking dimensionally and thinking modularly
- Building user-defined aggregates
- Using server-defined solve orders with user-defined aggregates
- Using dimensional calculations and solve orders as your friend
- Dealing with quotes in names
- Using sets to clarify logic
- MDX templates for building reports
- Constructing names

In addition, we will list out here some things you can't do:

- Calculate new values for member properties, captions, and so on
- Define new levels
- Define calculated members whose names are results of MDX

Thinking Dimensionally

In this author's opinion, the most important skill to develop to create effective queries is to think dimensionally. MDX is very strong at expressing calculations in a dimensional fashion, and by leveraging that capability you can perform a lot of work with only a little composition. When we say "thinking dimensionally," we mean using the whole dimensional framework of the underlying cubes to capture the computations you want. Many times (as with many numerical calculations), this will be straightforward. Other times, it may be subtle, and it may involve influencing the underlying database design to make sure that you have what you want as support for queries (for example, that you have utility dimensions or a particular set of member properties defined). Although this chapter deals with more than the dimensional aspects of queries, we hope that the examples we work through help to emphasize this.

Much of what an OLAP database or application developer needs to do when building an application is design MDX expressions. For example, in Microsoft OLAP/Analysis Server, all calculated members, security expressions, actions, and custom member formulas are MDX expressions in essence. All of these are generally defined before a user even connects to the database to start retrieving data. In some technical cases, however, you need to use a query in order do something. Some extremely common cases are the following:

- Define aggregations based on user selections
- Retrieve a set based on user selections
- Create named sets to make a calculation more efficient

Let us take aggregations of user selections as an example. Suppose that you want to let a user pick a set of customer members and query for the sum of measures over these customers, for some time and product. If the user picks customers [Zhou Tang], [Avi Roth], and [Leah Cornish], then a query that produces this total might look like the query in Figure 8.1.

Is there any way to express this total purely as a calculated member, of the form CREATE CALCULATED MEMBER [Sales].[Customer].[Total] AS 'Something' ? The quick answer is that there is no way to do it that is any simpler than generating the query like this. Technically speaking, you could accomplish it through ways that (in Analysis Services 2000) involve external functions and the StrTo-Val( ) function or use CELL CALCULATION clauses, but you still need to assemble a syntactically correct set at the time the query is actually issued.

Another case is when you want to retrieve a set of members based on user selection. For example, you want to select the top five products based on a

```
WITH
MEMBER [Customer].[Total] AS
'Sum ( {
  [Customer].[Zhou Tang], [Customer].[Avi Roth],
  [Customer].[Leah Cornish]
})'
SELECT
{ [Measures].AllMembers } on columns,
{ [Customer].[Zhou Tang], [Customer].[Avi Roth],
  [Customer].[Leah Cornish], [Customers].[Total]
} on rows
FROM [Sales]
WHERE [Time].[Q1, 2001]
```

Figure 8.1   Query involving aggregate of user-selected members.

user-selected date and region. You cannot encapsulate this in a cell calculation, as cell calculations only compute values for cells. If you define a global or session-named set, then its definition is fixed until it is deleted and re-created (and if you delete it, everything like a calculated member that depends on it becomes invalid). However, in a query, the retrieval is quite straightforward:

```
WITH
Set [Top 5 Products] AS
'TopCount (
  [Product].[Category].Members,
  5
  ([Measures].Sales, [Time].[Q2, 2001], [Geography].[Northeast])
)'
SELECT
[Top 5 Products] on columns,
[Time].[Q2, 2001] on rows
FROM [Sales]
```

(The user selected the values in italics.)

This lets us state a general rule:

When a calculation or retrieval involves a set of members selected by the user, it is easiest to package the calculation in a query as opposed to trying to put it in a calculated member or named set (or cell calculation in Analysis Services 2000).

Reporting an aggregate or other calculation on members of a user's choosing is a pretty common application requirement. We're going to use this now to try to present some themes again, this time trying to be clear in both thinking about the problem dimensionally, and also about how to use Microsoft's calculation architecture to make construction easy.

The query in Figure 8.1 requests Measures.AllMembers, which will return any calculated measures along with the base measures. If some of these calculated measures are ratios, then we may end up returning the sum of the ratios as opposed to the ratio of the sums, given that we implicitly have a solve order of zero for the [Customer].[Total] member. In our experience, Microsoft OLAP/Analysis Services calculates the measures dimension last within a solve order so measure ratios with a solve order of at least zero will be calculated from the sums, but as developers we don't like to lean on such default behavior too heavily.

How can we not lean on default solve order behavior? By picking a solve order for our server-side ratios that is going to be relatively unique. Can we do this and still create aggregations in queries? Absolutely—recall from Chapter 6 "The Many Ways to Calculate in Microsoft Analysis Services" that solve orders are all considered in one lump when answering a query, regardless of where the calculated member or cell calculation was defined. To be sure about our solve order numbers, we can (as a policy) make all server-based solve orders multiples of 10, and make all client-defined solve orders fit in between. For example, if we know that a the calculated measure [Average Sales Price] has a solve order of 20, we can re-cast the query of Figure 8.1 as the query in Figure 8.2 and be confident in getting the right results.

```
WITH
MEMBER [Customer].[Total] AS
'Sum ( {
  [Customer].[Zhou Tang], [Customer].[Avi Roth],
  [Customer].[Leah Cornish]
})', SOLVE_ORDER = 5
SELECT
{ [Measures].[Units], [Measures].[Average Sales Price] } on columns,
{ [Customer].[Zhou Tang], [Customer].[Avi Roth],
  [Customer].[Leah Cornish], [Customers].[Total]
} on rows
FROM [Sales]
WHERE [Time].[Q1, 2001]
```

Figure 8.2 Re-phrased query involving aggregate of user-selected members.

Dealing with Quotes in Member Names

One thing that you may need to deal with is quotes embedded within member names. This occurs if you allow a user to select a set of member for use in building a calculated member or named set. Consider a customer dimension that contains a set of business names to which you sell kitchen supplies. These might include [Awfully Good Bread], [Connie's Italian], and [Levi's Bagels]. A simple query that requests the sum of these three might start with

```
WITH MEMBER [Customer].[Total] AS
'SUM ( { [Customer].[Awfully Good Bread], [Customer].[Connie's Italian],
[Customer].[Levi's Bagels] } )'
SELECT ...
```

But this will run into a syntax error. The apostrophe in "Connie's" will be taken as the single-quote that closes the whole expression, and everything after that will not parse correctly. If quotes need to be embedded, they need to be doubled up. The only solution to this problem, if you are generating queries, is to make sure that the code that generates the query repeats quotes as necessary. The following will be correctly parsed and executed:

```
WITH MEMBER [Customer].[Total] AS
'SUM ( { [Customer].[Awfully Good Bread], [Customer].[Connie''s Ital-
ian],
[Customer].[Levi''s Bagels] } )'
SELECT ...
```

Building Names and Identifiers

In many applications, you won't need to actually know how to construct a member name. A generalized browser, for example, will discover meta data from the meta data rowsets, present member captions to the end user and keep the associated unique names internally. In an application where all names originate through discovery of meta data, you can pretty much treat a unique name as an opaque pointer.

However, you may well have an application where you need to construct the names to put into a query. (We have had to deal with this ourselves many times.) For example, an end user may pick a product or time frame from a list in a relational database. In this case, performing meta data lookup can be inefficient. It also could be the case (depending on the structure of your database) that you need to phrase a complete MDX query to retrieve the member information. (We'll talk about this later in this chapter.) Such a query is unnecessary if it is reasonable to assume that the member exists in the OLAP database as well as the relational database, so long as you can construct the name of the member. We discussed the format of unique names earlier, but we'll go into more depth here.

The most important names to build in MDX queries are member names. Dimension and level names are straightforward. There are several different ways to build a member name, and in Analysis Services, you can build and use member names that have a different style than the names you get from the meta data functions. (See Appendix B for a discussion of the MDX Unique Name Style and MDX Compatibility connection parameters.)

NOTE

The rest of this section will be specific to Microsoft Analysis Services. If you are building queries for use in another OLE DB for OLAP provider, then this discussion may not apply.

In Analysis Services, you can identify regular members either by member key or by name. Calculated members have no member key, so you need to identify them by name. Analysis Services can be very flexible in dealing with ambiguous names in a dimension, even to the point of allowing more than one child of a parent to have the same member name. Similarly, it can be flexible with ambiguity in the member keys, although no two children of the same parent can have the same key value. The greater the degree of duplication allowed in the dimension, the more qualification the member identifier is going to need if you are attempting to compose it. (Note: because the member can be identified by name or by key, we're going to try to use "identity" and "identify" as much as possible in this discussion.)

In the simplest case, to identify a member by name, you can combine the dimension name with the member name, as with

```
[Measures].[Unit Sales]
```

(The square braces are not strictly necessary unless the names have special characters in them, but we recommend their use.) If member names are unique within the dimension, that is all you really need. It's frequently not that easy. If member names are unique within the level of the member, you can combine the dimension name, the level name, and the member name (which requires you to know the right level name, although the application frequently dictates it). For example:

```
[Time].[Week].[WW 35, 2001]
```

If member names are not unique within the dimension or the level, then you need to either use member key notation, or add parent members into the name.

In our opinion, it's preferable to use keys when available (and try to make them available) as they are not only just as good, but they will likely be the same for relational queries against the underlying fact and dimension tables as for the MDX.

The key notation requires the key value to be prefixed by &[and followed by]. For example, the following provides the key for a week-level time member:

```
[Time].[Week].&[2001935]
```

If the keys are unique within the time dimension, this could be simplified to

```
[Time].&[2001935]
```

In parent-child dimensions, the keys are always unique in the dimension, so you can always identify members this way in a parent-child dimension.

Because identifying a member is so straightforward using one of these four techniques, we strive to enable unique names and/or unique keys in applications that we are responsible for. In most data marts and warehouses, member keys are unique at the leaf level anyway because that follows from best data warehousing practice. However, dimension columns for higher levels may or may not be unique, depending on the discipline used to build the tables.

If member names or keys are not unique within the dimension or the level, you do need to bring in parent member names (or risk selecting the wrong member). The complete path for a member using member names is

```
[Dimension].[Top Level Member].[2nd Level Member].[3rd Level
Member].[Target Member]
```

where the dimension name is followed by the ancestor at the top level followed by the ancestor at the next level down, and so on to the name of the member you are trying to uniquely identify.

Note that you can mix and match key and name identifiers if you need to. For example, the following member identifier combines a unique key and a non-unique name to specify the member as a child of another member. The following identifies the Valve 1 child of the member otherwise identified by a key value of 37015:

```
[Asset].&[37015].[Valve 1]
```

Names and "Large Levels"

In general, we would advise client applications to use the briefest and most unique names possible in an application. Smaller names mean less storage, and one of the benefits of defining levels as having unique names or keys should be more compact structures and faster lookups. However, this comes with a price in Microsoft's Analysis Services. A setting called the "large level" setting (discussed in Appendix B) controls how many members of a member are downloaded to a client when the client requests members of a level. If the level contains more members than the setting allows, then the member meta data is held back at the server. What this means is that a perfectly good identifier like [Customer].[Cust ID].&[1022834] may be rejected when a query is parsed, even though the member exists. The reason for this would be that the query which includes this name is being run before the meta data has been transferred to the client, and since queries are parsed on the client, it appears to be undefined. During the course of a client session, if the member identifiers used have all been discovered from meta data, this won't be a problem. However, if you save a query and re-run it in a later session, it can be a problem.

You could increase the large level threshold, but if your dimensions are substantially larger than the default of 1,000 members then clients may spend a great deal of time and memory downloading meta data when they connect to a cube. An alternative is to not use names that are this unique. For example, suppose another path to the member is [Customer].[All Customer].[CDN].[Alberta].[Calgary].&[1022834]. In this case, the parsing of the name from left to right introduces meta data to the client tier, and the member will be found.

Using Sets to Clarify Logic

As part of building queries, we recommend that you use named sets in queries for even moderately complicated set logic. If a set is going to be evaluated more than once (for example, the results of a Filter( ), Order( ) or Generate( )), you can usually get some query efficiency out of only creating it once. For queries that are fast enough, comprehensibility is also an issue. If a query is somewhat complicated, using a named set can make the text of the query briefer and easier to understand.

If you are generating queries on the fly through code, it might not seem to make much of a difference. You can generate the same text in more than one place in a query just about as easily as generating it in one place to define the set. However, if you ever have to debug a generated query, you may wish that it had already been simplified.

For example, suppose you have a report that lists the top five products in terms of units sold, along with the total of units for those five, and the percentage of the overall total units sold. (This would ideally allow the user to pick time frame, customer, and so on as well.) You'll need to reference the top-five set twice—once to get their sum and another time to list them in the axis. Without a named set, a sample query looks like the following:

```
WITH
MEMBER [Products].[Sum of Top 5] AS
'Sum (
  TopCount (
    { [Product].[Category].Members },
    5,
    [Measures].[Units]
  )
)', SOLVE_ORDER = 1
MEMBER [Products].[Ratio of Top 5 To All] AS
'[Products].[Sum of Top 5] / [Products].[All Products]'
, SOLVE_ORDER = 10
SELECT
{ [Measures].[Units] } on columns,
{
  TopCount (
    { [Product].[Category].Members },
    5,
    [Measures].[Units]
  ),
  [Products].[Sum of Top 5],
  [Products].[Ratio of Top 5 To All]
} on rows
FROM [Sales]
```

With the use of a named set, it becomes easier to understand:

```
WITH
SET [Top 5 Products] AS
'TopCount (
  { [Product].[Category].Members },
  5,
  [Measures].[Units]
)'
MEMBER [Products].[Sum of Top 5] AS
'Sum (
  [Top 5 Products]
)', SOLVE_ORDER = 1
MEMBER [Products].[Ratio of Top 5 To All] AS
'[Products].[Sum of Top 5] / [Products].[All Products]'
, SOLVE_ORDER = 10
SELECT
{ [Measures].[Units] } on columns,
{
  [Top 5 Products],
  [Products].[Sum of Top 5],
  [Products].[Ratio of Top 5 To All]
} on rows
FROM [Sales]
```

And, if you follow the examples in Chapter 4, you will see a number of other queries that benefit from this.

Report Templates and Modularity

One of the tasks that MDX makes simple is writing parameterized reports, where some of the query is built into the report and some of it is generated in response to user actions. While the question of how to build report templates in MDX has no one correct answer, you can use some principles. The modularity of MDX expressions makes sophisticated user interaction possible with simple templates for queries.

For example, in a simple case of a product profitability report, you may simply allow the user to select a set of time periods and distributors to view, for a product that is coded into the report. A requirement for this example is that the user can pick any set of time periods and distributors that they want. The MDX framework will be the same no matter what they pick. If we imagine a couple of application variables named sTimeSet and sDistribSet, we can (using VB syntax) describe the query as

```
sMDX = "SELECT " & _
"{ " & sTimeSet & "} on columns, " & _
"{ " & sDistribSet & " } on rows " & _
"FROM [Profitability] " & _
"WHERE ([Product].[Category].[Perishables], [Measures].[Profitability])"
```

All that we need to do is fill in sTimeSet and sDistribSet with the identifiers for their members. If more than one member is selected, we just need to make sure that commas separate the identifiers. (For the purposes of this example, we are going to wave our hands over the issue of how you come up with the member identifiers.) For example, if prior to building the overall query string we had simply made the following assignments, we would have our complete query ready to run:

```
sTimeSet = "[Time].[Q3-2001], [Time].[Q3-2000]"
sDistribSet = "[Distributor].[Alpha Industries], [Distributor].[Zorro
Sales]"
```

We'll talk about retrieving query results into your client program in Chapter 12, "Client Programming Basics."

Imagine that this report is a hit with your users. The next thing they realize that they want is an easy way to select the top or bottom 10 distributors in terms of profitability. As you may have already surmised, this basic query template won't need to change at all (or the code that represents its results to the user). All that will need to change is the contents of the sDistribSet variable. You will need to deal with what time period the top/bottom count is determined for. Imagine that you have an application variable named sTimeFrame that holds the member identifier for the time member at which top/bottom profitability is established, and another variable eCountType that holds one for a top-10 selection and two for a bottom-10 selection. You can build the sDistribSet variable with the following code:

```
if eCountType = 1 then
    sDistribSet = "TopCount"
else
    sDistribSet = "BottomCount"
end if
sDistribSet = sDistribSet & " ([Distributor].[Dist Acct].Members, 10,
([Measures].[Profitability], " & _
    sTimeFrame & "))"
```

At this point, sDistribSet holds a TopCount or BottomCount expression that can be used in place of a comma-separated set of member identifiers.

The important technique to understand is simply to turn the requirements of the reports that users need to interact with into a suitable template or set of templates, and then combine that with the necessary logic to fill in the blanks. There is no absolute right or wrong answer on how general or specific the templates should be; it is quite possible that a single template can cover more than one report.

Client application environments including Knosys' ProClarity and Business Objects' BusinessQuery MD provide a framework for doing much the same modeling of queries using an internal object model for the portions of a query. If you are using a client system that provides such a model, you may find that you rarely need to actually code MDX. However, for reports that are awkward or not supported by these platforms, you can use their objects with your own templates to get the best of both worlds.

MDX Queries to Retrieve Member Meta Data

One situation that some applications find themselves in is a need to present a list of members to a user that is different than a list that the application gets from the OLAP meta data. For example, a user may need to be able to pick a location from an alphabetically-sorted list of locations, but the locations have a hierarchical structure so that you have all of the cities alphabetically within each state, and all states alphabetical within each region. With only 50 or so cities, a simple sorted list is far more efficient for the user to flip through. In an application that supports multiple languages, an alphabetical ordering at the database is likely to be ordered in only one of the languages anyway—depending on the language the client is using, the alphabet used for sorting into alphabetical order will be different.

How can we get this list? Well, although an MDX query always implies a set of cells, we don't actually need to retrieve the cells. We can just request a set of members on one axis, and ignore any cells that are returned. (In the case of Microsoft Analysis Services, we won't incur any noticeable overhead for retrieving cells unless we actually start to reference the cells in the returned data set.) So, we can issue a query for these members and any member properties that we want. For example, to get the unique names and display captions for the cities in the geography dimension sorted by member caption, we can use the following query (the unique names and captions are automatically retrieved):

```
SELECT
{ Order (
  [Geography].[City].Members,
  [Geography].CurrentMember.Properties ("Caption"),
  BASC
) }
on Axis(0)
FROM [Reporting]
```

This can also be used to sort products by sales price or color, or employees in an org chart by name or ID number. Some applications call for retrieving a set of members whose names or some member property matches a pattern (for example, contains the string "Airlines" anywhere in it). This can be satisfied by a simple filter expression, using the VBA InStr( ) function:

```
SELECT
{ Filter (
  [Customer].[Line Customer].Members,
  InStr (
    1,
    [Customer].CurrentMember.Name,
    "Airlines"
  ) > 0
) }
on Axis(0)
FROM [Reporting]
```

Summary

We have taken a look at some of the basics of building a query in MDX and cases where you need to express what you want in a query. We've also looked at how to leverage MDX queries to retrieve meta data information that you might not have thought of issuing a query for. Although this only scratches the surface of query construction, this should be useful in considering how to support end users of your analytical applications.

CHAPTER 9

Advanced Operations and Commands—Drill-Through and Actions

O LAP-based systems are usually intermediaries—they draw on detail data that was collected from various operations, and supply results that are used in making decisions. Frequently, we would like them to extend their reach a little bit in both directions, so that we may see the raw data that they derived their results from and to help us implement the actions that their results suggest. Enabling these two possibilities is the subject of this chapter, and for Microsoft these are provided by *drill-through* and *actions*. Drill-through is an industry-standard term for reaching into the underlying fact table records for a cell or cells in an OLAP system. An action is a term created by Microsoft and used in the OLE DB for OLAP specification for a textual command that can be generated by the OLAP database for use in an arbitrary application, for example to implement a decision. Let's look at each of these.

Using Drill-Through

Drill-through enables a client application to access data from the tables that underlie a cube. For example, suppose that a cell for quarterly sales for a particular region shows a number for which an analyst wishes to look at the supporting transaction detail. Figure 9.1 shows the relationship of the underlying table to the cell, and represents the result that the analyst would like to see.

	Q1-2000		Q2-2000		Q3-2000	
	Hours	Revenue	Hours	Revenue	Hours	Revenue
Detroit	450	450	400	450	425	8500
Lansing	305	6010	350	7000	380	7400
Columbus	275	5500	280	5600	325	6500
Toledo	405	8100	400	8000	350	7000
Bowling Green	550	11000	510	1020	470	9400
Lexington	120	2400	115	2300	175	3500

Location	Date	Customer	Hours	Billing
Columbus	April 06, 2000	Acme Mfg	50	1000
Columbus	April 23, 2000	Bower's Flowers	20	400
Columbus	May 14, 2000	Acme Mfg	35	700
Columbus	May 30, 2000	Specialty Inc.	75	1500
Columbus	June 12, 2000	eXen Design	100	2000

Figure 9.1   Representation of drill-through.

To perform a drill-through, the client issues a drill-through query in MDX, which is very similar to an ordinary query. The result of the drill-through query is an OLE DB rowset that appears the same as one that results from an SQL query. A client that uses ADO can access this result as a regular read-only ADODB.Recordset object. (Although the MDX query causes SQL to be generated under the hood, there is no way to access the SQL query. Sometimes, multiple SQL queries actually may be generated.) Drill-through must be specifically enabled in the cube, and each partition of the cube may have different settings for drill-through. If a client makes a drill-through query on a cube or partition that has no drill-through specified for it (including local cubes), the query will fail.

MDX for Drill-Through

An MDX query that drills through is simply a single-cell query that starts with DRILLTHROUGH. For example, assuming that drill-through is set up on our inventory cube, the following query will retrieve rows for products made by Acme in Warehouse 8 for August 2000 (results shown in Figure 9.2):

```
DRILLTHROUGH
SELECT
FROM [Inventory]
WHERE (
  [Product].[ByManufacturer].[All Product].[Acme],
  [Warehouse].[Whse 8],
  [Time].[Aug. 2000]
)
```

Because the major syntactic requirement for a drill-through query is that no more than one member be specified for each axis, the following would result in the same rowset:

```
DRILLTHROUGH
SELECT
{ [Product].[ByManufacturer].[All Product].[Acme] } on axis (0),
{ [Warehouse].[Whse 8] } on axis (1),
{ [Time].[Aug. 2000] } on axis (2)
FROM [Inventory]
```

Product	Date	Mfg	Qty_In	Qty_Out	Qty_OnHand
Crate	Aug 5, 2000	Acme Mfg	60	50	400
Barrel	Aug 8, 2000	Acme Mfg	20	0	120
Crate	Aug 12, 2000	Acme Mfg	0	30	370
Barrel	Aug 12, 2000	Acme Mfg	50	100	70
Barrel	Aug 18, 2000	Acme Mfg	100	0	170
Crate	Aug 20, 2000	Acme Mfg	0	30	340
Barrel	Aug 20, 2000	Acme Mfg	20	0	190
Barrel	Aug 26, 2000	Acme Mfg	30	40	180
Barrel	Aug 27, 2000	Acme Mfg	30	10	200
Crate	Aug 31, 2000	Acme Mfg	50	0	390

Figure 9.2 Results of a drill-through query.

Drill-through can be from a leaf-level cell or an aggregate cell for a base measure. You cannot drill through from a cell related to a calculated member. If a default member in any of the dimensions is a calculated member, you must override it with a specific non-calculated member for that dimension as a result. For example, if you are using a calculated measure as the default measure, to drill through you must pick an arbitrary non-calculated measure (perhaps with [Measures].Members.Item(0)).

When you drill through on a regular cube, it does not matter what measure you drill through on (because measures are derived from columns and drill-through queries can only affect the rows returned). When you drill through on a virtual cube, the measure you drill through on can make a difference because the measure implies the underlying regular cube and each cube may return different sets of columns from a different collection of tables.

The type of dimension you drill through on does not make a difference. If you drill through on a cell for a parent member in a parent-child hierarchy, all rows that contributed to that cell, including the cells of the children members, will be included in the result.

Drilling through on Multiple Partitions

When you drill through a cell, the records may be taken from multiple partitions in a number of ways. An aggregate cell may be drawn from multiple partitions, depending on the partitioning scheme of the underlying cube. In a budgeting cube, drill-down may have been set up on the write-back partition so that from any cell you can view the audit trail for the cell. However, owing to the structure of virtual cubes, you cannot drill down on a cell and obtain records from multiple cubes.

Programmatic Aspects of Drill-Through

A drill-through query can return one rowset, or it can return one rowset per partition involved. Through ADO, when multiple rowsets are returned, they can be accessed by the NextRecordSet( ) method of the RecordSet object. (We have observed that calling NextRecordSet( ) on the last recordset generates an exception in ADO 2.6 instead of Nothing, although you can test for an AbsolutePage property value of adPosEOF as a proxy.) Figure 9.3 lists Visual Basic code that executes a drill-through query and iterates through all of the recordsets. Through OLE DB, when multiple partitions contribute to the result, they can be accessed as multiple separate rowsets by retrieving an IMultipleResults object from the drill-through query instead of an IRowset object. If a single IRowset object is retrieved from the query, then the resulting rowset contains the union of all columns with the union of all rows from the individual partitions accessed.

NOTE
█████ The OLE DB rowset(s) and the ADO recordset(s) returned are read-only.

```
Dim cn As New ADODB.Connection
cn.ConnectionString = "Provider=MSOLAP;Data Source=localhost;Initial
Catalog=My Cube;"
cn.Open

Dim rs As New ADODB.Recordset
Dim cmd As New ADODB.Command

cmd.CommandText = "DRILLTHROUGH SELECT FROM Sales2 WHERE
([Time].[2001], [Store].[Tacoma], [Product].[Household])"
cmd.ActiveConnection = cn
Set rs = cmd.Execute

Dim AllDone As Boolean

While Not AllDone

    While Not rs.EOF
        'Do something with record
        rs.MoveNext
    Wend

    ' If "rs Is Nothing" below generates an exception, try this
instead:
    If rs.AbsolutePage = adPosEOF Then
        AllDone = True
    Else
        Set rs = rs.NextRecordset
    End If

    ' Ideally, this works
    'If rs Is Nothing Then
    '     AllDone = True
    'End If

Wend
```

Figure 9.3 VB Code that executes a drill-through and loops through the resulting rowsets.

If you want to only deliver one partition's drill-through rows to the client, you can use the FIRSTROWSET clause of the drill-through query. For example, the following query fragment sets up a result from only the second partition of the query:

```
DRILLTHROUGH
FIRSTROWSET 2
SELECT ...
```

However, effective use of this option requires the knowledge of how many rowsets you might have returned, which is not directly provided through any interface, and there is no guarantee that we know of as far as what the order of returned partition rowsets will be. You will always be able to retrieve FIRSTROWSET 1 because at least one rowset will be returned. A client could iterate through increasingly higher numbers until no rowset was returned.

MDX for Drill-Through

As we described earlier, a drill-through query in MDX is any query that returns a single cell, does not use any calculated members, and begins with DRILLTHROUGH. The general form is

```
DRILLTHROUGH
[FIRSTROWSET N]
[MAXROWS N]
SELECT
...
FROM Cube
[WHERE ...]
```

It does not matter at all how dimensions map to query axes or to the slicer.

The FIRSTROWSET option is followed by a positive integer and specifies the relative partition from which the drill-through rows will be obtained. For example, FIRSTROWSET 1 indicates to return rows from the first partition that contributes to the drill-through cell; FIRSTROWSET 2 indicates to return rows from the second partition, and so on.

The MAXROWS option is followed by a positive integer and specifies the maximum number of records to retrieve from each partition. Note that you do not get the opportunity to specify an ordering for the records, so the set returned will be essentially arbitrary. If the underlying OLE DB provider does not support the DBPROP_MAXROWS property, then this value is ignored. There is no way to limit the number of overall rows returned, except by combining this with the FIRSTROWSET option.

Although you cannot reference calculated members, you can reference items from named sets in the query. For example, if a client application had created a set [Customer Set] as {[Customer].[Cust 007], [Customer].[Cust M]}, then the following would be perfectly valid:

```
DRILLTHROUGH
SELECT
FROM [Purchases]
WHERE ([Customer Set].Item (0))
```

Note that no WITH clause is available in a drill-through query, so you cannot define sets in the context of the query.

Using Actions

Actions is a feature that allows a string to be generated by the analysis system along with a suggestion as to how it should be used by a client application. This allows the developer of the analysis system to include application functionality that a relatively generic client can invoke. An application developer can also include functionality that is very specific their application alone. They are sort of like a stored procedure that is limited to returning a string. Like a calculated member, every action is defined against a particular cube. The string that the action returns can be the result of any MDX string expression that can be invoked against the cube. The action can also be directed against some context in the cube: the entire cube, a dimension, a level, a member of a dimension, a cell within the cube, or a set defined for the cube.

The main part of an action is simply a string expression, expressed in MDX. Any MDX expression that results in a string can be used, which includes simple operators and functions that return strings and any combinations that result in strings as well. The result is a single string, as if it were the result of calculating a single cell in a query.

Somewhat surprisingly, only a little language aspect is used to invoke an action; they are not invoked like MDX commands and queries are. Mostly, invoking an action requires a client application to prepare a data structure and use it as a means of restricting the rows. In OLE DB, you prepare a set of restrictions on the schema rowset for actions (a table interface used to retrieve meta data). In ADO MD, you prepare an array of restriction values for the Actions schema recordset. One of the restrictions is the context for the action, which can be a string identifying a dimension, a level, a member, a tuple, or a set name. (When you define an action to use on a set, note that the set name must be passed in when obtaining the action string. You cannot pass in a set expression instead of a set name.) We'll look at Visual Basic code for invoking actions using ADO MD later in this section. (We won't elaborate on OLE DB for OLAP programming. If you are familiar with OLE DB and a suitable language like C++, the techniques for invoking actions using OLE DB for OLAP are quite similar.)

What Can You Do with an Action?

The strings returned by the execution of an action can be interpreted in a variety of ways. The point, however, is to try to use some result from the analysis system to influence the world outside of itself, beyond just contributing a number to a graph or spreadsheet. An action type associated with each action indicates to a client application how to treat the result string. Following the OLE DB for OLAP 2.0 specification, Table 9.1 lists the types of action types supported by Analysis Services 2000.

Two of the predefined action types are connected with Web usage. The first, URL, results in a string that should be suitable for use as a browser's URL. For example, it could be the name of a Web page, or the URL of an ASP or CGI script adorned with one or more arguments to the script. For example, the expression

```
"http://www.dsslab.com/search.dll?" + Product.CurrentMember.Properties
("SKU ID")
```

will concatenate the URL of the search DLL with the SKU ID property associated with the product context's member, perhaps producing the following as a result:

```
http://www.dsslab.com/search.dll?WUY3391
```

The second type, HTML, provides interesting possibilities. For example, an action directed against a set can build an HTML table of member names and default cell values (identified through the default members of all other dimensions) with the following:

```
"<HTML><TABLE>" +
"<TR><TD>Name</TD><TD>Value</TD></TR>" +
"<TR><TD>" +
Generate (
  ActionParameterSet,
  ActionParameterSet.Current.Item(0).Properties ("Caption") +
    "</TD><TD>" +
    iif (Not IsEmpty ([Measures].CurrentMember),
      CStr ([Measures].CurrentMember),
      ""
    )
  , "</TD></TR><TR><TD>"
) +
"</TD></TR></TABLE></HTML>"
```

This uses the string version of Generate( ) to emit rows of the table; for each row, a column of member captions (appropriately localized, if set up in the database!) and associated value is produced. We use the [Measures].Current-Member.Value as a proxy for "current cell;" current cell has no syntax so we simply reference the current member of one of the cube's dimensions, and

Table 9.1   Action Types Supported by Analysis Services 2000

CODE	MEANING
URL	The resulting string is a URL, preferably launched using an Internet browser.
HTML	The resulting string is HTML. The string should be rendered using an Internet browser, usually by saving it to a file first. A whole script may be executed as part of the generated HTML.
STATEMENT	The resulting string is a statement that needs to be executed in OLE DB or OLE DB for OLAP. In OLE DB, set the ICommand:SetText method of a command object to the string and call the ICommand:Execute method. In ADO, set the CommandText of a Command or Connection object and call Execute on it. If the command does not succeed, an error should be returned to the client application.
DATASET	The resulting string is a Multidimensional Expressions (MDX) query to execute. In OLE DB, set the ICommand:SetText method of a command object to the string and calling the ICommand:Execute method with a requested interface ID (IID) of IDataset. In ADO MD, set the CommandText of a Cellset object to the result text and open it. The client application should allow the user to browse or manipulate the returned data set.
ROWSET	Similar to DATASET. In OLE DB, instead of requesting an IID of IDataset, the client application should request IID of IRowset. In ADO, the result string should be used to set the CommandText of a Recordset object, and that Recordset should be opened against a connection. The client application should allow the user to browse or manipulate the returned rowset.
COMMANDLINE	The resulting string is a command line. The client application should execute it.
PROPRIETARY	The resulting string is meaningful to some other application. A client application should not display or execute the action unless it has specific knowledge of the specific action. A proprietary action is not returned to the client application unless the client application explicitly asks for it by setting the appropriate restriction on the application name.

every cube always has a dimension called Measures. Because CStr( ) will return an error if the underlying value is NULL, we test for the cell value being empty first and substitute an empty string if the cell is NULL. Note the use of the special set name ActionParameterSet. For an action that is targeted at sets, the name of the set to run it on may not be known when the action is created. ActionParameterSet is set to the contents of the set that the action is actually invoked on.

An example of code (in Visual Basic) that would invoke a set-scoped action and retrieves the resulting content is shown in Figure 9.4. It assumes that a cube named [Sales2] has a set called [Picked Customers] and an action called [Set Action], and it retrieves the action without regard to the invocation type or the action type. Note that none of the names in the restriction are enclosed by [ ]; if any of them were, the name would not be recognized and the action content would not be retrieved! This is a case where unique names should not be enclosed by [ ].

Three of the other types—STATEMENT, DATASET, and ROWSET—are geared for use with the client's OLE DB and OLE DB for OLAP connections. The result of an action of these types should be capable of being executed as a database query or command would be (for example, CREATE MEMBER, UPDATE CUBE, DRILLTHROUGH SELECT, and so on). The OLE DB for OLAP specification does not specify whether the command is to be presented as an OLAP command or a SQL command; in general, you should be cautious in your assumptions, and know what your client applications are going to do. A DATASET action is only useful against an OLE DB for OLAP or ADO MD con-

```
Dim cn As New ADODB.Connection
cn.ConnectionString = "Provider=MSOLAP;Data Source=localhost;Initial
Catalog=OLAP Database;"
cn.Open

Dim rs As ADODB.Recordset

Set rs = cn.OpenSchema(adSchemaActions, Array( _
    Empty _
  , Empty _
  , "Sales2" _
  , "Set Action" _
  , Empty _
  , "Picked Customers" _
  , 5 _
  ))

Dim sResult as String
If Not rs.EOF Then
    ' Get the action text
    sResult = rs.CONTENT
End If
```

Figure 9.4 Code to retrieve a set action's results.

nection, but a ROWSET or STATEMENT might be useful against a relational OLE DB or ADO connection as well.

The COMMANDLINE action type indicates that the client should execute the returned string as an operating system command line. Use of this type may require you to be aware of the operating system that your clients are running and applications that they have installed.

Actions whose type is PROPRIETARY are meant to be executed by a particular client program. In order to execute a proprietary action, a client must fill the name of the application into the APPLICATION_NAME restriction that is passed to the OLE DB schema rowset or ADO MD recordset. Third-party browser tools may publish specifications for actions that they will accept, and in addition you can define your own. If you are developing a client that may use proprietary actions, take care to create an application name that is unlikely to collide with anyone else's. Incorporating your company name ("DSS Lab.Special Browser") increases the odds of uniqueness, and using the string form of a GUID virtually ensures uniqueness along with the potential of factoring action functionality by the GUIDs of objects that know how to interpret the action.

One class of very useful actions requires that the statements be presented to an RDBMS connection. An MDX query could result in a set of rows, and using a statement such as

```
INSERT INTO MyTable
SELECT * FROM OpenQuery (
  OurOLAPServer,
  'SELECT
  { [Measures].[Calculated Potential] } on columns,
  { [Current Customer Set] } on rows
  FROM PredictionCube'
)
```

Web Server Security Note for COMMANDLINE Actions

If you are providing a Web interface to OLAP and are running the PivotTable Service on the Web server, you should very carefully evaluate how you run actions of COMMANDLINE type, if you do at all. Actions are useful in the context of a Web server, as the logic of the action remains on the server. However, executing a command line on the server raises significant security concerns. If a client of the Web server (for example, a browser) can pass MDX to be executed, they can pass a CREATE ACTION statement to the server that creates a COMMANDLINE action, and then request execution of the action.

could transfer data calculated or filtered by the OLAP system into a table for use in preparing a mailing list in the RDBMS. However, the overall statement would need to be presented to an RDBMS connection. This could be addressed by using the Proprietary action type instead, although for more than one commercial client to support this the related application name would need to indicate that RDBMS statements are the purpose of this action.

Targets for Actions

Each action can be targeted against a different region or element of a cube as in Table 9.2.

When an action is invoked, the context for the action starts with all dimensions at their default members. If the scope of the action is Member or Cell, then the member(s) provided as the argument to the action will alter this default context. For example, in a typical cube, the default member for every non-measures dimension is the All member, and the default measure is the first one

Table 9.2 Action Types

SCOPE OF ACTION	APPLICATION
Cube	Actions that are global to a cube (not to be parameterized).
Dimension	Actions that apply across a dimension, but are not defined specifically for any member(s) or level(s) within it. The dimension is supplied when the action is invoked.
Level	Actions that apply to an entire level of a dimension, but are not defined specifically for any member in that dimension. The dimension and level are supplied when the action is invoked.
Member	Actions that apply to a specific member of a dimension or a level of a dimension. The dimension and member are supplied when the action is invoked.
Cell	Actions that apply to a specific cell. One or more members that define the cell are supplied when the action is invoked (the remaining dimensions are set to their default members for the user role invoking the action).
Set	Actions that apply to a named set. The name of the set is supplied when the action is invoked. In order to allow the action to be generic with respect to the actual set, the name *ActionParameterSet* is used in the action expression to refer to the set that is the argument.

listed in the cube definition. A cube-scoped action that returned a constant string would be independent of any members, whereas a cube-scoped action defined by

```
Time.CurrentMember.UniqueName + ": " + CStr
(Measures.CurrentMember.Value)
```

would return a string like [Time].[All Time]: 948235350. If the same expression were used for a cell-scoped action and it was invoked with a coordinate of ([Time].[Quarter].[Q3, 2000], [Measures].[Profit], [Department].[Clothing]), then the string returned might be [Time].[Quarter].[Q3, 2000]: −2123.95.

Defining an Action

Actions are defined using MDX CREATE ACTION statements. Ordinarily, actions are defined in DSO Command objects at the server and downloaded to the PivotTable Service when the cube or cube role is accessed for the first time. However, you can also issue CREATE ACTION commands from within the PivotTable Service and then invoke them.

The general form of a CREATE ACTION statement is

```
CREATE ACTION CubeName.ActionName FOR Target
AS 'MDXExpression'
[, TYPE = 'ActionType']
[, INVOCATION = 'ActionInvocation']
[, APPLICATION = 'ApplicationName']
[, DESCRIPTION = 'Description']
[, CAPTION = '<MDX expression>']
```

Or, using the ALTER CUBE syntax:

```
ALTER CUBE CubeName
  CREATE ACTION ActionName FOR Target
  AS 'MDXExpression'
  [, TYPE = 'ActionType']
  [, INVOCATION = 'ActionInvocation']
  [, APPLICATION = 'ApplicationName']
  [, DESCRIPTION = 'Description']
  [, CAPTION = '<MDX expression>']
```

If the CREATE ACTION statement is held in the Commands collection of a server-side cube or cube role, or it is in the COMMANDS section of a local cube definition, then you can use CURRENTCUBE in place of the cube name because the target is obvious.

The ActionName needs to be unique among the actions defined for that cube. The *Target* identifies the scope in which the action applies. The

MDXExpression is the MDX expression evaluated when the action is executed. The following list contains the options for the *Target*:

TARGET OPTIONS

CUBE

DimensionName [MEMBERS]

LevelName [MEMBERS]

CELLS

SET

The following list contains the kinds of actions that can be specified. If none is specified, then the default given to the action is PROPRIETARY.

ACTION TYPES

URL

HTML

STATEMENT

DATASET

ROWSET

COMMANDLINE

PROPRIETARY

The following list contains the types of invocations that can be specified. Although these names are suggestive, it is the responsibility of the client program to interpret and use these invocation types; nothing in Analysis Services actually executes all of the relevant actions on opening a cube or in batch, for example. The INTERACTIVE option is meant for designation actions in response to user gestures. If no option is specified, then the default given to the action is INTERACTIVE.

ACTION INVOCATIONS

INTERACTIVE

ON_OPEN

BATCH

The CAPTION is actually an MDX expression that is evaluated as the action's schema rowset is retrieved. This allows the displayed name of the action to reflect the coordinate that you pass in the restrictions as well as other data in the database. This is separate from the DESCRIPTION, which (if provided) should simply describe what the action is to do.

For example, the following statement creates a command-line action whose target is cells (tuples) in the Budgeting cube and whose intended invocation is batch. It specifies an executable file with the customer and time keys (as text) and the textual form of the identified cell as arguments. When viewed by a user interface, its displayed caption is generated from the time and customer as well, so a user might see its name as Mark projection current for Laredo, Wk 43 2000 instead of An Action:

```
CREATE ACTION [Budgeting].[An Action]
FOR CELLS
AS
'   "\\CentralServer\Processes\MarkCurrent.EXE " +
    Customers.CurrentMember.Properties ("KEY") + " " +
    Time.CurrentMember.Properties ("KEY") + " " +
    CStr (Measures.CurrentMember.Value)
'
, TYPE = 'COMMANDLINE'
, INVOCATION = 'BATCH'
, DESCRIPTION = 'Mark projections as current for this customer/time'
, CAPTION =
'"Mark projection current for " + Customers.CurrentMember.Properties
("CAPTION") + ", " Time.CurrentMember.Properties ("CAPTION")
'
/* possible result:

\\CentralServer\Processes\MarkCurrent.EXE TX_005 200143 65000.75

*/
```

Programmatic Aspects of Actions

In Figure 9.4, we saw an example of programming an action. We'll talk a little more about that now. In order to invoke an action (as well as to find out what actions are available to invoke in the first place), you need to restrict the Actions schema rowset. The lengthy Array( ) construct in Figure 9.4 contained a set of restrictions. Table 9.3 shows the set of restriction columns (also contained in the OLE DB for OLAP and Analysis Services documentation).

Something that is not provided in the ADO libraries but provided in the C++ header files with Analysis Services are the numerical codes for specifying action restrictions.

The codes for coordinate types are listed in Table 9.4.

The codes for action types are listed in Table 9.5. They can be ORed together or added together (except for the zero no-restriction value) to obtain multiple types of actions in the resulting rowset.

Table 9.3 Restriction Columns

COLUMN	REQUIRED/OPTIONAL	TYPE
CATALOG_NAME	Optional	String
SCHEMA_NAME	Optional	String
CUBE_NAME	Required	String
ACTION_NAME	Optional	String
ACTION_TYPE	Optional	Integer
COORDINATE	Required	String
COORDINATE_TYPE	Required	Integer
INVOCATION	Optional	Integer

Table 9.4 Target Scopes and Numerical Codes

COORDINATE TYPE	NUMERICAL CODE
CUBE	1
DIMENSION	2
LEVEL	3
MEMBER	4
SET	5
CELL	6

Table 9.5 Action Types and Numerical Codes

ACTION TYPE	NUMERICAL CODE
(no restriction)	0
URL	1
HTML	2
STATEMENT	4
DATASET	8
ROWSET	16
COMMANDLINE	32
PROPRIETARY	64

The codes for invocation types are listed in Table 9.6. We haven't discussed invocation types yet, but we will later on.

For example, the code in Figure 9.5 will retrieve all batch command-line actions for the tuple ([Time].[Week 43, 2001], [Customers].[Laredo, TX]) on the Budgeting cube and execute them (assuming that you trust them . . .).

Table 9.6 Invocation Types and Numerical Codes

INVOCATION TYPE	NUMERICAL CODE
(no restriction)	0
INTERACTIVE	1
ON_OPEN	2
BATCH	3

```
Dim cn As New ADODB.Connection
cn.ConnectionString = "Provider=MSOLAP;Data Source=localhost;Initial
Catalog=OLAP Database;"
cn.Open

Dim rs As ADODB.Recordset

Set rs = cn.OpenSchema(adSchemaActions, Array( _
     Empty _
   , Empty _
   , "Budgeting" _
   , Empty _
   , 32 _
   , "([Time].[Week 43, 2001], [Customers].[Laredo, TX])" _
   , 6
   , 3 _
   ))

Dim sResult as String
While Not rs.EOF
    ' Get the action text
    sResult = rs.CONTENT
    ' Execute it
    If 0 = Shell sResult, vbMinimizedFocus Then
          'Handle error
    End If
Wend
```

Figure 9.5 Example of more sophisticated action invocation.

Dropping an Action

Like other created objects, the client can drop actions at any time. Two variations on the syntax for this are

```
ALTER CUBE CubeName
   DROP ACTION ActionName

DROP ACTION CubeName.ActionName
```

Summary

This chapter has been devoted to two topics: understanding the MDX, and the essential programming required to use Microsoft's drill-through capability and OLE DB for OLAP/ADO MD actions. Drill-through queries are very simple MDX with great utility in exploring the underlying data. Actions can provide an end user with additional application functionality. Actions make use of MDX string expressions to provide their results, so understanding the MDX string functions available can be important. In the next chapter, we will change gears and look at MDX functions that affect the user dimension and cube environment.

CHAPTER 10

Changing the Cube and Dimension Environment through MDX

I n Analysis Services, it is possible to significantly alter the given cube environment through a client application. Some of the things that you can alter for a user's session regardless of the source of the cubes are

- Create a new virtual cube in your session

- Alter the default member for a dimension

- Refresh the cell data and dimension members

If the dimension has write-back enabled (which requires a server-based cube), you can

- Create a new member

- Drop a member

- Move a member within the hierarchy

- Update the custom member formula or member properties associated with the member

If a cube has write-back enabled, you can also update data cells within it, either programmatically or with the UPDATE CUBE statement.

These commands enable you to build applications, such as budgeting and forecasting, where end users can alter the database without being granted administrative access to the cubes or using DSO code to update the databases.

The result of each command in this last set of four is that the database and all-sessions connected to it immediately see the changes to the dimension structure, and the table that underlies the dimension is immediately updated. As a result, a certain amount of collaborative construction and analysis is supported.

Note that creating a new member in a write-back dimension is not the same as creating a new calculated member, and updating a member is not the same as altering the definition of a calculated member. These operations actually affect the underlying dimension table and cause the results to be visible to all users connected to their cubes, while calculated members do not exist in dimension tables and only really exist in the context of a user's own session. For the collaborative application, differences in solve order and execution order for calculated members and custom member formulas can be significant. We discuss these issues in Chapter 6, "The Many Ways to Calculate in Microsoft Analysis Services."

Creating a New Virtual Cube for Your Session

You can create a new virtual cube within your session. A session virtual cube (called a grouping cube in any error messages you encounter) is a limited form of a regular virtual cube. It is limited in that it can include dimensions and measures from one or more cubes, but it cannot include dimensions from other cubes, nor can it have levels of its dimensions disabled. Like a regular virtual cube, it can use data mining dimensions as well as regular dimensions. It can also hide dimensions and measures, and it can rename measures like a virtual cube does. Also like a regular virtual cube, it will not automatically incorporate any calculated members from its input cubes. (If you want to do that, you will need to use the EXPRESSION schema column that Analysis Services provides for members and measures, or otherwise gain access to the formulas that define calculated members in the input cubes.) One advantage over a regular virtual cube is that it can include one or more regular virtual cubes as its own input cubes.

The general syntax for creating a virtual cube in your session is

```
CREATE [SESSION] CUBE VCubeName
FROM Cube [, Cube ... ]
(
MEASURE Cube.MeasureName [ HIDDEN ] [ AS MeasureName ]
    [ , MEASURE ... ]
```

```
, DIMENSION Cube.DimensionName [ HIDDEN ]
   [ , DIMENSION ... ]
)
```

Unlike the CREATE CUBE statement that builds local cube files, you cannot specify MDX commands in this statement, nor can you control the levels, member properties, or member ordering in the dimensions or functions or formatting of the measures.

For example, imagine that you have a manufacturing cube named [Process-Cost] and a sales cube named [Sales], and you want to create a cube named [Profitability] that incorporates the [Product] and [Time] dimensions from each cube and the customer dimension that exists only in the [Sales] cube. The following statement would accomplish that:

```
CREATE CUBE Profitability
FROM [ProcessCost], [Sales]
(
  MEASURE [Sales].[Units] AS [Unit Sales]
  , MEASURE [Sales].[Dollar Sales]
  , MEASURE [Sales].[Rebate Offered]
  , MEASURE [ProcessCost].[Units] AS [Units Produced]
  , MEASURE [ProcessCost].[Dollars] AS [Dollar Cost]

// shared dimensions: doesn't matter whether from Sales or ProcessCost

  , DIMENSION [Sales].[Time]
  , DIMENSION [Sales].[Product]
  , DIMENSION [Sales].[Customer]
)
```

Although we will not go into the creation of data mining models in this book, you can also create session virtual cubes that incorporate mining dimensions from a mining model that you have built. The syntax for incorporating a mining dimension is

```
DIMENSION DimensionName  [ HIDDEN ] NOT_RELATED_TO_FACTS
FROM MiningModelName COLUMN MiningColumn
```

NOTE

The following command will drop a cube created by CREATE CUBE:
DROP CUBE *CubeName*

If the cube named in *CubeName* is a cube in a local cube file, it will be dropped from the file.

Altering the Default Member for a Dimension in Your Session

Every dimension in each cube has a default member, which is the member chosen when the dimension is not referenced in a query or by the *Dimension* .DefaultMember function. This default is chosen by the DBA or database designer and can be for the dimension as a whole, within the cube, or for the user's login role. However, this default can also be changed by MDX during the course of a session.

The general syntax to do this looks like the following:

```
ALTER CUBE Cube
    UPDATE DIMENSION Dimension, DEFAULT_MEMBER = 'MDX Rule'
```

The MDX rule can be any valid MDX expression that results in a single member of that dimension. It could be the name of a member, but it could also be the results of selecting an item from a named set, or the result of an external function. Whatever it is, it is evaluated right then; if it is an expression that relies on changing data, it will need to be re-evaluated to pick up the changes in the data.

For example, suppose the rule was 'Tail([Time].[Day].Members, 1).Item (0).Item(0)', which will pick up the last day defined in the time dimension. An incremental update of the time dimension during the session might introduce a new last day that would be available in metadata, but the default member would not be changed until the ALTER CUBE statement was run again. Suppose you had an external function that returned the name of the time member to use. If the rule was 'StringToSet (ExternalDayNameFunction()).Item(0) .Item(0)', then this rule would be evaluated at the moment the ALTER CUBE statement was run, and once again, the default will not be changed until the ALTER CUBE statement is run again.

Dimension Writeback Operations

If your cube contains write-enabled dimensions, then you can use the following Microsoft-specific MDX commands to manipulate these dimensions. These commands each take effect immediately, regardless of the transaction isolation mode in effect for the session. They also commit immediately, unlike the UPDATE CUBE and cell write-back operations that require an OLE DB or ADO commit in order to take effect on the server. Although they are phrased as ALTER CUBE . . . , they affect the dimension in every cube that the dimension appears in, so they can affect many cubes at once.

Creating a New Member

To create a new member in a dimension, you can use the ALTER CUBE CRE-ATE DIMENSION MEMBER statement. The general syntax for this is

```
ALTER CUBE Cube
    CREATE DIMENSION MEMBER [ParentUniqueName.]MemberName
    [ AS 'MDXExpression' ] , KEY='KeyValue'
    [ PropertyName = 'PropertyValue' [, PropertyName = 'PropertyValue'
. . . ]]
```

The result of this command is that a new row is actually entered into the underlying dimension table.

The property names are database-defined member properties like [Manager Name] or [Reporting Units], not OLE DB member properties like FORMAT_STRING.

For example, given a parent-child dimension that is write-enabled, the following will add a new [Family Assistance] member under the [Human Resources] member, with a calculation that draws data from another cube:

```
ALTER CUBE IntegratedReporting
CREATE DIMENSION MEMBER [Accounts].[Net Cash].[Expenses].[Human
Resources].[Family Assistance]
AS
'LookupCube (
  "HumanDevelopment",
  "([Measures].[Expenses], " + Time.CurrentMember.UniqueName + ","
    + Geography.CurrentMember.UniqueName + ")"
)'
, KEY='175'
, [RollupColumn] = '+'
```

Moving a Member within Its Dimension

If a member already exists, but it needs to be moved, you can move it with the UPDATE CUBE MOVE DIMENSION MEMBER command. The general syntax of this command is

```
ALTER CUBE Cube
    MOVE DIMENSION MEMBER MemberUniqueName
[, SKIPPED_LEVELS = '<value>'] [WITH DESCENDANTS]
    UNDER MemberUniqueName
```

If you specify the WITH DESCENDANTS clause, then the entire subtree of members starting with the member and extending to the roots is moved under the new parent. Otherwise, the member alone is moved, and the member's children immediately prior to the command's execution become the children of the member's original parent (or root members if it was a top-level member). The effect of the operation on the underlying dimension table is simply to alter the values of the parent key column for the row that defined the member, and possibly for the rows that defined its immediate children. The new parent key is that of the member listed in *MemberUniqueName*. If the SKIPPED_LEVELS clause is used, then the member is effectively placed that many hierarchical steps below the parent member, so that it will appear in metadata requests for members at that deeper level from the parent or root.

Note that this does not always provide a good means to make the member a root member. If the dimension does not have a database-defined all level, there is no way that this member can become a child member of anything and be a root member. You can, of course, work around this by moving the member under a dummy member and then deleting the dummy.

Dropping a Member

You can delete a member from the dimension by using the UPDATE CUBE DROP MEMBER command. The general syntax for the command is

```
ALTER CUBE Cube
    DROP DIMENSION MEMBER MemberUniqueName
    [WITH DESCENDANTS]
```

This simply deletes the member and the corresponding row in the dimension table. If the WITH DESCENDANTS clause is included, then all descendants (and their dimension table rows) are also deleted. If the WITH DESCENDANTS clause is omitted, then the children of the member become the children of the member's parent. If the member being dropped is a root member and WITH DESCENDANTS is omitted, then the member's children become root members.

NOTE
This command does not drop a calculated member. Use the DROP MEMBER command instead.

Updating a Member's Definition

You can also update some aspects of a member's definition by using the UPDATE CUBE UPDATE DIMENSION MEMBER command. This command enables you to alter the custom member formula associated with the member and one or more property values as well. The general syntax for the command is

```
ALTER CUBE Cube
    UPDATE DIMENSION MEMBER MemberUniqueName
[ AS 'MDXExpression' ] [ , Property = 'Value' [, Property = '<value>'
. . . ]]
```

or simply (no *MDXExpression*)

```
ALTER CUBE Cube
    UPDATE DIMENSION MEMBER MemberUniqueName
    Property = 'Value' [ , Property = 'Value'  . . . ]
```

The definition of the calculated member formula and/or member property values are updated in the OLAP database and also in the underlying dimension table.

Although the second variant (without the *MDXExpression*) is documented by Microsoft, in the RTM version, the first variant works with an empty expression. For example, the following will alter the rollup operator associated with our member to subtraction ("−"):

```
ALTER CUBE IntegratedReporting
UPDATE DIMENSION MEMBER [Accounts].[Net Cash].[Expenses].[Human
Resources].[Family Assistance]
  , [RollupColumn] = '+'
```

NOTE This command does not alter the formula for a calculated member. In order to do that, you will need to drop the calculated member and then re-create it.

Refresh Cell Data and Dimension Members

During the course of a client session, it is possible for data to be updated at the server. These updates can include new members appearing, cell data changing, member property values changing, and in some cases, members being deleted or renamed as well. Ordinarily, after some time lag, the PivotTable Service component will detect these changes and begin to provide the new or altered members and data to new queries. However, depending on connection settings, the time it takes for these to appear may be too long. It will always be possible for a client to refresh its data with the REFRESH CUBE command. The general syntax for refreshing a cube is as follows:

```
REFRESH CUBE CubeName
```

For example, the following command will refresh the Sales cube:

```
REFRESH CUBE [Sales]
```

Note that only one cube at a time can be updated with this command. Also, although the members of dimensions may have changed, any named sets defined on the Sales cube will not be updated.

When a client is connected to a local cube file as opposed to a server-based cube, the REFRESH CUBE command will cause the cube contents to be re-built from its definition and tables. (Local cube files are discussed in Chapter 13, "Working with Local Cubes").

Writing Data Back to the Cube

Writing data back to the cube (assuming that the cube has been write-enabled) can be done in two ways. One way (supported by standard OLE DB for OLAP) is through data structures, while the other way uses Microsoft's UPDATE CUBE statement. We'll talk about both of these here, although we will discuss UPDATE CUBE in much greater detail. UPDATE CUBE can be used in place of the standard write-back facility as well.

Standard Cell Write-Back

The standard cell write-back capability involves programmatically changing the data value for a cell that has already been retrieved from the database. This requires that a query has already been formulated to produce the cell. From OLE DB for OLAP, when the results of the query are requested into a range rowset (via IMDRangeRowset:GetRangeRowset), it is possible for the cells to be updated by obtaining an IRowsetChange interface on the range rowset and altering the cell values as though they were updatable fields in a relational database. The details for this are covered pretty well in the OLE DB for OLAP documentation. Through ADO MD, after retrieving the results of a query into a Cellset object, you can update a cell value by simply assigning a new data value to the cell. You must remember two important details about Microsoft's Analysis Services:

- Only leaf-level cells of a cube can be updated by writing back to the data structures. This means that no cell for a calculated member can be updated. If the cells are not leaf cells in a regular cube, they cannot be written back to. For a virtual cube, if a regular cube does not expose all of its dimensions to the virtual cube, there is no way to write back to the underlying regular cube because no query can retrieve its leaf-level cells through the virtual cube. However, if a cell in a virtual cube is a leaf-level cell in the underlying regular cube, it may be written back to.

- Only the Value column (or ADO MD .Value property of the Cellset object) can be written to. Formatted_Value and the other cell properties cannot be written to.

In ADO MD, the following snippet of VB code updates the cell:

```
Dim ResultCS As ADOMD.CellSet
Dim cmd AS ADODB.Command

Set ResultCS = cmd.Execute ("SELECT  . . . ")

ResultCS (1, 1) = 45    ' update cell 1,1 with the value 45
```

Commit and Rollback

Note that updating cell data in the actual database will always involve programming in addition to using MDX. Cell updates are controlled via OLE DB transactions. When you update cell data through the techniques described in this section, you initially update data held in the session cache. This enables you to perform a variety of what-if calculations. (You cannot drop the results of a particular update; if you want to "roll back" a particular what-if, you need to remember what the change was and apply its opposite. You can roll back all uncommitted changes issued so far, however.) If you want to update the shared database so that your database will persist the results and all users can see your changes, then you need to programmatically commit the work. Through OLE DB, you will use IRowsetUpdate:Update( ), and in ADO MD, you will use the ADODB's Connection.CommitTrans method to commit all updates for the connection. Similarly, you can also use IRowsetUpdate:Undo( ) and Connection. RollbackTrans to undo changes.

When a transaction is committed in Microsoft Analysis Services, all accumulated deltas for changed cells are written to the writeback table. If a cell has been changed more than once, only one row is entered into the writeback table that contains the sum of all deltas.

The Microsoft documentation states that Analysis Services automatically begins a transaction when another transaction commits or rolls back. We have found that the automatic transaction will commit but not roll back. You can issue an ADO Connection.BeginTrans call to explicitly start a transaction, and then rollback will recognize that there is a pending transaction.

Using UPDATE CUBE

Microsoft's UPDATE CUBE extension to MDX provides a couple of enhance-ments over the standard cell update mechanism. Functionally, it enables aggre-gate cells to be updated and provides a set of options for allocating data to leaf-level cells. It also provides a language-based interface which makes the description of the task to perform easier than lower-level programming, which requires opening a query and programmatically placing new data into the cell data structures returned by the query. As with standard write-back, cells asso-ciated with calculated members cannot be updated. Also, the measure associ-ated with the cell must be aggregated by SUM.

NOTE
━━━━ Updating a cell associated with a member from a level-based dimension actually causes the associated leaf cells to be updated via one of four allocation functions. This is true even for parents in parent-child dimensions where non-leaf data may be entered from underlying fact tables, unless you use the .DataMember function to specify that data should be written back for the parent only.

When Analysis Services executes an UPDATE CUBE statement, it first deter-mines the set of leaf-level cells that will be affected by the update, and then it calculates new values or deltas for them. The outcome will be that the updated cell will have the value specified by the UPDATE CUBE command, but when multiple cells contribute to the aggregated cell, the values in those cells may change in different ways. We will describe the allocation methods in the course of describing the syntax.

The general syntax for the UPDATE CUBE command is as follows:

```
UPDATE [CUBE] CubeName
SET tuple [.VALUE] = New_aggregate_value
[ USE_EQUAL_ALLOCATION |
  USE_EQUAL_INCREMENT |
  USE_WEIGHTED_ALLOCATION [BY Weight_value_expression ] |
  USE_WEIGHTED_INCREMENT [BY Weight_value_expression ]
]
```

The *tuple* must be specified by naming members. For example, ([Platform].[Bering 0244], [Q3 2002]) is a valid tuple specification. You cannot use an expression to construct the tuple. For example, Set1.Item(0) cannot be used as a tuple specification. If a dimension in the cube does not have a mem-ber listed in the tuple, the current default member for that dimension is used. Notice that no quotes are around either the *New_aggregate_value* or the *weight_value_expression*.

NOTE
You cannot use any member of a virtual dimension in an UPDATE CUBE command except the All member. Analysis Services will generate an error if you attempt to. This means that you must ensure that only non-virtual dimensions are incorporated into the tuple specification.

Four different allocation methods are available:

1. **USE_EQUAL_ALLOCATION**. Every leaf-level cell contributing to the updated cell will be assigned the same value. *New leaf cell value = New_aggregate_value*/Count (*leaf cells related to aggregate cell*)

2. **USE_EQUAL_INCREMENT**. Every leaf-level cell contributing to the updated cell will be changed by the same increment: *New leaf cell value = Original leaf cell value + (New_aggregate_value - Original aggregate value)*/Count(*leaf cells related to aggregate cell*)

3. **USE_WEIGHTED_ALLOCATION**. Every leaf-level cell contributing to the updated cell will be assigned the same value. *New leaf cell value = New_aggregate_value * Weight value expression*

4. **USE_WEIGHTED_INCREMENT**. Every atomic cell contributing to the updated cell will be changed by an individual increment. *New leaf cell value = Original leaf cell value + (New_aggregate_value - Original aggregate value) * Weight value expression*

If the *Weight_value_expression* is not provided, the following expression is assigned to it by default:

```
Original leaf cell value/Original aggregate cell value
```

Regardless, you should ensure that the *weight_value_expression* evaluates to a number between 0 and 1 per cell. If the sum of all the leaf-level cell evaluations is 1, then the sum of the leaf cells after the UPDATE CUBE has been executed will be *New_aggregate_value*. However, if the sum of all the leaf-level cell evaluations for *weight_value_expression* is not 1, then the result of the UPDATE CUBE will be that the cell specified will have a value proportionately greater than or less than *New_aggregate_value*. Generally speaking, you will use a *weight_value_expression* that generates a ratio of some measures across multiple levels in one or more dimensions, which will guarantee that the sum of the weights is 1. Remember, the calculations in weight_value_expression can be influenced by cell calculations, custom member formulas, and all other techniques of calculating available when executing an expression.

The USE_EQUAL _ALLOCATION and USE_EQUAL_INCREMENT methods guarantee that each of the associated leaf cells ends up with a value. If some of the cells were empty prior to the UPDATE CUBE command, they will have appropriate data values afterwards. Cells that contained data values prior to the execution of the command will be adjusted.

NOTE

Because USE_EQUAL_ALLOCATION and USE_EQUAL_INCREMENT ultimately assign a data value to every leaf-level cell associated with the aggregate cell, assigning a cell with many associated leaf cells can consume a great deal of memory and take substantial time.

The USE_WEIGHTED_ALLOCATION and USE_WEIGHTED_INCREMENT methods increment data values for cells that already have data. For related leaf-level cells that are empty, they do not create new cells, unless all of the cells related to the aggregate cell are empty. If that is the case, the first cell (the cell related to the first leaf descendant in database ordering along each of the dimensions) related to the aggregate cell is assigned the entire *New_aggregate_value.*

Each of these allocation options can be useful for different purposes in budgeting and forecasting applications. For example, when leaf-level cells already contribute different quantities to an aggregate cell, USE_EQUAL_INCREMENT preserves the absolute differences between the cells (albeit changing empties into non-empty cells), while USE_WEIGHTED_INCREMENT can be used to maintain their proportional differences while not assigning values to empty cells.

For example, the following statement updates the month-level, store-level, and Provision-VAT account cells related to Q2-2002 and Austria, incrementing the current values by the ratio of the related store-month estimated sales:

```
UPDATE CUBE [Transfer Budget]
SET (
    [Time].[Q2-2002]
  , [Operating Unit].[Austria]
  , [Account].[Provision-VAT]
) = 65000
USE_WEIGHTED_INCREMENT BY
   [Account].[Est Sales]
   / ([Operating Unit].[Austria], [Time].[Q2-2002], [Account].[Est
Sales])
```

If the [Account].[Provision-VAT] member is itself a parent member, the previous expression would write back to each of its leaf-level descendants as well. To avoid that and have the values calculated and written back to the [Account].[Provision-VAT] member itself, use the following:

```
UPDATE CUBE [Transfer Budget]
SET (
    [Time].[Q2-2002]
  , [Operating Unit].[Austria]
  , [Account].[Provision-VAT].DataMember
) = 65000
USE_WEIGHTED_INCREMENT BY
   [Account].[Est Sales]
   / ([Operating Unit].[Austria], [Time].[Q2-2002], [Account]. [Est
Sales])
```

Summary

The commands that we have covered in this chapter are useful for a number of applications. In particular, the virtual cube version of CREATE CUBE and the ALTER CUBE UPDATE DIMENSION can be used by any application to adjust the cubes and dimensions provided by the DBA. The other commands that we have discussed are important pieces of interactive budgeting and collaborative analysis applications. These commands complement the queries and calculations that we have covered in the first six chapters. In the next chapter, we will look more specifically at MDX in cube and dimension design.

CHAPTER 11

Advanced Applications in Cube Design

I n this chapter, we consider some of the MDX topics that a database designer may need to deal with when constructing dimensions and cubes. This includes time analysis "utility" dimensions, the design of virtual cubes in general, the design of cubes that integrate two or more versions of the same (or similar) dimensions. In the preface, we stated that "awesome MDX can overcome awkward cube designs." Although the design of an OLAP system in Microsoft Analysis Services is usually clean, a few aspects of cube design can be awkward. In this chapter, we provide some pointers to simple solutions within your application, as well as illuminate techniques that you can apply to different situations.

NOTE We discuss a number of techniques for designing virtual cubes in this chapter. The database designer can use these techniques when creating virtual cubes at the server. To the degree that supporting meta data (cubes, dimensions, and member properties) exist in the database, these techniques can also be applied to virtual cubes created on the fly by the CREATE CUBE DDL statement. See Chapter 10, "Changing the Cube and Dimension Environment through MDX," for more details on how to create these cubes.

Time Analysis Utility Dimensions

One fairly common design theme is to provide multiple types of time-series analysis for multiple periodicities in time. For example, an application may need to support queries for year-to-date sums, rolling 12-month or rolling 52-week averages, period-to-year-ago difference, and period-to-period difference. At least in Microsoft OLAP/Analysis Services, a very clean way to support these is to introduce a periodicity dimension into a database. This dimension will have one regular member (let's call it [Current]) to which all measured data is related, and a set of calculated members. One calculated member will have a formula for year-to-date sum at the [Current] member, another will have period-to-year ago percentage at the [Current] member, and so on. (At least some of the members in this dimension cannot be regular members with custom formulas because solve order cannot be controlled in custom formulas.) In this scenario, if you want the end user to be able to select a set of customers and see the period-to-year-ago percent change in total sales for them, you need to be able to set the solve order of the sum to be less than the solve order of the percent-change member. Meanwhile, another query for the rolling 12-month average of [Units] and [Average Sales Price] will want the 12-month average calculation to either have a higher or lower solve order than the [Average Sales Price] calculation, but in either case to have a higher solve order than the sum of the customers picked in the query.

For example, the MDX to create the Period-To-Period Pct Diff member and the Year-To-Date Total member would look like the following:

```
CREATE MEMBER CURRENTCUBE.[Periodicity].[Period-To-Period Pct Diff] AS
'([Periodicity].[Current] /
  ([Periodicity].[Current], [Time].CurrentMember.PrevMember)) - 1'
, SOLVE_ORDER = 20, FORMAT_STRING = '0.0%'

CREATE MEMBER CURRENTCUBE.[Periodicity].[Year-To-Date Total] AS
'Sum(
  PeriodsToDate (
    [Time].[Year],
    [Time].CurrentMember
  ),
  [Periodicity].[Current]
)'
, SOLVE_ORDER = 3, FORMAT_STRING = '0.0%'
```

Note that each of these formulas references the one regular member named [Periodicity].[Current]. That is the member at which the data to be operated on exists, and without that reference we would end up with infinite recursion in the Periodicity dimension. Given the periodicity dimension that we have just described, to retrieve the year-to-date aggregate for any particular time member, you just retrieve that time member and the year-to-date periodicity. If you want to see year-to-date and period-to-year-ago percent change, you just retrieve both of those periodicity members.

Multiple Time Hierarchies

You may need to support time-series analysis in cubes that use more than one time hierarchy. For example, year-to-date totals and period-to-period variance may be calculated in the fiscal, operational, and calendar hierarchies. In Microsoft Analysis Services, each hierarchy is implemented as a separate dimension, and there is no one "time dimension." Of course, users won't understand this, they just want to see time-series functions. We can make them work, but we need to add a little more MDX.

Consider how multiple time hierarchies are used. It is unlikely that a user will be analyzing data along more than one time hierarchy in any report. (In what cases would a cross-tab of fiscal time and calendar time be meaningful?) So, we can look at which time hierarchy-dimension is being analyzed along, and choose the appropriate dimension within which to do our member referencing. We can determine the hierarchy-dimension by looking at the level; if the level is below the top, then it must be this dimension. (For this reason, we suggest adding an All level to time dimensions.) Assume that there are now two time dimensions: Time.ByFiscal and Time.ByCalendar. We can modify our two earlier time analysis utility calculations to accommodate these as follows:

```
CREATE MEMBER CURRENTCUBE.[Periodicity].[Period-To-Period Pct Diff] AS
'iif (
  [Time].[ByFiscal].CurrentMember.Level.Ordinal > 0,
  ([Periodicity].[Current] / ([Periodicity].[Current],
              [Time].[ByFiscal].CurrentMember.PrevMember))
    - 1,
  ([Periodicity].[Current] / ([Periodicity].[Current],
              [Time].[ByCalendar].CurrentMember.PrevMember))
    - 1,
, SOLVE_ORDER = 20, FORMAT_STRING = '0.0%'

CREATE MEMBER CURRENTCUBE.[Periodicity].[Year-To-Date Total] AS
'iif (
  [Time].[ByFiscal].CurrentMember.Level.Ordinal > 0,
  Sum(
    PeriodsToDate (
      [Time].[ByFiscal].[Year],
      [Time].[ByFiscal].CurrentMember
    ),
    [Periodicity].[Current]
```

```
  ),
  Sum(
    PeriodsToDate (
      [Time].[ByCalendar].[Year],
      [Time].[ByCalendar].CurrentMember
    ),
    [Periodicity].[Current]
  ),
)'
, SOLVE_ORDER = 3, FORMAT_STRING = '0.0%'
```

If we had more than these two time hierarchies, we would add more nested iif( ) conditions to determine which hierarchy-dimension had a current member's level below the top.

Constructing Virtual Cubes: Integrating Similar Measures across Common Dimensions

Virtual cubes are an important mechanism for solving a variety of cube construction issues in Microsoft OLAP Services. Whether a cube is real (instantiated) or virtual, when an end user connects to that cube and begins navigating within it, the conceptual model that we frequently want to support is that of a set of measures organized by common dimensions. For a regular cube this model is automatic, but for virtual cubes this model requires additional effort. The reason for this is that all the measures for each base cube that forms an input to the virtual cube are placed in parallel, even if the base cubes have exactly the same dimensions. They can join along every dimension but the measures, and we would like to have them appear to join on the measures as well.

For example, consider a virtual cube for budget analysis that is based on two regular cubes, one holding actual data and another holding budget data. Each of the regular cubes is associated with one slice of a Scenario dimension, so the budget analysis cube may use the Scenario dimension. Each of these cubes has identical dimensionality: time, geography, products, customers, and sales channels. Each of the cubes also has identical measures: units, sales, direct costs, and indirect costs. However, when the cubes are combined in the virtual budget analysis cube, two of every measure is present: two sales measures, two units measures, and so on. An MDS of the applicability ranges for the measures is shown in Figure 11.1a, and a sample report that compares actual to budget sales for a set of stores and months is shown in Figure 11.1b. As you can see, the display leaves something to be desired in terms of easy comprehensibility.

a) MDS of measure application ranges

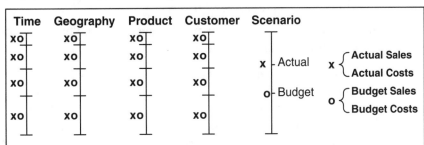

b) Query result for actual and budget sales

		1995		1996	
		Act. Sales	Bud. Sales	Act. Sales	Bud. Sales
Northeast	Actual	125		160	
	Budget		160		150
Southwest	Actual	110		140	
	Budget		130		110

Figure 11.1 Applicability range of measures within virtual cube created from identically dimensioned regular cubes.

The duplication we see won't just create empty patches on a screen. Any inter-scenario calculations that are formed will need to involve not just different scenarios, but different, related measures as well. This is something that query builders (human and software) need to deal with over and over. The benefit of having a Scenario dimension is somewhat diminished if our measures are the major source of scenario identification. If we discard the Scenario dimension, we have lost important conceptual leverage over our scenario-based analysis.

We cannot get away from dealing with this in the database, but we can at least hide it under a layer so that end users and query builders alike deal with a cleaner dimensional model for the cube. We're going to create a set of integrating measures that mask the difference in applicability ranges for the original measures. To do this, we need to employ the following features and attributes in concert:

- Calculated measures
- Solve orders

- The Hidden property of a measure (Analysis Services 2000) or the IsInternal property (OLAP Services 7.0)
- The independence of a virtual cube's measure name from the corresponding base cube's measure name

The dimensionality of the cube is fine, and the members of all non-measures' dimensions are also all fine. It is just the relationships between measures that we wish to alter. What we want to achieve is a set of calculated measures that each represents a single measure (like Units Sold) rather than independent measures that represent Actual Units Sold and Budget Units Sold. When someone is using the base cubes, they will see names for certain measures and expect to see those names in the new cube as well.

We need to take care of a few details in setting up our cube before we get into the MDX. Our base cubes may each have measures with the same name. When we define the virtual cube, we can redefine the names of the measures to be different with each other, and to not collide with our desired name. For example, the Units Sold measure from the Actual cube can be named "Actual Units Sold" in the virtual cube, and the Units Sold measure from the budget cube can be named "Budget Units Sold." Also, we should set the Hidden property of each of these measures in the virtual cube to Yes through the Analysis Manager (IsInternal to Yes through the OLAP Manager in 7.0) so they do not appear in the meta data that a client can access. (They can still be used in queries and calculations; they will just have to be accessed by name.)

We then need to create a set of calculated measures, one for each measure duplicated in the base cubes. These calculated measures won't perform any calculations of note; they will just access the correct base measure for the particular Scenario member being accessed. For example, the Analysis Services formula for our calculated Units Sold measure would be as follows:

```
'iif (
  [Scenario].CurrentMember IS [Scenario].[Budget],
  [Measures].[Budget Units Sold],
  [Measures].[Actual Units Sold]
)'
```

Note that this uses the IS operator of Analysis Services, which is more efficient as well as more logical than the method of comparing the name of the Scenario member to "Budget" that standard MDX enables.

We could also have phrased this as a sum of the measures from the various cubes, as with

```
'Sum ({[Measures].[Actual Units Sold],
     [Measures].[Budget Units Sold]})'
```

If for any given scenario you either have Actual or Budget units but not both, then the numbers returned should be correct. However, OLAP/Analysis Services will need to query each base cube involved to create the sum. We exchange the overhead of the IS operator for the overhead of accessing both of the base cubes instead of only one or the other. We do not yet have benchmark results to tell us which is better, but we expect that using IS will perform better as the sizes of the cubes and the number of cubes involved grow.

Finally, we need to pay close attention to our solve orders. Most, if not all other calculations in this virtual cube that are generated by a client, will come after this range-masking calculation, so we probably want the solve order number associated with each of these calculated measures to be zero. We therefore want all other calculated members on any dimension to have a solve order number of at least one. As we noted in Chapter 5, "MDX Context and Execution," solve order numbers can range up to more than 2,000,000,000, so adopting a practice in which all client solve orders start at, say, 1,000 will give you plenty of solve order headroom for both server-defined and client-defined calculated members.

When we are done, we will be able to browse a logical space whose MDS looks like that shown in Figure 11.2a. This logical space results in reports that look like those shown in Figure 11.2b. The client no longer has to deal with empty spaces of measures when comparing actual to budget. Furthermore, the budget absolute and percentage difference from actual formulas now looks like this:

```
CREATE MEMBER [Budget Perf].[Scenario].[Budget Difference With Actual]
AS
'[Scenario].[Budget] - [Scenario].[Actual]'

CREATE MEMBER [Budget Perf].[Scenario].[Budget Percentage From Actual]
AS
'[Scenario].[Budget] / [Scenario].[Budget Difference With Actual]'
```

NOTE This technique in Analysis Services has one odd limitation. The RTM version requires that in a virtual cube, at least one base measure needs to be visible. This means that we can hide all but one of the individual scenario cube's measures, and hope that the extra measure doesn't confuse our users.

Redimensioning One or More Cubes

Sometimes, we need to present a more dimensional view of data than our tables and cubes originally contained. For example, a fact table may contain many

a) MDS of altered measure application ranges

Time	Geography	Product	Customer	Scenario	
xo	xo	xo	xo		x - Sales
xo	xo	xo	xo	xo – Actual	o - Costs
xo	xo	xo	xo	xo – Budget	
xo	xo	xo	xo		

b) Query result for actual and budget sales, costs, and differences between actual and budget

		1995		1996	
		Sales	Costs	Sales	Costs
Northeast	Actual	125	80	160	190
	Budget	160	90	150	180
	Difference	−35	−10	10	10
	Percentage	−0.22	−0.11	0.07	0.06
Southwest	Actual	110	90	140	120
	Budget	130	90	110	140
	Difference	−20	0	30	−20
	Percentage	−0.37	0	0.27	−0.07

Figure 11.2 Applicability range of combined measures within virtual cube and sample report view from it.

different columns, which correspond to a set of measures with different scenarios from a planning system. However, in order to cleanly integrate the cube with the rest of the environment, we want to treat this one set of cube measures as if they had two dimensions: Scenario and Measure. Or we may be trying to combine information from a cube that treats its measures as a regular dimension (as with an accounts dimension) and a cube that has its measures across a measures dimension. In both cases, we are trying to augment or alter the apparent dimensionality of the cubes. In each of these cases, we want to combine cube and dimension structural design with some MDX to present useful cubes to the end user. Along the way, we'll look at some additional virtual cube construction issues, such as adding dimensions to a virtual cube that aren't in its base cubes.

Let's start with the first case, where we want to break out a set of scenario measures in one cube into a scenario dimension and measures for analysis. For example, a [Planning] cube built directly from the planning fact table may have measures of Pessimistic Sales, Pessimistic Units, Expected Sales, Expected Units, Optimistic Sales, and Optimistic Units. We also have a [Sales] cube that contains our actual Sales and Units. (For simplicity's sake, let's assume that the two regular cubes have the same set of dimensions otherwise.) We'd like to present the user with the ability to do scenario analysis over Pessimistic, Expected, Optimistic, and Actual.

Of course, to do that, we will need a separate scenario dimension. In our RDBMS, we will need to provide a table that lists the scenario names, as shown in Figure 11.3. The Scenario dimension based on this table will have only one level (no All level).

As of this point in our design, neither [Planning] nor [Sales] contains this Scenario dimension, and yet we want to use it in our virtual cube that integrates the two cubes. The Analysis Manager interface won't let us put this dimension into the virtual cube, although the server will. This has three solutions: include it in one or both of the base cubes, use some DSO code to put this dimension into the virtual cube, and create a dummy cube with this scenario dimension and add that cube into the virtual cube. DSO programming is beyond the scope of this book, so we won't explore that now (although in practice that provides the cleanest conceptual solution). From a performance point of view, creating a dummy cube just to hide its measure(s) so as to sneak in a dimension seems awkward, especially because we have to add a dummy fact table with one row into the RDBMS to create this cube; however, it will provide the best overall performance without our custom programming. Because we don't need to alter the dimensionality and aggregation structure of either of the base cubes, it will be very small, and it will never be queried. So, we create a third cube named [Scenario Dummy] with a single measure [Dummy]. In the Analysis Manager, we can mark the [Scenario Dummy] cube itself as Hidden so that clients won't have to deal with it. (If we were going to perform this scenario analysis in the [Planning] cube, we would just have added the dimension there.)

Scenario_ID	Scenario_Name
101	Actual
102	Expected
103	Pessimistic
104	Optimistic

Figure 11.3 Table for Scenario members.

Now, we create our [Scenario Analysis] virtual cube from the [Planning], [Sales], and [Scenario Dummy] cube. We make sure that the [Dummy] measure is marked as hidden. Because we're only going to expose calculated members for Units and Sales, we also want to mark all of the measures from [Planning] and [Sales] as hidden. We also make sure that the names of the measures from the base cubes are in two clean parts: the name of the scenario and the name of the measure. For the measures that come from the sales cube, we add the Actual scenario name for consistency's sake.

At this point, we have a Scenario dimension with the member names "Actual," "Expected," "Optimistic," and "Pessimistic," We also have measures named "Actual Units," "Actual Sales," "Expected Sales," "Expected Units," and so on. Now, we can write some simple MDX to pick out the right measure based on the scenario. We can create our main [Units] and [Sales] members for the virtual cube with the following MDX:

```
CREATE MEMBER [Scenario Analysis].[Measures].[Units]
AS
'StrToTuple (
   "Measures.[" + Scenario.CurrentMember.Name + " Units]"
)', SOLVE_ORDER = 0

CREATE MEMBER [Scenario Analysis].[Measures].[Sales]
AS
'StrToTuple (
   "Measures.[" + Scenario.CurrentMember.Name + " Sales]"
)', SOLVE_ORDER = 0
```

Analyzing and Generalizing the Technique

This technique relies on the fact that in any MDX expression, you can both obtain the name of an object and convert a string into a reference to an object or to data. In this case, we're exploiting regularity between member names in one dimension and pieces of member names in another. You may also have worked in the past with planning or forecasting tables that listed data for each month in a separate column. This technique could also work with measures whose names are the same as members in the time dimension or in any other dimension. We can generalize this not only in terms of what dimension you are pivoting off of the columns, but also in terms of how many dimensions there are and how you obtain the names of the measures.

For example, you may have multiple related cubes that each contain non-additive facts for different levels of granularity in more than one dimension (by time and by market region, for example). For example, we may have [Mkt

Penetration Pct] for all products, quarters, and regions in one cube, all products, months, and counties in another cube, and so on. We'd like to make a single virtual cube that gives you an integrated view of all these different cubes, which really vary only by granularity. A virtual cube built by combining these cubes will give us sets of measures in the virtual cube that are different only in levels to which they refer for certain dimensions. For example, we'd have a [Quarter Region Mkt Penetration Pct] measure and a [Month County Penetration Pct]. (The product level is not necessary in the measure names, as the levels of product granularity are the same in each base cube.)

We can use our same general technique to pick out the right base cube measure based on the time and region level names. In this case, instead of using .CurrentMemeber.Name, we'll use .CurrentMember.Level.Name, and we'll combine them from both the time and region dimensions. This leads to the following expression:

```
StrToTuple (
  "[Measures].["
  + Time.CurrentMember.Level.Name + " "
  + Region.CurrentMember.Level.Name
  " Mkt Penetration Pct]"
)
```

Another thing we can generalize on is how we obtain the names of the measures. We have managed to keep things simple by matching the names of the measures to the names of the members or levels. If for some reason the names of the non-measures' members can't be part of the measure names, we can add a member property to the appropriate dimensions and fill its values with the appropriate part of the measure names. We could then use the .Properties( ) function to look up the piece of the name in StrToTuple( ):

```
'StrToTuple (
  "Measures.["
  + Scenario.CurrentMember.Properties ("Integration Name")
  + " Units]"
)', SOLVE_ORDER = 0
```

Integrating Similar Dimensions from Different Cubes

A cube may end up with multiple dimensions that are very similar to each other through a variety of ways, and you want to present the user with a single dimension for querying and analysis. For example, you may have a virtual cube that combines a linked cube with a local cube. In a linked cube, all dimensions are private dimensions. Even if your local cube uses shared dimensions built from the same dimension tables (for example, either replicated copies or the exact same tables from the same relational source), these dimensions will be treated as different. For example, if you combine a local cube built using the same time dimension as the linked cube's, the virtual cube that combines these two cubes will have two different time dimensions. To combine the measures and to perform any meaningful time-based analysis on the measures from the two base cubes, you will need to integrate the time dimensions somehow. (You may also need to integrate the other dimensions of the cubes, not just the time dimension.) This same issue can occur with any cube that has private dimensions, not just linked cubes.

Another case, which will occur less often but is still sometimes an issue, is trying to present users with a dimension that is the union of two different dimensions from other cubes. This may happen, for example, if you are using data provided by a syndicated data provider and you wish to integrate data provided by the syndicate with your own internal data. You may also be in a position where you are trying to provide integrated views of cube data before the underlying data marts themselves are integrated. Perhaps different departments have each created their own similar cubes, and you are tasked with presenting an integrated view. One of the advantages of using a platform like Microsoft Analysis Server is that you can use the OLAP layer to create a clean and integrated view of the underlying data, even if the underlying data mart(s) is not clean and integrated yet.

A separate but similar case occurs when you want to integrate members that exist in multiple hierarchy-dimensions within a regular or virtual cube. For example, simultaneous allocation down multiple hierarchies will require that, for a member on one of the hierarchies, its counterpart on another hierarchy can be located and referenced. We'll treat this in the next section.

The following issues arise: determining how the version(s) of the dimensions appear to the client, ensuring that the correct version is available, and constructing appropriate references to measures so that the resulting virtual cube is coherent to a client application.

Multiple Versions of the Same Dimension

In the case of integrating multiple versions of the same dimension, you will need to decide how many different versions of the dimension a client application will need to see and what those versions (or that version) should be. If they need to see more than one, you may not have to do much integrating work at all. If they should only see one dimension (one time dimension, one product dimension, and so on), you will need to decide which dimension is the one they should see, and hide the others. If the dimension versions are guaranteed to stay in synch with each other, the choice will be arbitrary. If the versions might differ in a meaningful way, then you should decide what dimension version should be visible. It is possible that you will want to construct an additional dimension version that is the union of the other versions.

In the simplest case, the dimensions are just duplicates. They have the same levels and member keys. In this case, you can hide one of the versions, and use simple calculated members or calculated cells to make the right member references. For example, a simple case would be a linked cube and a regular cube with a time dimension built from the same timetable. Each contributes a time dimension, and these dimensions are always in synch due to how the dimensions and cubes are processed.

In a less simple case, one version is a superset of the other. In this case, you will need to decide which you want to use, and hide the other(s). For example, you may want to expose the superset version and hide the subset version. In the least simple case, the dimensions overlap or are entirely disjoint from each other. In this case, you will need to build an "integrating" dimension from scratch for the virtual cube that represents the dimension you wish to present to the user. You can use MDX queries and DTS or linked servers to construct a dimension table that contains the union of all members.

Let us turn our attention to the MDX that makes the data appear as though only one version of the dimension were present. The LinkMember( ) function plays an important role; if you are unfamiliar with it, you might want to take a quick look at its description in Appendix A. In our simplest case of a virtual cube with two versions of the time dimension, the dimensions are identical in terms of levels and keys. Let us assume that the local [Orders] cube is being combined with the linked [Inventory] cube into an [Orders Inventory] virtual cube. The time dimension of the local [Orders] cube is to be shown, while the time dimension of the linked [Inventory] cube is marked as hidden. To show data from the [Units Over 90 Days Old] measure from the [Inventory] cube, we will give it the name [Units Over 90 Days Old − Base] in the virtual cube, hide it, and create a calculated [Units Over 90 Days Old] measure to access with MDX statement shown in Figure 11.4.

No calculation is really occurring, only a reference to the measure at the related time member. If a query accesses a [Units Over 90 Days Old] value at [Time].[December, 2001], this will be translated into a request for the [Units Over 90 Days Old − Base] at ([Inventory^Time].[December 2001]). We use ValidMeasure( ) around the reference because [Units Over 90 Days Old − Base] isn't dimensioned by [Time]. We also give it a low solve order number so that calculations in other dimensions (particularly time) will not be calculated before it: if this were computed for a calculated time member with a lower

```
CREATE MEMBER [Orders Inventory].[Measures].[Units Over 90 Days Old]
AS

// Note the extra set of parentheses around the tuple;
// these are required when ValueMeasure() takes a
// multidimensional tuple as opposed to single member.

'ValidMeasure ((
  [Measures]. [Units Over 90 Days Old - Base],
  LinkMember ([Time].CurrentMember, [Inventory^Time]),
))'
, SOLVE_ORDER = 0
```

Figure 11.4 Basic pattern for linking members from different dimensions using keys.

solve order number, we would not get a result because the calculated time member won't exist in the [Inventory^Time] dimension. We would want the computation of [Units Over 90 Days Old] for a calculated time member to take as its inputs the [Units Over 90 Days Old] value for base time members instead. If we are going to have important functions in other dimensions with a solve order number of zero, we need to either rely on the fact that a solve order tie between dimensions is lost by the measures dimension (and won by a non-measures dimension), or to give this an even lower solve order number (like −1, although we generally try to stay away from negative solve orders).

We could also use the calculated cells feature of Analysis Services to avoid creating a parallel set of calculated measures in the first place. In this case, we don't change the name of the [Units Over 90 Days Old] measure when we bring it into the virtual cube. Calculated cells provide an alternate way of computing values for any cells in the cube, regardless of whether they are for base measures/members or calculated measures/members. (We discussed cell calculations in Chapter 6, "The Many Ways to Calculate in Microsoft Analysis Services.") The corresponding calculated cells definition would be

```
CREATE CELL CALCULATION [Orders Inventory].[Match Inventory] FOR
'(
  {[Measures].[Units Over 90 Days Old] }
)' AS
'CalculationPassValue (
  ValidMeasure ((
    [Measures].CurrentMember,
    LinkMember ([Time].CurrentMember, [Inventory^Time])
  ))
```

```
    , 0
    , ABSOLUTE
    )'
  , SOLVE_ORDER = 0
```

This single definition can include more or all of the inventory measures by modifying the set containing the [Units Over 90 Days Old] measure.

You may have considered using a custom rollup function to perform this reference. You could define a custom rollup on each level in the time dimension with a formula similar to

```
Iif (
    [Measures].CurrentMember IS [Measures].[Units Over 90 Days Old],

    // reference at the linked member
    ([Time].Ignore,
     LinkMember ([Time].CurrentMember, [Inventory^Time])),

    // reference right here
    [Time].Ignore
)
```

The .Ignore function is used here to prevent recursion on the time dimension. In the false section of the iif( ) function, the value for the current measure will now be referenced at the same time member. Resolving this reference will require looking at the time dimension and, as part of that, stepping recursively back into this function. The .Ignore function stops this recursion. In the true branch of the iif( ), the LinkMember( ) function converts a member of Time into a member of [Inventory^Time], but does not change the [Time] member, so without [Time].Ignore this branch would recurse as well. We did not put a reference to [Measures].CurrentMember in either branch of the iif( ) because it is redundant in this formula. If we are going to use ValidMeasure( ), we could use

```
Iif (
    [Measures].CurrentMember IS [Measures].[Units Over 90 Days Old],
    ValidMeasure ((
      LinkMember ([Time].CurrentMember, [Inventory^Time]),
      [Time].Ignore
    )),
    ValidMeasure (
      [Time].Ignore
    )
)
```

Or:

```
Iif (
    [Measures].CurrentMember IS [Measures].[Units Over 90 Days Old],
    ValidMeasure (
      ([Measures].CurrentMember,
```

```
      LinkMember ([Time].CurrentMember, [Inventory^Time]),
      [Time].Ignore)
   ),
   ValidMeasure (
      ([Measures].CurrentMember,
      [Time].Ignore)
   )
)
```

Performance for this technique should be similar to calculated cells. In addition, custom rollups are executed before almost every other data calculation technique, including calculated cells and calculated members. This minimizes any concerns over getting your solve orders and calculation passes right. Note that if multiple measures are being exposed from the inventory cube, you should OR together all of the [Measures].CurrentMember IS xxx terms in the test section of the iif( ) function. Unfortunately, there is no more direct way in MDX to obtain the base cube from which a virtual cube's measure comes. If we could create custom rollups on the measures dimension, we could get rid of the iif( ) logic in this formula. However, this gets the job done.

Merging Dimensions That Are a Subset/Superset of Each Other

If the dimensions being matched are proper subsets or supersets of each other in terms of their members and levels, then you can use the techniques we have just been describing for accessing data at related members of related dimensions. You should keep in mind the following, though.

If the dimension that is a superset is the visible dimension, then LinkMember( ) will cause a cell error to be generated for members in the superset that are not in the subset. Unfortunately, you cannot test for LinkMember(. . .) IS NULL because the cell error stops evaluation of the formula before the IS NULL can be executed; no NULL member reference is returned. The only way around this is through additional data or logic. For example, if you can add it into the OLAP database schema, a member property in the superset dimension may flag the existence of the member in the subset dimension(s). Then, the reference expression would read something like

```
'iif (
   [Product].CurrentMember.Properties ("Exists in Special Products") =
"Y",
   ValidMeasure ((
      LinkMember (
         [Product].CurrentMember,
         [Special Products]
      )
```

```
    )),
  NULL
)'
```

This could prove unwieldy if more than a couple of subset dimensions are present. For any more complex a situation (too many subset dimensions, or you are not able to add the member property), you will want to consider one of the techniques we describe in the section, "When the Keys Don't Match," further along.

If the subset dimension is the visible dimension, there will be no difficulty accessing data, as every member in the visible dimension will have a counterpart in the hidden dimension.

Merging Dimensions That Are Disjoint

If the two dimensions to be combined are disjoint or perhaps overlapping for some members and not for others, we can still combine and use them, but we need to first create a dimension that contains all of the members that we require in our analysis cube. Thus, to tie together two dimensions, we need a third. We'll call this third dimension an *integrating* dimension.

In Analysis Services, one of the tasks toward constructing the integrating dimension is building the dimension table that it will be based on. This can be accomplished by many means, but we want to ensure a couple of things along the way.

First, for each member in the integrating dimension, we have the name or key of the corresponding member in the dimension that the data will actually be drawn from. If possible, we would build the dimension so that the member keys in the integrating dimension are the same as the member keys in the integrated dimensions. Second, that we have a column in the table that encodes the dimension that the data actually is drawn from. This could be a code or the actual name of the dimension in the cube.

For example, let's say that three manufacturing plants (A, B, and C) have each built their own cubes to cover the products that they produce. Each makes different products. Their product names are different, but their member keys are not unique, so we need to integrate them using member names. When we create linked cubes of their cubes and a virtual cube that will integrate them, we will need to build an integrating product dimension and add that into the virtual cube (and then hide the [A^Product], [B^Product], and [C^Product] dimensions).

The integrating product dimension, named [Int Product], will have as its leaf level the leaf level products from the [A^Product], [B^Product], and [C^Product] dimensions. It also has two member properties at that level to help reference the data from the appropriate dimension and cube. [Source] names the plant that makes the product. [Mbr Name] holds a member identifier for the product member from that plant. (In the case of key path member identifiers, these can be compact and readily generated within the RDBMS.)

As we bring the three regular cubes together in the virtual cube, we will end up with three separate sets of measures that we can integrate using the techniques from the opening of the chapter. However, because the source defines not only a set of product members but also a set of measures, we will put the source name into the measures that come from each source. Thus, we will have measures, like [A Units Produced], [B Units Produced], [A Closing Inventory], [C Closing Inventory], and so on that we will combine into [Units Produced] and [Closing Inventory]. We will use the [Source] member property of the Product dimension to choose the appropriate base measure. The following is an obvious CREATE MEMBER statement, which unfortunately is wrong (as we will see in a little bit):

```
CREATE MEMBER [Measures].[Units Produced] AS
'ValidMeasure ((
  StrToTuple(
    "[Measures].["
    + [Int Product].CurrentMember.Properties ("Source")
    + "]"
  )
))', SOLVE_ORDER = 0
```

We also need to select the right private product dimension to go along with this, for every product. The simplest way to do this is a custom rollup formula on the leaf level of the dimension. (This will also handle the issue of how to aggregate the leaf-level product data up any hierarchy in our integrating product dimension, as the results of this custom rollup will automatically be aggregated up the integrating product hierarchy on the fly.) Our custom rollup formula will read

```
StrToTuple (
  "["
  + [Int Product].CurrentMember.Properties ("Source")
  + "^Product]."
  + [Int Product].CurrentMember.Properties ("Name")
  + "]"
)
```

Why was the calculated member definition wrong, when it was so like the ones we discussed early in this chapter? It has to do with solve order. Custom rollups are ordinarily calculated from a much earlier solve order than our calculated member. Therefore, for any integrating product and measure, the measure formula will first select the underlying base measure, and then the custom rollup will select the underlying dimension. However, if we don't select the underlying dimension and member in the calculated measure, its call to ValidMeasure( ) will leave us with the top member in the underlying dimension. We need to set this all up so we select the underlying product member first and then perform the ValidMeasure( ).

An easy way, though one we hesitate to recommend in general, is to set the solve order of the integrating measure to below −5,119 (for example, to −5,200). This will limit our ability to use the results of this formula in other custom rollups.

Another way would be to define the custom rollup so as to embed the measure lookup and ValidMeasure( ) operations as well. In this case, the formula for the rollup would look like

```
ValidMeasure ((
  StrToTuple(
    "( [Measures].["
    + [Int Product].CurrentMember.Properties ("Source")
    + "],["
    + [Int Product].CurrentMember.Properties ("Source")
    + "^Product]."
    + [Int Product].CurrentMember.Properties ("Name")
    + "]"
  )
))
```

All the work of the integrating measure is being done in the rollup, so what should the measure's formula be? Nothing at all. Well, it needs to have some formula by the rules of MDX, but it can be a simple NULL. More interestingly, we need to set the solve order to below that of custom rollups (for example, to something like −5,200). That way, the calculated member itself will never be executed because the custom rollup will intersect all cells and always have a higher solve order.

When the Keys Don't Match

All of the examples so far have highlighted the use of LinkMember( ) to connect dimensions based on common member keys at common levels. It is entirely possible that your dimensions do not have common member keys. In this case, you need to have something in common between the members of each dimension. If a value isn't shared between them in the names, keys, or properties, then there isn't any way at all to match up members between the dimensions. For one application, we've also used a variation on this technique to match dimensions that have similar names and different structures.

If they share member names, then you can use the same general techniques for looking up the corresponding member between two members with different

MDX functions. Perhaps one cube's dimensions were built using the member names as the keys, whereas the equivalent dimension in another cube was built using the data warehouse's integer join key for the member. The actual lookups will be slower, but then you've also saved the time it would have taken to make the databases and tables conform to each other. The functions that you can use depend on names and strings manipulation.

For example, let's use our example of two time dimensions from a linked cube and a local cube in a virtual cube again. We can't use LinkMember, but we can use the Members( ) or StrToTuple( ) functions with the unique name of the member. What we will do is transform the name of the member on the visible dimension to the name of the member in the hidden dimension, and then turn it into a member reference with Members( ).

Each time that we employ this strategy, we need to deal with how unique names in the visible dimension are generated. In Analysis Services, this technique may require specifying that the "name path" style of unique names is in use. This is set by the MDX Unique Name Style connection parameter or the HKLM\Software\Microsoft\OLAP Server\CurrentVersion\MDXUniqueNames registry key on the server; see Appendix B for more information. If our dimension has unique member names throughout, then we don't really care—a name will be as good as a unique name.

Let's say we don't have unique names in our dimensions, so we are using name path convention. For a unique member name in the [Time] dimension, like "[Time].[All Time].[2002].[January]," we want to create the character string "[Inventory^Time].[All Time].[2002].[January]" because that is the unique name of the matching member in the [Inventory^Time] dimension. All we need to do is replace the first "[" in the first string with "[Inventory^". This will be pretty easy using the VBA string manipulation function Mid( ). The MDX in Figure 11.5 is functionally equivalent to the LinkMember( ) example in Figure 11.4. If names in the two dimensions are unique throughout the dimension (which we ordinarily recommend in a time dimension), then we could also substitute .Name for .UniqueName in the definition in Figure 11.5.

If we cannot obtain one member's name from another's, then we are left with using member properties through the .Properties( ) function. For example, we could use a construct such as the following to translate a member property into a member reference:

```
Members (
  "[Product].["
  + [Material].CurrentMember.Properties ("SKU Code")
  + "]"
)
```

```
CREATE MEMBER [Orders Inventory].[Measures].[Units Over 90 Days Old]
AS

// Note the extra set of parentheses around the tuple;
// these are required when ValueMeasure() takes a
// multidimensional tuple as opposed to single member.

'ValidMeasure ((
  [Measures]. [Units Over 90 Days Old - Base],
  StrToTuple (
    "[Inventory^" +
    Mid (
      [Time].CurrentMember.UniqueName,
      1
    )
  )
))'
, SOLVE_ORDER = 0
```

Figure 11.5 Basic pattern for linking members from different dimensions using names.

One thing we would avoid at all costs unless the dimensions involved were extremely small would be to look up a member based on the value of some property for that member. This is because there is no efficient way at all to do the lookup. Whereas the Members() and StrToTuple() functions can take advantage of some internal index of names, in order to look up a member based on a member property, we will need to perform a Filter() of a level's members or the entire dimension.

Integrating Related Hierarchies

The last topic that we would like to discuss in this chapter is how to use related hierarchies within a single cube for analysis. In this case, we're not interested in how to reference data across dimensions when connecting cubes, but how to reference data across dimensions within a single cube. One powerful application for this is in budgeting and planning, when we need to allocate data down from multiple hierarchies, or allocate down from one hierarchy and use it in another hierarchy. (Remember, in Microsoft OLAP/Analysis Services, different hierarchies are different dimensions.)

For example, let's say that we are a manufacturer that sells our products through different chains of stores ("Federalized" and "Shopper's Galaxy"). Thanks to our supply chain software, we know how much of our product is sold in each store of the chains. We have two hierarchies in our Outlet dimension: by region and by chain. These are called [Outlet].[ByRegion] and [Outlet].[ByChain]. Figure 11.6 illustrates the two hierarchies. We are trying to understand the regional impact of sales efforts by each of the chains. In one cube, we have chain-level estimates of sales growth of 12 percent for Federalized and 9 percent for Shopper's Galaxy for Q2 next year compared with Q2 of this year. (We're not using the UPDATE CUBE feature to allocate data down to the leaf levels of the cube, due to the number and size of the dimensions.) Given actual sales for this year, we want to take this growth and arrive at an estimate of regional sales across the stores.

One part of our formula will be the multiplication of a growth rate by last year's sales. Given actual store sales (at the store level), if we were calculating this along the [Outlet].[ByChain] hierarchy, the formula would look like

```
CREATE MEMBER [Planning].[Measures].[Projected Sales] AS
'(
    [Measures].[Growth Factor],
```

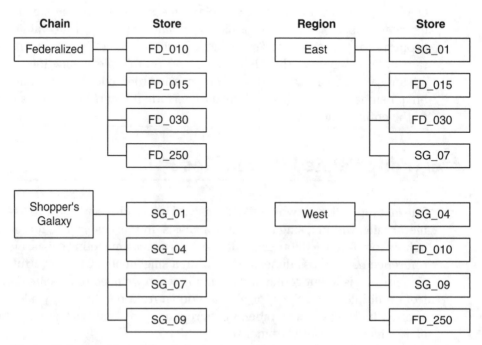

Figure 11.6 Two hierarchies of stores.

```
    Ancestor (
      [Outlet].[ByChain].CurrentMember,
      [Outlet].[Chain]
    )
  ) *
  (
    [Measures].[Sales],
    ParallelPeriod ([Time].[Year], [Time].CurrentMember)
  )'
```

To calculate this along the [Outlet].[ByRegion] hierarchy, we need to use LinkMember( ) again:

```
CREATE MEMBER [Planning].[Measures].[Projected Store Sales] AS
'ValidMeasure ((
  [Measures].[Growth Factor],
  Ancestor (
    LinkMember (
      [Outlet].[ByRegion].CurrentMember,
      [Outlet].[ByChain]
    ),
    [Outlet].[ByChain].[Chain]
  )
)) *
(
  [Measures].[Sales],
  ParallelPeriod ([Time].[Year], [Time].CurrentMember)
)'
```

The other part will be the logic that connects the regions we want to report on to the chains doing the selling. Because the two hierarchies share the same stores, we're going to involve the store-level descendants of the region member we're calculating for. This formula will look something like

```
CREATE MEMBER [Planning].[Measures].[Projected Region Sales] AS
'Sum (
  Descendants (
    [Outlet].[ByRegion].CurrentMember,
    [Outlet].[ByRegion].[Store]
  ),
  [Measures].[Projected Store Sales]
)
```

Figure 11.7 depicts the flow of access through Descendants( ), LinkMember( ), and Ancestor( ). If we wanted to roll all of this functionality into one calculated measure, we can instead use

```
CREATE MEMBER [Planning].[Measures].[Projected Region Sales] AS
'Sum (
  Descendants (
    [Outlet].[ByRegion].CurrentMember,
    [Outlet].[ByRegion].[Store]
```

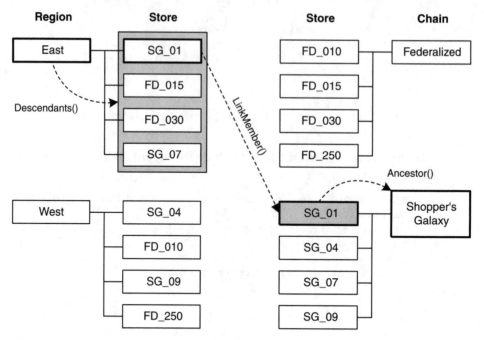

Figure 11.7 Flow of access through the reference functions.

```
      ),

ValidMeasure ((
  [Measures].[Growth Factor],
  Ancestor (
    LinkMember (
      [Outlet].[ByRegion].CurrentMember,
      [Outlet].[ByChain]
    ),
    [Outlet].[ByChain].[Chain]
  )
)) *
(
  [Measures].[Sales],
  ParallelPeriod ([Time].[Year], [Time].CurrentMember)
)
)'
```

With this formula, changes to our sales growth projections per chain can be immediately calculated over regions. This will help us plan our inventory and shipping logistics, and perhaps our manufacturing too.

Summary

In this chapter, we have attempted two things. The first was to introduce some very concrete and practical constructs for solving cube and dimension design problems that come up from time to time. The second was to expose you to generalized techniques for combining data from between cubes and within a cube based on dimension relationships. As with techniques we have presented in the other chapters, your own applications may use these same general constructs with functions or operators that we haven't even touched on in this chapter (like Microsoft's own LookupCube( ), StrToValue( ), and so on). Given the flexibility of MDX operators and constructs, many possibilities are available.

CHAPTER 12

Client Programming Basics

W e've spent the majority of this book describing the use of MDX without very much discussion on how a client program issues MDX and retrieves results from a query. As with SQL, we can consider data structures and analyses in the abstract, but to bring our system to a user, we do need to involve some code. This chapter will briefly introduce programming issues related to the use of MDX. Our point will not be to construct a full-fledged client browser, but rather to expose you to bread-and-butter issues that every type of client application may need to deal with.

Although SQL works with several different APIs, as we write this, MDX works with only one API: Microsoft's OLE DB for OLAP. Another API that is layered on top of OLE DB for OLAP is ADO MD, which is generally used by programmers developing clients using Visual Basic or ASP. With Microsoft's forthcoming XML for Analysis specification, the distinction between using VB or Java and C/C++ or Delphi will diminish; OLE DB for OLAP will be available for all client types. As we write this chapter, we (including the author) can and do write in C++ for OLE DB for OLAP as well as in VB for ADO MD. However, because it is simpler and more likely to be used by more developers, we will demonstrate programming in ADO MD using Visual Basic. We will assume that you are familiar with ADO, but not necessarily with ADO MD.

NOTE

Various third-party client tools, including Knosys' Proclarity and BusinessObjects' BusinessQuery MD, also provide their own APIs that layer on top of OLE DB for OLAP, and they provide additional GUI and application support as well. In particular, each of these products' APIs contains an object model for all (or almost all) the components of an MDX query. This can be extremely handy for building customized applications. We will not explore the programming of these clients in this book.

ADO MD Basics

Using ADO MD is similar to using regular ADO in that you are presented with an object model of meta data and query results, but also with a different set of objects and properties. Some of the ADO objects are also used with ADO MD, such as the Connection object. These objects behave appropriately to the OLAP application. For example, the OpenSchema method of a Connection object that has an OLE DB for OLAP provider open retrieves a tabular form of meta data for OLAP constructs such as cubes, dimensions, and members. Although in ADO DB the result of a query is a Recordset, in ADO MD the result of an MDX query is usually a Cellset, which is a multidimensional object that represents the axes and cells returned.

You can also request a Recordset result, in which case the resulting axes and cells for a normal MDX query are flattened according to the OLE DB for OLAP-flattening algorithms. If you pose an SQL query to a cube, you will get back a Recordset as well. We describe the effects of flattening an MDX query result later in this chapter. Requesting a Recordset to be returned from an MDX query is also how you obtain results from a DRILLTHROUGH query in Analysis Services 2000.

A general-purpose client may need to perform various tasks, including but certainly not limited to the following:

- Getting meta data
- Listing databases and cubes
- Listing dimensions, hierarchies, and levels
- Listing members
- Listing sets
- Listing external functions
- Listing actions
- Listing cell calculation functions

ADO MD (as of MDAC 2.6, which is distributed with Analysis Services 2000 and available by a separate download from www.microsoft.com/data) supports all of these activities. Listing sets, actions, and external functions are relevant to the MDX a client may attempt to execute, but little programming is required to handle the results of these meta data inquiries. (Listing cell calculation functions is more awkward than listing the other types of meta data through VB.) Executing MDX statements may affect which sets, external functions, and actions are defined (as well as the members). The programming side of executing these DDL statements is simple and we will cover it in this chapter.

Prerequisites

Using ADO MD requires using the ADO library as well. In order to develop a client using ADO MD using Visual Basic, your project will need to have two references in it: one to the ADO library (ActiveX Data Objects) and another to the ActiveX Data Objects (Multidimensional) library.

Making a Connection

Establishing a connection in ADO MD is basically the same as in ADO. The provider name in the connection string needs to be an OLE DB for OLAP provider (such as MSOLAP). The data source needs to be the name of the server to which you want to connect. In the case of a Microsoft cube file, the path and name of the cube file should be used for the data source. If you know the database that you want to connect to, you can provide that in the Initial Catalog field; otherwise, you can select it by setting the DefaultDatabase property of the Connection object.

For example, the following code will create a connection to the local machine and set the database to Sales Development:

```
Dim cn as New ADOMD.Connection


cn.Open "Provider=MSOLAP;Data Source=localhost;Initial Catalog=Sales
Development;"
```

With the Enterprise Edition of Analysis Services, you can also connect to an OLAP server through HTTP. In this case, the URL of the server is the data source. In addition, you may also need to pass in user ID and password credentials, as in the following:

```
cn.Open "Provider=MSOLAP;Data
Source=http://www.dsslab.com/Analyses/OLAP;Initial Catalog=Sales
Development;User ID=deannay;Password=Safe&Secure;"
```

The OLE DB for OLAP provider may also support additional connection properties that affect client behavior, including how meta data is represented and how MDX is executed. We provide a full list of connection properties for Microsoft Analysis Services in Appendix B.

Executing a Query

A central programming activity in MDX is executing a query or statement and retrieving the query results. To execute a query, you need to be familiar with a few objects:

- Cellset object
- Axes and Axis objects
- Cell object

The Cellset is the primary object that executes MDX and that holds query results in ADO MD. Unlike an ADO Recordset, which can be generated by executing a query, you need to create a Cellset object before it is used. It needs to have a connection associated with it, and it also needs to have the query text set in advance of executing the query. The following overall setup is required of a Cellset in order to retrieve data from it:

```
Dim cs As ADOMD.Cellset

' create it explicitly if it doesn't already exist
Set cs = New ADOMD.Cellset

' set the connection that the cellset is going to execute on
Set cs.ActiveConnection = cn

' set the text of the MDX command
cs.Source = "SELECT [Customers].[Northeast].Children FROM [Budgeting]"

cs.Open

' ... do things

cs.Close   ' when we're done with it
```

To execute a DDL statement such as CREATE ACTION or DROP SET, you can also execute the command directly against the connection

```
cn.Execute "DROP SET [Budgeting].[Delicate Customers]"
```

Once the query has been successfully executed, you can begin to work with the axis and cell information of the Cellset. If the query fails, an error will be raised and you will need to handle it.

Axes Hold Axis Information

Within the Axes collection of the Cellset, each axis holds one of the query's axes. The contents of the Axes collection are ordered so that the first item (Cellset.Axes(0)) holds the set of tuples for axis 0 (the columns), the second item holds the results for axis 1 (the rows), and so on. The slicer axis defined by the WHERE clause is held in a separate FilterAxis property of the Cellset. If the query has no axes defined (a zero-dimensional query, as described in Chapter 2, "MDX in More Detail"), then the Axes collection is empty. The Axes collection will also be empty if the Cellset has been used to execute an MDX DDL statement such as CREATE MEMBER or USE LIBRARY.

All dimensions not referenced in the axes of the query (if the MDX was a query) will end up in the FilterAxis. Remember from Chapter 5, "MDX Context and Execution," that if the members of a dimension are not placed in one of the other axes, the default member of that dimension forms part of the context for the query. That context is reflected in the FilterAxis; all dimensions of the cube will end up being reflected in either the axes or the slicer if the MDX that was executed was a query.

Each Axis object holds the number of dimensions reflected in that axis in its DimensionCount property. If the axis exists, this number should be at least 1. This DimensionCount can be used to set up user displays. Each axis also holds each result tuple in its Positions collection. Each Position corresponds to a single tuple from the query. Note that if a query returns an empty set for an axis, the Positions collection will be empty (as will the set of result cells).

Each Position contains a list of members, one member for each dimension in the tuple. The first dimension represented in the tuple will be the one listed first in the MDX query for the axis. If the query started off with

```
SELECT
CrossJoin (
  [Time].[2001].Children,
  [Salesperson].[Eastern].Children
) on columns
...
```

then, in each position in the Axes(0).Positions collection, the first member will be a Time member and the second will be a Salesperson member.

Each member in the Members collection of a position will contain information about the member, including its name, unique name, display caption, and some OLE DB-defined properties that will assist in displaying the member. Additionally, if the query requested any member properties for members of that dimension, their names and values will be held in the Properties collection of the member.

For example, the following loop will retrieve all of the member captions for the tuples of the columns axis and place them in the fixed columns of an MSFlex-Grid object named fg1 (ignoring any layout issues for the row headers):

```
Dim i As Integer, j as Integer
Dim iCol As Integer

' only for this example...
' One row in the grid for each dimension in the axis
' For MSFlexGrid, Rows must be > FixedRows
fg1.Rows = cs.Axes(0).DimensionCount + 1
fg1.FixedRows = cs.Axes(0).DimensionCount

' if we were accounting for row headers, count would be adjusted
fg1.Cols = cs.Axes(0).Positions.Count

' Loop over Positions
For i = 0 To cs.Axes(0).Positions.Count - 1
' if we were accounting for row headers, iCol would be adjusted from i
    iCol = i

    ' Loop over Members per Position
    For j = 0 to cs.Axes(0).DimensionCount - 1
        fg1.TextMatrix(j, iCol) = _
            cs.Axes(0).Positions(i).Members(j).Caption
    Next j
Next i
```

Cells Hold Cell Information

A Cellset also holds a collection of Cell objects in its Item collection. Each Cell object in the Item collection holds various properties for each retrieved cell. The Value property contains the raw, unformatted number or string value for the cell and is the default, so simply requesting a value from the Cellset's collection of Items will retrieve the unformatted value. The FormattedValue property is also available by name. Other cell properties can be retrieved through the cell's Properties collection (such as through cs.Item(iCol, iRow).Properties ("FORE_COLOR")).

In MDX, the names of the cell properties that you can retrieve are listed here and are repeated in Appendix C:

BACK_COLOR

CELL_EVALUATION_LIST   *Microsoft extension*

CELL_ORDINAL

FONT_FLAGS

FONT_NAME

FONT_SIZE

FORE_COLOR

FORMAT_STRING

FORMATTED_VALUE

NON_EMPTY_BEHAVIOR *Microsoft extension*

SOLVE_ORDER *Microsoft extension*

VALUE

You would use these names to retrieve the cell properties from the cell's list of properties. You may also retrieve the properties by ordinal in the cell's list of properties; the properties will be placed in the collection in the order that they were listed in the CELL PROPERTIES section of the query.

NOTE

Remember that if you ask for any specific cell properties, you need to request every cell property that you are interested in. By default, you get back VALUE, FORMATTED_VALUE, and CELL_ORDINAL.

If you are aiming to present information in Microsoft Excel or through another interface that enables the user to perform further calculations against the retrieved data, it may be helpful to retrieve the raw value and the format string in each query. If you retrieve the formatted value only, then the number of decimal places may be limited and the numbers represented may not be correct for further calculations. If you retrieve the raw value only, you lose the formatting information provided by the database designer. If you retrieve both the raw value and the format string, you can combine them at the client layer by Excel's cell formatting or with the VBA Format( ) function and still retain the exact number as calculated.

For example, the code in Figure 12.1 retrieves formatted value and color information from a query that requests these cell properties. The code then places the colored text into an MSFlexGrid named fg1.

Further Details on Retrieving Information from a Query

A couple more common details are worth bringing up here: how to retrieve member properties from a result set, and how to retrieve and use additional member information provided by OLE DB for OLAP and ADO MD.

```
Dim iRow as Integer

For i = 0 To cs.Axes(0).Positions.Count - 1
    iCol = i
    fg1.Col = iCol
    For j = 0 To cs.Axes(1).Positions.Count - 1
        iRow = j
        fg1.Row = iRow
        fg1.Text = cs.Item(i, j).FormattedValue
        fg1.CellForeColor = _
              cs.Item(i, j).Properties ("FORE_COLOR")
        fg1.CellBackColor = _
              cs.Item(i, j).Properties ("BACK_COLOR")
    Next j
Next i
```

Figure 12.1   Code to retrieve cell data from a cellset.

Retrieving Member Property Information

The following are always going to be returned into specific named properties of the Member object:

- Caption
- Name
- UniqueName
- Description
- LevelName
- LevelDepth

For example, the caption for the member can always be retrieved by referencing Member.Caption.

These properties can also be retrieved by specifically listing them in the DIMENSION PROPERTIES clause of the query's specification for that axis. In that case, their values will also appear in the Properties collection of the Member object. Database-defined member properties will also be listed in that clause and retrieved in the member's Properties collection.

Member properties retrieved through the Properties collection are named using unique names, which can cause some complication to your code if you need to search them by name or translate the name to a user-readable format. The unique name style for member properties is discussed in Chapter 2, "MDX in More Detail." A human-accessible caption can usually be inferred by isolating the text enclosed by the rightmost "[" and "]" characters in the string.

One important use for member unique names returned from queries, apart from holding them for insertion into subsequent queries, is to augment the members retrieved from the database with ancestor information, which may not have been retrieved in the query. For example, the default formatting for a time dimension in Microsoft Analysis Services gives each day member the day of the month as its name, so 12 members are in each year with a name of [1]. If a query retrieves only day-level members, a user has no way of clearly knowing which month or year the days belong to. That information is contained in the Unique-Name, but we'd also like to hide unique names as much as possible and display captions instead.

We can add in ancestor information to our display simply by using the Unique-Name property along with the Connection's OpenSchema method to walk the parents up. In addition, we would want to ensure that the LevelDepth for the member is greater than 0. If it is 0, then it has no ancestors. For example, the following loop will prepend all ancestor's captions to a given member's caption, separating the captions with "/":

```
Dim oMember As ADOMD.Member
Dim sCaption As String
Dim sTmpCaption As String
Dim rs As ADODB.Recordset

' ... Retrieve an arbitrary member into oMember

sCaption = oMember.Caption

If oMember.LevelDepth > 0 Then
    iLevel = oMember.LevelDepth

    ' Use the Members schema rowset for efficient object traversal
    ' Note that we need the name of the cube
    ' in the third restriction column.

    Set rs = cn.OpenSchema(adSchemaMembers, _
        Array(Empty, Empty, "budgeting", Empty, Empty, _
            Empty, Empty, Empty, oMember.UniqueName))

    sTmpUniqueName = rs!PARENT_UNIQUE_NAME
    rs.Close

    While Not (iLevel = 0)

        Set rs = cn.OpenSchema(adSchemaMembers, _
```

```
                    Array(Empty, Empty, "budgeting", Empty, Empty, _
                        Empty, Empty, Empty, sTmpUniqueName))

            sTmpCaption = rs!MEMBER_CAPTION
            sCaption = sTmpCaption & "/" & sCaption
            If (IsNull(rs!PARENT_UNIQUE_NAME)) Then
                rs.Close
                GoTo Out1
            End If

            sTmpUniqueName = rs!PARENT_UNIQUE_NAME
            iLevel = rs!LEVEL_NUMBER

    Wend
    rs.Close
Out1:
    ' Done with loop here
End If

' Now sCaption holds full hierarchy of captions
' e.g. "2001/Q3/October/31"
```

Rather than try to traverse the object hierarchy of the cube to figure out the dimension and level of the member and then walk up the ADO MD object trees, we make use of the underlying schema rowsets to first access the member's parent unique name. Then we would use the rowsets to access for each parent its caption and its own parent's unique name, repeating as necessary to move up the hierarchy until all ancestors have been accounted for. If we used the ParentSameAsPrev property described in the next section, we could probably economize our searching. (We're assuming only one parent per member here, which won't be a valid assumption for providers like TM1.) In order to understand the specifics of the OLE DB for OLAP schema rowsets, you should refer to the OLE DB for OLAP documentation.

Retrieving Additional Member Information

In addition to standard and database member properties, the following properties will also be returned for each member in a Position's collection of members:

- DrilledDown
- ParentSameAsPrev
- ChildCount

The DrilledDown flag basically indicates if a parent member is immediately followed by one of its children. This can be useful for indicating to an end user whether an action on the parent member will initiate a drill-down or -up. If the client is attempting to render children together under a parent, perhaps by using indenting or HTML table rows, ParentSameAsPrev provides a low-cost way to the client to determine, as it loops through result tuples, whether it should break out of a child group to start a new parent or not. ChildCount is an approximate count of the number of children that a member has. It is not reliable (OLE DB for OLAP specifies that the number returned here need only be an approximation but doesn't say how good the approximation needs to be), but in general if the ChildCount is zero then a member cannot be drilled down on, and if it is greater than zero, then it can be.

Further Details about Retrieving Cell Data

The code in Figure 12.1 shows the use of multiple indices to retrieve data from a Cellset. In this variation, we use one index per axis of the result set. This works when our code that retrieves the cell data knows the number of axes in the result set ahead of time. If it does not, and we also don't want to litter our code with conditions to test for one-dimensional, two-dimensional, three-dimensional, and other cases, we can use one index instead. In this case, the single index value we use will combine the offset that we want to retrieve data for in each axis. The position number in each axis will be multiplied by the product of the number of positions at each lower-numbered axis. The column position number will be multiplied by 1, because no lower-numbered axes exist.

Let's say that we have a three-dimensional result set with four columns, five rows, and six pages. If we want to access the cell at position $(2, 3, 1)$, then we will calculate the cell index as $(2 * 1) + (3 * 4) + (1 * 20) = 34$. The cell at position $(2, 3, 2)$ would be at index $(2 * 1) + (3 * 4) + (2 * 20) = 54$. When the query is executed, an array can be filled with the multipliers of 1, 4, and 20, and a short function can use this to convert any array of coordinate values from the user interface into a cell index. (If performance on queries with more than two dimensions is an issue, you may seriously want to implement your client code in C++ or Delphi with OLE DB for OLAP instead of ADO MD.)

In the case of a zero-dimensional result set, we have no axes for our result set, but we do have a slicer. We can reference cell 0 to obtain the sole cell returned by the query.

Retrieving Cell Data or Drill-Through Data as a Recordset

Given a connection to an OLE DB for OLAP provider that supports flattening, we can get our results back in table form by executing an MDX query against the connection, instead of a SQL query, and retrieving it into a Recordset. In addition to the tabular presentation of cube cells, this is also how we will perform a drill-through query.

For example, the following code will retrieve an MDX query as a Recordset that can be bound to a control or used to render an HTML page:

```
Dim rs As ADODB.Recordset

Set rs = cn.Execute ( _
"SELECT { [Measures].[Profit], [Measures].[Margin Pct] } on columns," _
& " { PeriodsToDate ([Year], [Time].[Dec., 2001]) } on rows" _
& " FROM [Budgeting] " _
)

' rs is ready to use!
```

Executing Actions

As described in Chapter 9, "Advanced Operations and Commands—Drill-Through and Actions," OLE DB for OLAP actions are not executed by issuing MDX. Instead, an action is executed by retrieving a text value from an ADO SchemaRowset (or an OLE DB for OLAP schema rowset). The action text is retrieved from the CONTENT field of the actions table after specifying restrictions on the Recordset. As with the preceding example that prepended ancestor captions to a member name, we use the ADO/OLE DB technique of providing column restrictions through an Array of column values and retrieving a Recordset. Some of the restrictions are typical, such as the name of the action, the name of the cube in which it is found, and the type of the action.

However, one key restriction (at the fifth position in the array) provides whatever argument the action may require, such as the tuple for a cell action, the set name for a set action, the member name for a member action, and so on. This restriction needs to be coordinated with the restriction value provided in the sixth position, which indicates how to interpret the coordinate. The actual numerical codes to provide are detailed in Chapter 9.

The following code snippet executes a cell action named Retrieve Details and retrieves the value into the string sActionToDo:

```
Dim rs As ADODB.Recordset
Dim sActionToDo As String

Set rs = cn.OpenSchema(adSchemaActions, Array( _
     Empty _     ' schema
   , Empty _     ' catalog
   , "Budgeting" _   ' cube name
   , "Retrieve Details" _ ' name of action
   , Empty _     ' type of action (URL, HTML, etc.), assume we know what
to do here
```

```
    , "([Time].[Q1, 2002], [Customers].[NJ], [Products].[Clothing])" _
    , 6 _         ' code for cell coordinate action
    ))

  sActionToDo = rs!CONTENT  ' e.g. "DRILLTHROUGH SELECT  . . . "
```

Note that the names provided are not unique names, nor are they delimited by brackets or another character. By way of another example, the following code snippet executes a statement-type set action named Update Selected with a set named Picked Customers and retrieves the statement text into the string sActionTodo:

```
Set rs = cn.OpenSchema(adSchemaActions, Array( _
    Empty _    ' schema
    , Empty _  ' catalog
    , "Budgeting" _  ' cube name
    , "Update Selected" _ ' name of action
    , 3 _    ' type of action (3 = STATEMENT)
    , "Picked Customers" _
    , 5      ' code for set action _
))

  sActionToDo = rs!CONTENT  ' e.g "UPDATE INVENTORY_REQ  . . . "
```

As you can see, integrating actions with the rest of your client code involves different programming techniques.

Handling ADO MD Meta Data Caching

If you are going to use the ADO MD meta data objects in your client, you need to understand the following regarding the caching of meta data in its ADO MD objects.

ADO MD, as distributed in the MDAC 2.5 and 2.6, has one very important issue to contend with regarding meta data caching. Typically, a client will traverse the Dimensions, Hierarchies, and Levels collections to reach member meta data. (Member meta data is actually handled separately from the Member objects that are returned from a query.) When ADO MD reads in the members for a level, it assumes that it has read in all of the members for that level and does not check the source again during the life of that connection. As a result, if your client creates new calculated members or alters the members through the UPDATE CUBE commands, they will not be picked up in the meta data objects, although they can be used by queries and commands and will be fully available through their corresponding schema Recordset. With Microsoft's OLAP/Analysis Services, the same is true for changes to a dimension via incremental processing.

In order to account for changes, you need to execute the Refresh method of the meta data collection in question. For example, if a client executes a CREATE MEMBER statement to add a calculated measure, this measure member will only be visible in the meta data objects if you refresh the collection of measures for the cube. The following code snippet demonstrates the technique:

```
Dim oCube as ADOMD.Cube

' Assume oCube set to appropriate cube

oCube.Dimensions ("Measures").Hierarchies(o).Levels(o).Members.Refresh
```

Handling "Flattened" MDX Results

In some programming situations, you may need to use the results of an MDX query as though they came from an SQL query. This may occur because you are using the MDX query in a SQL Server Data Transformation Services (DTS) step or through a SQL Server-linked server. You also may be using the MDX results in an application that uses tables and which you cannot adequately modify to use cell sets. Regardless, you can provide the results of an MDX query so that a program sees them as if they were the results of SQL.

OLE DB and Tabular Results for MDX Queries

OLE DB (of which OLE DB for OLAP is a part) is a fairly general data-transport interface that is based on COM. An important interface abstraction in OLE DB is the rowset, which behaves conceptually like a table. A rowset has a set of columns, each of which has a name and a data type. A rowset also provides a software interface through which a client program can obtain rows of information from it. Because the results of an SQL query are in the form of rows and columns, they fit easily into the OLE DB rowset model. DBMS meta data, such as lists of tables, lists of columns, indexes, and the like, are also easily represented as rowsets. For the most part, OLE DB for OLAP uses the same mechanisms as general OLE DB. For example, it provides its own rowsets for an OLAP database's dimensions, hierarchies, levels, members, measures, cubes, and properties.

Although an MDX query specifies an N-dimensional result space, an OLE DB for OLAP client can specify two different formats in which to return the data when it submits the query. One format is as a multidimensional data set and the other is as a normal tabular rowset. The multidimensional data set is normally requested by an OLAP client because it retains the full dimensional layout of the query. However, the client can request that the results be returned in tabular form, even though the query is in MDX. In this case, the client will receive a result data rowset that is almost indistinguishable from the result data rowset coming from any SQL query. There are some restrictions on what data comes back from an MDX query when it is requested as a rowset, which we will discuss in this section. In addition, the column names will not be like those from an SQL database. However, neither of these poses an obstacle.

The OLE DB for OLAP specification documents the table layout. The process of laying out the tabular format is called "flattening" the result set. We will explain in this section the aspects of the flattening you need to understand in order to use the results. (If you are programming an application that will directly use OLE DB or ADO to retrieve the rows, you will want to refer to the programming documentation for OLE DB for OLAP and the PivotTable Service to get additional programming details.) Let's look at how a query is mapped into tabular form.

An MDX query specifies results that are organized along a set of axes. Flattening orients the axes of the result set into rows and columns. There is a special division between axis 0 (the "columns" axis) and the other axes of the query. To prevent confusion between MDX "columns" and table columns, we will refer to the axes of an MDX result set as "axis 0" and "non-axis 0."

Axis 0

Each tuple from axis 0 will appear as its own column of the result rowset. For each of these columns, the column name will be formed from the unique names of the tuple's members, joined together by periods. (This naming can be quite awkward to use.) For example, the following tuple on axis 0,

```
([Time].[All Time].[1965], [Geography].[USA].[IL].[Chicago])
```

would correspond to a column named

```
[Time].[All Time].[1965].[Geography].[USA].[IL].[Chicago]
```

On each row of the resulting table, the columns for the axis 0 tuples will contain cell-related values. Since the actual cell values can be of any type and the type may change from row to row, the values will be returned as COM Variants. Only the cell values will be returned. If the query requests specific cell properties (as listed in Appendix A), the request will be ignored. Member properties cannot be returned for the dimensions of axis 0. An MDX query can request member properties for axis 0 without generating an error, but the request will be ignored.

Other Axes

The tuples for the non-axis 0 axes are essentially cross-joined together and placed in the result rows. The information that is returned for each dimension can be divided into two different cases depending on whether or not any properties have been specified in the query for the axis that contains the dimension (through the PROPERTIES ... on axis clause).

When no properties have been specified on the axis, then for each dimension of each of the non-axis 0 axes there will be one result column for each level of that dimension from its root down to the lowest level of that dimension for which there will be a result member. (The All level, if it exists in a dimension, will not have a corresponding column.) Each column will have a name that consists of the level's unique name and "[CAPTION]," joined by a dot (.). For example, consider the use of a geography dimension that has country, region, state/province, and city levels. If a query only requests region members there will be one column for that dimension's region level and another for its country level. If a query results in a mix of country members, region members, and city members, there will be a column for each of the country, region, state/province, and city levels (even though no state/province was specifically requested). In the event that the members returned for any dimension are not all from the same level, some rows will have NULL member values. For example, using our geography dimension as just described, a query for

```
{[Geography].[France], [Geography].[France].[Bordeaux],
 [Geography].[France].[Bordeaux].[Cadillac]}
```

will produce the names for the following members in the rows:

[Geog]. [Country]. [CAPTION]	[Geog]. [Region]. [CAPTION]	[Geog]. [State/Province]. [CAPTION]	[Geog]. [City]. [CAPTION]
France	<null>	<null>	<null>
France	West	Bordeaux	<null>
France	West	Bordeaux	Cadillac

Note that by the same token, the [Geography].[All Geography] member would be represented by a NULL in each column.

When any level's member properties are specified for an axis, there will be one column for each member property that is listed in the properties clause. Intrinsic properties like ID, KEY, and NAME can be requested, along with any member properties defined by the database. It is important to note that only the properties you list will have corresponding columns. For example, the following axis specification will only return a column for Manufacturer property values in the rowset:

```
CrossJoin ([Product].[Brand].Members, [Time].[Quarter].Members) PROPER-
TIES [Product].[Brand].[Manufacturer] on rows
```

If you also wanted a single column for each dimension's member names, you would need to specify the following:

```
CrossJoin ([Product].[Brand].Members, [Time].[Quarter].Members) PROPER-
TIES [Product].[Brand].[Manufacturer], [Product].Name, [Time].Name on
rows
```

Note that all slicer information is lost when an MDX query is flattened into a rowset. No member information will be returned for any dimensions that you fail to place on an axis. If it is important to retain the slice context for the cell data, place all relevant dimensions into an explicit axis of the query (for example, axis 2).

From ADO MD, obtaining and using MDX results in recordset form is trivially easy. The following code sample demonstrates this:

```
Dim rs As ADODB.Recordset

' create it explicitly if it doesn't already exist
Set rs = New ADODB.Recordset

' set the connection that the cellset is going to execute on
Set rs.ActiveConnection = cn

' Open the recordset with an MDX query
rs.Open "SELECT [Customers].[Northeast].Children FROM [Budgeting]"

' ... do things with it like any other recordset

rs.Close  ' when we're done with it
```

The only major difference between how we used this recordset and how we used any other is that we executed an MDX query, and we used it on a connection to an OLAP database instead of a relational database.

Summary

We have touched on the very basics of client programming in ADO MD using Visual Basic for the purposes of executing MDX. Any given client that you are going to create will need to use the techniques that we have outlined here. Your clients will doubtlessly involve a great deal more; we could have devoted several chapters to building a client in ADO MD and in OLE DB for OLAP. However, if this topic is new to you, we hopefully have demonstrated that it can be quite straightforward to interact with an OLAP database and put your MDX to use.

CHAPTER 13

Working with Local Cubes

L ocal cube files provide a way for users to work with data in a disconnected client setting. In fact, local cubes are required if your users are to access data without being connected to a server. As far as client software is concerned, a local cube can be very similar to a server cube that is created in a limited database. Only a few areas of MDX do not work with a local cube, such as DRILLTHROUGH, UPDATE CUBE, and any ALTER CUBE statements that change the position or existence of members (though you can use ALTER CUBE to change the default member for a dimension). It is possible, for a variety of application requirements and constraints, to construct applications where a user can work with either server cubes or local cubes and not see any difference between them.

This chapter will detail the syntax and semantics of these MDX statements along with some subtle wrinkles in their use, and talk about some of the logistics of creating and managing local cubes. We'll discuss some of the capabilities and limitations of local cubes along the way, although that is not our primary focus in this chapter. We'll also focus on the local cube capabilities of Analysis Services 2000.

Overview of the Process

Creating a local cube involves specifying the outline structure of a local cube through the CREATE CUBE statement, and then populating the local cube by use of an MDX INSERT INTO statement, which will contain a SQL SELECT clause. Both components (CREATE CUBE and INSERT INTO . . . SELECT) are character strings, which are placed into OLE DB/ADO connection properties. At the ADO/OLE DB layer, opening a connection to the cube file when these connection properties are set will cause the cube to be created. Depending on the details of the INSERT INTO statement, the cube can be populated with data right then, and the cube is available for use.

Once a cube has been created, it can be updated by using the REFRESH CUBE statement (described in Chapter 10, "Changing the Cube and Dimension Environment through MDX") as well as by re-creating it from scratch.

Anatomy of the CREATE CUBE Statement

At its heart, the CREATE CUBE statement consists of the following framework:

```
CREATE CUBE CubeName (
Dimension definitions
Measure definitions
Command definitions
)
```

Dimensions are defined first, followed by measures, followed by any commands. The following is a very simple CREATE CUBE statement:

```
CREATE CUBE Sales
(
   DIMENSION [Time] TYPE TIME
,     LEVEL [All Time] TYPE ALL
,     LEVEL [Year]
,     LEVEL [Month]

, DIMENSION [Customer]
,    LEVEL [All Customer] TYPE ALL
,    LEVEL [State]
,    LEVEL [City]
,    LEVEL [Customer]

, DIMENSION [Product]
,    LEVEL [All Product] TYPE  ALL
```

```
    ,   LEVEL [Type]
    ,   LEVEL [Product]

    ,   MEASURE [Units]
        FUNCTION SUM

    ,   MEASURE [Dollars]
        FUNCTION SUM
        FORMAT 'Currency'

    , COMMAND ( CREATE MEMBER CURRENTCUBE.[Measures].[Avg Price] AS
        '[Measures]].[Dollars] / [Measures].[Units]' )
    )
```

Within each dimension definition, hierarchy, level, and member property, information is spelled out. Within each measure definition, data type, measure aggregation function, and default formatting, information is specified. Following measures, one or more commands can optionally be specified as well.

Note that a comma is placed between the DIMENSION information and the LEVEL information, but no comma is placed between each MEASURE and its FUNCTION or FORMAT.

Defining Dimensions

The definition of each dimension begins with the DIMENSION keyword and the name of the dimension. (Note: We will assume that you have at least some familiarity with the characteristics of Analysis Services dimensions.) You can define regular level-based dimensions, parent-child dimensions, and ragged variations on level-based and parent-child dimensions. You can also define data mining dimensions. Dimensions can contain multiple named hierarchies as well. As with a server-based dimension, you can define member properties at each level, and you can declare dimensions and hierarchies as hidden.

You can also define custom rollup expressions for each level; in conjunction with Microsoft's RollupChildren( ) extension to MDX, you can provide the functionality found in server-based rollup operators. (According to Microsoft documentation, rollup operators are directly supported, but in the RTM version, they result in a cell retrieval error (#ERR) with the message "syntax error—unexpected end of expression." Hopefully, by the time you read this, a service pack that fixes this error will be available.) Although you can't directly define custom member formulas, you can define a custom rollup expression for the level that executes an MDX formula stored in a member property, which accomplishes the same thing.

Overall Dimension

The overall dimension is defined with the following general expression:

```
DIMENSION DimName [ TYPE TIME ] [ DIMENSION_STRUCTURE PARENT_CHILD ]
[ HIDDEN ] [ OPTIONS Options ] ,
```

The allowable options to use for *Options* are:

ALLOWSIBLINGSWITHSAMENAME	Let sibling members (having different member keys) have the same name (the impact of this is discussed in Chapter 2, "MDX in More Detail" and Chapter 8, "Building Queries in MDX").
UNIQUE_NAME	Declare that every member in the dimension has a unique name.
UNIQUE_KEY	Declare that every member in the dimension has a unique key.
NOTRELATEDTOFACTTABLE	Specifies a mining dimension.

If the ALLOWSIBLINGSWITHSAMENAME is set to true (default is false), then a query for a particular member by name or unique name (following the OLAP Services 7.0 unique name style), or for a set of members, may turn up two or more members that have the same name, and two members with the same name (but different member keys) may be children of the same parent. We discuss the impact of this in Chapter 2 and Chapter 8.

If the dimension is PARENT_CHILD, then only one level (and perhaps also an ALL level) may be defined for it. Depending on whether the dimension is PARENT_CHILD or not, different options are available. If the dimension is to appear as a time dimension to MDX functions, then the TIME keyword must be specified.

Named Hierarchies

If named hierarchies are provided in the dimension, the very next thing after the dimension expression is the hierarchy name expression, which has the general form of:

```
HIERARCHY HierName [ HIDDEN ] ,
```

As you may guess, the hierarchy may be hidden. Following the HIERARCHY expression, or following the DIMENSION expression, if no named hierarchies are present, comes the level expressions.

Levels

Levels are listed for the dimension or hierarchy in order from the root level down. If the top level is to be an intrinsic ALL level, then its form is

```
LEVEL LevelName TYPE ALL ,
```

Otherwise, its form is (for the levels of non-parent-child dimensions)

```
LEVEL LevelName [ TYPE LevelType ]
[ FORMAT_NAME name_format [ FORMAT_KEY key_format ]]
[ OPTIONS ( level_options ) ] [ HIDDEN ]
[ HIDE_MEMBER_IF hide_options ]
[ CUSTOM_ROLLUP_EXPRESSION rollup_expression ]

,
```

For a parent-child dimension, the level you define has the following form (which adds one option):

```
LEVEL LevelName [ TYPE LevelType ]
[ FORMAT_NAME name_format [ FORMAT_KEY key_format ]]
[ OPTIONS ( level_options ) ] [ HIDDEN ]
[ HIDE_MEMBER_IF hide_options ]
[ ROOT_MEMBER_IF root_member_options ]
[ CUSTOM_ROLLUP_EXPRESSION rollup_expression ]

,
```

(In a parent-child dimension, if you are looking to define a ragged dimension where children can be more than one level below their parent, you will set that option in the INSERT INTO statement.) In either case, if the level holds member properties, then they are defined immediately after (and we will get to them shortly). The allowed options are as follows:

LEVEL TYPES

YEAR

QUARTER

MONTH

WEEK

DAY

DAYOFWEEK

DATE

HOUR

MINUTE

SECOND

LEVEL OPTION	MEANING
SORTBYNAME	Sort sibling by name
SORTBYKEY	Sort siblings by key value
SORTBYPROPERTY *member_property*	Sort siblings by value of *member_property*. (Must define the property)
UNIQUE	Members are fully unique in level.
UNIQUE_NAME	Member names are unique in level.
UNIQUE_KEY	Member keys are unique in level.
NOTRELATEDTOFACTTABLE	Level is a mining level.

HIDE OPTION	MEANING
ONLY_CHILD_AND_BLANK_NAME	Member hidden if no other siblings and name is blank
ONLY_CHILD_AND_PARENT_NAME	Member hidden if no other siblings and name is same as its parent's
BLANK_NAME	Member hidden if its name is blank
PARENT_NAME	Member hidden if its name is the same as its parent's

ROOT MEMBER OPTION	MEANING
ROOT_IF_PARENT_IS_BLANK	Member is considered a root if its parent name is empty.
ROOT_IF_PARENT_IS_MISSING	Member is considered a root if its parent key is NULL.
ROOT_IF_PARENT_IS_SELF	Member is considered a root if it is listed as its own parent.
ROOT_IF_PARENT_IS_BLANK_OR _SELF_OR_MISSING	Member is considered a root if any of the other conditions is met.

For example, a time dimension with levels of All, Year, Quarter, and Month that sorted its members by key value (derived from an appropriate column) would be minimally defined by the following snippet:

```
DIMENSION [Time] TYPE TIME,
  LEVEL [All Time] TYPE ALL,
  LEVEL [Year] TYPE YEAR OPTIONS (SORTBYKEY),
  LEVEL [Quarter] TYPE QUARTER OPTIONS (SORTBYKEY),
  LEVEL [Month] TYPE MONTH OPTIONS (SORTBYKEY),
```

A ragged geography dimension with levels of Country, Region, City, and Store (ragged in cities and stores) would be minimally defined by the following snippet:

```
DIMENSION [Geography],
   LEVEL [All Geography] TYPE ALL,
   LEVEL [Country],
   LEVEL [Region],
   LEVEL [City] HIDE_MEMBER_IF BLANK_NAME,
   LEVEL [Store] HIDE_MEMBER_IF BLANK_NAME,
```

Member Properties

Each member property in a level of a dimension is defined with the following:

```
PROPERTY PropertyName [ TYPE PropType ] [ HIDDEN ]
[ CAPTION Caption ] ,
```

A comma must separate each property definition from the next thing being defined (be it dimension, hierarchy, level, property, or measure). The *Caption* can be any string (in double quotes). The property types accepted can be one of the following:

PROPERTY TYPE NAMES

REGULAR

ID

RELATION_TO_PARENT

ORG_TITLE

CAPTION

CAPTION_SHORT

CAPTION_DESCRIPTION

CAPTION_ABREVIATION

WEB_URL

WEB_HTML

WEB_XML_OR_XSL

WEB_MAIL_ALIAS

ADDRESS

ADDRESS_STREET

ADDRESS_HOUSE

ADDRESS_CITY

ADDRESS_STATE_OR_PROVINCE

ADDRESS_ZIP

ADDRESS_QUARTER

ADDRESS_COUNTRY

ADDRESS_BUILDING

ADDRESS_ROOM

ADDRESS_FLOOR

ADDRESS_FAX

ADDRESS_PHONE

GEO_CENTROID_X

GEO_CENTROID_Y

GEO_CENTROID_Z

GEO_BOUNDARY_TOP

GEO_BOUNDARY_LEFT

GEO_BOUNDARY_BOTTOM

GEO_BOUNDARY_RIGHT

GEO_BOUNDARY_FRONT

GEO_BOUNDARY_REAR

GEO_BOUNDARY_POLYGON

PHYSICAL_SIZE

PHYSICAL_COLOR

PHYSICAL_WEIGHT

PHYSICAL_HEIGHT

PHYSICAL_WIDTH

PHYSICAL_DEPTH

PHYSICAL_VOLUME

PHYSICAL_DENSITY

PERSON_FULL_NAME

PERSON_FIRST_NAME

PERSON_LAST_NAME

PERSON_MIDDLE_NAME

PERSON_DEMOGRAPHIC

PERSON_CONTACT

QTY_RANGE_LOW

QTY_RANGE_HIGH

FORMATTING_COLOR

FORMATTING_ORDER

FORMATTING_FONT

FORMATTING_FONT_EFFECTS

FORMATTING_FONT_SIZE

FORMATTING_SUB_TOTAL

DATE

DATE_START

DATE_ENDED

DATE_CANCELED

DATE_MODIFIED

DATE_DURATION

VERSION

None of these property type codes conveys the meaning of "function," which would be handy if you were using a member property to hold either MDX functions that simulate Analysis Server custom member formulas or unary rollup operators for use by RollupChildren( ).

For example, the following snippet defines a customer dimension with an All level and a single customer level, ordered by a [Zip Code] property, and the [Zip Code] property itself:

```
DIMENSION [Customer],
  LEVEL [All Customer] TYPE ALL,
  LEVEL [Customer] OPTIONS SORTBYPROPERTY [Zip Code],
    PROPERTY [Zip Code],
```

FORMAT_NAME and FORMAT_KEY

If FORMAT_KEY and/or FORMAT_NAME are specified, they each take a format string like that used for a calculated member (surrounded by double quotes) and generate a textual name (or textual member key) that corresponds to that format. For example, consider the following:

```
DIMENSION [Time] TIME,
  LEVEL [Year]  FORMAT_NAME "yyyy" FORMAT_KEY "yyyy",
  LEVEL [Day]   FORMAT_NAME "mmm dd, yyyy"
```

When these two levels are created from columns having a datestamp data type, the names for the year members will be the year portion of that datestamp and the internal member keys for the years will also be the four-digit text form of the year (for example, "2001"). The day names will be of the form "Aug 27,

2001." The day key is left unspecified by this, which is probably a good idea because generally, we want compact numbers (like integers and possibly date-stamps) and not text strings for our member keys. If we specified FORMAT_NAME "mmm dd, yyyy" for our member keys as well, then our days would be ordered alphabetically within our years (for example, [Apr 01, 2001], . . . [Dec 31, 2001] . . . [Jan 01, 2001] . . .) unless we also specified an appropriate member property and OPTIONS (SORTBYPROPERTY).

FORMAT_NAME and FORMAT_KEY can be used to format strings from data types other than datestamps, such as adding currency formatting, thousands separators, or percentages to numbers.

Note that use of FORMAT_NAME and FORMAT_KEY is a convenience; the formatting facilities may well be available in the SQL SELECT clause of the INSERT INTO (described below), but by using the FORMAT_NAME and FORMAT_KEY, you won't have to adjust your SQL to any particular dialect.

Defining Measures

After all of the dimension information for the cube is defined, you list the measures for the cube. The cube must have at least one measure. The general form for a measure is much simpler than that for a dimension. It consists of the following:

```
MEASURE MeasureName AggregationFunction [ FORMAT format_string ]
[ TYPE OLEDB_type_def ] [ HIDDEN ]
```

A comma must separate a measure from its following measure or command definition, if one follows.

The *AggregationFunction* can be one of the following (DISTINCT COUNT is not supported):

AGGREGATION FUNCTIONS

SUM

COUNT

MAX

MIN

The *format_string* can be any measure format string. See Appendix C, "Intrinsic Cell and Member Properties" for the format strings accepted (in general, these follow VBA and Excel format strings).

The *OLEDB_type_def* can be one of the following (refer to OLE DB documentation if necessary for their meaning):

OLE DB MEASURE TYPE DEFINITION

DBTYPE_I1

DBTYPE_I2

DBTYPE_I4

DBTYPE_I8

DBTYPE_UI1

DBTYPE_UI2

DBTYPE_UI4

DBTYPE_UI8

DBTYPE_R4

DBTYPE_R8

DBTYPE_CY

DBTYPE_DECIMAL

DBTYPE_NUMERIC

DBTYPE_DATE

Adding Commands

After all of the measures are defined for the cube, you can list a set of commands that will be executed when the cube is opened. These commands include USE LIBRARY, CREATE MEMBER, CREATE SET, and ALTER CUBE UPDATE DIMENSION.

Each command is listed individually, using command syntax virtually identical to that if you were executing it at a client session or defining it at the server using DSO. You must get used to one important syntactic wrinkle, due to the general form of the command definition in a local cube. This general form (which looks innocuous enough at high level) is:

```
COMMAND command
```

The wrinkle comes in because if *command* contains any spaces, then the executable MDX command needs to be wrapped in matched delimiters. Interestingly, these delimiters are somewhat up to you: Both square-braces [] and parentheses () can be used. Parentheses are easy to use. If you wrap the expression in square braces and some part of the command (for example, a unique name uses square braces as well), then you need to remember how MDX nests braces. A nested right-brace is represented by two adjacent right-braces,]]. So, a command may look like (literally)

```
COMMAND [ CREATE MEMBER CURRENTCUBE.[Measures]].[Price]] AS
'[Measures]].[Dollars]] / [Measures]].[Units]]' ]
```

although it would be rendered most easily as

```
COMMAND ( CREATE MEMBER CURRENTCUBE.[Measures].[Price] AS
'[Measures].[Dollars] / [Measures].[Units]' )
```

If you are writing code to automatically place command expressions into local cubes, you should use parentheses, or make sure that your code transforms the right-braces appropriately.

ROLAP versus MOLAP

It is possible to create local cubes to be either ROLAP or MOLAP. In a MOLAP local cube, the data is read from the relational data source at the time the cube is connected to and stored in the local cube file. Only the leaf-level data is stored; no pre-calculated aggregates are stored in the file. In a ROLAP cube, by comparison, data is only read from the relational data store when cells are needed by queries (mitigated, of course, by caching in the PivotTable Service).

By default, if no options are specified, a MOLAP cube will be created. In the INSERT INTO statement, the OPTIONS keyword controls how the cube data will be treated. The "Options for INSERT INTO" section later in the chapter discusses the conditions under which one kind or the other is built.

Note that if you create a ROLAP local cube, you need make sure that the relational database login is set up appropriately. The Source_DSN property provided, when the cube is created, is retained in the cube file, whereas any information provided in the Source_DSN_Suffix property must be supplied at every subsequent connection to the cube. This means that if a user ID and/or password is required, embedding it in the Source_DSN will place it in the cube definition, whereas placing it in the Source_DSN_Suffix will require the application to provide it in subsequent uses (which you may want for security purposes).

ROLAP cubes mean smaller cube files, although cube file size frequently isn't much of a problem. If the size of a cube file is a problem for transmission over a slow network (or modem) link, remember that they compress very well using Zip compression.

Note that the options used when constructing a cube affect what members appear in each dimension. If a ROLAP cube is built, then the dimensions for the cube will include all members listed in the dimension tables regardless of whether they join to facts or not. This appears to be enabled because the PTS can parse the SQL and can internally create SQL SELECT against the underlying database that obtain dimension information. In the RTM version, though, if a MOLAP cube is built without any member properties, then the only members created for each dimension are those that actually have corresponding facts in the fact table. The difference between these two modes is important. However, if a dimension has member properties defined for it, for a MOLAP cube that is created without the SELECT query being passed through, that dimension will have all members listed. This difference between how dimensions are constructed may be accidental, but if you want a MOLAP cube to be created using all members from a dimension table regardless of whether they have facts in the fact table, you can harmlessly add a member property to the leaf level of that dimension (for example, one that holds the member name or a constant string value).

The PTS will return an error if PASSTHROUGH and DEFER_DATA are specified together.

Anatomy of the INSERT INTO Statement

Whereas the CREATE CUBE statement lays out the outline of the cube, the INSERT INTO statement describes the connection of that cube structure to relational columns and contains a SQL SELECT statement that fills the cube with data. The INSERT INTO statement lists all of the levels, member properties, and measures of the cube, which are matched to columns in the SELECT clause. It is somewhat analogous to the INSERT INTO . . . SELECT statement in SQL.

The framework of the INSERT INTO statement is as follows:

```
INSERT INTO CubeName (
Target1,
Target2,  . . .
)
[ OPTIONS options ]
SELECT ...
```

The order of cube entities (levels, member properties, and measures) in the list of targets should not make any difference, although for consistency, we tend to follow the same order as they are listed in the CREATE CUBE statement. To repeat ourselves a little, the order of columns in the SELECT clause must match the order of targets. The following is a very simple INSERT INTO statement:

```
INSERT INTO Sales (
   [Time].[Year]
 , [Time].[Month]
 , [Time].[Day]
 , [Customer].[State]
 , [Customer].[City]
 , [Customer].[Customer]
 , [Product].[Product]
 , [Measures].[Units]
```

```
,  [Measures].[Dollars]
)
SELECT
 t.year_name
,t.month_name
,t.day_name
,c.cust_state
,c.cust_city
,c.cust_name
,p.prod_name
,s.units
,s.dollars
FROM sales s, timetable t, customer c, product p
WHERE s.time_id = t.time_id AND s.cust_id = c.cust_id AND s.prod_id =
p.prod_id
```

Cube Targets

A few options are available for the targets. For any level, you can specify the key and name columns separately, and you can specify some options for the construction of a time dimension.

The All type level of a dimension is never a target for a column (as in a server-defined dimension).

Regular Dimension Levels

A regular dimension level can be specified by one or two columns. If it is specified by one column, then the name and key of the members in the level are the same. In this case, you would just name the level with its name or unique name. We'll use unique names in our examples:

[Dimension].[Level] *or* [Dimension].[Hierarchy].[Level]

If it is specified by two columns, then you append .Name to the reference for the name column and .Key to the reference for the key column, like

```
[Time].[Month].Name,
[Time].[Month].Key
```

Any member properties for the level would be defined as described later in the chapter.

Parent-Child Dimensions

A parent-child dimension has only one internal level, and this level requires at least member and parent columns. To define the members, you don't actually list the name of the level, but instead list the name of the dimension. As with a regular level, if the key and name are provided by separate columns, you use .Name and .Key to identify them, otherwise you list the dimension name only once. You also use .Parent to identify the parent column. For a parent-child dimension named account, the following snippet identifies three columns as corresponding to member key, member parent (key), and member name:

```
[Account].Key,
[Account].Parent,
[Account].Name
```

Parent-child dimensions can also be created as ragged, which in their case, requires a column that identifies the number of levels to insert between a member and its parent. The .SkipLevelColumn term is used to indicate that column, as in

```
[Account].SkipLevelColumn
```

Any member properties for the parent-child dimension would be defined as described later in the chapter.

Time Dimension

According to Microsoft's documentation, for a dimension that has been defined to be of type Time, its levels that have been defined to have one of the predefined time-level types will all be populated from a single column in the SELECT statement that has a datetime data type. In this case, even though multiple levels may have been defined for the time dimension, you only list the name of the time dimension. In this case, if you had a time dimension defined, for example, as

```
CREATE CUBE MyCube (
DIMENSION [Period] TYPE TIME
, LEVEL [Year] TYPE YEAR
, LEVEL [Month] TYPE MONTH
...
```

then the corresponding INSERT INTO would simply list the name of the [Period] dimension and supply a column expression that had a datetime data type:

```
INSERT INTO MyCube (
  [Period],
...
) SELECT
  t.period_datestamp
...
```

According to our own work with the RTM product, however, this syntax does not work; the PTS complains that a column expression for level [Year] is not found. If FORMAT_NAME and FORMAT_KEY options are specified for the levels, then a SQL error results instead when the RDBMS is Microsoft Access, so it may be that you need to provide these options after a service pack fixes the SQL generator. You can populate time levels as though they were ordinary levels, though, using the .Key and .Name placeholders. Because you will ordinarily want time members to sort in date-sequential order rather than alphabetical order, make sure to define the levels with OPTIONS (SORTBYKEY) or OPTIONS (SORTBYPROPERTY *property*) and provide an appropriate key column or member property as well.

Member Properties

For each level that has member properties, each member property is identified just by naming it. For example, if a member property [Address] has been defined for the Customer.Customer level, then the following reference would indicate it in the selected columns:

```
[Customer].[Customer].[Address]
```

If the member property is defined on a parent-child dimension, then you just use the name of the dimension as the name of the level:

```
[Account].[Ledger Code]
```

If you use the name for the internal level that you provided in the CREATE CUBE statement, you will get an error message stating that it cannot find the column expression for level *PropertyName*.

NOTE In the RTM version of Analysis Services 2000, an INSERT INTO with OPTIONS PASSTHROUGH will cause an "unexpected internal error" if a member property is specified for any level of a level-based dimension.

Custom Rollups

A custom rollup operator would be specified by listing the name of the level (or dimension name if it is a parent-child dimension) and .Custom_Rollup. An example of this would be

```
[Account].Custom_Rollup
```

Measures

Each measure is identified just by naming it, as with

```
[Measures].[Units Sold]
```

Column Placeholders in the Targets

If for some reason the SELECT clause returns columns that are not going to be used by the INSERT INTO targets, you can use the SKIPCOLUMN keyword in the target list at the position or positions in which the column to ignore appears. For example

```
SKIPONECOLUMN
```

Options for the INSERT INTO

The OPTIONS clause that can appear between the INSERT INTO (. . .) and the SELECT clauses governs how the PivotTable Service will populate the cube and how it will attempt to interpret the SELECT statement.

The options available can be divided into *analysis* and *defer* options. You can specify zero or one of each in the OPTIONS section of the INSERT INTO.

DEFER OPTION	MEANING
DEFER_DATA	Do not populate the cube with data (build a ROLAP cube).
ATTEMPT_DEFER	Try not to populate the cube with data (depends).
ANALYSIS OPTION	MEANING
PASSTHROUGH	Do not try to interpret the SELECT statement.
ATTEMPT_ANALYSIS	Try to interpret the SELECT statement.

The following table indicates what the results are for the different combinations of options:

DEFER OPTION	ANALYSIS OPTION	CUBE FORM SUCCESSFUL PARSE	CUBE FORM FAILED PARSE
(none)	(none)	MOLAP	(Error)
(none)	PASSTHROUGH	MOLAP	(can't fail)
(none)	ATTEMPT_ANALYSIS	MOLAP	MOLAP
DEFER_DATA	(none)	ROLAP	(Error)
DEFER_DATA	PASSTHROUGH	(Error)	(can't fail)
DEFER_DATA	ATTEMPT_ANALYSIS	ROLAP	(Error)
ATTEMPT_DEFER	(none)	ROLAP	MOLAP
ATTEMPT_DEFER	PASSTHROUGH	MOLAP	(can't fail)
ATTEMPT_DEFER	ATTEMPT_ANALYSIS	ROLAP	MOLAP

NOTE

■■■■ For some reason, in the RTM version, having the OPTION PASSTHROUGH by itself causes an internal error when creating a cube with a PC dimension or when creating a member property on a level.

The SELECT Clause

The SELECT statement is an ordinary SQL-compatible SELECT statement, although if you do not specify the PASSTHROUGH option, then it can only use a subset of available SQL-89 syntax. The reason for this is that the PivotTable Service will attempt to parse the SQL to some degree, and it is not facile with either a large subset of SQL or any RDBMS's particular extensions. If for some reason your SELECT statement is not being parsed correctly, or you get a mysterious "column expression cannot involve multiple tables" error message, you may need to either hide table joins under a view (if you need a ROLAP cube) or use OPTIONS PASSTHROUGH.

The order of columns selected by the SELECT statement must match the order of levels, properties, and measures identified in the INSERT INTO statement. This is similar to the requirements on a SQL INSERT INTO (. . .) SELECT . . . statement.

The following discussion is most relevant if you are using OPTION ATTEMPT_ANALYSIS or leaving out OPTION PASSTHROUGH, as it is most concerned with the SQL that the PTS can parse. If you use OPTION PASSTHROUGH, then the syntax limitations of the PS won't come into play.

The SELECT statement can use the following syntax if the PivotTable Service is to attempt/succeed at parsing it, and use it against a relational database:

```
SELECT
  ColumnRef [ AS ColumnAlias1]
  [, ColumnRef [AS ColumnAlias2] ...]
FROM
  Table1 [ [AS] TableAlias1]
  [, Table2  [[AS] TableAlias2] ...]
WHERE
  Where-clause
```

Each *ColumnRef* can consist of a column name or a table.column pair, an expression enclosed by parentheses, or an ODBC scalar function of columns. For example, the following are acceptable:

```
CustomerCity,
A.CustomerState,
(B.Price * B.Qty) AS Total,
MONTH(TimeTable.Day_Date) AS Month
```

However, because there is no provision for a GROUP BY clause, aggregate functions such as Sum( ) or Count(*) are of limited use.

The FROM clause cannot contain SQL-92 join clauses (INNER JOIN, OUTER JOIN, and so on). It can only contain a list of table names, each one optionally with a corresponding table alias.

The WHERE clause can contain zero or more equi-join clauses and zero or more constraint clauses. Individual join and constraint clauses can be combined with AND. The equi-join clauses can only be of the form ColumnA = ColumnB or (ColumnA = ColumnB), as in the following:

```
WHERE
    T.Day_ID = Tx.Day_ID AND (P.SKU = Tx.SKU)
```

The constraint clauses can be combined with OR as well as AND, and NOT can be used to negate them.

If you are going to include constraints, like (T.Day_ID < 366), then you need to enclose all of your constraints in parentheses. Otherwise, it will complain of too many tables being involved in the query. Although Microsoft does not document any join constraint besides = being usable, we find that comparisons such as < and >= can be used as well as constructs like (p.prod_id in (select prod_id from Johnson_products)), so we really can't say what the true limits are.

Select Statements that Are Not SQL

If you provide OPTION PASSTHROUGH or ATTEMPT_ANALYSIS in the INSERT INTO statement, then the contents of the SELECT clause do not need to necessarily be SQL at all. It needs to be understood by the underlying data ODBC source or OLE DB provider as something that will result in rows, but the only key is that it returns suitable rowsets for constructing a cube.

We need to provide the caveat that we have attempted to make this work, but as of the time of this writing, have not found a working case. Theoretically, it should be possible to issue an MDX SELECT statement and get the result as a flattened rowset that can be read as a cube, but we have only seen data type errors or "parameter type incorrect" errors after the query has run for some time.

More Advanced Programming: Using Rowsets in Memory

Instead of a FROM clause, the SELECT statement can select columns from an OLE DB rowset already initialized in memory by using a rowset option. This allows an application to build a local cube from anything that represents its information as an OLE DB rowset, without resorting to a full SQL interface. In this case, there will be no FROM, no tables listed, and no any WHERE clause. The options and meanings are listed in the following table:

ROWSET OPTION	MEANING
DIRECTLYFROMCACHEDROWSET *hex-number*	Populate from rowset found at address *hex-number*
DIRECTLYFROMMARSHALLEDROWSET *hex-number*	Populate from marshalled rowset found at address *hex-number*

The PivotTable Service is an in-process OLE DB provider, which means that it operates in the same address space as the process that is creating the connection to the cube file. If that process holds a pointer to an OLE DB rowset, the text form of the pointer value converted into hexadecimal is passed as the *hex-number* value following the rowset option. The following would be an example of this (assuming that the rowset has columns named Col1, Col2, and Col3):

```
SELECT
Col1, Col2, Col3
DIRECTLYFROMCACHEDROWSET 87e011c0
```

Tips for Construction

Overall, the following connection properties are relevant when you are creating a local cube:

CreateCube

Data Source

InsertInto

Source_DSN

Source_DSN_Suffix

UseExistingFile

We encourage you to review their descriptions in Appendix B, "Correction Parameters That Affect MDX."

If you are creating multiple local cubes for a user, you can package them into a single cube file. All you need to do is specify the name of an existing cube file when you create the cube, and the cube will be added to the file or updated if it already exists. By use of the UseExistingFile connection parameter, you can also direct the PTS to preserve the cube, or to fail to create the cube if the file does not already exist. (See Appendix A for a full description of this property.)

When you do create multiple cubes in a single cube file, keep in mind that each cube appears in its own catalog or database having the same name. This means that the cubes are separate and cannot be combined in a session virtual cube.

As far as maintaining the cube files go, keep in mind that the REFRESH CUBE statement will refresh the MOLAP data when executed. It is roughly the same as a full process of a cube on a Microsoft OLAP/Analysis Services server—all data is re-read from the source databases and the MOLAP storage is re-built. Along the way, the dimensions are fully refreshed too. This means that you don't have to go through the process of re-specifying and executing the full CREATE CUBE/INSERT INTO process. Of course, if any of the dimension levels change, any measure definitions change, or commands change, you will need to re-create the cube from scratch.

Local Cubes from Server Cubes

One very frequent use of local cubes is to provide disconnected access to server-resident cubes. In many cases, this is straightforward, but you should keep a few things in mind.

You can create local cubes from a SQL query against a server cube. We will not discuss the SQL syntax supported by Analysis Services (this is, after all, a book on MDX). It is a reasonably restricted and easy-to-understand subset of SQL that treats the entire cube as a table.

If the server cube is a virtual cube that combines measures with differing leaf levels in their regular cubes or with different base dimensionality, you will need to pay attention to which measures you are querying for and from where. All measures in the local cube will have the same dimensionality and enter at the leaf level of its dimensions, so you may need to provide placeholder members at the leaf level for one or more measures for one or more dimensions to make all measures enter at the leaf level. In addition, although you can create a UNION ALL query in standard SQL to combine multiple separate table queries, you cannot create a UNION ALL query against multiple regions of an Analysis Services cube to query separate regions of the virtual cube and combine them into one rowset. However, you can readily compose a UNION ALL query that combines each fact table that feeds the virtual cube, and inserts placeholder members if necessary to ensure that all data actually feeds into the leaf level.

Rollups and Custom Member Formulas

In order to use unary rollup operators, you need to be able to define a custom rollup formula. The following ought to work for a dimension named [Account] that holds its rollup operators in a property named [RollupOp]:

```
CUSTOM_ROLLUP_EXPRESSION
'iif (
  IsLeaf ([Account].CurrentMember),
  [Account].Ignore,
  RollupChildren (
    [Account].CurrentMember,
    [Account].CurrentMember.Properties ("RollupOp")
  )
)'
```

In order to simulate custom member formulas, you can use a custom rollup formula that references a member property that contains the member formula. The formula would look like the following:

```
CUSTOM_ROLLUP_EXPRESSION
'iif (
  [Account].CurrentMember.Properties ("CustomFunc") = ""
  [Account].Ignore,
  StrToVal (
    [Account].CurrentMember.Properties ("CustomFunc")
  )
)'
```

The whole definition of the dimension would look like

```
DIMENSION [Account] DIMENSION_STRUCTURE PARENT_CHILD
, LEVEL [Account1]
ROOT_MEMBER_IF ROOT_IF_PARENT_IS_BLANK_OR_SELF_OR_MISSING
CUSTOM_ROLLUP_EXPRESSION
'iif (
  [Account].CurrentMember.Properties ("CustomFunc") = ""
  [Account].Ignore,
  StrToVal (
    [Account].CurrentMember.Properties ("CustomFunc")
  )
)'
, PROPERTY CustomFunc
```

And, where a dimension has both custom member formulas and custom rollup operators, the formula overrides the operators for a member, so simulating that would require the following:

```
CUSTOM_ROLLUP_EXPRESSION
'iif (
```

```
     [Account].CurrentMember.Properties ("CustomFunc") = "",
     /* no function, check for operators */
     iif (
       IsLeaf ([Account].CurrentMember),
       [Account].Ignore,
       RollupChildren (
         [Account].CurrentMember,
         [Account].CurrentMember.Properties ("RollupOp")
       )
     ),
     /* got a function, execute it */
     StrToVal (
       [Account].CurrentMember.Properties ("CustomFunc")
     )
   )'
```

Summary

In this chapter, we have focused on the mechanics of building and maintaining local cube files, and we have explored the Microsoft MDX syntax required to describe and populate these cubes. Combined with at least a basic understanding of good dimension and cube design principles, you should be able to build and use local cube files for delivering data and analyzing it in a variety of ways.

CHAPTER 14

Optimizing MDX

J ust like any other language, there is more than one way to say the same thing in MDX. Some alternatives, however, may be more efficient than others in their execution. In this chapter, we look at some of the factors that control efficiency (in terms of CPU and memory used) when executing MDX in Microsoft Analysis Services. If you are interested in efficiency but use a different OLE DB for OLAP provider, some of the techniques described may still apply.

We are not going to discuss optimal database design in this chapter. In our experience building analysis systems using OLAP and Analysis Services, we have found many other issues and factors in total system efficiency, some of which affect MDX execution. However, in keeping with the thrust of this as an MDX book, we will restrict our discussion to the issues most directly connected to composing and using MDX, and only look at one design issue that trades MDX work for cube construction work.

Although we will present different areas of optimization, it is also important to remember that faster is not necessarily "better." If your applications respond too slowly, then something may need to be made faster. If it's fast enough and it works, it doesn't need to be fixed. Composing queries that are optimal from a resource point of view may require more cumbersome database designs or front-end query builders as well. But when you need to tune it up, this chapter may help.

Controlling Location of Execution

One aspect of Analysis Services query performance is where the query actually executes. We have generally described calculations performed by Analysis Services, without specifying either the PivotTable Service or the server as the location of calculations. The location for the calculations depends on a few criteria. The first factor is the value of the Execution Location connection parameter. If this is set to 2, then all aspects of queries are executed in the PivotTable Service. If this is set to 3, then queries are resolved as much as possible on the server. If left to its default value or set to 1, then internal heuristics decide whether the query is executed in the PivotTable Service or at the server. The only heuristic we can locate is whether or not the "large-level" limit was exceeded for the query. By default, OLAP Services defines a large level as 1,000 members, though this default can be changed for the server and also can be specified by the client when opening a connection (see the description of the "Large Level Threshold" connection property in Appendix B).

Using the default as an example, PivotTable Services would consider a query as requiring the aggregation of a large level if the results require the run-time aggregation of 1,000 or more members of a dimension level. If the query does not involve any large level, then all calculations occur at the client. If the query involves a large level, then the query is evaluated at the server (however, in tests it appears that the supporting data is also passed along to the client because subsequent variations on the query that used the same low-level data were not forwarded to the server).

This issue of the location of calculations is particularly important for you to understand if you are making use of ROLAP or HOLAP partitions. An MDX query that cannot be satisfied from a stored aggregate and that does not cross the large-level threshold on members involved will cause the required records from the fact table to be aggregated in the PivotTable Service. This means that clients that make queries that involve lots of fact table aggregation will only require the Analysis Services server to spend a negligible amount of CPU and no measurable additional RAM to satisfy the query. The amount of work performed at the client may be significant, however, because even on an SMP client, the PivotTable Service will devote only one thread's worth of processing to the task. It also means that the results will not be cached at the server, only at the client. If more than one client needs the same aggregated data, then each client will perform the same aggregation of leaf-level data. By adjusting the large-level threshold, you will allow more of these queries to be handled and cached at the server. Whether this makes sense or not for your situation will depend on the mix of queries posed to your server.

On a query-by-query basis, there is no way for the client to make the request, "Please execute this at the server; I don't have the resources here." (There is also no direct way for the client to make the request, "Please execute this here; I don't want to tie up the server resources if I can't answer it myself.") There is an indirect way to specify that large calculations take place at the client, however. Any use of a named set, whether defined by CREATE SET or WITH SET, will pin the query at the client. If you first create a named set at the client that contains the large level's members, then using that set in a query will cause the query to be executed at the client. Forcing the calculation to take place at the client also forces all of the required cell data to cross the network to the client.

All calculated members are not equal as far as controlling the location of execution. A calculated member defined at the server (using CREATE MEMBER) can be used in a query either at the client or at the server. A calculated member defined using WITH MEMBER can also be executed either at the client or the server. However, a calculated member defined with CREATE MEMBER that is created during the course of a session cannot be used at the server; any query that involves such a calculated member will be executed at the client.

Cell calculations also may or may not pin the execution of a query to the client, depending on how they are defined. A cell calculation defined at either the server or the client using CREATE CELL CALCULATION will enable the query to be executed at the server. A cell calculation defined at the client using WITH CELL CALCULATION will be executed at the client, however.

Optimizing Set Operations

When the PivotTable Service executes queries, it behaves as though every set were fully materialized in memory prior to use. This introduces significant resource issues for both the client and the server. The server lets you tune the size of a "large level." The server will handle calculations that involve members from a single dimension level that are greater in number than this large-level size. Calculations that involve fewer members can be handled in the PivotTable Service at the client. Note that this issue affects the use of members from a single dimension. For example, the expression

```
Topcount ([Customer].[Individual Customer].Members, 50,
    [Measures].Sales)
```

will be evaluated at the server if the number of members in the [Customer].[Individual Customer] level is greater than this threshold, and at the client if it is less. However, this threshold is for members of a level, not tuples in a set. Assume that the threshold is set at 1,000 (the default). Suppose that you have 500 customers, which is safely below the threshold, and 100 product categories. Suppose also that you request the following:

```
Topcount (
  CrossJoin(
    [Customer].[Individual Customer].Members,
    [Product].[Category].Members
  ),
  50,
  [Measures].[Sales]
)
```

You will get the top 50 customer-product tuples in terms of sales. In this case, the 50,000 combinations will be generated and examined on the client, perhaps pushing the memory consumed by the PivotTable Service past the limits of your machine. If the combinations were generated on the server, this would still be a burden.

To obtain good performance, you may need to rephrase very resource-intensive calculations. The key to rephrasing is breaking up an operation on a large set into a set of operations on smaller sets. We'll work through some common types of set-related optimizations now. A common thread that runs through them is replacing an expensive CrossJoin() with a less expensive series of operations.

Sums along Cross-Joined Sets

For example, sums across multiple dimensions that are phrased as the sums of sums of individual dimensions will be less resource-intensive than will a single sum of a cross-join. That is, instead of this expression,

```
Sum (
  CrossJoin (
    Descendants (
      [Customer].CurrentMember,
      [Customer].[Individual Customer]
    ),
    Crossjoin (
      Descendants (
        [Time].CurrentMember,
        [Time].[Day]
      ),
      Descendants (
        [Product].CurrentMember,
        [Product].[Category]
      )
    )
  ),
  [Measures].[Sales in Euros] *
```

```
    ([Measures].[Currency Conversion],
      Ancestor ([Geography], [Geography].[Country]))
  )
```

you would want to express it as follows:

```
Sum (
  Descendants (
    [Customer].CurrentMember,
    [Customer].[Individual Customer]
  ),
  Sum (
    Descendants (
      [Time].CurrentMember,
      [Time].[Day]
    ),
    Sum (
      Descendants (
        [Product].CurrentMember,
        [Product].[Category]
      ),
      [Measures].[Sales in Euros] *
      ([Measures].[Currency Conversion],
        Ancestor ([Geography], [Geography].[Country])
) ) )
```

This avoids the CrossJoin () and provides exactly the same result. When you are calculating the results, the order of dimensions is not likely to make any semantic difference. However, if you nest the larger sets within the smaller sets, the Sum() will execute noticeably more quickly. For example, if the number of customer descendants in the previous Sum() is likely to be larger than the number of product descendants, you should move the customers to be inside of the products. The performance boost will vary as a function of the number of dimensions and members involved, but it can easily make a difference of 5 to 20 percent on the time it takes to calculate. (See "Optimizing Summation" further along for more notes.)

Filtering across Cross-Joined Sets

Frequently, you will need to filter the results of one or more cross-joined sets. Depending on what your filter criterion is, you may or may not be able to create a high-performing expression.

Let's take the simplest case: filtering out tuples with associated empty cells. In straightforward, standard MDX, you might express this as

```
Filter (
  CrossJoin (
    [Geography].[Region].Members,
```

```
CrossJoin (
  [Product].[Category].Members,
  [Payment Terms].[Terms].Members
 ),
 ),
Not IsEmpty ([Measures].[Sales])
)
```

In Analysis Services, cross-joining is pretty expensive, as the entire cross-joined set appears to be instantiated in memory prior to any filtering taking place. However, if the [Sales] measure is directly fed into the cube from a fact table, you can make this much more efficient by using Microsoft's own NonEmpty-CrossJoin( ), as in the following:

```
NonEmptyCrossJoin (
  [Geography].[Region].Members,
  [Product].[Category].Members,
  [Payment Terms].[Terms].Members,
  { [Measures].[Sales] },
  3
)
```

We'll leave the detailed definition of this function to Appendix A. You can see that it accepts more than two sets for its input. Analysis Services uses internal information gleaned from reading fact table information to provide the most rapid response it can.

The NonEmptyCrossJoin(. . .) works much better than Filter (CrossJoin (. . .), Not IsEmpty(. . .)). However, NonEmptyCrossJoin( ) doesn't deal with calculated members on any dimension. If you need to factor calculations in (for example, members calculated by custom member formulas or calculated members), then you should use Generate( ):

```
Generate (
  [Geography].[Region].Members,
  CrossJoin (
    [Geography].CurrentMember,
    Generate (
      [Product].[Category].Members,
      CrossJoin (
        [Product].CurrentMember,
        Filter (
          [Payment Terms].[Terms].Members,
          Not IsEmpty ([Measures].[Calculated Member])
) ) ) ) )
```

The previous is much faster than the equivalent filter of a large number of CrossJoin( ) operators. In our own lab testing on sample data sets, when the difference is noticeable it takes about twice as long as the NonEmptyCrossJoin( ), but only about a third of the time as the straightforward filter of a CrossJoin( ).

Optimizing TopCount() and BottomCount()

TopCount() and BottomCount() are valuable and somewhat resource-intensive operations. If you are simply taking the top or bottom count against members of a single dimension, you can't really optimize the MDX used. However, if you are taking the top or bottom count of a set of tuples formed from a CrossJoin(), then you can significantly optimize the processing through MDX. Consider the following extreme example, which potentially generates a huge set in memory:

```
TopCount (
    { [Customer].[Individual Customer].Members
    * [Time].[Day].Members
    * [Product].[Category].Members },
    50,
    [Measures].[Qty Returned]
)
```

Creating the set and then accessing the top members is very time- and memory-consuming. However, it can be broken up into the following to get the same result:

```
TopCount (
    Generate (
        [Customer].[Individual Customer].Members,
        TopCount (
            { [Customer].CurrentMember } *
            [Time].[Day].Members * [Product].[Category].Members,
            50,
            [Measures].[Qty Returned]
        )
    ),
    50,
    [Measures].[Qty Returned]
)
```

This last expression means "for each customer, generate a top-50 set, combine all of these top-50 sets, and take the top 50 from them." The overhead of creating the larger number of smaller sets is less than the overhead of extracting the top 50 from the single larger set, and the results will be the same.

Note that TopPct () and BottomPct() cannot be optimized in this way, as the inner TopPct() will remove tuples and cell values that need to be considered by the outer TopPct().

Optimizing Sorting: Order()

Fortunately, the Order( ) function doesn't need a lot of optimizing in Analysis Services 2000. When a set of tuples is to be ordered, the ordering expression is evaluated once over the set, the results are placed into a work area, and the tuples are sorted off of that. This means that complex expressions are only evaluated once per tuple, and any converting of data types (for example, text versions of member properties into dates or numbers) will also only happen once.

There isn't any straightforward way of optimizing the sorting of cross-joined sets; you cross-join the sets and then you order them. If you are both ordering and filtering a set, it is usually most efficient to filter the set first and then order it, unless the filter condition is somehow dependent on the ordering.

Optimizing Summation

When discussing dimensional calculations in Chapter 8 and time analysis calculations in Chapter 11, we looked very briefly at expressing a calculation across measures as a calculation on another dimension that would intersect existing measures. In various examples in Chapter 3, we created calculated mesures that would aggregate another measure. One technique creates a calculated member that, when combined with a measure, produces the right calculation for the measure, while the other technique puts all of the calculation logic into its own calculated measure. Although computationally equivalent, there is a surprising performance difference between the two ways to express a calculation. Summation is the most common calculation that this will be seen in.

To recap, consider the two possible ways of phrasing the summation of two measures for a given set of customers, products, and channels:

```
WITH
MEMBER [Customer].[Total] AS
'Sum ( { Set of Customers } )'
MEMBER [Product].[Total] AS
'Sum ( { Set of Products } )'
MEMBER [Channel].[Total] AS
'Sum ( { Set of Channels } )'
SELECT
{ [Measures].[Units], [Measures].[Revenue] } on columns,
{ [Time].[Quarter].Members } on rows
FROM Sales
WHERE ([Customer].[Total], [Product].[Total], [Channel].[Total])
```

and

```
WITH
MEMBER [Measures].[Total Units] AS
'Sum (
  { Set of Channels },
  Sum (
    { Set of Products },
    Sum (
      { Set of Customers },
      [Measures].[Units]
) ) )'
MEMBER [Measures].[Total Sales] AS
'Sum (
  { Set of Channels },
  Sum (
    { Set of Products },
    Sum (
      { Set of Customers },
      [Measures].[Sales]
) ) )'
SELECT
{ [Measures].[Total Units], [Measures].[Total Revenue] } on columns,
{ [Time].[Quarter].Members } on rows
FROM Sales
```

Both of these will result in exactly the same set of cell values, although they will have slightly different measure names. However, there is a notable performance difference between them. Although your mileage will vary depending on the query, we have seen the second phrasing take only 60 percent of the time of the first phrasing. In short, the more dimensionally compact phrasing can easily be 40 percent slower. Both take time in proportion to the number of measures being aggregated, so querying for fewer measures or more measures in the first phrasing of the query will not affect the time despite the fact that the number of formulas hasn't changed.

Although the more dimensional phrasing is slower, remember that in many cases the difference will be negligible. Also consider that the phrasing lends itself to a simple way of constructing ratios and further calculations on those sums at the server.

External Functions

Although the use of external functions in a query requires the function library to be installed on the client tier, the presence of external function calls does not force the execution of the query to the client tier. Analysis Services divides a query up into resolving the sets that comprise the axes of the query and then filling in the cell values. If the external function exists on the server as well as on the client, then the query can be resolved on either tier. If the external function is not involved in determining the axes of the query, then the bulk of the query can be resolved at the server, regardless of whether the function is on the server or not. Of course, if the function exists only on the client, then the query will be executed on the client.

External functions may well be faster than recursive or complex calculated members, and be used to optimize calculations themselves. If the definition of a calculated member requires a naturally iterative operation, or if it requires creating a set two or more times and referencing related cell values at least once, then it is a good candidate. We provide a simple example of this in Chapter 3, "MDX in Use," where we describe how to implement Pareto analysis.

Designing Calculations into Your Database (Member Properties into Measures)

We have seen over and over that there are certain useful calculations that junior designers will initially compose against member properties, but which are more efficient and manageable when put directly into OLAP cubes. This is an area that is straightforward to explain, so even though it delves into cube design as well, we will describe it here.

A number of simple numerical data types are often expressed as member properties. Typical examples include the square footage of each store or the number of days in a month (or a higher level time period). As a member property, these are relatively straightforward to use in calculations on the level they are defined for:

```
CREATE MEMBER [Sales].[Sales Per Square Foot] AS
'[Measures].[Sales] / Val ([Store].CurrentMember.Properties ("Store Sq
Ft"))'
```

However, these calculations are desirable at any level, so there is an impetus to define a calculated member that works at any level:

```
CREATE MEMBER [Sales].[Sales Per Square Foot] AS
'[Measures].[Sales] / Sum (
  Descendants (
    [Store].CurrentMember,
    [Store].[Individual Store]
  ),
  Val ([Store].CurrentMember.Properties ("Store Sq Ft"))
)'
```

If you have more than one calculation that involves square footage (costs per square foot, employees per square foot, and shrinkage per square foot), you may also define a calculated member that is just the square footage aggregated appropriately:

```
CREATE MEMBER [Sales].[Store Square Feet] AS
'Sum (
  Descendants (
    [Store].CurrentMember,
    [Store].[Individual Store]
  ),
  Val ([Store].CurrentMember.Properties ("Store Sq Ft"))
)'
CREATE MEMBER [Sales].[Sales Per Square Foot] AS
'[Measures].[Sales] / [Measures].[Store Square Feet]'
```

However, this makes for unnecessary work in every query that executes against the cube. It also forces you to deal with any client-side and logistical issues that arise because [Store Square Feet] is not a "real" member, but a calculated one.

The simplest way to provide this calculation that is also the most efficient is to create a one-dimensional cube with a measure of [Store Square Feet], using the Store dimension. (Although cubes generally have a time dimension, they don't have to, and in fact you are ignoring the time dimension by having the square footage as a member property instead of a measure anyway.) Then combine this one-dimensional cube with your original cube into a virtual cube. Now your sales per square foot calculated member will only need to be defined as

```
CREATE MEMBER [Sales].[Sales Per Square Foot] AS
'[Measures].[Sales] / [Measures].[Store Square Feet]'
```

Similarly, the number of days per time period can be placed into a one-dimensional cube by simply counting the number of day-level time dimension records (or by summing the number 1). If your time dimension starts above the day level, you can use an appropriate column function or a stored column value in the time dimension table to bring in the right number.

Less frequently, applications make use of the first day that a customer, product, or piece of apparatus becomes active. Date/time serial numbers can also be used in cubes and aggregated by the MIN or MAX aggregation function, so the same cube-combining technique can be used for date values as well.

Use of WITH CACHE and CREATE CACHE to Optimize Caching

Analysis Services leverages precalculated aggregates where it can to assist in answering a query. These aggregates may be stored in optimized MOLAP storage or in relatively unoptimized ROLAP (relational) storage. Precalculated aggregates are only useable if they are available, and sometimes they are not. For example, in a cube with 12 dimensions and only two levels per dimension, the number of possible precalculated aggregates to create rises to 4,096, and if only one of those dimensions has four levels, the number of possible aggregates is 16,384. It is only practical to create pre-calculated aggregates for a small percentage of these, and a great many queries may end up being satisfied by accessing leaf-level cells and aggregating up. If the storage mode of the cube is ROLAP or HOLAP, then these queries will initially be answered by accessing the fact table. Also, if the query is being directed to a local cube (whether MOLAP mode or ROLAP mode; see Chapter 13 for information on local cubes), there are no precalcuated aggregates at all to leverage. When queries are insufficiently supported by aggregates for one reason or another, we can sometimes speed them up by directing Analysis Services to create and/or cache relevant aggregates in memory.

Drill-down analysis (by definition as well as by practice) starts with a high-level query that is followed by additional low-level queries. Unfortunately, if a query is not being satisfied from a pre-calculated aggregate, a high-level query is likely to add data to the query cache at a high level. When the client drills down, the leaf-level data must be entirely re-queried from the lowest level (and perhaps also from the fact table). However, it is possible to essentially warm up the cache for a drill-down analysis through use of the CREATE CACHE statement. For example, let's say that you anticipate the following query to run more slowly than you'd like, and you expect the user to drill down from one of the quarters to the months in 2000:

```
SELECT
{ CrossJoin (
  [Time].[2000].Children,
  { [Measures].[Units], [Measures].[Avg Price] }
) } on columns,
{ [Product].[CPU].Children } on rows
FROM [Forecasts]
```

The following CREATE CACHE statement will set aside a usable cache that will support both that query and a drill-down from it. The CREATE CACHE statement itself will take about the same amount of time that the query would have to execute, but after the cache is created, the query should execute entirely from RAM (in milliseconds):

```
CREATE CACHE FOR [Forecasts] AS
'(
  Descendants (
    [Time].[2000],
    [Time].[Month]
  ),
  [Product].[CPU].Children
)'
```

Note that we do not specify the measures in the CREATE CACHE statement itself; all base measures of the cube are loaded into the cache. Also note that if the [Units] or [Avg Price] measures are calculated from data outside the cell region that we specified in the CREATE CACHE statement, the query will still need to go out and retrieve the appropriate data. (There isn't a way to say "load data necessary for this calculated member/measure across this cell region.") We may eventually want to drop this cache eventually to make room for other cache data. However, in Analysis Services 2000, there is no equivalent DROP CACHE statement. (Executing a REFRESH CUBE statement does not free up the memory, either.)

The applications for WITH CACHE are less frequent than those for CREATE CACHE, as the cache created by WITH CACHE lasts only as long as the query. Perhaps surprisingly, we have found that WITH CACHE actually tends to slow queries down. When Analysis Services responds to a query, it first resolves the axes and their contents, and then returns a multidimensional data set to the client. As the client retrieves cell values from the multidimensional data set, calculations such as calculated member take place and cell data gets retrieved from the server. (This is relatively optimal when not all of a set of cells gets used out of a query.) Use of WITH CACHE can cause the overall query to be satisfied more quickly in some cases since the entire set of cells specified by WITH CACHE is brought to the client before the multidimensional data set is returned. In an application accesses the server through a fast LAN, the performance difference should not be noticeable. In an application that accesses the server over a modem connection or a wide area network (WAN) link, the query results may take longer to begin appearing since more work is done up front, but they are likely to take less overall time to fully retrieve.

When should you use CREATE CACHE or WITH CACHE? In general, only after you find out that a query or set of queries takes too long and that the cache actually speeds things up. CREATE CACHE often will speed up queries, and WITH CACHE sometimes will. However, a query that someone runs only once will usually not be any faster, as it takes time to build the cache. Also, when you specify a cache, you specify a full sub-cube of data to be returned to the Pivot-Table Service. Many queries that access a large number of cells don't actually access all those cells. For example, they may only access certain tuples out of the full cross-join of all members specified in the cache. The extra time (and memory) it takes to cache cells that you are not going to reference may not compensate the decrease in performance. There is a general truism in software development that premature optimization is a mistake. We have found this to be especially true with respect to cache construction. CREATE CACHE and WITH CACHE can help you, but you should try them out only on queries that seem to need optimizing in the first place.

Summary and Takeaway Rules

Some general rules that you should take away from this chapter include the following:

- You need to determine what level of server resources you are willing to use to support client queries because this will impact your choice of default large levels. This will involve looking at the query mix and client machine resources. You can adjust the server-side large-level setting and the client-side large-level and execution location settings in order to push more queries to the server or to the clients.

- CrossJoin( ) can be expensive. The relationship between CrossJoin( ) and Generate( ) can be leveraged when operations that involve sorting and selection are involved to make the operation more efficient. The relationship is as follows: CrossJoin(A, B) is equivalent to Generate(A, CrossJoin({A.Current}, B)). Any sort of filtering done on the results of a cross-join can be transformed into this, and if the difference in time is noticeable, then using Generate( ) will be faster.

- Consider using NonEmpty CrossJoin() instead of CrossJoin() when appropriate; it is much faster.

- The commutative nature of SUM (and MIN and MAX) can be leveraged when operations that involve aggregating over multiple dimensions are involved. That is, Sum({A} * {B} * {C}, d) is equivalent to Sum({A}, Sum ({B}, Sum ({C}, d))). Operations involving Count( ) need to be treated a little differently: Count({A} * {B} * {C}) is equivalent to Sum ({A}, Sum ({B}, Count ({C}))).

MDX Function and Operator Reference

This appendix is a detailed reference to the functions and operators of both standard MDX and Microsoft's extensions as implemented in Analysis Services 2000. The main body of the appendix lists the functions and operators in alphabetical order, along with any arguments and the result's data type. We have included a pair of indexes at the beginning to help you navigate.

Index to Functions

We have found that two different indexes are useful for looking up a function or operator: by name and by return type.

Alphabetical Index

Return Type Index

The functions are all listed here by return type:

Number

String

Logical

Member

Tuple

Set

Dimension, Hierarchy, and Level

The following functions return a reference to a dimension:

Miscellaneous

Basic Operators

This section lists the basic operators for manipulating strings, numbers, and logical conditions.

Value Operators

Table A.1 lists the basic operators. A *ValueExpr* can be either numeric or string, but it must be the same type on both sides of the operator. An *ObjectExpr* can refer to any meta data object or to NULL.

Table A.1   List of Operators

OPERATOR	RESULTS IN
NumericExpr + *NumericExpr*	Addition
NumericExpr − *NumericExpr*	Subtraction
NumericExpr * *NumericExpr*	Multiplication
NumericExpr / *NumericExpr*	Division
− *NumericExpr*	Unary negation
StringExpr + *StringExpr*	String concatenation (*extension to OLE DB for OLAP*)
StringExpr ‖ *StringExpr*	String concatenation (*standard MDX*)
ValueExpr < *ValueExpr*	Less than
ValueExpr > *ValueExpr*	Greater than
ValueExpr <= *ValueExpr*	Less than or equal to
ValueExpr >= *ValueExpr*	Greater than or equal to
ValueExpr <> *ValueExpr*	Not equal to
ValueExpr = *ValueExpr*	Equal to
BooleanExpr **AND** *BooleanExpr*	True if both expressions are true, false otherwise
BooleanExpr **OR** *BooleanExpr*	True if either expression is true
NOT *BooleanExpr*	True if expression is not true, false otherwise
BooleanExpr **XOR** *BooleanExpr*	True if either of the expressions is true but not both of them, and false otherwise
ObjectExpr **IS** *ObjectExpr*	True if the two object expressions refer to the same object, and false otherwise. Any reference to a non-existent object will return True when combined with NULL, as in Time.[All Time].Parent IS Null. (*extension to OLE DB for OLAP*)

Expressions can be grouped with parentheses ( ) to make the ordering of operations clear.

Constructing Tuples

```
( member [, member . . .] )
```

Tuples can be explicitly constructed by listing members from one or more dimensions, separated by commas, and enclosing that dimension or dimensions within parentheses. If only one dimension is present in the tuple, the parentheses can be omitted as well. Any member specification will work, not just explicitly named members. For example, the following examples are all tuple specifications:

```
[Time].[1997]
([Time].[1997])
([Time].[1997], [Customer].[All Customers])
([Time].[1997], {[Customer].Members}.Item (0))
```

Note that when a function requires that a tuple be one of its arguments within parentheses, the parentheses must be placed around the tuple as well as within. For example, the following would be a correct tuple specification to be passed to TupleToStr( ):

```
TupleToStr( ([Time].[1997], [Customer].[All Customers]) )
```

Trying to create an empty tuple with ( ) will result in a syntax error.

Constructing Sets

```
{ tuple or set  [, tuple or set  . . . ] }
```

Sets can be explicitly constructed by enclosing one or more tuples or sets with the same dimensionality within curly braces, "{" and "}". Each tuple or set specification must be separated from the next by a comma. For example, the following are all sets:

```
{ [Time].[1997] }
{ ([Time].[1997], [Customer].[All Customers]) }
{ [Time].[All Time], [Time].[Year].Members, { [Time].[Quarter].Members
}}
```

The first two are sets of one tuple each, and the last one is a set comprised of one member and two sets in order. Note that in the last example, the second set within it is also enclosed in curly braces. This is not required, and it does not affect the interpretation in any way. Although an empty set is not usually of much practical use, it may be created with an empty pair of curly braces:

```
member : member
```

This operator constructs a set from two members and uses the two members as endpoints. The two members must be on the same level; if they are not, a parse error will occur. By using the database ordering of the members in the dimension, all members between the endpoints will be included. It is not an error for the two members to be the same (that is, {[Time].[1998] : [Time].[1998]}).

In Microsoft Analysis Services, if the member on the right-hand side of the colon is earlier in the database ordering than the member on the left, a range is constructed from the member on the right to the member on the left (as though the members were flipped around the colon). If either of the members is invalid, a parse error occurs.

In the first release of Microsoft OLAP Services, if the member on the right-hand side of the colon is earlier in the database ordering than the member on the left, a range is constructed from the left-hand member to the last member on the level. If only one member is invalid and the other is valid, a range is constructed from the valid member to the end of the level. An invalid left-hand member creates a range from the first member in the level, and an invalid right-hand member creates a range to the last member in the level. If both are invalid, an empty set is returned.

Standard MDX Operators Not Supported by Microsoft OLAP/Analysis Services

The CASE operator is not supported in any variation, and the || operator is not used for string concatenation. Instead, the + operator is supported for string concatenation.

Function and Operator Reference

A

AddCalculatedMembers(*set***)**   Returns: set   *Extension*

By default, when a set of members is specified using a function that retrieves a set based on meta data (like .Members, .Children, Descendants( ), and so on), only base members are returned, even though calculated members may be within that range. The AddCalculatedMembers( ) function adds in all of the calculated members that are siblings of the members specified within the *set*. Each calculated member that was not already in the set is added in database order after its last sibling member in the set.

The set is limited to only one dimension. Note that this function adds all calculated members defined, whether they were defined by CREATE MEMBER at the server or at the client, or in the query through WITH MEMBER.

See also: .AllMembers, StripCalculatedMembers( )

Aggregate(*set* **[,** *numeric value expression***])**   Returns: number

This function aggregates the cells formed by the *set* according to the default aggregation operator for any measures in context. If a *numeric value expression* is provided, then this function sums the expression's set of values over the cells. In the event that the cells are of a measure that aggregates by COUNT, MIN, or MAX, then COUNT, MIN, or MAX, respectively, is the aggregation operation used; otherwise, the aggregation operation used is summation. Although you may specify an expression to be evaluated by this function, this function does not work if you use calculated members as its inputs. (If a calculated member "M" has a higher SOLVE_ORDER than a calculated member on a different dimension that is performing the Aggregate( ), then "M" will use the results of the aggregating member.)

This comes in handy when you have a set of different measures with different aggregation rules that are all being queried for. Calculated members performing period-to-date aggregations as well as aggregations on other dimensions will often be best constructed out of this operator. (Essentially, this is the implicit operation carried out within OLAP Services's hierarchies.) Consider the following calculated member:

```
CREATE MEMBER [Time].[MonthsOf1998ToDate] AS
'Aggregate ( {[Time].[Jan 1998] : [Time].[May 1998]} )'
```

When combined with a summing measure, this member will yield the sum of its values over the range of January through May 1998. When combined with a measure aggregating by MAX, this member will yield the MAX of its values over that same time period.

Note: In Analysis Services 2000, measures aggregated by DISTINCT COUNT cannot be aggregated by this function.

See also: Sum( ), Count( ), Min( ), Max( ), Avg( )

dimension.**AllMembers**   Returns: set   *Extension*

hierarchy.**AllMembers**   Returns: set   *Extension*

level.**AllMembers**   Returns: set   *Extension*

Generally, the .AllMembers functions are semantically equivalent to AddCalculatedMembers(*Scope*.Members), but they provide a more intuitive syntax. Although the Microsoft documentation only refers to .AllMembers for dimensions and levels, we note that in the case of multiple hierarchies on a dimension, you can only use this against one hierarchy.

The only case where .AllMembers and AddCalculatedMembers( ) differ is when no members are visible in the scope of [Dimension].Members, [Hierarchy].Members, or [Level].Members. This can occur on the measures dimension if all measures are hidden in a cube.

The following two statements will generally return the same set:

```
[Measures].AllMembers
AddCalculatedMembers([Measures].Members)
```

See also: AddCalculatedMembers( ), StripCalculatedMembers( )

Ancestor(*member, level***)**   Returns: member

Ancestor(*member, distance***)**   Returns: member

This function finds the source *member*'s ancestor at the target *level* or *distance*. If the target *level* is the level of the source member, then the source member is returned. If a *distance* number is specified, it is the number of hierarchical steps above the *member*. A *distance* of 0 will return the source member. The behavior of Ancestor( ) is shown in Figure A.1.

See also: Descendants( ), .Children

Ancestors(*member, level***)**   Returns: set

Ancestors(*member, distance***)**   Returns: set

ANCESTOR

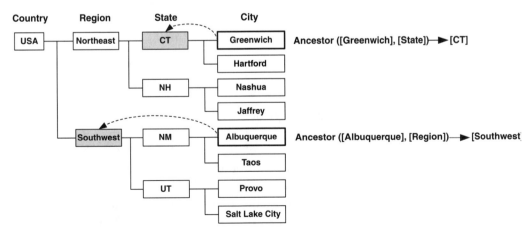

Figure A.1   Behavior of Ancestor( ).

This function finds the set of ancestors for the source member at the target level. If the database supports multiple parents for a single member in a hierarchy (as Applix TM1 does), then this function may return multiple members. Other databases (like Microsoft Analysis Services) will return a set of one member. If the target level is the level of the source member, then the source member is returned as a set.

The target level can be expressed either by name as a string expression or by distance as a numeric expression where 1 represents a parent, 2 represents a grandparent, and so on. Using 0 as a distance will return the member itself.

Note that although this function in theory may return multiple ancestors, the ancestors must be from the same hierarchy and the same level.

See also: Ancestor( ), Ascendants( ), Descendants( ), .Children

expr1 **AND** *expr2*

The AND operator returns true if both *expr1* and *expr2* are true, and false otherwise. In Microsoft Analysis Services, if expr1 is false, then *expr2* is not evaluated (there is no need to; the result is guaranteed to be false).

Ascendants(*member***)**   Returns: set   *Extension*

This function returns the full set of ancestors for the given *member* all the way up to the root of the hierarchy or dimension. The ancestors are ordered bottom-up, so that parents follow children. The given *member* is included in the set. It is very useful in queries when you want to include all higher level totals for a given member or set of members. The behavior of Ascendants( ) is shown in Figure A.2.

Note that the order of the resulting set must be changed by using Hierarchize( ) to get a top-down ordered set before being used in conjunction with any of the drill-related or VisualTotals( ) functions.

See also: Ancestor( ), Ancestors( ), Descendants( ), .Children

Avg(*set* **[,** *numeric expression***])**   Returns: number

This function takes the average of the non-empty values found across cells related to the *set*. If a numeric expression is supplied, then its values are averaged across the cells in the *set*. Note that the average is formed out of the sum of the cells divided by the count of the non-empty cells. If you want to take the average over all cells, treating empty as zero, then you can either create a *numeric value expression* that converts missing to zero, or you can take the Sum( ) over the set divided by the Count( ) of the set, including empty cells.

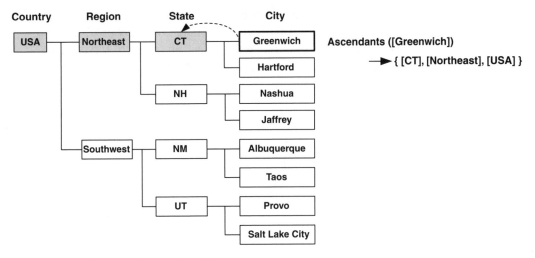

Figure A.2 Behavior of Ascendants( ).

Avg( ) over an empty set returns a double-length floating-point overflow value, not a NULL value.

See also: Aggregate( ), Sum( ), Count( ), Min( ), Max( )

Axis(*Axis number***)**   Returns: set   *Extension*

This function returns a set of members that are included in a specified axis. Axis(0) returns the row members, Axis(1) returns the column members, and so on. This function is likely to be used most often in client applications when building queries. The following example uses Axis( ) in conjunction with Generate( ) and TopCount( ) to select the top two stores for each of the four quarters of 1999. Note that this statement will return results for all selected stores for each of the four quarters:

```
SELECT
Generate(
  Axis (1),
  TopCount(
    [Store].[Store Name].Members,
    2,
    ([Measures].[Amount],
     Axis(1).Current)
  ),
  ALL
) on 0,
{[Time].[1997].Children} on 1
FROM Sales
```

You can use this set as the source for various set-related functions, like .Count, Extract( ), Distinct( ), Except( ), and so on. The .Item( ) function can be used as well. To use this function to select the top two stores based on the first member in the set down the rows, we would write the following:

```
SELECT
TopCount(
  [Store].[Store Name].Members,
  2,
  ([Measures].[Amount],
   Axis(1).Item(0))
) on 0,
{[Time].[1997].Children} on 1
FROM Sales
```

Regardless of which dimensions were involved in the rows, the query would work fine (so long as [Store] is not in the rows!).

However, the execution of a query (building the axes and calculating cell values) does not provide a context on its own for iterating over the tuples in the set. For example, the following results in an error with the message that .Current cannot be used in this context:

```
WITH
MEMBER [Measures].[Disp] AS
'[Measures].[Unit Sales]',
FORE_COLOR = 'iif (Axis(1).Current.Item(0).Level.Ordinal > 1, 0, 5)'
SELECT
{ [Time].[Quarter].members } on 0,
{ Ascendants ([Customers].[Name].&[2659]) } on 1
FROM Sales
WHERE [Measures].[Disp]
CELL PROPERTIES FORMATTED_VALUE, FORE_COLOR
```

This can be explained by the fact that the filter is always evaluated first. However, the following will also fail with the same error:

```
WITH
MEMBER [Measures].[Disp] AS
'[Measures].[Unit Sales]',
FORE_COLOR = 'iif (Axis(1).Current.Item(0).Level.Ordinal > 1, 0, 5)'
SELECT
{ CrossJoin (
    [Time].[Quarter].members,
    { [Measures].[Disp] }
) } on 0,
{ Ascendants ([Customers].[Name].&[2659]) } on 1
FROM Sales
CELL PROPERTIES FORMATTED_VALUE, FORE_COLOR
```

B

BottomCount(*set*, *index* [, *numeric expression*]**)**   Returns: set

See the description for TopCount( )

BottomPercent(*set*, *percentage*, *numeric expression***)**   Returns: set

See the description for TopPercent( )

BottomSum(*set*, *value*, *numeric expression***)**   Returns: set

See the description for TopSum( )

C

CalculationCurrentPass( )   Returns: number (integer)   *Extension*

This returns the current pass number for which the expression is being calculated. Typically, this will be used with iif( ) to pick out a particular expression based on the pass number. The lowest pass number is 0. Calculated cells begin calculations with pass 1.

See Also: CalculationPassValue( ), iif( )

CalculationPassValue(*numeric expression*, *pass number* [, *flag*]**)**
Returns: number   *Extension*

CalculationPassValue(*string expression*, *pass number* [, *flag*]**)**
Returns: string   *Extension*

This function evaluates the given expression at the calculation pass identified by *pass number* and returns the value to the current calculation pass. If the *flag* is specified, it may be one of the following:

FLAG	DESCRIPTION
ABSOLUTE	The *pass number* is the absolute number of a pass (starting from zero). If you refer to a pass number that is higher than the currently executing pass, you will begin invoking the higher numbered pass for the cells that are referenced in the expression if they have not already executed that pass.
RELATIVE	This indicates to take the value from the pass that was *pass number* passes later. A negative *pass number* will refer to an earlier pass, and a positive pass number will invoke a later pass. A pass number that would refer to a pass earlier than pass 0 will.

See Also: CalculationCurrentPass( ), iif( )

Call UDF-Name (*arguments*)   Returns: NULL *Extension*

This function executes a registered external function that does not return anything (that is, a procedure in Visual Basic). Data can be passed to the function as if it were any other external function. The Call itself will return an empty cell value. Unlike other MDX functions and operators, this one cannot be combined with any other operators or functions; when used in an expression, the sole contents of the expression will be the Call invocation. Here's an example:

```
Call MailMsgToUser (
  [Employee].CurrentMember.Properties ("Email Address"),
  "Look at department" + [Department].CurrentMember.Name
  )
```

*member.***Children**   Returns: set

This function returns the children of the given member. member.Children is equivalent to {member.FirstChild : member.LastChild}. As you might expect, if you apply member.Children to a leaf member, the result is no members. Figure A.3 illustrates the behavior of the .Children function.

See also: Ancestor( ), Descendants( ),.Parent, .Siblings

ClosingPeriod([*level* **[,** *member*]]**)**   Returns: member

See description of OpeningPeriod( )

CoalesceEmpty(*value expression* **[,** *value expression* . . .]**)**
Returns: number or string

This function evaluates the first *value expression* listed. If it is not NULL, then the value of that expression is returned. If it is NULL, then the second

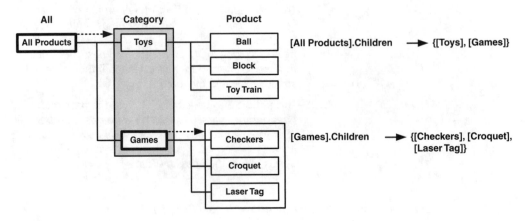

Figure A.3   member.Children.

value expression is evaluated and returned if it is not NULL. Each subsequent expression, if present, is evaluated in turn; if the last one is NULL, the entire operator returns NULL.

CoalesceEmpty( ) can either take all number-valued expressions and return a number or it can take all string-valued expressions and return a string.

See also: iif( )

Correlation(*set, y numeric value expression* **[,** *x numeric value expression***])**

This function calculates a correlation coefficient between x-y pairs of values. The *y numeric expression* is evaluated over the set to get the y values for each pair. If the *x numeric expression* is present, then it is evaluated over the set. Otherwise, the cells formed by the set are evaluated within the current context, and their values are used as the x values. The formula for the correlation coefficient is as follows:

$$\frac{n\sum_{i=1}^{n} x_i y_i - \sum_{i=1}^{n} x_i \sum_{i=1}^{n} y_i}{\sqrt{n\sum_{i=1}^{n} x_i^2 - \left(\sum_{i=1}^{n} x_i\right)^2}\sqrt{n\sum_{i=1}^{n} y_i^2 - \left(\sum_{i=1}^{n} y_i\right)^2}}$$

If either the y or the x numeric expression is a logical or text value, or if the value is NULL, then that tuple and its related values are not included in the correlation. Zero values for y and x are included.

Count(*set* **[, INCLUDEEMPTY | EXCLUDEEMPTY])** Returns: number (integer)

This function counts the cells in the range formed by the set (as opposed to counting the tuples in the set). Without the INCLUDEEMPTY flag, only non-empty cells are counted; with the flag, all cells are counted. INCLUDEEMPTY is the default.

See also: .Count, Sum( ), Avg( )

*Set.***Count** Returns: number (integer) *Extension*

This function counts the tuples present in Set. It is equivalent to Count (Set, INCLUDEEMPTY) but is syntactically simpler.

See also: Rank( ), Count( ), Avg( ), Set.Item( )

*Tuple.***Count** Returns: number (integer) *Extension*

This function counts the dimensions present in *Tuple*.

See also: Tuple.Item( )

Cousin(*member*, *ancestor_member***)**   Returns: member

This function returns the member that has the same relative position under a specified ancestor member as the initial member specified. The Cousin( ) function is best understood by walking through its algorithm. Figure A.4 shows the behavior of the Cousin( ) function. From the *member*'s level to the *ancestor_member*'s level, Cousin( ) tracks which sibling it is related to under its ancestor at that level. [March 1998] is the third child of the first child of [1998]. The same path is then followed from the ancestor member down to the level of member. [March 1999] is the third child of the first child of [1999]. Because of the straightforwardness of this algorithm, it works best when you can guarantee the same number of descendants under each ancestor. For example, it is likely that years, quarters, and months or days, hours, and minutes can be used with Cousin( ), because each of these levels

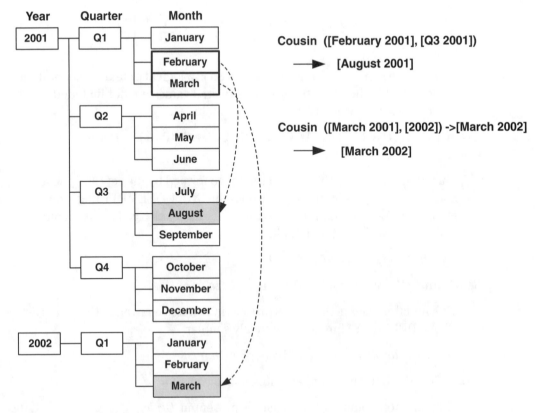

Figure A.4   Cousin( ) function.

has a fixed relationship within itself. However, a cousin of January 31 in February will not exist because February will not have a thirty-first day.

See also: ParallelPeriod( ), PeriodsToDate( )

Covariance(*set, y numeric expression* **[,** *x numeric expression***])**   Returns: number

CovarianceN(*set, y numeric expression* **[,** *x numeric expression***])** Returns: number

These functions calculate the statistical covariance across x-y pairs of values. The y numeric expression is evaluated over the set to get the y values for each pair. If the x numeric expression is present, then it is evaluated over the set. Otherwise, the cells formed by the set are evaluated within the current context, and their values are used as the x values. The biased population formula for covariance is as follows:

$$\frac{\sum_{i=1}^{n}(\bar{x} - xi)(\bar{y} - yi)}{n}$$

Covariance( ) calculates the population covariance and uses the biased population formula (dividing by the number of x-y pairs). CovarianceN( ) calculates the sample covariance and uses the unbiased population formula (dividing by the number of x-y pairs minus 1). If either the y or the x *numeric value expression* is a logical or text value, or if the value is NULL, then that tuple and its related values are not included in the correlation. Zero values for y and x are included.

CrossJoin(*set1, set2***)**   Returns: set

set1 * set2   Returns: set   *Extension*

These functions return a set formed out of the Cartesian product of the two sets. The two sets must represent different dimensions. Microsoft OLAP Services will signal an error if the same dimension appears in either of them. CrossJoin( ) only takes two sets as arguments. However, because it takes two sets as input and returns a set as its output, you may nest multiple calls to CrossJoin( ) to take the Cartesian product of three or more dimensions. Following the same rules used for composing tuples by hand, the order of the dimensions in the resulting tuples is the same as the order of dimensions in the set arguments. Using an asterisk between two sets, as with {set1 * set2}, is a Microsoft-specific synonym for CrossJoin( ). The expression set1 * set2 * set3 is the same as CrossJoin(set1, CrossJoin(set2, set3)).

See also: Extract( ), Generate( ), Distinct( ), NonEmptyCrossJoin( )

Set.**Current**   Returns: tuple

This function returns the current tuple from a set within an iteration over the set. Conceptually, this is the same as Dimension.CurrentMember, except that set.Current is only valid while there actually is an iteration occurring over the set. Also, it only returns a full tuple from the set, as opposed to the dimension's member from the current tuple in that set.

See also: .CurrentMember, Generate( )

dimension[**.CurrentMember**]   Returns: member

This function returns the current member in that dimension. "Current" is relative to the context that the calculation is taking place in. That context may be the axis of a query being executed or a Generate( ) function within that query. We indicate that .CurrentMember is optional. The default operator applied to a dimension is .CurrentMember.

Note that the MDX specification states that .CurrentMember may be applied to any set to return the current tuple. The first release of Microsoft OLAP Services restricts the application of this operator to a set that has a single dimension, which will then return a single member. The .Current operator is applied to an arbitrary set to retrieve a tuple.

See also: .Current

D

Member.**DataMember**   Returns: member   *Extension*

This function returns the system-generated data input member associated with a member (as opposed to the input data). This function generally applies to parent-child dimensions where data is input at the parent level and also calculated by aggregating the parent's children. The following example would produce both the input individual salary and the aggregated organizational salary for each employee:

```
WITH MEMBER [Measures].[Individual Salary] AS
'([Employees].CurrentMember.DataMember, [Measures].[Salary])'
SELECT
{ [Employees].Members } on columns,
{ [Measures].[Salary], [Measures].[Individual Salary] } on rows
FROM HRCube
```

Note that when using the UPDATE CUBE command, the .DataMember function enables you to write data to the actual member, as opposed to the member's leaf descendants.

dimension.**DefaultMember**

hierarchy.**DefaultMember**

> Each of these returns the default member for the dimension or hierarchy. If the dimension has an All level and member, then the default member is the All member. If the dimension does not have an All member, then an arbitrary member from its top level will be the default member. Microsoft Analysis Services also allows you to override these defaults at the server or through their ALTER CUBE UPDATE DIMENSION command; see section "Altering the Default Member for a Dimension in Your Session" in Chapter 10.

Descendants(*member*, [*level* [, *desc_flag*]])

Descendants(*member*, *distance* [, *desc_flag*])

> This function returns a set of descendants of the given member using the given level, or numeric distance from the specified member's level, as a reference point. The *desc_flag* parameter is used to pick from the many possible sets of descendants. If no *level* or *desc_flag* is provided, then the member and all of its descendants are returned. Figures A.5 through A.12 illustrate the behavior of the Descendants( ) operator. The flags are as follows:

SELF	SELF_AND_AFTER
AFTER	SELF_AND_BEFORE
BEFORE	SELF_BEFORE_AFTER
BEFORE_AND_AFTER	LEAVES

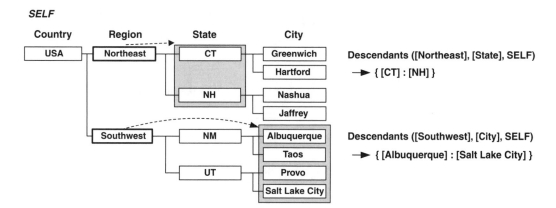

Figure A.5 Behavior of descendants( ) with SELF FLAG.

AFTER

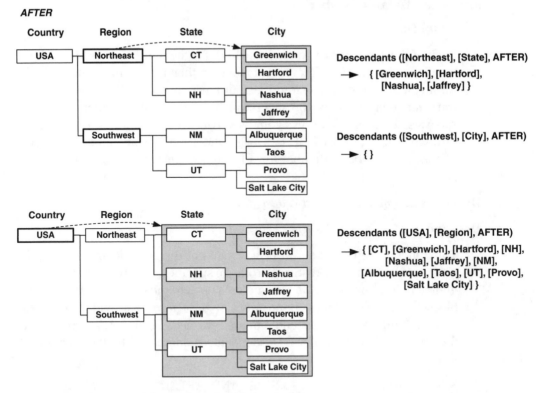

Descendants ([Northeast], [State], AFTER)

→ { [Greenwich], [Hartford],
    [Nashua], [Jaffrey] }

Descendants ([Southwest], [City], AFTER)

→ { }

Descendants ([USA], [Region], AFTER)

→ { [CT], [Greenwich], [Hartford], [NH],
    [Nashua], [Jaffrey], [NM],
    [Albuquerque], [Taos], [UT], [Provo],
    [Salt Lake City] }

Figure A.6 Behavior of descendants( ) with AFTER flag.

BEFORE

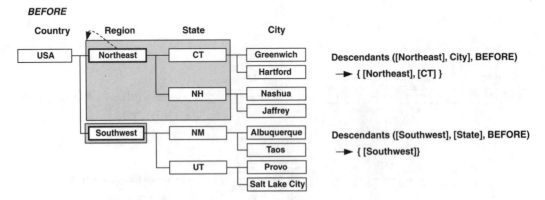

Descendants ([Northeast], City], BEFORE)

→ { [Northeast], [CT] }

Descendants ([Southwest], [State], BEFORE)

→ { [Southwest]}

Figure A.7 Behavior of descendants( ) with BEFORE flag.

SELF_AND_AFTER

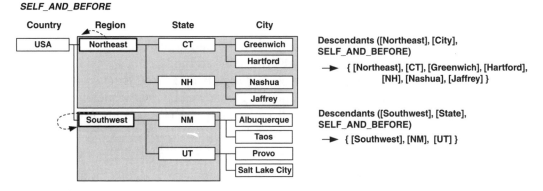

Descendants ([Northeast], [State], SELF_AND_AFTER)

→ { [CT], [Greenwich], [Hartford], [NH], [Nashua], [Jaffrey] }

Descendants ([Southwest], [Region], SELF_AND_AFTER)

→ { [Southwest], [NM], [Albuquerque], [Taos], [UT], [Provo], [Salt Lake City] }

Figure A.8   Behavior of descendants( ) with SELF_AND_AFTER flag.

SELF_AND_BEFORE

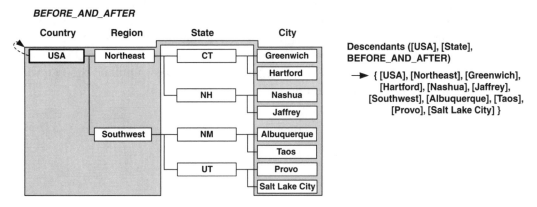

Descendants ([Northeast], [City], SELF_AND_BEFORE)

→ { [Northeast], [CT], [Greenwich], [Hartford], [NH], [Nashua], [Jaffrey] }

Descendants ([Southwest], [State], SELF_AND_BEFORE)

→ { [Southwest], [NM], [UT] }

Figure A.9   Behavior of descendants( )with SELF_AND_BEFORE flag.

BEFORE_AND_AFTER

Descendants ([USA], [State], BEFORE_AND_AFTER)

→ { [USA], [Northeast], [Greenwich], [Hartford], [Nashua], [Jaffrey], [Southwest], [Albuquerque], [Taos], [Provo], [Salt Lake City] }

Figure A.10   Behavior of descendants( ) with BEFORE_AND_AFTER flags.

SELF_BEFORE_AFTER

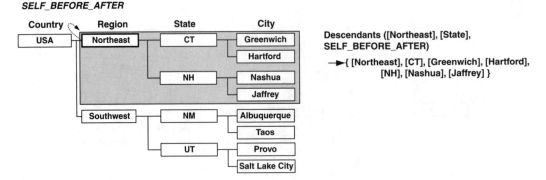

Figure A.11 Behavior of descendants() with SELF_BEFORE_AFTER flags.

SELF refers to the level listed as the second argument and means to take the members at that level. AFTER refers to the level or levels that appear below the level listed as the second argument. BEFORE refers to the level or levels that appear above the level listed and below the member given as the first argument. The BEFORE_AND_AFTER, SELF_AND_AFTER, SELF_AND_BEFORE, and SELF_BEFORE_AFTER flags combine these basic options, as shown in Figures A.5 through A.12.

The LEAVES flag is used in conjunction with a depth number and is intended for use with ragged and parent-child hierarchies. If a depth number is specified without LEAVES, then only members that are at that depth are returned. If a depth number is specified with LEAVES, then any leaf members encountered up to that depth are retained. You cannot specifically request all leaf-level members below a member, but you can approximate this by using a depth number that is as large as the number of levels in the dimension. There is no way to derive this number in MDX unless you know the name of the leaf level, in which case you can use the .Ordinal function to provide the number. You can pick a large number, though, without any errors. For example,

```
Descendants (
  [Accounts].CurrentMember,
  50,
  LEAVES
)
```

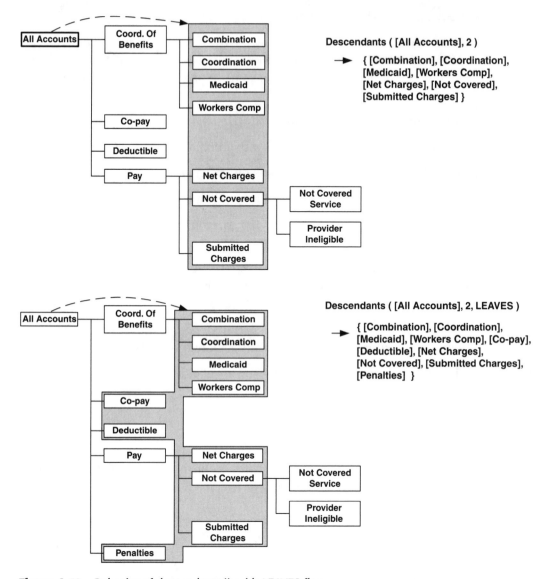

Figure A.12 Behavior of descendants( ) with LEAVES flag.

will return all leaf members under the current [Accounts] member (assuming that the dimension has fewer than 50 levels).

If no flag is specified, the default behavior is SELF.

See also: Ancestor( ), Ancestors( ), Ascendants( ), .Children

Hierarchy.**Dimension**   Returns: dimension   *Extension*

This function returns the dimension that the hierarchy is in. Because Microsoft OLAP Services and Analysis Services semantically treat different hierarchies as different dimensions, this function is essentially a "no-op" in those products.

Level.**Dimension**   Returns: dimension   *Extension*

The function returns the dimension that contains Level.

Member.**Dimension**   Returns: dimension   *Extension*

This function returns the dimension that contains Member.

Dimensions(*numeric expression***)**   Returns: dimension   *Extension*

This function returns the dimension whose zero-based position within the cube is *numeric expression*. Note that the Measures dimension is always Dimensions(0), while the order of the other dimensions depends on the order in which they were added to the cube when it was being constructed (and/or modified).

Dimensions(*string expression***)**   Returns: dimension   *Extension*

This function returns the dimension whose name is given by *string expression*.

See also: Dimension.*Name*

Distinct(*set***)**   Returns: set

This function removes any duplicates from the set. The first instance of each tuple is retained in the order in which it appears.

See also: DistinctCount( ), Except( ), Extract( )

DistinctCount(*set***)**   Returns: set   *Extension*

This function counts the distinct, non-empty tuples in a set. It is equivalent to Count (Distinct (set),EXCLUDEEMPTY). Only a measure can use this function. If you define a calculation on another dimension that uses DistinctCount( ), you will get a syntax error. (If you want this functionality on another dimension, you can use the equivalent Count(. . .) expression.)

When this function is used to calculate a cell, the distinct tuples in *set* are determined, and the non-empty cells formed by intersecting those tuples with the current member in every other dimension are counted. This function can be used to simulate the DistinctCount measure aggregation type in Analysis Services, but its strength is when you want the distinct count along only a subset of cube dimensions (one or two), when you are limiting the scope within the dimensions, when you are taking the distinct count at aggregate members in one or more of the dimensions, or when one or more dimensions involve a calculated member. Remember that the DistinctCount aggregation is handled to some degree by the server during cube aggregation, while this function is calculated at client query time.

See also: Distinct( ), Count( ), .Count

DrillDownLevel(*set* [, *level*])   Returns: set

This function returns a set resulting from a particular drill-down operation performed by the function. The Set1 can be of arbitrary dimensionality; *set2* must be of only one dimension. When the level argument is specified, all members or tuples in set that are in level are drilled down onto the next lowest level (if there is one). When the level argument is not specified, only those members or tuples that are at the lowest level in the first dimension of the set are drilled down, and they are drilled down to the next lower level. The behavior of DrillDownLevel( ) is shown in Figure A.13. All children are inserted immediately after their parents; otherwise, the order is preserved. If level is specified but there is no member at level in the set, then the given set is returned without modification.

NOTE

If one or more children of a member to be drilled down on immediately follows a parent in set, then that parent will not be drilled down on.

DrillDownLevel(*set*, , *index*)   Returns: set *Extension*

This variation is a Microsoft OLAP Services-specific extension to Drill-DownLevel( ). It enables the dimension to be drilled down on by leaving the level field empty and providing a zero-based dimension index to specify which dimension you should drill down on. This is really only useful when set has tuples with more than one dimension. The first dimension to drill down on is at index 0, the second dimension is at index 1, and so on. As with the rules for the standard version of DrillDownLevel( ), tuples containing the lowest level members of that dimension are drilled down on.

NOTE

If one or more children of a member to be drilled down on immediately follows a parent in set, then that parent will not be drilled down on.

DrillDownLevelBottom(*set*, *index* [,[*level*]

[, *numeric expression*]])   Returns: set

Similar to DrillDownLevel( ) and DrillDownLevelTop( ), this function drills down all members in set that are at the specified level, if level is provided

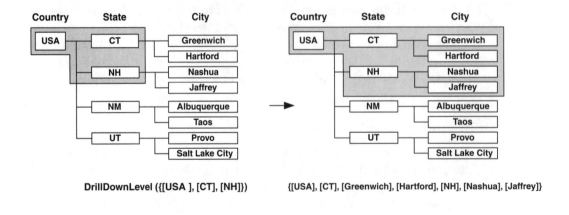

DrillDownLevel ({[USA], [CT], [NH]})

{[USA], [CT], [Greenwich], [Hartford], [NH], [Nashua], [Jaffrey]}

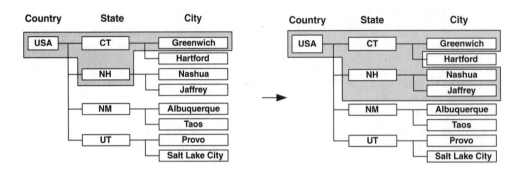

DrillDownLevel ({[USA], [CT], [Greenwich], [NH]})

{[USA], [CT], [Greenwich], [NH], [Nashua], [Jaffrey]}

Figure A.13   DrillDownLevel().

(or the lowest level of members that are present in the set if level is not provided). However, instead of returning all children, this function returns only the bottom index members or tuples. The set can be of arbitrary dimensionality. The ranking is determined through the numeric expression, if one is provided, or through the values of cells found in the default context when the set is evaluated, if the numeric expression is left out. Figure A.14 illustrates the behavior of DrillDownLevelBottom().

NOTE

If one or more children of a member to be drilled down on immediately follows a parent in set, then that parent will not be drilled down on.

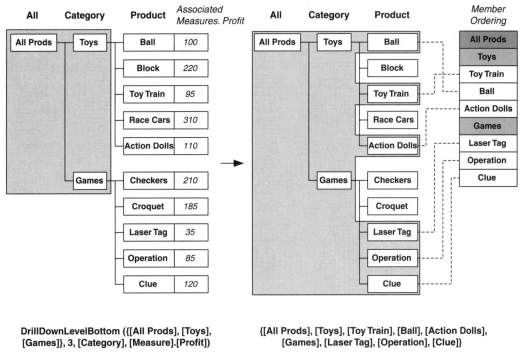

DrillDownLevelBottom ({[All Prods], [Toys], [Games]}, 3, [Category], [Measure].[Profit])

{[All Prods], [Toys], [Toy Train], [Ball], [Action Dolls], [Games], [Laser Tag], [Operation], [Clue]}

Figure A.14 DrillDownLevelBottom( ).

DrillDownLevelTop(*set*, *index* [, [*level*]

[, *numeric expression*]])   Returns: set

Similar to DrillDownLevel( ) and DrillDownLevelBottom( ), this function drills down all members in set that are at the specified level, if level is provided (or the lowest level of members that are present in the set if level is not provided). However, instead of returning all children, this function returns only the top index members or tuples. The set can be of arbitrary dimensionality. The ranking is determined through the numeric expression, if one is provided, or through the values of cells found in the default context when the set is evaluated, if the *numeric value expression* is left out. Figure A.15 illustrates the behavior of DrillDownLevelTop( ). As with Drill-DownLevel( ), if a member at level is immediately followed by one of its children, it will not be drilled down on.

NOTE
If one or more children of a member to be drilled down on immediately follows a parent in *set*, then that parent will not be drilled down on.

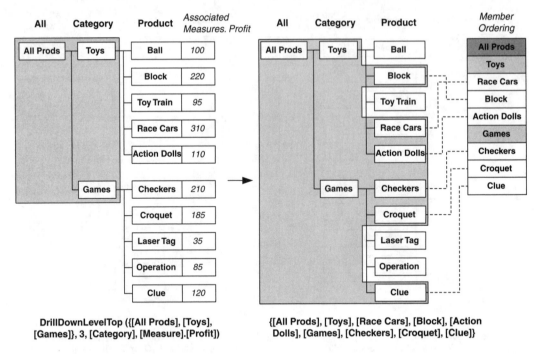

DrillDownLevelTop ({[All Prods], [Toys], [Games]}, 3, [Category], [Measure].[Profit])

{[All Prods], [Toys], [Race Cars], [Block], [Action Dolls], [Games], [Checkers], [Croquet], [Clue]}

Figure A.15 DrillDownLevelTop( ).

DrillDownMember(*set1*, *set2* [, RECURSIVE])   Returns: set

This function returns a set that is formed by drilling down one level on each member in *set1* that is present in *set2*. *Set1* can be of arbitrary dimensionality; *set2* must be of only one dimension. The ability for *set1* to consist of more than one dimension is an extension to the OLE DB for OLAP specification.

If *set1* contains tuples, this function will return a set that is formed by drilling down each tuple in *set1* that has a matching member from *set2* in it. If RECURSIVE is not specified, then only one pass through *set1* is performed, matching each member or tuple with each member in *set2*. If RECURSIVE is specified, then the set resulting from the first pass is again matched with each member in *set2*, and so on until no more members in the set being constructed are found in *set2*. Figure A.16 illustrates the behavior of DrillDownMember( ).

NOTE

If one or more children of a member to be drilled down on immediately follows a parent in set, then that parent will not be drilled down on.

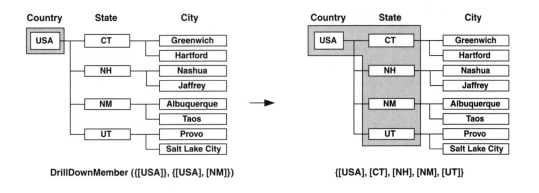

DrillDownMember ({[USA]}, {[USA], [NM]})

{[USA], [CT], [NH], [NM], [UT]}

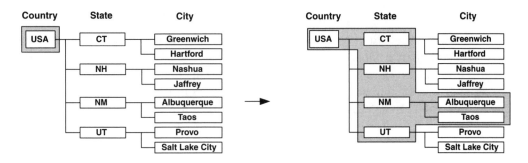

DrillDownMember ({[USA]}, {[USA], [NM]}, RECURSIVE)

{[USA], [CT], [NH], [NM], [Taos], [Albuquerque], [UT]}

Figure A.16 DrillDownMember().

DrillDownMemberBottom(*set1*, *set2*, *index* **[**, *numeric expression***][**, RECURSIVE])**   Returns: set

Much like DrillDownMember, this function returns a set that is formed by drilling down one level on each member in *set1* that is present in *set2*. However, it returns the bottom *index* children for a parent rather than all children. *Set1* can be of arbitrary dimensionality; *set2* must be of only one dimension.

If *set1* contains tuples, this will return a set that is formed by drilling down each tuple in *set1* that has a matching member from *set2* in it. If RECURSIVE is not specified, then only one pass through *set1* is performed, matching each member or tuple with each member in *set2*. If RECURSIVE is specified, then the set that results from the first pass is again matched with each member in *set2*, and so on until no more members in the set being constructed are found in *set2*. At each step of drilling, the bottom index child members or tuples are returned instead of all children. The ranking is based on the numeric expression, if specified; otherwise, values from the set of children are evaluated in the current context, and those results are used. Figure A.17 illustrates the behavior of DrillDownMemberBottom( ).

DrillDownMemberTop(*set1*, *set2*, *index* **[,** *numeric expression***][, RECURSIVE]])**   Returns: set

Like DrillDownMember( ), this function returns a set that is formed by drilling down one level on each member in *set1* that is present in *set2*. However, it returns the top *index* children for a parent rather than all children. *Set1* can be of arbitrary dimensionality; *set2* must be of only one dimension.

If *set1* contains tuples, this will return a set formed by drilling down each tuple in *set1* that has a matching member from *set2* in it. If RECURSIVE is not specified, then only one pass through *set1* is performed, matching each member or tuple with each member in *set2*. If RECURSIVE is specified, then the set that results from the first pass is again matched with each member in *set2*, and so on until no more members in the set being constructed are found in *set2*. At each step of drilling, the top *index* child members or tuples are returned instead of all children. The ranking is based on the

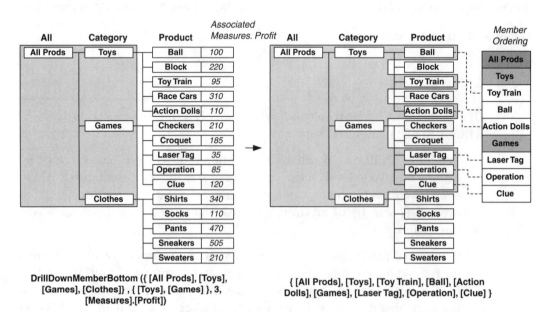

DrillDownMemberBottom ({ [All Prods], [Toys], [Games], [Clothes]} , { [Toys], [Games] }, 3, [Measures].[Profit])

{ [All Prods], [Toys], [Toy Train], [Ball], [Action Dolls], [Games], [Laser Tag], [Operation], [Clue] }

Figure A.17   DrillDownMemberBottom( ).

numeric expression, if specified; otherwise, values from the set of children are evaluated in the current context, and those results are used. Figure A.18 illustrates the behavior of DrillDownMemberTop( ).

DrillUpLevel(set [, level]**)**   Returns: set

This function strips away all members in the set that are below the given level. If the level is not provided, then it is assumed to be one level higher in the hierarchy than the level of the lowest level member(s) in set (the lowest level members in the set are removed). Figure A.19 illustrates the behavior of DrillUpLevel( ). A set returned by DrillDownMember( ) or DrillDown-Level( ) will be suitable for cleanly drilling up with this function.

DrillUpMember(set1, set2 **)**   Returns: set

This step strips away members in set1 that are descendants of members in set2. Figure A.20 illustrates the behavior of DrillUpMember( ). Set1 can contain tuples of arbitrary dimensionality; set2 must contain only members of one dimension.

Note that only descendants that are immediately after the ancestor member in set2 are stripped away. If an ancestor member specified in set2 is not

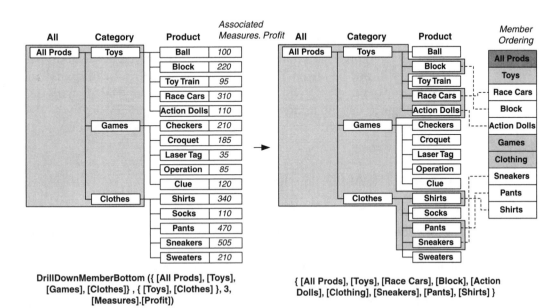

DrillDownMemberBottom ({ [All Prods], [Toys], [Games], [Clothes]} , { [Toys], [Clothes] }, 3, [Measures].[Profit])

{ [All Prods], [Toys], [Race Cars], [Block], [Action Dolls], [Clothing], [Sneakers], [Pants], [Shirts] }

Figure A.18   DrillDownMemberTop( ).

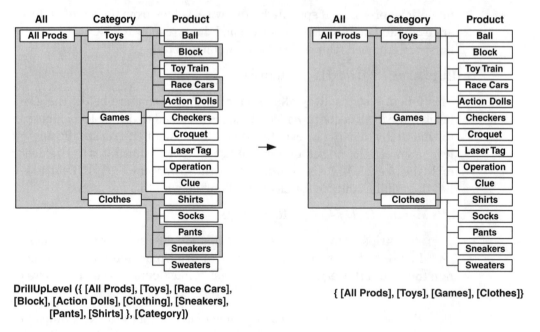

DrillUpLevel ({ [All Prods], [Toys], [Race Cars],
[Block], [Action Dolls], [Clothing], [Sneakers],
[Pants], [Shirts] }, [Category])

{ [All Prods], [Toys], [Games], [Clothes]}

Figure A.19 DrillUpLevel( ).

present in *set1*, any descendants will remain. Descendants that precede the ancestor or that appear after another member that is not a descendant has intervened will not be stripped away. A set returned by DrillDownMember( ) or DrillDownLevel( ) will be suitable for drilling up cleanly with this function. Figure A.20 illustrates the behavior of DrillUpMember( ).

E

Except(*set1*, *set2* **[, ALL])**   Returns: set

set1–set2   Returns: set   *Extension*

The Except( ) function removes all elements from *set1* that also exist in *set2*. The ALL flag controls whether duplicates are retained or eliminated. When ALL is specified, duplicates in *set1* are retained, though any tuples matching them in *set2* are discarded. When ALL is not specified, no duplicates are returned. The members returned are determined by the order in which they appear in *set1*.

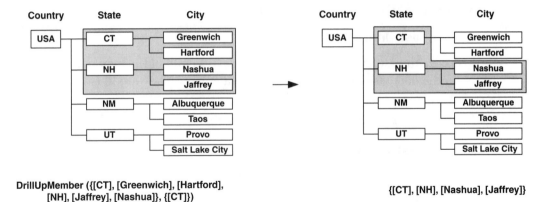

DrillUpMember ({[CT], [Greenwich], [Hartford], [NH], [Jaffrey], [Nashua]}, {[CT]})

{[CT], [NH], [Nashua], [Jaffrey]}

Figure A.20 DrillUpMember( ).

Microsoft OLAP Services also provides "-" as an alternate way of specifying Except( ). Duplicates are removed from the resulting set. The expression Set1– Set2 is equivalent to Except (Set1, Set2).

See also: Union( ), Intersect( ), Extract( )

Extract(*set, dimension*[, *dimension* ...])   Returns: set

This function behaves as an opposite to the CrossJoin( ) function. The resulting set consists of tuples from the extracted dimension elements. For each tuple in the given set, the members of the dimensions listed in the arguments are extracted into new tuples. Since this could result in a great deal of redundancy, this function always removes duplicates from its results.

See also: CrossJoin( ), Generate( )

F

Filter(*set, search condition*)   Returns: set

Filter returns those tuples of *set* for which the search condition (a logical expression) is true. If none are true, an empty set is returned. The tuples in the resulting set follow the same order in which they appeared in the original set. Note that the *search condition* must be phrased as a Boolean expression; you cannot use the assumption that a non-zero numerical result means "true" and a zero numerical result means "false."

See also: iif( ), CoalesceEmpty( )

member.**FirstChild**   Returns: member

member.**LastChild**   Returns: member

These functions return the first child or last child of the member according to the database ordering of the child members. They are illustrated in Figure A.21.

See also: .FirstSibling, .LastSibling, .Children, .Siblings

member.**FirstSibling**   Returns: member

member.**LastSibling**   Returns: member

Figure A.22 shows the behavior of the member.FirstSibling and member.LastSibling operators. The first child of a parent is its own first sibling, and the last child is its own last sibling. If no parent exists, then the first member in that level is the first sibling and the last member in the level is the last sibling. For example, the All member of a dimension is its own first and last sibling. In a dimension without an All level, the first member of the top level is the first sibling of all members at that level, and the last member of the top level is the last sibling of all members at that level.

See also: .Siblings, .FirstChild, .LastChild

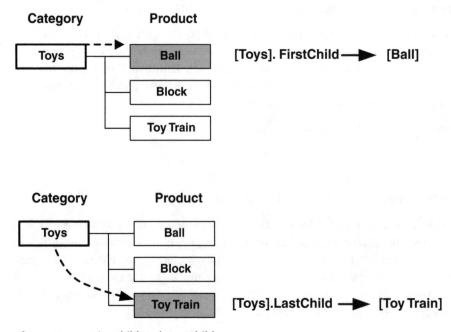

Figure A.21   .FirstChild and .LastChild.

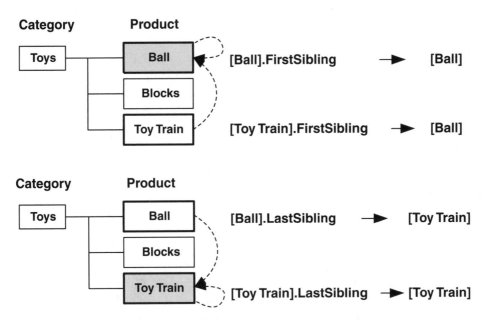

Figure A.22 .FirstSibling and .LastSibling.

G

Generate(*set1, set2* [**, ALL**]**)** Returns: set

Generate(*set, string expression,* [*delimiter*]**)** Returns: string *Extension*

The set version of Generate( ) iterates over each tuple in *set1*, and for each element in *set1*, it puts every element specified by *set2* into the result set. The dimensionality of the result set is the dimensionality of *set2*. If ALL is specified, then duplicate result tuples are retained. If ALL is not specified, duplicates after the first are removed. *Set1* and *set2* may be composed of completely different dimensionality, or they may be composed of exactly the same dimensionality. When *set2* is a relatively static set of members, this function behaves much like CrossJoin( ). Generate( ) gains its iterative power when *set2* is an expression that depends on the current member or tuple in *set1*. The string version of this function iterates over each tuple in the set specified as the first argument, evaluates the string expression for the current member of the set, and returns the concatenated result, optionally with a delimiter.

See also: CrossJoin( ), Extract( )

H

Head(*Set* [, *Count*]**)**   Returns: set   *Extension*

This function returns a set of the first *Count* elements from the given set. The order of elements in the given set is preserved. If *Count* is omitted, the number of elements returned is 1. If *Count* is less than 1, an empty set is returned. If the value of the *Count* is greater than the number of tuples in the set, the original set is returned.

See also: Tail( ), Subset( ), Rank( ), .Item( )

Hierarchize(*set***)**   Returns: set

Hierarchize(*set***, POST)**   Returns: set   *Extension*

Hierarchize( ) returns the set that it is given after it puts all the members in each dimension into hierarchical order. By default, within each level, members are put into their database ordering, top down. Children are sorted to immediately follow after their parents. The optional POST keyword returns the members in bottom-up rather than top-down order; that is, the children precede their parents. When the tuples are composed of more than one dimension, they are sorted primarily on the first dimension, then on the second dimension, and so on. Any duplicate tuples are retained.

In Analysis Services, Hierarchize( ) is similar to sorting on the members' internal ID property.

See also: Order( ), Ascendants( ), Ancestor( ), .Parent

level.**Hierarchy**   Returns: hierarchy

This function returns the hierarchy that contains the level. Because OLAP Services semantically treats different hierarchies as different dimensions, this function is essentially equivalent to *Level*.Dimension.

member.**Hierarchy**   Returns: hierarchy

This function returns the hierarchy that contains the member. Because OLAP Services semantically treats different hierarchies as different dimensions, this function is essentially equivalent to *Member*.Dimension.

I

dimension.**Ignore**   Returns: member   *Extension*

When used in an expression, .Ignore fixes the member of *Dimension* at the current one in the context and prevents any further recursion along that dimension. In recursive calculations, sometimes a cell reference will end up being circular. For example, the level-wide custom rollup expression

```
IIf (IsLeaf ([Accounts].CurrentMember),
  [Accounts].CurrentMember,
  RollupChildren ( [Accounts].CurrentMember,
    Accounts.CurrentMember.Properties ("UNARY_OPERATOR") )
)
```

becomes recursive at leaf levels, because the evaluation of the [Accounts].CurrentMember at the leaf level will still result in another cycle through the whole iif( ) clause. Modifying the expression to

```
IIf (IsLeaf ([Accounts].CurrentMember),
  [Accounts].Ignore,
  RollupChildren ( [Accounts].CurrentMember,
    Accounts.CurrentMember.Properties ("UNARY_OPERATOR") )
)
```

fixes the problem; no more recursion will take place on the Account dimension.

Iif (*search_condition*, *true_part*, *false_part*)

This function evaluates *search_condition*, which needs to be a logical value. If the result is true, then the *true_part* expression is evaluated and returned. If the result is not true, then the *false_part* expression is evaluated and returned. The iif( ) function can either take numerical expressions for the true part and the false part and return a number, or it can take string expressions for the true part and the false part and return a string.

Note that because the search condition must contain a logical expression that involves comparison operation's and NULL cells compare as equal to zero with any comparison operator, the result of the search condition cannot be NULL. However, either the *true_part* or the *false_part* may evaluate to NULL, in which case NULL will be the result when that condition is met.

Also note that in Analysis Service, if either the *true_part* or the *false_part* is the NULL token, the iif( ) is interpreted to be a numerical operation. There is no way to express iif (search-condition, "text", NULL). The nearest workaround is iif (search-condition, "text", ""), which may or may not be suitable for your application.

See also: CoalesceEmpty( ), Filter( )

Intersect(*set1*, *set2* [,ALL])   Returns: set

The ALL flag controls whether duplicates are retained or eliminated. When ALL is not specified, only the unique tuples appearing in *set1* that also appear in *set2* are returned. When ALL is specified, then duplicated tuples in *set1* that appear anywhere in *set2* are returned. If duplicates of a tuple occur in *set2*, only the duplicates that exist in *set1* will end up in the resulting set. The members are returned in the order in which they appear in *set1*. For example, the expression

```
Intersect (
    {[Customer].[AZ].[Phoenix], [Customer].[AZ].[Scottsdale],
        [Customer].[KS].[Pittsburg], [Customer].[AZ].[Phoenix]},
    {[Customer].[NM].[Albuquerque], [Customer].[AZ].[Phoenix],
        [Customer].[AZ].[Scottsdale], [Customer].[AZ].[Phoenix]},
)
```

yields the following set:

```
{ [Customer].[AZ].[Phoenix], [Customer].[AZ].[Scottsdale] }
```

The expression

```
Intersect (
    {[Customer].[AZ].[Phoenix], [Customer].[AZ].[Scottsdale],
        [Customer].[KS].[Pittsburg], [Customer].[AZ].[Phoenix]},
    {[Customer].[NM].[Albuquerque], [Customer].[AZ].[Phoenix],
        [Customer].[AZ].[Scottsdale], [Customer].[AZ].[Phoenix]},
    , ALL
)
```

yields the following set:

```
{ [Customer].[AZ].[Phoenix], [Customer].[AZ].[Scottsdale],
    [Customer].[AZ].[Phoenix]}
```

object1 **Is** *object2*   Returns: boolean   *Extension*

The Is operator is used to determine if two objects are equivalent. For example, in the FoodMart 2000 database, the expression

```
[Customers].[All Customers].[Canada].[BC].[Vancouver] IS
[Store].[Store City].[Vancouver]
```

would return TRUE. You can compare objects with NULL as well to see if they exist. For example, if the first month in the Time dimension is [Jan 2000], then the expression

```
[Jan 2000].PrevMember IS NULL
```

will return TRUE.

IsAncestor(*AncestorMember, StartingMember***)**   Returns: boolean   Extension

This function returns True if the *AncestorMember* is indeed an ancestor of *StartingMember*, and False otherwise. No error is returned if the two members are from different dimensions (just False).

See also: IsGeneration, IsSibling( ), IsLeaf( ), iif( ), Is, .Ordinal

IsEmpty(*ValueExpression* **)**

This function returns true if the *ValueExpression* is NULL, and false otherwise. In Microsoft Analysis Services, if the *ValueExpression* is a tuple instead of a simple member reference, then it must be enclosed by parentheses, as with

```
IsEmpty ( ([Measures].[Units], [Time].PrevMember) )
```

Also, at least in the RTM version of Analysis Services, if you use the value retrieved by .Properties( ) as an argument to IsEmpty( ), you will get a syntax error.

See also: iif( ), IS

IsGeneration(*member, generation_number***)**   Returns: boolean   *Extension*

This function returns True if the *member generation_number* steps from the leaf level, and false otherwise. The definition of a generation is as follows: The leaf level is considered to be generation 0. For every non-leaf member, the generation number is 1 plus the range of generation numbers from all of the children of its parent. In an irregular hierarchy, this means that a member may belong to more than one generation. For example, the generation numbers for a simple hierarchy are shown in Figure 8.23

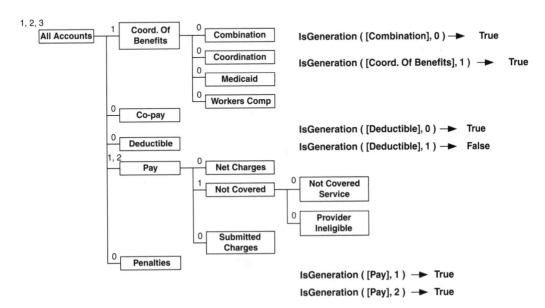

Figure A.23   IsGeneration().

In the case of a ragged level-based dimension, the generations are counted from the visible members. If a leaf member has a hidden parent and a visible grandparent, for example, the visible grandparent will be considered to be generation 1.

The expression IsGeneration ([Account].CurrentMember, 0) is equivalent to IsLeaf ([Account].CurrentMember).

See also: IsAncestor, IsSibling( ), IsLeaf( ), iif( ), IS, .Ordinal

IsLeaf(*Member***)**   Returns: boolean   *Extension*

This function returns True if the *Member* is a leaf member in its dimension, whether the dimension is a parent-child dimension, or if it is a regular dimension.

In the case of a ragged level-based dimension, a member is considered to be a leaf member if it has no visible children.

See also: IsAncestor, IsSibling( ), IsGeneration( ), iif( ), IS, .Ordinal

IsSibling(*Member1***,** *Member2***)**   Returns: boolean   *Extension*

This function returns True if the *Member1* is a sibling of *Member2*.

In a ragged, level-based dimension, the sibling relationship is determined by the visibility of members. If a parent has one hidden child and one visible child, and the hidden child has a visible child, the two visible children will be considered as siblings.

See also: IsAncestor, IsLeaf( ), IsGeneration( ), iif( ), IS, .Ordinal

*tuple***[.Item](***index***)**   *Extension*

This function returns the member at the index position within the tuple. The index is based at 0. For example, ([Product].[Jackets], [Time].[1996]).Item (0) is [Product].[Jackets], and ([Product].[Jackets], [Time].[1996]).Item (1) is [Time].[1996]. We indicate that Item( ) is optional because it is the default operator. The following are equivalent:

```
Tuple(index)
Tuple.Item(index)
```

*set***[.Item](***index***)**

*set***[.Item](***string expression***[** *,string expression* . . . **])**

The first variation of the .Item( ) operator returns the tuple at the index position within the set. The index is based at 0. For example, consider:

```
{ [Time].[1996], [Time].[1997] }.Item (0) is [Time].[1996]
{ [Time].[1996], [Time].[1997] }.Item (1) is [Time].[1997]
```

The second variation returns the first tuple in the set whose name is matched by the string expressions. When using the string form, you can use either one string or more than one string. If you use one string, it must contain a complete tuple specification. If you use more than one string, than the number of strings must match the number of dimensions, but each string will identify only one member from one dimension. In either case, the order of dimensions listed in the string(s) must match the order of dimensions in the set. If some member from the strings is not found in the meta data when the expression is parsed, then a parse error results. If the member is found in the meta data, but not in any tuple in the set, then an empty tuple is returned. For example, the following two item specifications are identical:

```
Crossjoin ([Time].[Year].members, _[Customer].[State].Members).Item(
"[1997]", "[FL]")
Crossjoin ([Time].[Year].members, _[Customer].[State].Members).Item(
"([1997], [FL])")
```

Note that in the tuple specifications, member expressions can be used as well as named members. For example, the following are also equivalent to the two-item specifications just given:

```
Crossjoin (
   [Time].[Year].members,
   [Customer].[State].Members
).Item( "[1998].lag(1)", "[FL]")
Crossjoin (
   [Time].[Year].members,
   [Customer].[State].Members).Item( "([1997].[Q1].Parent, [FL])")
```

We indicate .Item( ) as being optional because it is the default operator. The following are equivalent:

```
Set(index)
Set.Item(index)
```

Remember: If you are trying to use Rank( ) to pick out an index for Item( ), that Rank returns a 1-based index, and you will need to subtract 1 from it to use it with Item( ).

L

*member.***Lag(***index***)**   Returns: member

.Lead( ) returns the member that is *index* number of member after the source *member* along the same level, and .Lag( ) returns the member that is *index* number of member before the source *member* on the same level. .Lead(0) and .Lag(0) each result in the source member itself. Lagging by a negative amount is the same as leading by the positive quantity and vice versa. Figure A.24 shows examples of .Lead( ) and .Lag( ).

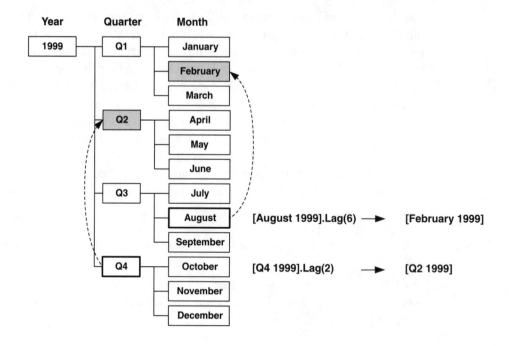

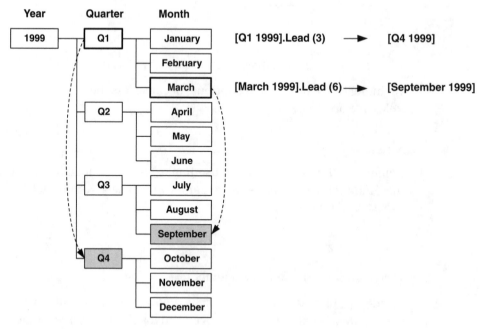

Figure A.24 .Lag( ) and .Lead( ).

member.**LastChild**   Returns: member

See definition for .FirstChild

LastPeriods(*index* **[,** *member* **])**   Returns: set

This function returns the set of index periods from member back to the member lagging by index-1 from member. This is *almost* equivalent to

```
{ member.LAG(index - 1) : member }.
```

If *member* is not specified, then it defaults to the current member of the Time-typed dimension in the cube. If the *index* is a negative number, then the range goes forward from the member to *index*-1 members instead of backward. If *index* is 0, then an empty set is returned (which makes it slightly different than by using .Lag( )). If *member* is omitted, and no dimension in the cube is marked as being Time-typed, the statement will parse and execute without error. However, when a client attempts to retrieve a cell calculated in part by the LastPeriods( ) function, a cell error will occur.

The behavior of LastPeriods( ) is shown in Figure A.25.

See also: OpeningPeriod( ), ClosingPeriod( ), .Lag( ), .Lead( )

member.**LastSibling**   Returns: member

See definition for .FirstSibling

member.**Lead(***index***)**   Returns: member

See definition for .Lag( )

member.**Level**   Returns: level

This function returns a member's level.

Levels(*string expression***)**   Returns: level

This function returns the level whose name is given by *string expression*. It is typically used with user-defined functions (UDFs) that return a name. The *string expression* can be any expression that results in a level reference. For example, the string "[Time].[Year]" will result in the year level of the Time dimension. However, the string "[Time].Levels(1)" in a Time dimension where the year level is the first one down from the root level will also result in the year level. (See the following description for the *Dimension*.Levels( ) function as well.)

Dimension.**Levels(** *numeric expression* **)**   Returns: level

This function returns the dimension level specified by *numeric expression*. The number is zero-based, starting at the root level. If the levels of the

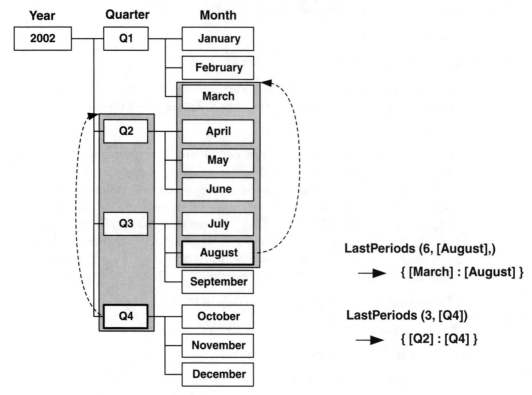

Figure A.25   Behavior of LastPeriods( ).

[Time] dimension are [All], [Year], and [Month], then [Time].Levels(0) returns the [Time].[All] level, and [Time].Levels(2) returns the [Time].[Month] level.

LinkMember(*member, dimension***)**   Returns: member

The LinkMember( ) function is used to reference a member in one hierarchy based on a member from another related hierarchy. The hierarchies may either be from the same dimension (where a dimension has multiple hierarchies) or from different dimensions. (Remember that different hierarchies *are* different dimensions in Microsoft OLAP/Analysis Services.) The members are matched by key rather than by name, so members with the same key but with different names will be linked. For example, the expression

```
Hierarchize(
    Ascendants(
```

```
            Linkmember([Time].[Calendar].[Jan 1 1999],[Time].[Fiscal])
   ))
```

will return the ascendants in the fiscal hierarchy for the calendar hierarchy member [Jan 1 1999].

LinRegIntercept(*set, y numeric expression* [, *x numeric expression*]**)**
Returns: number

This function returns the intercept of the linear regression line calculated from the given data points (where the regression line intersects 0). For the linear equation $y = ax + b$, which will be determined over some set of y and x, the values of the *y numeric expression* are evaluated over the *set* to get the y values. If the *x numeric expression* is present, then it is evaluated over the *set* to get the values of the x axis. Otherwise, the cells formed by the *set* are evaluated within the current context and their values are used as the x values. Empty cells and cells containing text or logical values are not included in the calculation, but cells with zero values are included.

Once the linear regression line has been calculated, this function returns the x-intercept of the line (represented by b in the equation $y = ax + b$). Also see the other LinRegXXX functions.

LinRegPoint(*numeric expression, set, y numeric expression* [, *x numeric expression*]**)** Returns: number

This function returns the value of the calculated linear regression line $y = ax + b$ for a particular value of x. For the linear equation $y = ax + b$, which will be determined from a *set* of y and x values, the values of the *y numeric expression* are evaluated to get the y values. If the *x numeric expression* is present, then it is evaluated over the *set* to get the values of the x axis. Otherwise, the cells formed by the *set* are evaluated within the current context and their values are used as the x values. Empty cells and cells containing text or logical values are not included in the calculation, but cells with zero values are included.

Once the linear regression line has been calculated, the value of $y = ax + b$ is calculated for the value given in the x slice numeric expression and is returned.

LinRegR2(*set, y numeric expression* [, *x numeric expression*]**)** Returns: number

This function returns the statistical R^2 variance of the given data points to the linear regression line calculated from them. For the linear equation $y = ax + b$, which will be determined over some set of y and x, the values of the *y numeric expression* are evaluated to get the y values. If the *x numeric expression* is present, then it is evaluated over the set to get the values of the x axis. Otherwise, the cells formed by the set are evaluated within the current context and their values are used as the x values. Empty cells and cells containing text or logical values are not included in the calculation, but cells with zero values are included.

Once the linear regression line has been calculated, this function returns the statistical R^2 variance between the points on it and the given points. See also the other LinRegXXX functions.

LinRegSlope(*set* [, *y numeric expression* [, *x numeric expression*]**)**
Returns: number

This function returns the slope of the linear regression line calculated from the given data points. For the linear equation y = ax + b, which will be determined over some *set* of y and x, the values of the *y numeric expression* are evaluated to get the y values. If the *x numeric expression* is present, then it is evaluated over the *set* to get the values of the x axis. Otherwise, the cells formed by the *set* are evaluated within the current context and their values are used as the x values. Empty cells and cells containing text or logical values are not included in the calculation, but cells with zero values are included.

Once the linear regression line has been calculated, this function returns the slope of the line (represented by a in the equation y = ax + b). See also the other LinRegXXX functions.

LinRegVariance(*set, numeric expression* [, *numeric expression*]**)** Returns: number

This function returns the variance of fit of the calculated linear regression line to the actual points given for it. For the linear equation y = ax + b, which will be determined over some *set* of y and x, the values of the *y numeric expression* are evaluated to get the y values. If the *x numeric expression* is present, then it is evaluated over the *set* to get the values of the x axis. Otherwise, the cells formed by the *set* are evaluated within the current context and their values are used as the x values. Empty cells and cells containing text or logical values are not included in the calculation, but cells with zero values are included.

Once the linear regression line has been calculated, this function returns the statistical variance between its points and the given points. See also the other LinRegXXX functions.

LookupCube(*cube string, numeric expression***)** Returns: number *Extension*

LookupCube(*cube string, string expression***)** Returns: string *Extension*

LookupCube( ) can be used to retrieve a single value from another cube. This function can look up values from a regular cube or a virtual cube. The expression can also reference calculated members within the designated cube. The function is most likely to be used as part of a calculated member or custom rollup expression, although care must be taken to ensure that the result is as expected, because LookupCube( ) returns only a single value and does not respect the context of the current query. This means that any necessary current members need to be placed in the *numeric expression* or *string expression*. For example, the following calculated member only makes sense if we are looking at the All level on the other dimensions:

```
WITH MEMBER [Measures].[Store Net Sales] AS
'[Measures].[Store Sales] - LookupCube("Budget","[Account].[Total
Expense]")'
```

The following will include time and product dimensions from the sales cube:

```
WITH MEMBER [Measures].[Store Net Sales] AS
'[Measures].[Store Sales] - LookupCube("Budget",
  "([Account].[Total Expense]," + [Time].CurrentMember.UniqueName +
","
  + [Product].CurrentMember.UniqueName + ")"
)'
```

See also: StrToVal( )

M

Max(*set* **[,** *numeric expression***])** Returns: number

This function returns the maximum value found across the cells of the set. If a numeric expression is supplied, then the function finds the maximum of its non-empty values across the set.

See also: Min( ), Median( )

Median(*set* **[,** *numeric expression***])** Returns: number

This function returns the median value found across the cells of the set. If a numeric expression is supplied, then the function finds the median of its values across the set.

See also: Min( ), Max( )

dimension.**Members**   Returns: set

hierarchy.**Members**   Returns: set

level.**Members**   Returns: set

Each of the variations of the .Members function returns the set of all members within the scope of the given meta data object in the database's default order. Figure A.26 shows the scope of the members operator. Dimension.Members, shown in Figure A.26a, returns the members of the entire dimension and includes the All member of the hierarchy if present. Because in OLAP/Analysis Services a hierarchy is implemented as a dimension, the Hierarchy.Members function is also shown. Level.Members, shown in Figure A.26b, selects all members in the specified level.

See also: .AllMembers, AddCalculatedMembers( ), StripCalculatedMembers( )

Members(*string expression***)**   Returns: member   *Extension*

This function returns the member whose name is given by *string expression*. (Yes, it only returns a single member, even though its name is plural.) The most common use for this function is to take a string from a user-defined function (UDF) that identifies a member and convert it to a member. For example, consider a UDF named UDF_GetMySalesTerritory on the client that returned the member name for the user's sales territory. Given this UDF, the following expression,

```
([Measures].[Sales], Members ( UDF_GetMySalesTerritory() ) )
```

would refer to the sales value for that user's sales territory.

See also: StrToMember( ), StrToTuple( ), StrToSet( ), .Name, .UniqueName

MemberToStr(*member***)**   Returns: string

This function returns the unique name of a member. In Analysis Services, the MDX Compatibility and MDX Unique Name Style connection parameters will determine the format of the name generated. This is identical in function to .UniqueName.

See also: Member.*UniqueName*

Min(*set* **[,** *numeric expression***])**   Returns: number

This function returns the minimum value found across the cells of the *set*. If a *numeric expression* is supplied, then the function finds the minimum of its values across the set.

See also: Max( ), Median( )

A) *DIMENSION*.Members
    HIERARCHY.Members

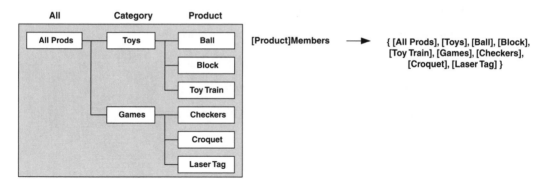

B)   *LEVEL*.Members

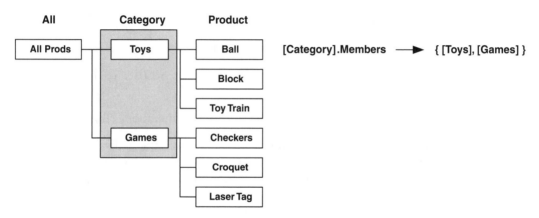

Figure A.26   Members selected by .Members operator.

MTD([*member*])   Returns: set

MTD( ) is the equivalent of PeriodsToDate( ) with the level set to Month. If member is not specified, it defaults to the current member of the Time-typed dimension. If no Time-typed dimension is in the cube, or if it does not have a level tagged as a Month, then a parser error results.

See also: PeriodsToDate( ), YTD( ), QTD( ), WTD( )

N

*dimension.***Name**   Returns: string   *Extension*

This function returns the name of the dimension.

See also: .UniqueName, Dimensions( )

*hierarchy.***Name**   Returns: string   *Extension*

This function returns the name of the hierarchy.

See also: .UniqueName

*level.***Name**   Returns: string   *Extension*

This function returns the name of the level.

See also: .UniqueName, .Ordinal, Levels( )

*member.***Name**   **Returns: string**   *Extension*

This function returns the name of the member.

See also: StrToMember( ), StrToTuple( ), StrToSet( ),TupleToStr( ), .UniqueName

NameToSet(*membername***)**   Returns: set (of one member)   *Extension*

This function returns a set containing one member specified by the *membername*. If no member can be found with this name, then the set is returned empty (and it cannot be identified with .Dimension). The contents of *membername* must be only a member name or unique name. It cannot be a member expression, as StrToSet( ) would enable.

See also: Member.UniqueName, StrToSet( ), StrToMember( )

*member.***NextMember**   Returns: member

See description of .PrevMember

NonEmptyCrossJoin(*set1, set2* **[,***set3* **. . .] [, set-count])**   Returns: set
Extension

This function returns the non-empty cross-join of two or more sets. It is based on data actually present in fact tables. This means that it filters out all tuples involving calculated members.

Non-emptiness is a characteristic of cells as opposed to tuples. NonEmpty-CrossJoin( ) takes a different approach to specifying the cells than the other functions that deal with empty/non-empty cells associated with tuples. If the *set-count* is present, then the number specified for it will be used as the number of sets (starting at *set1*) to actually cross-join. The remaining sets listed will be used to form the slices used to find the cells that are non-empty. (Any dimensions not listed will have their current member used to determine cells.)

If the *set-count* parameter is provided, then only that number of sets (in the order that they appear) will contribute tuples to the resulting set. The remaining sets will provide the context or add members for consideration in the non-emptiness. The other sets may have only one member, or they may have multiple members. If they have multiple members, it is possible that more than one contributes to result tuples. Only the distinct tuples from the dimensions listed in the first *set-count* sets will be returned, though.

Note that if a measure field is NULL in the underlying fact table, Analysis Services will treat the measure as zero, so the associated tuple will show up in the non-empty set (unless all measures in the row are NULL).

This function is by far the most efficient technique for obtaining its results. See Chapter 14, "Optimizing MDX," for a discussion of efficiency and creating non-empty sets that involve calculated results.

See also: CrossJoin( ), Extract( ), Except( ), Union( ), Intersect( )

NOT *expr*　Returns: Boolean

The NOT operator returns false if *expr* is true, and false otherwise.

O

OpeningPeriod([*level* [, *member*]]**)**　Returns: member

ClosingPeriod([*level* [, *member*]]**)**　Returns: member

The OpeningPeriod and ClosingPeriod operators are essentially first-descendant and last-descendant operators that are intended primarily to be used with the Time dimension, though they may be used with any dimension. The OpeningPeriod function returns the first member among the descendants of member at level. For example, OpeningPeriod(Month, [1991]) returns [January, 1991]. If no member is specified, then the default is the current member of the Time-type dimension in that cube. If no level is specified, then it is the level immediately below that of member. OpeningPeriod (*level, member*) is equivalent to Descendants(*member, level*).Item(0). ClosingPeriod( ) is very similar, only it returns the last descendant instead of the first descendant. OpeningPeriod( ) and ClosingPeriod( ) are illustrated in Figure A.27.

If member is omitted, and no dimension in the cube is marked as being Time-typed, the statement will parse and execute without error. However,

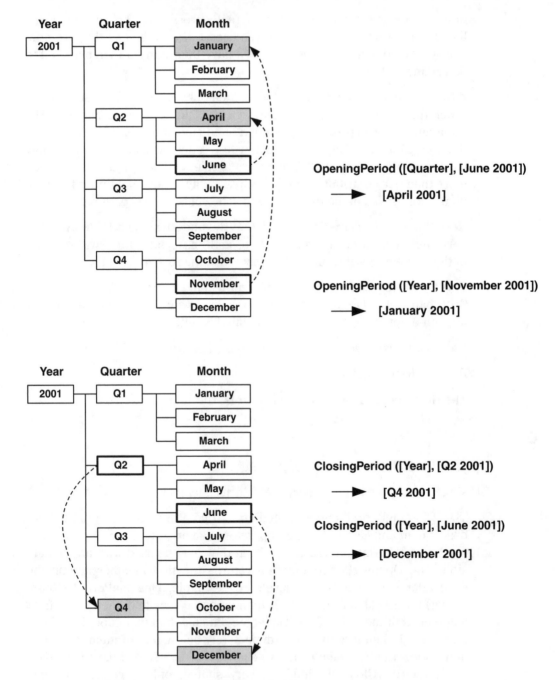

Figure A.27 OpeningPeriod( ) and ClosingPeriod( ).

when a client attempts to retrieve a cell calculated in part by the Opening-Period( ) or ClosingPeriod( ) function, a NULL member reference will occur in Analysis Services. This is different from the behavior in OLAP Services 7, in which a cell error will occur.

See also: PeriodsToDate( ), ParallelPeriod( ), Is

expr1 **OR** *expr2*   Returns: boolean

The OR operator returns TRUE if either expr1 is TRUE or expr2 is TRUE. In Analysis Services, if expr1 evaluates to TRUE, then expr2 is not evaluated (because the result is already guaranteed to be TRUE).

See also: AND, NOT, XOR, iif( ), Filter( )

Order(*set***,** {string_expression|numeric expression} **[,ASC | DESC | BASC | BDESC])**   Returns: set

Order( ) returns the set that it is given after it sorts it based on the given expression. If a numeric or string value expression is provided, then that is used to sort the tuples; otherwise, the values of the cells in context are used. This function also takes an optional flag to indicate how to sort. The default ordering is ASC (ascending without breaking the hierarchy).

Order( ) has two modes for sorting: breaking hierarchy and preserving hierarchy. The BASC and BDESC options break the hierarchy, while ASC and DESC do not. When the hierarchy is broken, the values associated with each tuple in the set are treated as peers, and the set is ordered only by the values. When the hierarchy is preserved, a more complex ordering algorithm is used, which can lead to very useful results.

Note that there is no explicit way to sort a set based on more than one criterion. For example, if you want to sort a set based primarily on a string member property and secondarily on a numerical value, no good way is available for specifying this. We do describe techniques for performing this in Chapter 4, "More MDX in Use."

Preserving Hierarchy: Set Containing One Dimension

When the set consists only of one dimension's worth of members, sorting and preserving the hierarchy orders each parent before its children. At each level of members from the top down, the children of each parent are sorted relative to each other. For example, the product hierarchy for a fictional fishcake manufacturer is shown in Figure A.28 and the units shipped per product are shown in Figure A.29. Ordering these members while preserving the hierarchy would give us the orderings shown in Figure A.30.

Category	Product Name
Premium	Ancient Mariner
Premium	Gobi Crab Cakes
Premium	Moby Dick
Premium	Neptunes Glory
Diet	Silver Scales
Diet	Thin Fins
Standard	Anglers Choice
Standard	Briny Deep
Standard	Gill Thrill
Standard	Mako Steak-o

Figure A.28 Sample product hierarchy.

Product	Units
Ancient Mariner	221,871
Gobi Crab Cakes	223,351
Moby Dick	200,745
Neptunes Glory	210,745
Premium	856,274
Silver Scales	425,604
Thin Fins	434,482
Diet	860,086
Anglers Choice	207,662
Briny Deep	201,443
Gill Thrill	209,962
Mako Steak-o	215,521
Standard	834,588

Figure A.29 Units shipped in hierarchy.

ASC

Product	Units
Standard	834,588
Briny Deep	201,443
Anglers Choice	207,662
Gill Thrill	209,962
Mako Steak-o	215,521
Premium	856,274
Moby Dick	200,745
Neptunes Glory	210,745
Ancient Mariner	221,871
Gobi Crab Cakes	223,351
Diet	860,086
Silver Scales	425,604
Thin Fins	434,482

DESC

Product	Units
Diet	860,086
Thin Fins	434,482
Silver Scales	425,604
Premium	856,274
Gobi Crab Cakes	223,351
Ancient Mariner	221,871
Neptunes Glory	210,745
Moby Dick	200,745
Standard	834,588
Mako Steak-o	215,521
Gill Thrill	209,962
Anglers Choice	207,662
Briny Deep	201,443

Figure A.30   Hierarchy preserved in ordering.

Also, an extra sophistication in the sorting process is not immediately evident. Let us imagine that the category-level members [Standard], [Premium], and [Diet] were not part of the set being queried, while the ProductName members still were. Therefore, the category-level [Units] value does not come directly into play when the set is ordered. However, when sorting without breaking hierarchy, the [Units] value is still calculated at each parent member when Microsoft OLAP Services is trying to figure out how to order the groups of children relative to their cousins.

For example, suppose that the following set of product names was ordered by Units: {[Product].[Briny Deep], [Product].[Anglers Choice], [Product].[Ancient Mariner], [Product].[Gobi Crab Cakes], [Product].[Thin Fins]}. The ordering shown in Figure A.31 would be returned.

Preserving Hierarchy: Set Containing Multiple Dimensions

When the set consists of multiple dimensions, the tuples are sorted such that the hierarchical ordering of the first dimension in the tuples is the primary ordering. According to this ordering, within each member of the first dimension, the members of the second dimension are sorted. Within each

ASC

Product	Units	Parent's Units
Briny Deep	201,443	834,588
Anglers Choice	207,662	
Ancient Mariner	221,871	856,274
Gobi Crab Cakes	223,351	
Thin Fins	434,482	860,086

DESC

Product	Units	Parent's Units
Thin Fins	434,482	860,086
Gobi Crab Cakes	223,351	856,274
Ancient Mariner	221,871	
Anglers Choice	207,662	834,588
Briny Deep	201,443	

Figure A.31 Hierarchy preserved when ordering a set without parents.

([member from dim 1], [member from dim 2]) tuple, the members of the third dimension are sorted, and so on. For example, let us expand our example to include some customers and time periods and order the cross-join of

```
{ [Product].[Briny Deep], [Product].[Anglers Choice],
[Product].[Mako Steak-o] }
```

with

```
{ [Time].[Quarter 2], [Time].[Quarter 3] }
```

with

```
{ [Customer].[Supernaturalizes Food Service], [Customer].[Hanover
Distributors], [Customer].[Subcommittees Anticipates Farms] }.
```

The ordering and values shown in Figure A.32 will appear. The products are arranged in order of decreasing quantity over year and customer parent. For each product, the quarters are arranged in order of decreasing quantity based on that product and customer parent. For each (Product, Time) tuple, the customers are arranged in order of decreasing quantity. Where tuples are tied (at the blank cells), the original ordering of the tuples is retained rather than the dimension's ordering (which was alphabetical).

See also: Hierarchize( )

*Level.***Ordinal**   Returns: number (integer)

This function returns the zero-based index of the level in the cube. The root level of a cube is number 0, the next level down (if there is one) is number 1, and so on. This is typically used in conjunction with IIF( ) to test whether a cell being calculated is at, above, or below a certain level in the cube (for example, below the All level or below the Quarter level). No MDX function yields the number of levels in the cube.

See also: Is, .Name, Dimension.*Levels( ), Levels( )*

			Qty.
Mako Steak-o	Quarter 2	Subcommittee Anticipation Farms	119.00
		Supernatural Food Service	87.00
		Hanover Distributions	64.00
	Quarter 3	Hanover Distributions	185.00
		Supernatural Food Service	151.00
		Subcommittee Anticipation Farms	105.00
Anglers Choice	Quarter 3	Hanover Distributions	181.00
		Supernatural Food Service	179.00
		Subcommittee Anticipation Farms	
	Quarter 2	Supernatural Food Service	127.00
		Hanover Distributions	73.00
		Subcommittee Anticipation Farms	
Briny Deep	Quarter 3	Subcommittee Anticipation Farms	213.00
		Supernatural Food Service	
		Hanover Distributions	
	Quarter 2	Subcommittee Anticipation Farms	204.00
		Supernatural Food Service	
		Hanover Distributions	

Figure A.32 Hierarchy preserved when ordering a set with multiple dimensions.

P

ParallelPeriod([*level* **[,** *index* **[,***member***]]])**   Returns: set

This function is similar to the Cousin() function. It takes the ancestor of member at level (call it "ancestor"), then it takes the sibling of ancestor that lags by index (call it "in-law"), and it returns the cousin of member among the descendants of in-law. Figure A.33 illustrates the process of finding the parallel period. ParallelPeriod (level, index, member) is equivalent to Cousin(member, Ancestor(Member, Level).Lag(index).

See also: Cousin( ), OpeningPeriod( ), ClosingPeriod( ), Is

*member***.Parent**

This function returns the source member's parent member, if it has one. The behavior of Parent( ) is shown in Figure A.34.

See also: Ancestor( ), Ascendants( ), IsAncestor( ), IsGeneration( )

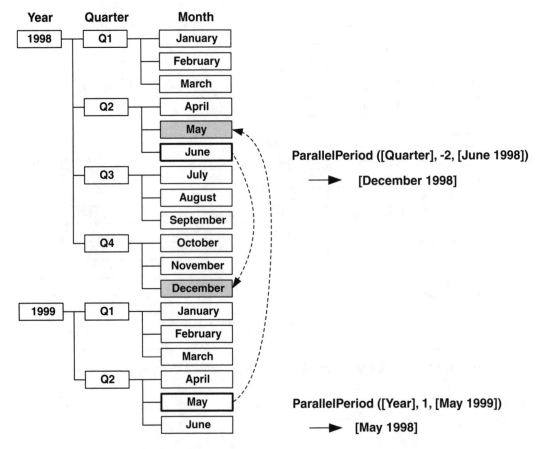

ParallelPeriod ([Quarter], -2, [June 1998])

$\longrightarrow$ **[December 1998]**

ParallelPeriod ([Year], 1, [May 1999])

$\longrightarrow$ **[May 1998]**

Figure A.33 ParallelPeriod( ) operator.

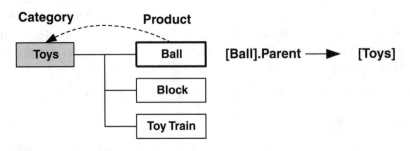

[Ball].Parent $\longrightarrow$ **[Toys]**

Figure A.34 Behavior of .Parent.

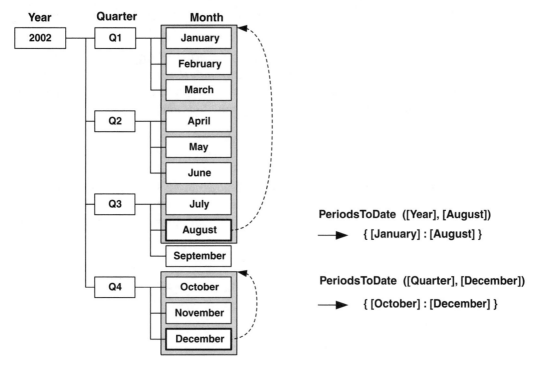

Figure A.35 Behavior of PeriodsToDate().

PeriodsToDate([*level*[, *member*]]**)** Returns: set

This function returns a set of members at the level of member, starting at the first descendant under member's ancestor at level and ending at member. If neither level nor member is specified, then the default member is the current member of the cube's Time-typed dimension, and level is the parent level of that member. If the level is specified but the member is not, then the dimension is inferred from the level, and the current member on that dimension is used. The function is identical to the following:

```
{ Descendants(Ancestor(member, level), member.Level).Item (0) :
member }
```

If member is omitted, and no dimension in the cube is marked as being Time-typed, the statement will parse and execute without error. However, when a client attempts to retrieve a cell calculated in part by the PeriodsToDate() function, a cell error will occur.

The behavior of PeriodsToDate is shown in Figure A.35.

See also: .Siblings, OpeningPeriod( )

Predict (*mining_moel_name,* *numeric_mining_expression*) Returns: Number *Extension*

Predict( ) evaluates the given *numeric_mining_expression* against the data mining model identified by *mining_model_name*. The actual syntax of the *numeric_mining_expression* is not part of MDX, but part of Microsoft's OLE DB for Data Mining specification.

member.**PrevMember**

member.**NextMember**

.PrevMember gives the previous member along the level implied by the member, while .NextMember gives the next member along the level implied by the member. Figure A.36 shows examples of .PrevMember and

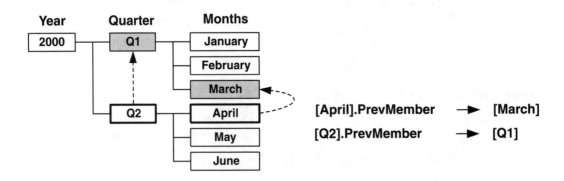

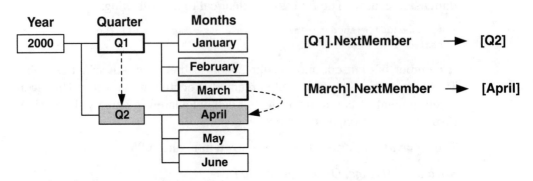

Figure A.36   .NextMember and .PrevMember.

.NextMember. Note that these functions return the next or the previous member within the same level regardless of whether the new member shares the same parent or not.

See also: OpeningPeriod( ), ClosingPeriod( ), Is

*member.***Properties(***property name***)**   Returns: string

The .Properties( ) function returns the value of the named member property at the *member,* for use in an MDX expression. The *property name* may be a string expression. Generally, this will be a constant string (like Zip Code), but it may also be a string-valued expression, such as a string returned by an external function. The property name string expression will be evaluated cell by cell every time the property reference is.

Note that even though Analysis Services supports member properties in a variety of data types, the return value of the .Properties( ) function is coerced to be a string.

In Analysis Services, every member has associated properties named CAPTION, NAME, ID, and KEY.

See also: StrToMember( ), StrToSet( ), StrToTuple( ), StrToValue( ), Members( ), Dimensions( ), Levels( )

Q

QTD([*member***])**   Returns: set

QTD( ) is the equivalent of PeriodsToDate( ) with the level set to Quarter. If member is not specified, it defaults to the current member of the Time-typed dimension. If no Time-typed dimension is in the cube, or if one is in the cube without a level tagged as a Quarter, then a parser error results.

See also: PeriodsToDate( ), YTD( ), MTD( ), WTD( )

R

Rank(*tuple, set***)**   Returns: number (integer)

Rank(*tuple, set, numeric expression***)**   Returns: number (integer)   *Extension*

This function returns the (one-based) index of the *tuple* in the *set*. If the *tuple* is not found in the *set*, Rank( ) returns 0.

If the optional *numeric expression* is provided, then it is evaluated for *tuple*, and then *numeric expression* is evaluated for the neighbors of *tuple*. If two or more tuples share the same value in the set, then the rank number returned is the tied rank. Note that if the set is not sorted by the same

MEMBER	SALES	UNITS
Leather Jackets	100	5
Leather Pants	120	4
Leather Gloves	150	200
Leather Bags	150	16
Leather Skirts	200	4

numeric expression, then the rank numbers will reflect the (possibly tied) rank according to the set as it is actually sorted.

Consider the following examples against a simple set of numbers:

Against this set of tuples (which we will call *Set1*) and associated values, the following is true:

Rank ([Product].[Leather Pants], Set1) is 2.

Rank ([Product].[Leather Bags], Set1, [Measures].[Sales]) is 3 (tied with leather gloves).

Rank ([Product].[Leather Skirts], Set1, [Measures].[Units]) is 5 (the tie with leather pants is not noticed).

Note that the .Item( ) and Subset( ) functions use a zero-based index; the rank of Set.Item(0) is 1.

See also: .Item( ), Subset( ), Head( ), Tail( )

RollupChildren(*member, string expression***)**   Returns: number   *Extension*

This function is used to return the value generated by rolling up the children of a specified parent member using the specified unary operator. The *string expression* is evaluated once per child of *member*. You can use a constant string value for the expression, but while the unary operator can be any of +, −, *, /, %, and ~, using the operators *, /, or % as the string expression will cause an error because these operators cannot be used for the first child of a parent member. Frequently, a reference to a member property ([Dimension].CurrentMember.Properties ("Some Property")) will be the *string expression*. You may also use a string expression based on a property. For example, the following expression will create the positive sum of all children that would ordinarily be subtracted from the sum

```
iif ([Accounts].CurrentMember.Properties ("UNARY_OPERATOR") <> "-",
    "~",
    "-"
)
```

This function could be used, for example, in a budgeting application where there may be more than one way to rollup the Accounts dimension, perhaps some costs are ignored in the alternate rollup. You could create a member property "alternate operators" to hold the operators of this alternate rollup. The following expression would return the results of this alternate rollup (note that the current member is evaluated once per child of [Account].[Net Profit]):

```
RollupChildren([Account].[Net Profit],
     [Account].CurrentMember.Properties("ALTERNATE_OPERATORS") )
```

Note that if you use this function as a custom rollup operator (for example, in a local cube), you may need to use it in conjunction with an iif( ) test and the .Ignore function to avoid infinite recursion at leaf-level members.

See also: Sum( )

S

SetToArray(*set* **[,** *set* . . . **][,** *numeric or string expression***])**

The SetToArray( ) function creates an array as a COM Variant type that holds an array of values. The only use for this function in OLAP and Analysis Services is to pass the constructed array to an external function that is defined as taking an array.

The constructed array will hold values of only one type (which might be, for example, long integer, single float, double float, or string). That type is determined by the type of the first value that is actually placed into the array. The dimensionality of the array that is created is determined by the number of sets that appear as arguments to SetToArray( ). If the optional numeric or string expression is provided, it is evaluated over the cross-join of the sets, and the values are placed in the array. If the numeric or string expression is not provided, then the cross-join of the sets is evaluated in the current context, and the results obtained are placed in the array.

SetToStr(*set***)**   Returns: string

This function constructs a string from a set. It will frequently be used to transfer a set to an external function that knows how to parse the string, even though the string is syntactically suitable for OLAP Services to parse into a set. OLAP Services constructs the string as follows: the first character is { and the last character is }. Between the braces, each tuple is listed in order. A comma and a space separate each tuple from the next name. If the set contains only one dimension, then each member is listed using its unique name. If the set contains more than one dimension, then each tuple begins with an open parenthesis ("(") and ends with a closing parenthesis (")"). The unique name of the member from each dimension is listed in the order of the dimensions in the set, separated by a comma and a space. For example, in a Time dimension that has 3 years, the expression

```
SetToStr ([Time].[Year].Members)
```

would yield the following string:

```
"{[Time].[All Times].[1998], [Time].[All Times].[1999], [Time].[All
Times].[2000]}"
```

Moreover, the expression

```
SetToStr ( {([Time].[1998], [Customer].[Northeast]), ([Time].[1999],
[Customer].[Southwest])} )
```

yields the following string:

```
"{([Time].[All Times].[1998], [Customer].[All Customers].[North-
east]), ([Time].[All Times].[1999], [Customer].[All
Customers].[Southwest])}".
```

Fairly large strings (greater than 16K) will take significant time to create, and the first release of OLAP Services was released with problems that led to the truncation of strings. The further down the hierarchy the members are, the longer and more numerous their unique names are likely to be. So, you may need to perform your own performance evaluations when using this function.

The style of the unique names generated into the string by this function will be affected by the MDX Unique Name Style and MDX Compatibility settings (see Appendix B for more information).

See also: Generate( ), StrToValue( ), StrToSet( ), StrToMember( ), LookupCube( )

*Member.***Siblings**   Returns: set   *Extension*

This function returns the set of meta data siblings of a specified member in the database's default order. The resulting set includes the specified mem-

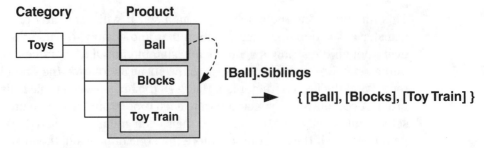

Figure A.37   Diagram of .Siblings.

ber itself. It does not include calculated members. Figure A.37 diagrams the selection of .Siblings.

See also: .Children, .FirstSibling, .LastSibling

StdDev(*set* **[,** *numeric value expression***])**   Returns: number

StdDevP(*set* **[,** *numeric value expression***])**   Returns: number

StDev(*set* **[,** *numeric value expression***])**   Returns: number

StDevP(*set* **[,** *numeric value expression***])**   Returns: number

These functions return the standard deviation of a numeric expression evaluated over a set. If the *numeric value expression* is not supplied, these functions evaluate the set within the current context to determine the values to use. The formula for obtaining the standard deviation is as follows:

$$\sqrt{\frac{\sum_{i=1}^{n}(\overline{x} - x_i)^2}{n}}$$

StDev( ) calculates the sample standard deviation and uses the unbiased formula for population (dividing by n − 1 instead of n). On the other hand, StDevP( ) calculates the population standard deviation and uses the biased formula (dividing by n). StdDev( ) and StdDevP( ) are aliases of StDev( ) and StDevP( ), respectively.

StripCalculatedMembers(*set***)**   Returns: set   *Extension*

The StripCalculatedMembers( ) function returns the members of set after removing all the calculated members. The set is limited to only one dimension. Note that this function removes all calculated members defined, whether they were defined by CREATE MEMBER at the server or at the client, or in the query through WITH MEMBER.

See also: AddCalculatedMembers( ), .AllMembers

StrToMember(*String Expression***)**   Returns: member

This function refers to a member identified by the string expression. This will frequently be used along with external functions to convert a string returned by the external function to a member reference within the query. The string expression can be dynamic as well as a fixed string. It can contain an MDX expression that evaluates to a member as well as just the name of a member.

See also: Members( ), StrToTuple( ), StrToSet( ), .Properties( )

StrToSet(*string expression***)**   Returns: set

This function constructs a set from a string expression. This will frequently be used to transfer a set specification returned by a UDF back to the MDX statement. The string must be a syntactically valid MDX set specification relative to the cube in whose context it is executed. For example, the set of all years in a Time dimension that has three year-level members could be created by passing either of the following strings into StrToSet:

```
"{[Time].[All Times].[1998], [Time].[All Times].[1999], [Time].[All
Times].[2000]}"
"[Time].[Year].Members"
```

See also: StrToTuple, SetToStr( ), TupleToStr( ), Members( ), .Properties( ), .Name, .UniqueName

StrToTuple(*string expression***)**   Returns: tuple

This function constructs a tuple from a string expression. This will frequently be used to transfer a tuple specification that is returned by an external function back to the MDX statement. The string must be a syntactically valid MDX tuple specification relative to the cube in whose context it is executed. For example, the following two strings would give identical results in the customer dimension, where [AZ] is a child of [Southwest], in that both would result in the Southwest region member:

```
"[Customer].[Southwest]"
"[Customer].[AZ].Parent"
```

See also: StrToSet( ), SetToStr( ), TupleToStr( ), Members( ), .Properties( ), .Name, .UniqueName

StrToValue(*string expression***)**   Returns: number or string

This function takes the results of an arbitrary string expression and evaluates it as an MDX expression in the current context of the cube or query. The string expression can be dynamic as well as a fixed string. The MDX expression can be arbitrarily complicated so long as it returns a single cell value.

See also: StrToSet, SetToStr( ), TupleToStr( ), Members( ), .Properties( ), .Name, .UniqueName

Subset(*set, start* **[,** *count***])**   Returns: set   *Extension*

This function returns up to *count* elements from *set*, starting at *start*. The *start* index is zero-based (like Rank( )): the first element in the set is at index 0, and the last is at one less than the number of tuples in the set. If *count* is not specified or is greater than the number of elements in the *set* following Start, all elements from Start to the end of the set are returned. If *count* is less than 1, then an empty set is returned.

See also: Head( ), Tail( ), Index( ), .Count, Count( ), Rank( )

Sum(*set* **[,** *numeric value expression***])**   Returns: number

This function returns the sum of values found across all tuples in the *set*. If *numeric value expression* is supplied, then it is evaluated across set and its results are summed; otherwise, *set* is evaluated in the current context and the results are summed.

See also: Aggregate( ), Avg( ), Count( ), .Count, Min( ), Max( )

T

Tail(*set* **[,** *count***])**   Returns: set   *Extension*

This function returns a set of the last *count* elements from the given *set*. The order of elements in the given set is preserved. If *count* is omitted, the number of elements returned is 1. If *count* is less than 1, an empty set is returned. If the value of the *count* is greater than the number of tuples in the set, the original set is returned.

See also: Subset( ), Head( ),Index( ), .Count, Count( ), Rank( )

ToggleDrillState(*set1***,** *set2* **[, RECURSIVE])**   Returns: set

This function returns a set in which those members or tuples in *set1* that are drilled up are drilled down and those members or tuples in *set1* that are drilled down are drilled up. This function combines the operations of DrillUpMember( ) and DrillDownMember( ). *Set1* can contain tuples of arbitrary dimensionality; *set2* must contain only members of one dimension. A member or tuple in *set1* is considered drilled down if it has any descendant immediately following it and is considered drilled up otherwise. When a member is found without a descendant immediately after it, DrillDownMember( ) will be applied to it, with the RECURSIVE flag if the RECURSIVE is present.

See also: DrillDownMember( ), DrillUpMember( )

TopCount(*set, index* **[,** *numeric expression***])**   Returns: set

BottomCount(*set, index* **[,** *numeric expression***])**   Returns: set

TopCount( ) returns the top *index* items found after sorting the *set*. The set is sorted on the *numeric expression* (if one is supplied). If there is no *numeric expression*, the cells found in the evaluation context are used. The BottomCount( ) function is similar to TopCount( ), except that it returns the bottom *index* items. TopCount( ) returns elements ordered from largest to smallest in terms of the cells or expression used; BottomCount( ) returns them ordered from smallest to largest. Any duplicate tuples are retained during sorting, and those that make the cutoff are retained.

These functions always break the hierarchy. If members from multiple levels are combined in the set, then they are all treated as peers. If duplicate values exist for some of the cells in set, these functions may pick an arbitrary set. For example, suppose the set of values (when sorted) is as follows:

FRUIT	VALUE
Strawberries	12
Cantaloupes	10
Peaches	8
Apples	8
Kiwis	8
Bananas	4

In this case, selecting the top three or bottom two fruits based on values will cause an arbitrary choice to be made at the value of 8. The results are functionally equivalent to Head(Order(set, numeric value expression, BDESC), index) and Head(Order(set, numeric value expression, BASC), index).

See also: TopSum( ), BottomSum( ), TopPercent( ), BottomPercent( )

TopPercent(*set, percentage, numeric expression***)**   Returns: set

BottomPercent(*set, percentage, numeric expression***)**   Returns: set

TopPercent( ) returns the top *percentage* tuples of *set*, based on numeric expression if specified. The cells or expression are summed over the set, and the top set of elements whose cumulative total of the numeric expression is at least percentage is returned. Percentage is a numeric expression. For example, using the sorted set of fruits and values, TopPercent(fruit, 50, Value) will result in {Strawberries, Cantaloupes}. Strawberries is 24 percent of the total, Cantaloupes + Strawberries is 44 percent of the total, and Peaches would push the set over the 50 percent limit to 56 percent.

BottomPercent( ) behaves similarly, except that it returns the bottom set of elements whose cumulative total from the bottom is less than the specified *percentage*. TopPercent( ) returns elements ordered from largest to smallest in terms of the cells or expression used; BottomPercent( ) returns them ordered from smallest to largest.

The percentage is specified from 0 to 100 (not 0 to 1.0). These functions always break the hierarchy. Like TopCount( ) and BottomCount( ), they may pick an arbitrary cutoff when some cells have the same values. Any duplicate tuples are retained during sorting, and those that make the cutoff are retained. Note that these functions do not have anything to do with taking tuples in the top or bottom percentile ranges according to the statistical definition of percentiles.

See also: TopCount( ), BottomCount( ), TopSum( ), BottomSum( )

TopSum(*set, value, numeric expression***)**   Returns: set

BottomSum (*set, value, numeric expression***)**   Returns: set

TopSum( ) returns the subset of set, after sorting it, such that the sum of the cells (or *numeric value expression*, if supplied) is at least value. This function always breaks the hierarchy. For example, given the sorted set of fruits and values, TopSum(fruit, 24, value) would return {Strawberries, Cantaloupes}. Strawberries' 12 is less than 24, and Strawberries + Cantaloupes is 22, while adding Peach's 8 to the 22 would push it over the limit of 24 to 30. The BottomSum( ) function behaves similarly, except that it returns the bottom set of elements whose cumulative total from the bottom is less than the specified value. TopSum( ) returns elements ordered from largest to smallest in terms of the cells or expression used; BottomSum( ) returns them ordered from smallest to largest.

These functions always break the hierarchy. Like TopCount( ) and Bottom-Count( ), they may pick an arbitrary cutoff when some cells have the same values. Any duplicate tuples are retained during sorting, and those that make the cutoff are retained.

See also: TopCount( ), BottomCount( ), TopPercent( ), BottomPercent( )

TupleToStr(*tuple***)**   Returns: string

This function constructs a string from a tuple. This will frequently be used to transfer a tuple specification to an external function. If the tuple contains only one dimension, the unique name for its member is placed in the string. (In this use, it is identical to Member.UniqueName.) If the tuple contains more than one dimension, OLAP Services constructs the string as follows. The string begins with an open parenthesis ("(") and ends with a closed parenthesis ("("). In between the parentheses, the member's unique name is placed in the string for each dimension in the order they follow in the tuple. Each member is separated by a comma and a space. For example, the expression

```
TupleToStr ( (Time.[1997], Customer.[AZ]) )
```

which uses names that are not quite the members' unique names, might return the following string:

```
([Time].[All Times].[1997], [Customer].[All Customers].[South-
west].[AZ])
```

If the tuple is a result of an invalid member reference, then the resulting string is empty (instead of an error result).

The style of name generated depends on the MDX Unique Name Style and MDX Compatibility settings (see Appendix B for more details).

See also: SetToStr( ), StrToTuple( ),.Name, .UniqueName, StrToMember( ), Members( ), StrToValue( ), LookupCube( )

U

Union(*set1*, *set2* **[, ALL])**   Returns: set

set1 + set2   Returns: set   *Extension*

This function returns the union of the two sets. The ALL flag controls whether duplicates are retained or eliminated; by default, they are eliminated. When duplicates of each tuple are eliminated, the first instance of each tuple is retained according to the order in which it appears. The effect of this function is that *set2* is appended to *set1*, and then all copies of each tuple are removed after the first instance of that tuple in the appended version. When duplicates are retained, any duplicates in the set1 are retained, and any additional copies in *set2* are also retained. The effect of the union is that *set2* is appended to set1. For example, the expression

```
Union (
    { [Customer].[AZ].[Phoenix], [Customer].[AZ].[Scottsdale],
      [Customer].[KS].[Pittsburg], [Customer].[AZ].[Phoenix] },
    { [Customer].[NM].[Albuquerque], [Customer].[AZ].[Phoenix],
      [Customer].[AZ].[Scottsdale], [Customer].[AZ].[Phoenix]
)
```

yields the following set:

```
{ [Customer].[AZ].[Phoenix], [Customer].[AZ].[Scottsdale],
  [Customer].[KS].[Pittsburg], [Customer].[NM].[Albuquerque] }
```

The expression

```
Union (
    { [Customer].[AZ].[Phoenix], [Customer].[AZ].[Scottsdale],
      [Customer].[KS].[Pittsburg], [Customer].[AZ].[Phoenix] },
    { [Customer].[NM].[Albuquerque], [Customer].[AZ].[Phoenix],
    [Customer].[AZ].[Scottsdale], [Customer].[AZ].[Phoenix] }
    , ALL
)
```

yields the following set:

```
{ [Customer].[AZ].[Phoenix], [Customer].[AZ].[Scottsdale],
[Customer].[KS].[Pittsburg], [Customer].[AZ].[Phoenix], [Cus-
tomer].[NM].[Albuquerque], [Customer].[AZ].[Phoenix],
[Customer].[AZ].[Scottsdale], [Customer].[AZ].[Phoenix] }
```

Microsoft OLAP Services and Analysis Services also provide + as an alternate way of specifying Union( ). Duplicates are removed from the resulting set. The expression Set1 + Set2 + Set3 is equivalent to Union (Set1, Union (Set2, Set3)).

See also: Intersect( ), Except( ), {}

*Dimension.***UniqueName**   Returns: string   *Extension*

This function returns the unique name of a dimension. In Microsoft's OLAP products, this does not include the name of the cube.

See also: .Name

*Level.***UniqueName**   Returns: string   *Extension*

This function returns the unique name of a level. In Microsoft's OLAP products, this does not include the name of the cube. It will be either [Dimension].[Level] or [Dimension].[Hierarchy].[Level], depending on the structure of the dimension.

See also: .Name, Levels( )

*Member.***UniqueName**   Returns: string   *Extension*

This function returns the unique name of a member. In Microsoft's OLAP products, this does not include the name of the cube, and the results are dependent on the MDX Unique Name Style connection property or the equivalent server-side setting (see Appendix B, Connection Parameters for more details).

See also: StrToMember( ), StrToTuple( ), StrToSet( ),TupleToStr( ), .Name

UserName   Returns: string   *Extension*

This function returns the username of the user executing the function. The name is returned in *Domain\Name* format. For example, if user Lisa in the domain ITCMAIN invokes a calculation that uses this function, it will return ITCMAIN\Lisa.

V

ValidMeasure(*tuple***)**   Returns: tuple   *Extension*

This function returns the value of the measure specified by the *tuple* where the measure has been projected to a meaningful intersection in a virtual cube. When a virtual cube joins two or more regular cubes that have different dimensionality, all base data values in the virtual cube are found at the ALL levels of each dimension that is not shared by all cubes. You can always reference these base data cells by explicitly qualifying the measure reference to the ALL level of each dimension (for example, ([Measures].[Employee Count], [Product].[All Products], [Customer].[All Customers])). This function is a convenience because you do not need to explicitly reference all of the dimensions that are not relevant to the measure.

The tuple may contain members from any dimensions of the virtual cube (and it does not need to have a measure in it). Any members for non-common dimensions for the measure are projected to the ALL member. Any members for dimensions that are in common are used to locate the value returned. The function can be used with regular cubes, but in that case it does nothing to change the location of reference for the measure.

Note that you need an extra set of parentheses to define the tuple if it contains more than one member

```
ValidMeasure ( ([Measures].[Qty Purchased], [Time].PrevMember) )
```

instead of

```
ValidMeasure ( [Measures].[Qty Purchased], [Time].PrevMember )
```

*measure***[.Value]**   Returns: number or string

The .Value operator returns the value of the specified *measure* at the location formed by the current members of all other dimensions in context. We show this operator as optional because it is the default operator on a measure in a calculation or query context. If you leave it off, you get the value of the measure anyway because the default interpretation of a measure is to take its value. This operator exists simply as a specific counterpart to the other functions that return aspects of a member, like .Name (which would return the name of the measure).

Var(*set* **[,** *numeric value expression***])**   Returns: number

Variance(*set* **[,** *numeric value expression***])**   Returns: number   *Extension*

VarianceP(*set* **[,** *numeric value expression***])**   Returns: number   *Extension*

VarP(_set_ **[,** _numeric value expression_**])**   Returns: number   _Extension_

These functions return the variance of a _numeric expression_ evaluated over a _set_. If the _numeric expression_ is not supplied, these functions evaluate the _set_ within the current context to determine the values to use. The formula for obtaining the variance is

$$\frac{\sum_{i=1}^{n}(\bar{x}-x_i)^2}{n}$$

Var( ) calculates the sample variance and uses the unbiased population formula (dividing by n-1), while VarP( ) calculates the population variance and uses the biased formula (dividing by n). Variance( ) and VarianceP( ) are aliases of Var( ) and VarP( ), respectively.

See also: Stdev( ), StdevP( )

VisualTotals(_set_**,** _pattern_**)**

This function returns a set that includes dynamically created calculated members that total up the given descendants for an ancestor. The function accepts a set that can contain members at any level from within one dimension. (The set can only include members from one dimension.) When a parent member is followed by one or more of its children in the given set, or an ancestor by one or more of its descendants, the function replaces that parent or ancestor member with a synthesized member that totals the values taken only from the children or descendants that follow it in the set. The name of the synthesized member is formed from the pattern given in the pattern argument. The order of the appearance of members is important; a parent that is to be replaced by a synthetic visual total must appear immediately before its children. The sets created by the DrillDownXXX functions are likely to fit VisualTotal( )'s member ordering requirements.

The synthesized members are named using the text from the pattern string. Wherever an asterisk appears in the string, the name (the simple name, not the unique name) of that parent member is inserted. A double asterisk (**) causes an asterisk character to appear in the name.

Consider the following VisualTotals( ) expression, which contains numerous parents and ancestors (its results as shown in Figure A.38).

```
WITH
MEMBER [Measures].[AvgPrice] AS '[Measures].[Total] /
[Measures].[Qty]', FORMAT_STRING = '#.00000'
SET [Rowset] AS 'VisualTotals (
{
```

	Qty	Total	Average Price
Quarter 1	1,811,965.00	44,166,000.00	24.37464
vt 2001	5,965,904.00	133,988,515.00	22.45905
January	620,829.00	16,343870.00	26.32588
February	572,194.00	13,863,990.00	24.26447
vt Quarter 2	1,186,056.00	23,660,064.00	19.94852
May	614,945.00	12,267,870.00	19.94954
June	571,111.00	11,392,190.00	19.94743
Quarter 1	1,811,965.00	44,166,000.00	24.37464
Quarter 2	1,774,860.00	35,934,600.00	20.24644
vt All Time	39,239.00	1,220,641.20	31.10786
Jan 01, 2001	16,127.00	492,969.90	30.56799
Jan 01, 2001	23,112.00	727,671.30	31.48457

Figure A.38   Sample results from VisualTotals( ).

```
[Time].[All Time].[1998].[Q1, 1998],
[Time].[All Time].[1998],
[Time].[All Time].[1998].[Q1, 1998].[January],
[Time].[All Time].[1998].[Q1, 1998].[February],
[Time].[All Time].[1998].[Q2, 1998],
[Time].[All Time].[1998].[Q2, 1998].[May],
[Time].[All Time].[1998].[Q2, 1998].[June],
[Time].[All Time].[1998].[Q1, 1998],
[Time].[All Time].[1998].[Q2, 1998],
[Time].[All Time],
[Time].[All Time].[1998].[Q1, 1998].[January].[Jan 01, 1998],
[Time].[All Time].[1998].[Q1, 1998].[January].[Jan 02, 1998]
}
, "vt *")'
SELECT
{ {[Measures].[Qty],  [Measures].[Total],  [Measures].[AvgPrice} }
on axis(0),
{ [Time].[All Time].[1997].[Quarter 1], [Rowset]
} on axis(1)
FROM cakes03
```

This highlights some of the useful aspects of VisualTotals( ) and also some of its quirks, which you will need to be aware of. Looking at the [vt All Time] member toward the bottom of the report, the All Time total is simply the sum of the two day-level members following it, and a similar look at the [vt Q2, 1998] shows that it is the sum of the two Q2 months following it. Looking at the Qty measure for [vt 1998], the value 252,984 is the sum of values found for January, February, [vt Quarter 2], [Quarter 1], and [Quarter 2]. In other words, [vt Quarter 2] was not double-counted with [May] and [June]. You do need to be careful in how you place descendants, however. [Quarter 1] and [Quarter 2] are included in the total without regard to the fact that their descendants have already been incorporated into the total.

The bottom three rows of the VisualTotals( ) expression just presented show that VisualTotals( ) can work against ancestors and descendants of arbitrary depth. The [All Time] member is the higher level member in the dimension, while each day is at the leaf level. If you observe the values for the [AvgPrice] measure in the query, you can see that it is calculated after the visual totals, despite the fact that it is at solve order precedence 0. The VisualTotals( ) aggregation is documented to be at solve order -4096, so calculated member definitions will ordinarily override VisualTotals( ) synthetic aggregates. Meanwhile, VisualTotals( ) synthetic aggregates should be calculated from the results of custom rollups, because they are at solve order -5119.

Note that the synthetic members in the set returned by VisualTotals( ) are almost fully equivalent to calculated members created by other means. They cannot exist outside of a set as a calculated member, so they will not appear as meta data items through OLE DB for OLAP. They can be part of a set held in a CREATE SET statement and are treated as another calculated member by StripCalculatedMembers( ). They can be filtered by name and unique name. They cannot, however, be referenced by a tuple reference in a formula because they are not entered into Microsoft Analysis Services's internal list of meta data objects.

W

WTD([*member*])   Returns: set

WTD( ) is the equivalent of PeriodsToDate( ) with the level set to Week. If *member* is not specified, it defaults to the current member of the Time-typed dimension. If no Time-typed dimension exists in the cube, or if it does not have a level tagged as a Week, then a parser error results.

See also: PeriodsToDate( ), QTD( ), MTD( ), YTD( )

X

expr1 **XOR** *expr2*   Returns: boolean

The result of this operator is true if only one of *expr1* or *expr2* is true, and false if they both are true or both false. Both expressions must be evaluated in order to determine this.

Y

YTD([*member***])**   Returns: set

YTD( ) is the equivalent of PeriodsToDate( ) with the level set to Year. If *member* is not specified, it defaults to the current member of the Time-typed dimension. If no Time-typed dimension exists in the cube, or if it does not have a level tagged as a Year, then a parser error results.

See also: PeriodsToDate( ), QTD( ), MTD( ), WTD( )

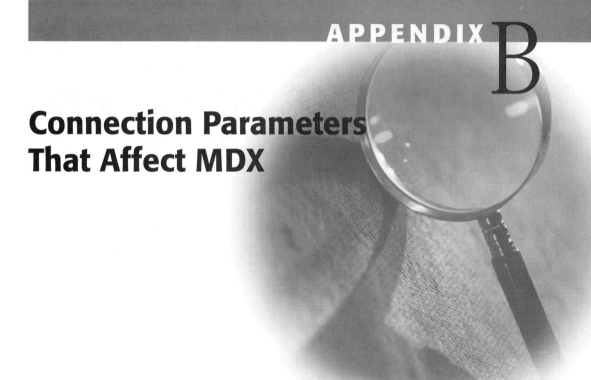

Connection Parameters That Affect MDX

This appendix distills all of the connection parameters that affect MDX usage and results in Microsoft OLAP and Analysis Services. The OLE DB for OLAP and ADO MD identifiers for them are both provided. This includes most of the implemented connection parameters for Analysis Services.

A table of the connection parameters and the Microsoft product versions that implement them are shown in Table B.1.

Auto Synch Period

This property controls the intervals (in milliseconds) for client/server synchronization.

Default setting: 10,000 (10 seconds).

Set: May be set when connecting, and you can change it during the session.

If you set this value to 0 or NULL, no automatic synchronization will occur. Instead, synchronization will only take place whenever a query goes to the server for resolution. Because data to resolve queries may be cached in the PivotTable Service, you may not get updates.

Table B.1 Connection Properties Affecting MDX and Query Results

ADO MD NAME	OLE DB FOR OLAP PROPERTY ID	OLAP SERVICES 7	ANALYSIS SERVICES 2000
Auto Synch Period	DBPROP_MSMD_ AUTOSYNCHPERIOD	Y	Y
CompareCaseNot SensitiveStringFlags	DBPROP_MSMD_ COMPARECASENOTSEN SITIVESTRINGFLAGS	Y	Y
CompareCaseSensitive StringFlags	DBPROP_MSMD_ COMPARECASESENSITIVE STRINGFLAGS	Y	Y
CreateCube	DBPROP_MSMD_ CREATECUBE	Y	Y
Data Source	DBPROP_INIT_ DATASOURCE	Y	Y
Default MDX Visual Mode	DBPROP_MSMD_DEFAULT _MDX_VISUAL_MODE	N	Y
Execution Location	DBPROP_MSMD_ EXECLOCATION	Y	Y
Initial Catalog	DBPROP_INIT_CATALOG	Y	Y
InsertInto	DBPROP_MSMD_ INSERTINTO	Y	Y
Large Level Threshold	DBPROP_MSMD_LARGE _LEVEL_THRESHOLD	Y	Y
Locale Identifier	DBPROP_INIT_LCID	Y	Y
Log File	DBPROP_MSMD_ LOG_FILE	N	Y
MDX Compatibility	DBPROP_MSMD_ MDXCOMPATIBILITY	N	Y
MDX Unique Name Style	DBPROP_MSMD_ MDXUNIQUENAMES	N	Y
OLE DB for OLAP Version	DBPROP_PROVIDER OLEDBOLAPVER	Y	Y
Roles	DBPROP_MSMD_ROLES	N	Y
Safety Options	DBPROP_MSMD_SAFETY _OPTIONS	N	Y
Secured Cell Value	DBPROP_MSMD_ SECURED_CELL_VALUE	Y	Y
Source_DSN	DBPROP_MSMD_SOURCE _DSN	Y	Y
Source_DSN_Suffix	DBPROP_MSMD_SOURCE _DSN_SUFFIX	Y	Y
UseExistingFile	DBPROP_MSMD_ USEEXISTINGFILE	Y	Y

The smallest value is 250 milliseconds (1/4 second). If you specify a number between one and 249, then 250 is used.

Connection string example: `Auto Synch Period=20000;`

CompareCaseNotSensitiveStringFlags

This property adjusts how case-insensitive string comparisons are performed for a specified locale.

Default: None (taken from CompareCaseNotSensitiveStringFlags registry entry on the client computer).

Set: Only when connecting; cannot be changed during session.

The value for this property is made up of discrete flags that can be combined via bitwise-OR. The flags specified in this property are used in case-insensitive string comparisons, and control string comparisons and sort order. This property also controls how comparisons are made in character sets that do not support uppercase and lowercase characters, such as Katakana (for Japanese) and Hindi.

If not specified, the default value is taken from the value of the Compare-CaseNotSensitiveStringFlags registry entry on the client computer. The client application can override this registry entry for case-insensitive string comparisons by setting this property in the connection string.

The PivotTable Service can have only one value for this property for each process. The value of this property, as set in the first connection of the process thread, affects all subsequent connections in that process thread. If the first connection specifies a value for this property and other connections are opened in the same process, each connection after the first connection must specify the same value as that of the first connection.

Table B.2 describes the meaning of each flag.

This setting overrides the setting found in following registry value:

```
HKEY_CLASSES_ROOT\CLSID\{a07ccd0c-8148-11d0-87bb-00c04fc33942}\
CompareCaseNotSensitiveStringFlags
```

Connection string example: `CompareCaseNotSensitiveStringFlags =52;`

Table B.2   Case-insensitive Comparison Settings and Meanings

VALUE	DESCRIPTION
1	Case is ignored.
2	Binary comparison. Characters are compared based on their underlying value in the character set, not on their order in their particular alphabet.
4	Nonspacing characters are ignored.
8	Symbols are ignored.
16	No differentiation is made between Hiragana and Katakana characters. Corresponding Hiragana and Katakana characters, when compared, are considered to be equal.
32	No differentiation is made between single-byte and double-byte versions of the same character.
64	Punctuation is treated the same as symbols.

CompareCaseSensitiveStringFlags

This property adjusts how case-insensitive string comparisons are performed for a specified locale.

Default: None (taken from CompareCaseSensitiveStringFlags registry entry on the client computer).

Set: Only when connecting; cannot be changed during session.

The value for this property is made up of discrete flags that can be combined via bitwise-OR. The flags specified in this property are used in case-insensitive string comparisons, and control string comparisons and sort order. This property also controls how comparisons are made in character sets that do not support uppercase and lowercase characters, such as Katakana (for Japanese) and Hindi.

If not specified, the default value is taken from the value of the CompareCase SensitiveStringFlags registry entry on the client computer. The client application can override this registry entry for case-insensitive string comparisons by setting this property in the connection string.

The PivotTable Service can have only one value for this property for each process. The value of this property, as set in the first connection of the process thread, affects all subsequent connections in that process thread. If the first connection specifies a value for this property and other connections are opened in the same process, each connection after the first connection must specify the same value as that of the first connection.

Table B.3 describes the meaning of each flag.

Note: The flag value 2 is not valid for use in this context.

This setting overrides the setting found in following registry value:

```
HKEY_CLASSES_ROOT\CLSID\{a07ccd0c-8148-11d0-87bb-00c04fc33942}\
CompareCaseNotSensitiveStringFlags
```

Connection string example: `CompareCaseSensitiveStringFlags=52;`

CreateCube

This property contains the CREATE CUBE statement that is used during creation of a local cube.

Default: None.

Set: Only when connecting; cannot be changed during session.

You can only use this property together with the InsertInto and Source_DSN properties.

Connection string example: `CreateCube=CREATE CUBE MyCube (...);`

Table B.3 Case-sensitive Comparison Settings and Meanings

VALUE	DESCRIPTION
1	Case is ignored.
4	Nonspacing characters are ignored.
8	Symbols are ignored.
16	No differentiation is made between Hiragana and Katakana characters. Corresponding Hiragana and Katakana characters, when compared, are considered to be equal.
32	No differentiation is made between single-byte and double-byte versions of the same character.
64	Punctuation is treated the same as symbols.

Data Source

This property specifies the name of the server computer or a local cube file.

Default: None.

Set: Only when connecting; cannot be changed during session.

This is a standard OLE DB property. For Microsoft OLAP/Analysis Server, the value given for this property will set the mode of operation.

Specifying a server name, LOCALHOST, LOCAL, an HTTP or HTTPS URL, or an IP address will attempt a connection with an OLAP/Analysis Server (only a server name or LOCALHOST will work with OLAP Services 7).

Specifying the path and name of a cube file (ending in .CUB) will attempt the creation or opening of a local cube file.

A null value will attempt the creation of a temporary cube file that will be deleted when the session ends. This file will be located in the directory named in the TMP environment variable.

Connection string example: `Data Source=C:\WorkFiles\Michael.cub;`

Default MDX Visual Mode

This property determines the behavior for automatic visual totals.

Default: DBPROPVAL_VISUAL_MODE_DEFAULT

Set: Only when connecting; cannot be changed during session.

Depending on the value set for this property, aggregate members may show either the true total for measures, or they may show the total only for their descendants that the user has queried for. (This property does not affect the ability of a client program to use the VisualTotals() function.) Table B.4 describes the meaning of the property's values.

Connection string example: `Default MDX Visual Mode=2;`

Execution Location

This property determines where queries will be resolved.

Table B.4 Visual Mode Values and Meanings

PROPERTY VALUE	DESCRIPTION
0	Provider-dependent. In Analysis Services 2000, this is equivalent to 2.
1	Automatic visual totals are enabled.
2	Automatic visual totals are not enabled.

Default: 0 (meaning of default subject to change in future versions).

Set: When connection is established, and at any time during session.

The two possible execution locations are client and server. A key driver of internal heuristics is the Large Level value in effect. Some queries cannot be executed on the server, including those that contain calculated members defined in a session or any form of named set.

Table B.5 lists the values and their meanings.

Connection string example: `Execution Location=3;`

Initial Catalog

This property is used to set the name of the database (or *catalog*) on the server when connecting.

Default: None.

Set: Only when connecting.

Connection string example: `Initial Catalog=FoodMart;`

InsertInto

This property contains the INSERT INTO statement used during creation of a local cube.

Default: None.

Set: Only when connecting.

Table B.5 Execution Location Values and Meanings

VALUE	MEANING
0	Default. For compatibility with OLAP 7, this means the same as 1.
1	The PivotTable Service selects the query execution location (client or server) based on internal heuristics.
2	Queries are executed on the client.
3	Queries that can be executed on the server are executed on the server.

This property must be used in conjunction with the CreateCube and Source_DSN properties. See Chapter 13, "Working with Local Cubes," for a description of the INSERT INTO command syntax.

Connection string example: `InsertInto=INSERT INTO MyCube (...);`

Large Level Threshold

This property determines the point at which a level is too large to be sent to the client application in a single piece, and at which the number of members used from a level force the PivotTable Service to try to execute it at the server.

Default: Set at server, server default is 1,000.

Set: Only when connection is established.

Using this property can help manage both memory and CPU usage for the client application. In meta data requests, a request for a level larger than this is broken up into a transmission of groups no larger than this size. If the level is smaller than this threshold, then the entire level is downloaded. Additionally, if a query involves more than this number of members from a single level, OLAP/Analysis Services will attempt to resolve the query on the server; below this threshold, it will resolve it on the client.

The minimum value for this property is 10. If a number less than 10 is used, then the value will silently be set to 10.

Connection string example: `Large Level=500;`

Locale Identifier

This OLE DB property is used to set the *locale ID* (LCID) of preference for the client application.

Default: Null.

Set: Only when connection is established.

The client application can modify the locale settings under which it runs by setting the Locale Identifier property when the connection is established. The locale will determine (among other things) how numbers, currency, and dates/times will be formatted. The LCID must be already installed through the Control Panel. If it is not, the attempt to set the LCID fails. By default, the Locale Identifier property is reported as null.

The PivotTable Service can use only one LCID for each process. If the first connection specifies an LCID and other connections are opened in the same process, each connection after the first connection must specify the same LCID as that of the first connection.

Refer to Microsoft platform documentation for how to obtain locale ID numbers.

Connection string example: `Locale Identifier=409;`

Log File

This property sets or returns the name of a file used to log queries and commands.

Default: None.

Set: Only when connection is established.

If you set a value for this property, then it is taken as the name of a file to log queries and commands into. This can be very useful for debugging queries generated by a client program. Queries are logged whether successful or not. The specified file is opened for exclusive write; any concurrent attempt by another connection to open the same file for write access will fail. The format of the log file is as follows:

Process_name : Process_ID

Date

Time

Command type (either MDX, SQL, or DM)

Query text

Each field is separated by a tab character and records are terminated by a carriage return/line feed pair. If the command contains carriage returns and/or line feeds, you should parse the log by looking for patterns of process name, process ID, and date/time.

Note: This may only be a pre-service pack condition, but if the log file exists when the connection is made, queries and commands are logged from the beginning of the file over the pre-existing contents. If this is the case in the version that you are working with (we are working with the RTM of Analysis Services 2000), then you should endeavor to either delete the log file or truncate it to zero bytes length prior to establishing the connection.

Connection string example: `Log File=C:\Temp\Debug MDX.log;`

MDX Compatibility

This property determines how placeholder members in ragged and unbalanced hierarchies are treated.

Default: 0 (same meaning as 1). The default meaning may change in future versions.

Set: When connecting, and at any time during a connection.

Ragged (level-based) hierarchies are implemented in Analysis Services 2000 either by hiding members in levels or by adding members to positions in the hierarchy. In a level-based ragged hierarchy, placeholder members are hidden to create the appearance of raggedness. In a parent-child hierarchy, members may be added to create the appearance of raggedness. This property determines how placeholder members in a ragged or unbalanced hierarchy are treated. Table B.6 describes possible values for this property.

NOTE

At least in the RTM version of Analysis Services 2000, in order to see the effect of non-default values of the MDX Unique Name Style property, you also need to ensure that this property is set to a value of 2. Exposing placeholder members neutralizes the special name algorithms.

Table B.6 MDX Compatibility Values and Meanings

VALUE	DESCRIPTION
0	Default. For compatibility with earlier versions, this is the same as Value 1. The meaning of this default value is subject to change in future versions.
1	Placeholder members are exposed.
2	Placeholder members are not exposed.

Setting this property overrides the setting found in following server registry key:

```
HKLM\Software\Microsoft\OLAP Server\CurrentVersion\MDXCompatiblityValue
```

Connection string example: `MDX Compatibility=2;`

At least in the RTM version of Analysis Services 2000, changing this setting during a session only affects names generated for databases subsequently loaded (for example, by setting a new value for the ADO Connection's DefaultDatabase property). Unique names for the database currently being accessed will not change.

MDX Unique Name Style

This property determines the algorithm used to generate unique names in OLAP meta data. (Note: this does not affect interpretation of names in any way.)

Default: 0 (means the same as 2).

Set: When connecting, and at any time during a connection.

The naming convention available to OLAP Services 7.0 is more tightly bound to hierarchical position than the naming conventions available in Analysis Services 2000, and they can be much larger when used in strings as well. Setting this property can cause Analysis Services to generate unique names using one of the following algorithms.

Table B.7   MDX Unique Name Style Values and Meanings

VALUE	ALGORITHM
0	Default. For compatibility with earlier versions, this is the same as Value 2. The meaning of this default value is subject to change in future versions.
1	Key path algorithm: [Dimension].&[Key1].&[Key2]
2	Compatible with version 7.0, name path algorithm: [Dimension].[Member1].[Member2]
3	Compatible with SQL Server 2000 Analysis Services. The algorithm uses as stable a name as can be derived from the underlying dimension and level settings.

NOTE

At least in the RTM version of Analysis Services 2000, in order to see the effect of values 1 or 3, you also need to ensure that the MDX Compatibility property is set to a value of 2.

At least in the RTM version of Analysis Services 2000, changing this setting during a session only affects names generated for databases subsequently loaded (for example, by setting a new value for the ADO Connection's DefaultDatabase property). Unique names for the database currently being accessed will not change.

Setting this property overrides the setting found in following key:

```
HKLM\Software\Microsoft\OLAP Server\Current Version\MDXUniqueNames
```

Connection string example: MDX Unique Name Style=3;

OLE DB for OLAP Version

This property indicates the OLE DB for OLAP version supported by the provider. (Deprecated; not recommended for current use.)

Set: Read only.

The version is a string of the form ##.##, where the first two digits are the major version and the next two digits are the minor version. If a provider returns "02.00," then it conforms to the 2.0 version of the OLE DB for OLAP specification.

Note: OLE DB for OLAP has been included in the OLE DB specification as of OLE DB's version 2.6. As such, this property is deprecated and not recommended for current use. This property contains the same value as the OLE DB Version property (DBPROP_PROVIDEROLEDBVER) for providers that comply with version 2.6 of the OLE DB specification. However, an OLAP 7 provider will require use of this property.

Roles

This property specifies the roles that a client application connects under.

Default: None.

Set: Only when session is established.

If specified, this property will contain a comma-delimited string of the role names under which the client application will connect to the server. The role names used need to be specified in the collection of database roles on that server. The user connecting to the server must be a member of these roles for the connection to succeed. This can be helpful for testing out the access of different roles. This is separate from using the User ID and Password connection properties, which may be required to authenticate you to the server as being a member of the stated role(s).

NOTE
Connecting under more than one role may get confusing because permissions are as though the least restricted role is connected.

Role names are case-sensitive. You should not include spaces between the role names (although if the role names contain spaces, you must use them).

Connection string example: `Roles=VP Sales;`

Safety Options

This property determines how safety and security for user-defined functions and actions is handled.

Default: DBPROPVAL_MSMD_SAFETY_OPTIONS_DEFAULT

Set: Only when session is established.

The value of the property determines whether "unsafe" libraries can be registered and loaded by PivotTable Service or the server. If safety checking is enabled and an attempt is made to load an unsafe library or reference an unsafe user-defined function, the PivotTable Service will return the following error message: "User defined functions are not allowed by security settings for current connection."

Table B.8 lists the possible values for this property.

Information about signing libraries as safe can be found at msdn.microsoft. com/workshop/components/activex/signmark.asp

Connection string example: `Safety Options=3;`

Secured Cell Value

This property determines the value returned for secured cells.

Default: 0 (Means same as 1). Meaning may change in future.

Set: Only when connection is established.

Depending on the value set through this property, a query that attempts to access a secured cell can return a specified error code and/or content for the

Table B.8 Safety Options Values and Meanings

VALUE	DESCRIPTION
0	For connections to a local cube or via an IIS server, this value is the same as 2. For all other connections, this value is the same as 1.
1	This value enables all user-defined function libraries without verifying that they are safe for initialization and scripting.
2	This value ensures that all classes for a particular user-defined function library are checked to ensure that they are safe for initialization and scripting. If a function is not safe, then an attempt to access a cell calculated by it will result in an error with the text, "A user-defined function from interface X is not safe to be called."
3	This value prevents user-defined functions from being used during the session. (Note: the Excel and VBA function libraries are exempt from this prohibition.)

Value and Formatted Value cell properties. The possible property values and results for proscribed cells are listed in the Table B.9.

NOTE

At least in the RTM version of Analysis Services 2000, when value 1 is in effect, sometimes retrieving the Value cell property results in an invalid variant structure (Error 2042).

This property interacts with the Default Isolation Mode setting of the query. Microsoft's RTM documentation indicates that it interacts with Execution Location as well, but we have not seen that in practice. If the Default Isolation Mode is set to True and Secured Cell Value is set to 2 or 5, then in our experience, it is the same as value 3 in the preceding table. If the Secured Cell Value is set to 1 or 4, then the default isolation mode does not matter.

Connection string example: `Secured Cell Value=5;`

Source_DSN

This property contains the OLE DB or ODBC connection string or ODBC data source name (DSN) for the relational database or server cube that will be used as the source for a local cube.

Table B.9   Secured Cell Value Settings and Meanings

VALUE	DESCRIPTION
0	Default. In Analysis Services 2000, this means the same as Value 1. The meaning of the default value may change in future versions.
1	OLE DB: HRESULT = NO_ERROR / ADO MD: no cell access error. Cell properties: Value holds nothing, Formatted Value holds "#NA".
2	OLE DB: HRESULT holds an error / ADO MD: Error raised accessing cell.
3	OLE DB: HRESULT = NO_ERROR / ADO MD: no cell access error. Cell properties: Value is NULL, Formatted Value is NULL.
4	OLE DB: HRESULT = NO_ERROR / ADO MD: no cell access error. Cell properties: Value is numerical zero (0), Formatted value holds the value zero formatted according to the active cell FORMAT_STRING.
5	OLE DB: HRESULT = NO_ERROR / ADO MD: no cell access error. Cell properties: Value is the string "#SEC," Formatted Value is the string "#SEC".

Default: None.

Set: Only when session is established.

This property is used only when creating a local cube. You must use this together with the CreateCube and InsertInto properties.

The value for this property is stored in the cube file and used every time a client opens the cube (in the case of a ROLAP cube) or whenever the cube is refreshed (in the case of a MOLAP cube). Different cubes in a cube file may have different values for Source_DSN (but the Source_DSN_Suffix, if any, are shared among them).

Connection string example (note the enclosing double quotes, and the specification of the server's initial catalog): `Source_DSN="Provider=SQLOLEDB; Initial Catalog=Sales Data Mart;";`

Source_DSN_Suffix

This property contains a string that is appended to the Source_DSN property value when creating or connecting to a local cube.

Default: None.

Set: Only when session is established.

This property holds connection information that is appended to the contents of the Source_DSN when a connection is established with a local cube. The primary purpose of this property is to separate out and contain information that should be provided each time the cube is opened, such as the username and password required to access the RDBMS that underpins a ROLAP cube, or when a MOLAP cube is refreshed. If you specify username and password in the Source_DSN, then they are stored in the cube definition and will be used every time the cube is opened. If you specify them in this property, then they must be supplied every time the cube is re-opened as well.

Connection string example (note that the contents are bounded by double quotes): `Source_DSN_Suffix="UserID=Adam;Password=1Eval;";`

UseExistingFile

This property indicates whether an existing local cube file is to be overwritten or appended to when creating a local cube file.

Default: None.

Set: Only when connecting.

The function of this property depends on the existence and contents of the cube file being created. If you do not set a value for this property, when the data source is opened any previous cube file is overwritten with the one cube specified in the CreateCube property. Table B.10 shows the interaction between the condition of the cube file and the value to which this property is set.

Manipulating this property will allow you to create and maintain multiple cubes in a single local cube file. Once a cube file contains a single cube, in order to add additional cubes to the file, you need to set this property to True.

Connection string example: `UseExistingFile=True;`

Table B.10   Effect of UseExistingFile Setting

FILE CONDITION	CUBE CONDITION	EFFECT WHEN TRUE	EFFECT WHEN FALSE
Does not exist	—	Returns E_FAIL (OLE DB for OLAP) when you open a new data source.	New file and cube are created when the data source is opened.
Exists	Not in file	Cube is created in file.	Cube is created in file.
Exists	Exists in file	No changes made to cube.	Cube overwritten in file.

APPENDIX C

Intrinsic Cell and Member Properties

OLE DB for OLAP gives you the ability to treat the members and cells returned by queries as groups of related properties. This enables multiple related pieces of information to be returned to a client for both members and cells. If you do not request specific cell or member properties in a query, then a default set is returned. This appendix provides a reference to aid you in specifying the properties in MDX queries. (You may also wish to refer to the documentation for OLE DB for OLAP or ADO MD for programmer-level information on how to extract and use the returned property information.)

When you are considering the use of member properties, it is important that you recognize that Microsoft Analysis Services does not make a syntactic distinction between intrinsic member properties and properties that you define (which might otherwise be called "member attributes"). This means that you should avoid creating member properties whose names collide with those of the intrinsic member properties. In Microsoft's OLAP products, you do not have the ability to define custom cell properties, so this is not yet a consideration for cell properties.

The main purpose of the cell properties supported in Microsoft's OLAP/Analysis Services is to assist in the rendering of cells. Client tools that look for these properties will be able to render results as these properties specify, whereas other clients will not. If you are interested in creating the functional equivalent of custom cell properties, you can always create additional calculated members that return their values and construct your front-end tool to look for them and interpret them accordingly.

Member Properties

A query specifies the member properties to return for a dimension in the axis specification that contains that dimension. This syntax is covered in Chapter 5, "MDX Context and Execution." To summarize, if the axis is to be retrieved with only default member information, then the axis will be specified as follows:

```
{ set specification } on axis
```

If member properties are to be retrieved, then the axis specification will look like the following: { set specification } [DIMENSION] PROPERTIES property-name [, property-name . . .] on axis

To request a specific set of member properties for the dimensions in an axis, you follow the set specification with DIMENSION PROPERTIES (or just PROPERTIES) and then list the unique names of each property. You would separate multiple property names by commas, and after the last property name, place the on axis as usual. For example, a query that requests the store manager name and mailing address on the rows axis would look like this:

```
SELECT
{ [Measures].[Target Inventory] } on columns,
{ [Geography].[Stores].Members }
  DIMENSION PROPERTIES [Geography].[Stores].[Manager],
  [Geography].[Stores].[Mailing Address] on rows
FROM Inventory
```

It is important to recognize that whereas the .Properties() function evaluates its property name on a cell-by-cell basis, each property name that you list in this example is bound to one and only one dimension level. If you have the same property name at two or more levels in the dimension, then you will want to qualify the name of the property with the unique name of the level (such as [Business Unit].[Store].[Manager] as opposed to [Business Unit].[Division]. [Manager]). All of the intrinsic properties are bound on a level-by-level basis.

The intrinsic properties supported for the members of a dimension and of a level are listed in Table C.1.

Because these are member properties and they are returned through the standard OLE DB for OLAP interface, they will all be returned through a column of type Variant. Names and unary operators are returned as Unicode strings (wide characters), and IDs are returned as 32-bit integers. A member key's type depends on its definition in the dimension.

Table C.1 Intrinsic Member Properties (Supported for Every Member in Analysis Services 2000)

MICROSOFT EXTENSION	PROPERTY NAME	TYPE	MEANING
	NAME	DBTYPE_WSTR	Name (not unique name) of the member.
	ID	DBTYPE_UI4	Internal database ordering number for the member; sorting on this provides hierarchical database ordering.
	KEY	*	Member key value as defined in the member key column from the dimension table.
*	UNARY_OPERATOR	DBTYPE_WSTR	The unary operator used for rollup operations (Only in parent-child dimensions, and not at the All level).
*	EXPRESSION	DBTYPE_WSTR	The custom member formula associated with the member (not the formula for a calculated member). Only in levels that have a custom member formula.

Intrinsic properties are only bound at the lowest level within a query by default. For example, consider the following query:

```
SELECT
{ [Measures].[Target Inventory] } on columns,
{ Descendants (
  [Geography].[France],
  [Geography].[Stores],
  SELF_BEFORE_AFTER
)}
  PROPERTIES [Geography].[ID] on rows
FROM Inventory
```

Although members from the country, province, and store levels will be retrieved, the ID property will only be retrieved at the [Stores] level. In order to query for the ID from all of the levels, you need to ask for it explicitly, as with

```
SELECT
{ [Measures].[Target Inventory] } on columns,
{ Descendants (
  [Geography].[France],
  [Geography].[Stores],
  SELF_BEFORE_AFTER
```

```
    )}
    PROPERTIES [Geography].[Country].[ID],
[Geography].[Province].[ID], [Geography].[Stores].[ID]
    on rows
FROM Inventory
```

This last query will not work with flattened rowsets because the three geography key columns would all get the same name [Geography].[ID].

The intrinsic properties listed in table C.2 may be queried for at the scope of an axis. Because these are queried for on axis scope, if the axis has more than one dimension, you will obtain whatever property you request for every dimensions in the axis.

By "axis scope" we mean that you cannot ask for these by dimension or level. When you request them, they will be provided for every dimension that appears in the axis. The following query succeeds:

```
SELECT
{ [Measures].[Target Inventory] } on columns,
{ [Geography].[Stores].Members }
    PROPERTIES MEMBER_UNIQUE_NAME on rows
FROM Inventory
```

whereas this query fails:

```
SELECT
{[Measures].[Target Inventory] on columns,
{ [Geography].[Stores].Members }
    PROPERTIES [Geography].MEMBER_UNIQUE_NAME on rows
FROM Inventory
```

When you specify member properties in a query that is to be returned as an MD data set, the member properties are returned in addition to the default properties: member unique name, caption, and so on. For a query that is to be returned as a "flattened" rowset, if you do not specify any member properties, then the (non-unique) names for members in each level of the query result will be returned. If the query does specify member properties for an axis, then only the properties that you request for the axis will be returned. When you request these axis properties in a query that is requested as a rowset, the rowset will contain one MEMBER_UNIQUE_NAME column and/or one MEMBER_CAPTION column per level that contributes a member to the results, as described in Chapter 12, "Client Programming Basics." Note that MEMBER_NAME is not a synonym for MEMBER_CAPTION in Analysis Services 2000; the caption may contain a different string and may depend on language settings for the connection.

You can mix requests for dimension- and level-scoped properties in the same query with axis-scoped dimension properties.

Table C.2 Member Properties Specified as Part of OLE DB for OLAP

MICROSOFT EXTENSION	PROPERTY NAME	TYPE	MEANING
	MEMBER_ CAPTION	DBTYPE_ WSTR	Name (not unique name) of the member.
	MEMBER_ NAME	DBTYPE_ WSTR	Name (not unique name) of the member.
	MEMBER_ UNIQUE_NAME	DBTYPE_ WSTR	Unique name of the member.
	CATALOG_ NAME	DBTYPE_ WSTR	Name of the catalog containing the cube(s).
	CHILDREN_ CARDINALITY	DBTYPE_UI4	Estimated child cardinality.
	CUBE_NAME	DBTYPE_WSTR	Name of the cube.
	DESCRIPTION	DBTYPE_WSTR	Description associated with the dimension.
	DIMENSION_ UNIQUE_NAME	DBTYPE_WSTR	Unique name of the dimension.
	HIERARCHY_ UNIQUE_NAME	DBTYPE_WSTR	Unique name of the hierarchy.
	LEVEL_NUMBER	DBTYPE_UI4	Unique name of the member.
	LEVEL_UNIQUE_ NAME	DBTYPE_WSTR	Unique name of the member.
	MEMBER_GUID	DBTYPE_GUID	Unique name of the member.
	MEMBER_ ORDINAL	DBTYPE_UI4	Unique name of the member.
	MEMBER_TYPE	DBTYPE_I4	Type code for the member. It will be one of the following: MDMEMBER_TYPE_REGULAR (1) for a regular member, MDMEMBER_TYPE_ALL (1) for an All member, MDMEMBER_ TYPE_FORMULA (3) for a formula member, MDMEMBER_ TYPE_MEASURE (4) for a measure, MDMEMBER_TYPE_ UNKNOWN (5) for a member not categorized by one of the other codes. A member calculated by a custom member formula is categorized as a regular member, not as a formula.

continued

Table C.2 Member Properties Specified as Part of OLE DB for OLAP (continued)

MICROSOFT EXTENSION	PROPERTY NAME	TYPE	MEANING
	PARENT_COUNT	DBTYPE_UI4	Number of parents (0 or 1 in Microsoft's OLAP).
	PARENT_LEVEL	DBTYPE_UI4	Level of the parent (will be 0 even if no parent).
	SCHEMA_NAME	DBTYPE_WSTR	Name of the schema containing the member.
	PARENT_UNIQUE_NAME	DBTYPE_WSTR	Unique name of the member's parent (NULL if no parent member).
*	IS_PLACEHOLDERMEMBER	DBTYPE_BOOL	True if the member is a generated placeholder in the hierarchy (only can be true in a ragged dimension).
*	IS_DATAMEMBER	DBTYPE_BOOL	True if the member represents a data member (only can be true in a parent-child dimension; see .DataMember).

Cell Properties

Any cell properties to be returned by a query are specified in the last clause. If the query has a WHERE slicer clause, then the cell properties clause follows it. If the query does not, then the cell properties follow the FROM clause. The syntax of the cell properties clause is as follows:

```
CELL PROPERTIES property-name [, property-name . . . ]
```

The intrinsic properties supported for a cell are shown in Table C.3.

By default (both for OLE DB for OLAP and Microsoft's OLAP products), if you do not explicitly request any cell properties in a query, the VALUE, FORMATTED_VALUE, and CELL_ORDINAL properties are returned for each cell. If you request any cell properties in a query, then only those that you request are returned. For example, if you are going to use the result of a query only to format a spreadsheet grid of numbers for display, then you may only want to query for the formatted values. If you are going to use the result of a query only to create a chart from the numerical values, then you may want to only query for the unformatted value. For example, the following query requests the formatted value plus font name, size, flags, and color information:

Table C.3 Cell Properties Supported in OLE DB for OLAP

MICROSOFT EXTENSION	PROPERTY NAME	TYPE	MEANING
	BACK_COLOR	DBTYPE_UI4	Color value for background color.
*	CELL_ EVALUATION_ LIST	DBTYPE _WSTR	Semicolon-delimited list of formula names (cell calcs, calculated members) that overlapped at the cell.
	CELL_ORDINAL	DBTYPE_UI4	Ordinal number of cell in result set (for use as index value).
	FORMAT_ STRING	DBTYPE_ WSTR	Format string used to render value into.
	FONT_FLAGS	DBTYPE_I4	Flags for font-rendering effects (bold, italic, strikethrough).
	FONT_NAME	DBTYPE_ WSTR	Name of font to use when rendering cell value.
	FONT_SIZE	DBTYPE_UI2	Font size to render value with.
	FORE_COLOR	DBTYPE_UI4	Color value for foreground color.
	FORMATTED _VALUE	DBTYPE_ WSTR	Formatted string of raw value for displaying formatted value.
*	NON_EMPTY_ BEHAVIOR	DBTYPE _WSTR	Name of measure that determines NON EMPTY behavior of the calculated measure (see Chapter 6 for more detail).
*	SOLVE_ORDER	DBTYPE _I4	Solve order number at cell.
	VALUE	*	Raw data value for the cell (returned in a Variant).

```
SELECT
{[Measures].[Sales], [Measures].[Peak Inventory]} on rows
{[Time].[Quarter].Members} on columns
FROM [StoreInfo]
CELL PROPERTIES [Formatted_Value], [Font_Name], [Font_Size],
[Font_Flags], [Fore_Color], [Back_Color]
```

No cell properties will be returned for an MDX query that is returned as a "flattened" rowset. Instead, the columns of the recordset/rowset that return cell values will return only values.

Format String Codes

C alculated members and cell calculations can specify the formatting applied to a cell value to transform it into a formatted value. The formatted value is a text string, whereas the raw value can be numeric or textual (and a numeric cell could represent a date or time serial number). This appendix lays out the codes specified by OLE DB for OLAP and used by Microsoft's OLAP and Analysis Services. The codes match the format arguments used by the Visual Basic Format() function.

Note that because calculated members and Microsoft's cell calculations can apply across cells having different types and meanings (string, number, date serial-number), finding the right format string for a particular calculation or query may be difficult. Unlike other display information such as font flag and color, Microsoft Analysis Services does not let you use MDX to construct the format string to apply to a particular cell.

Formatting Numeric Values

A format expression for numeric values can have from one to four sections, each section separated by semicolons. If the format argument contains one of the named numeric formats, only one section can be used. Table D.1 lists the section usage and interpretations of sections in format strings

Table D.1   Format Strng Sections and Interpretations

SECTION USAGE	INTERPRETATION
One section	The format expression applies to all values.
Two sections	The first section applies to positive values and zeros, the second to negative values.
Three sections	The first section applies to positive values, the second to negative values, and the third to zeros.
Four sections	The first section applies to positive values, the second to negative values, the third to zeros, and the fourth to null values.

The following example has one section, and formats a number with two decimal places:

```
"#.00"
```

The following example has two sections. The first section defines the format for positive values and zeros, and the second section defines the format for negative values. The result is that negative numbers are displayed within parentheses:

```
"#,##0%;(#,##0%)"
```

If you include semicolons with nothing between them, the missing section is printed using the format of the positive value. For example, the following format displays positive and negative values using the format in the first section and displays "Zero" if the value is zero:

```
"$#,##0;;\Z\e\r\o"
```

Table D.2 describes the characters that can appear in the format string for number formats.

In addition, the strings in Table D.3 may be used to identify pre-defined formats.

Date Values

Table D.4 describes the formatting characters that can appear in the format string for date/time formats. The numerical value is interpreted as a date serial number.

Table D.2 Formatting Code Characters and Interpretations

CHARACTER	DESCRIPTION
None	Displays the number with basic formatting (a decimal point if necessary).
0	Placeholder that displays either a digit or a zero, depending on whether the number would have a non-zero digit in that position. If the format expression has more zeros to either the right-hand or left-hand side of the decimal point than significant digits are in the number, leading or trailing zeros will be shown. If there are fewer zeros in the format expression than in significant digits to the right of the decimal point, the number will be rounded to as many decimal places as there are zeros to the right. If there are fewer zeros in the format expression to the left of the decimal point than there are digits to the left of the decimal point in the numerical value, then the extra digits in the number will be displayed.
#	Placeholder that displays a digit or nothing. If the numerical value has a digit in the same position as the # in the format string, the digit will be displayed. Otherwise, nothing is displayed in that position.
.	Placeholder for the decimal in some locales. (In other locales, a comma is the placeholder for the decimal separator.) This placeholder is used with the # and 0 placeholders to determine how many digits are displayed to the left and right of the decimal separator. If a 0 appears as the first digit placeholder to the left of the decimal separator, then a fractional number (smaller than 1) will begin with 0 (e.g., "0.5"). If the format expression contains only number signs (#) to the left of this symbol, numbers smaller than 1 begin with a decimal separator. Note: the actual character used as a decimal placeholder in the formatted output depends on your system and connection locale.
%	Placeholder for percentage representation. The numeric value is effectively multiplied by 100 (it has its decimal point shifted by two). The percent character (%) is inserted into the resulting string at the position where it appears in the format string.
,	Thousands separator in some locales. (In other locales, a period is used as a thousand separator.) The thousand separator separates thousands from hundreds within a number that has four or more places to the left of the decimal separator, and also millions from hundred thousands within a number that has seven or more places to the left of the decimal separator. Ordinary use of the thousand separator is specified if the format contains a thousand separator surrounded by the digit placeholders 0 or #. Two adjacent thousand separators, or a thousand separator immediately to the left of the decimal separator (whether or not

continued

Table D.2   Formatting Code Characters and Interpretations (continued)

, (continued)	a decimal is specified) means "scale the number by dividing it by 1,000, rounding as needed." For example, the format string "##0,, " indicates to represent 100 million as 100, and to represent numbers smaller than 1 million as 0. If 2,000 separators are adjacent anywhere other than immediately to the left of the decimal separator, they indicate simply to use a thousands separator in formatting the numerical value. Note: the actual character used as the thousands separator in the formatted output depends on your system and connection locale.
E– E+ e– e+	Scientific format. If the format expression contains at least one digit placeholder (**0** or **#**) to the right of **E–**, **E+**, **e–**, or **e+**, the number is displayed in scientific format and E or e is inserted between the number and its exponent. The number of digit placeholders to the right determines the number of digits in the exponent. Use **E–** or **e–** to place a minus sign next to negative exponents. Use **E+** or **e+** to place a minus sign next to negative exponents and a plus sign next to positive exponents.
– + $ ( )	Used to display one of these literal characters. To display any other character, precede it with a backslash (\) or enclose it in double quotation marks (" ").
****	Displays the next character in the format string. This can be used to display a character that has special meaning as a literal character. The backslash itself is not displayed. Using a backslash is the same as enclosing the next character in double quotation marks. To display a backslash, use two backslashes (\\). Examples of characters that cannot be displayed as literal characters are the numeric-formatting characters (#, 0, %, E, e, ,, and .), the date- and time-formatting characters (a, c, d, h, m, n, p, q, s, t, w, y, /, and :), and the string-formatting characters (@, &, <, >, and !).
"string"	Displays the string inside the double quotation marks (" ").

Table D.3   Predefined Format Code Strings

STRING	DESCRIPTION
Standard	Formats as a simple number (as if no format string were applied).
Currency	Formats as a currency value, using the locale in effect for currency symbol, thousands separator, and decimal separator. Provides two decimal places. Encloses the formatted number in parentheses if less than zero.
Percent	Formats as a percentage with two decimal places, and a negative sign if less than zero.

Table D.4 Date/Time Format Codes and Interpretations

CHARACTER	DESCRIPTION
:	Time separator in some locales. (In other locales, another character may be used to represent the time separator.) The time separator separates hours, minutes, and seconds when time values are formatted. Note: the actual character used as the time separator in formatting a string is determined by your system and connection locale.
/	Date separator. (In some locales, other characters may be used to represent the date separator.) The date separator separates the day, month, and year when date values are formatted. Note: the actual character used as the date separator in formatting a string is determined by your system and connection locale.
c	Displays the date as **ddddd** and displays the time as **ttttt**, in that order. Displays only date information if the date serial number has no fractional part. Displays only time information if no integer portion is present.
d	Formats the day's number without a leading zero (1–31).
dd	Formats the day's number with a leading zero (01–31).
ddd	Formats the abbreviated day name (Sun–Sat).
dddd	Formats the full day name (Sunday–Saturday).
ddddd	Formats the complete date including day, month, and year, formatted according to your system's short date format setting. In MS-Windows, the default short date format is **m/d/yy**.
dddddd	Formats a complete date including day, month, and year, formatted according to the long date setting recognized by your system. In MS-Windows, the default long date format is **mmmm dd, yyyy**.
w	Formats the weekday as a number (Sunday=1, Saturday=7).
ww	Formats the week of the year as a number (1–54).
m	Formats the month as a number without a leading zero (1–12).
m immediately after **h** or **hh**	Formats the minute without a leading zero (0–59).
mm	Formats the month as a number with a leading zero (01–12).
mm immediately after **h** or **hh**	Formats the minute with a leading zero (00–59).
mmm	Formats the month as an abbreviation (Jan–Dec).
mmmm	Formats the month as a full month name (January–December).
q	Formats the quarter of the year as a number (1–4).
y	Formats the day of the year as a number (1–366).

continued

Table D.4 Date/Time Format Codes and Interpretations (continued)

CHARACTER	DESCRIPTION
yy	Formats the year as a two-digit number (00–99).
yyyy	Formats the year as a four-digit number (100–9999).
h	Formats the hour as a number without leading zeros (0–23).
hh	Formats the hour as a number with leading zeros (00–23).
n	Formats the minute as a number without leading zeros (0–59).
nn	Formats the minute as a number with leading zeros (00–59).
s	Formats the second as a number without leading zeros (0–59).
ss	Formats the second as a number with leading zeros (00–59).
ttttt	Formats a time as a complete time (including hour, minute, and second), formatted using the time separator defined by the time format recognized by your system. A leading zero is displayed if the leading zero option is selected and the time is earlier than 10:00 (for example 09:59), in either the A.M. or the P.M. cycle. For Windows, the default time format is **h:mm:ss**.
AM/PM or **am/pm**	Formats the time using a 12-hour clock. Displays **AM** or **am/pm** with any hour from midnight until noon; displays an uppercase **PM** or **pm** with any hour from noon until midnight.
A/P or **a/p**	Formats the time using a 12-hour clock. Displays an uppercase **A** or lowercase **a** with any time from midnight until noon; displays an uppercase **P** or lowercase **p** with any hour from noon until midnight.
AMPM or **ampm**	Formats the time using a 12-hour clock. Displays the AM string literal as defined by your system with any time from midnight until noon; displays the PM string literal as defined by your system with any time from noon until midnight. The case of the string displayed matches the string as defined by your system settings. For Windows, the default format is **AM/PM**.

In addition, the following strings in Table D.5 may be used to identify pre-defined formats.

String Values

A format expression for strings can have one section or two sections separated by a semicolon (;).Table D.6 describes the sections and usage for string format strings.

Table D.5 Predefined Date/Time Format Code Strings

STRING	DESCRIPTION
Short Date	Formats the complete date including day, month, and year, formatted according to the locale's short date format setting.
Short Time	Formats a time as a complete time (including hour, minute, and second), formatted according to your system's short time format setting.
Medium Date	Formats the complete date including day, month, and year, formatted according to the locale's medium date format setting.
Medium Time	Formats a time as a complete time (including hour, minute, and second), formatted according to the locale's medium time format setting.
Long Date	Formats the complete date including day, month, and year, formatted according to the locale's long date format setting.
Long Time	Formats a time as a complete time (including hour, minute, and second), formatted according to the locale's long time format setting.

Table D.6 Sections in Format Strings for String Values

USAGE	RESULT
One section	The format applies to all string values.
Two sections	The first section applies to string data, whereas the second section applies to null values and zero-length strings ("").

The characters described in Table D.7 can appear in the format string for character strings.

For example, if the string value is "Flaxen," Table D.8 shows the results of four different string formats.

Table D.7   Format String Codes for Strings and Interpretation

CHARACTER	DESCRIPTION
@	Placeholder for a single character. If the string has a character in the position where the @ appears in the format string, it displays the character. Otherwise, it displays a space in that position. Placeholders are filled from right to left (right-justifying the string) unless an exclamation point (!) is in the format string. Note: if the string expression being formatted has more characters than there are @ and & symbols in the format string, the remainder of the string expression will be placed at the end of the formatted string.
&	Character placeholder. It displays a character or nothing. If the string has a character in the position where the & appears, it displays the character. Otherwise, no character is displayed. Placeholders are filled from right to left (right-justifying the string) unless an exclamation point (!) is in the format string. Note: if the string expression being formatted has more characters than there are @ and & symbols in the format string, the remainder of the string expression will be placed at the end of the formatted string.
<	Forces the result string to be in all lowercase.
>	Forces the result string to be in all uppercase.
!	Forces left-to-right fill of placeholders. This creates left-justification for the string. (The default is to fill placeholders from right to left.)

Table D.8   Format String Examples for String Values

FORMAT STRING	RESULT
@	"Flaxen"
@@@\F\o\o@@	"FlaFooxen"
!@@@@@@@@	"Flaxen"
<	"flaxen"

To use this CD-ROM, your system must meet the following requirements:

Platform/Processor/Operating System.

Pentium or Pentium-compatible computer running Windows NT 4.0 SP4 or higher, or Windows 2000 (server or workstation editions). Some software tools and sample code will work on computers running Windows 95, 98, or ME as well as NT 4.0/2000. If you are running Microsoft Analysis Services on a separate server machine, that system must be running Windows NT 4.0 SP4 or higher, or Windows 2000.

RAM.

128 MB minimum for use of sample database and tools on each machine.

Hard Drive Space.

In order to install the software tools, sample database, and sample code, you should have at least 150 MB free on your computer. If you are installing the sample database to a separate server machine, you should have 128 MB free on that server. If you are installing only the software tools and sample code to your local computer, you should have 22 MB of disk space free.

Peripherals.

A CD-ROM and a mouse are required to install and use the samples. Your video resolution should be at least 1024 x 768, or tools and samples may not display correctly.